Librarian's Guide
to Online Searching

Librarian's Guide to Online Searching

Third Edition

SUZANNE S. BELL

 LIBRARIES UNLIMITED

AN IMPRINT OF ABC-CLIO, LLC
Santa Barbara, California • Denver, Colorado • Oxford, England

Library of Congress Cataloging-in-Publication Data

Bell, Suzanne S.
 Librarian's guide to online searching / Suzanne S. Bell. — Third edition.
   pages cm
 Includes bibliographical references and index.
   ISBN 978-1-61069-035-5 (pbk.) — ISBN 978-1-61069-036-2 (ebook)
 (print)
   1. Database searching.   2. Electronic information resource searching.
 I. Title.
   ZA4460.B45   2012
   025.04—dc23   2012002168

ISBN: 978-1-61069-035-5
EISBN: 978-1-61069-036-2

16 15 14 13 12   1 2 3 4 5

This book is also available on the World Wide Web as an eBook.
Visit www.abc-clio.com for details.

Libraries Unlimited
An Imprint of ABC-CLIO, LLC

ABC-CLIO, LLC
130 Cremona Drive, P.O. Box 1911
Santa Barbara, California 93116-1911

This book is printed on acid-free paper ∞
Manufactured in the United States of America

The screen shots and their contents are published with permission of ProQuest LLC. Further reproduction is prohibited without permission. Inquiries may be made to: ProQuest LLC, 789 E. Eisenhower Pkwy, Ann Arbor, MI 48106-1346 USA. Telephone (734) 761-4700; E-mail: info@proquest.com; Web-page: www.proquest.com

To my grandfather, Augustus Hunt Shearer, librarian and teacher, and my father, Vern Coventry Bell, inventor and engineer. You may not have understood this book, but you would have appreciated it. Thank you both for the gifts that made it possible.

Contents

vii

Acknowledgments

Many thanks go to my colleagues at the University of Rochester, for once again putting up with my being out for most of a summer. Very special thanks go to Donna Berryman for being a fan and providing so much thoughtful, generous help on the PubMed section, even while in the throes of her dissertation. Huge thanks to Jennifer Gliere for reading and providing excellent feedback and funny comments from a nonlibrarian point of view, for being utterly ruthless about deleting commas, for website expertise, and for generally being even more insanely detailed than I am. Grateful thanks go to the faculty who use this book in their courses and were willing to be polled about changes and to share their thoughts. I apologize to the people whose choices I couldn't accommodate, but please know your input was deeply appreciated. Humble and delighted thanks go to the students in Michelynn McKnight's classes at Louisiana State University's School of Library & Information Science for their honest reactions, thoughtful comments, and excellent suggestions. The things you liked I tried to leave alone, and where you had suggestions I tried to incorporate them in this edition. (It's thanks to you that this edition will have a companion website, for example.)

Books don't happen without a publisher, and I have been truly blessed in this regard. My highly enthusiastic thanks go to Barbara Ittner, who answers emails at all hours of the day and night (which is when crazy authors write emails); to Cathleen Casey for being another fun, prompt, and helpful respondent; and to the wonderful Emma Bailey, production manager extraordinaire, for being patient, responsive, and flexible. You ladies are a total pleasure to work with.

My vision of the book as text supported by (lots of) screen shots would not have been possible without the vendors of these wonderful resources being willing to grant permission to use their material. I am deeply grateful to all the people who actually did the permission granting, who helped by getting my permission requests into the right hands, or who answered questions quickly and thoroughly. Particular thanks to Kim Stam and Kathleen McEvoy at EBSCO; Kim Landry and Sylvia Bonadio at Ovid; Jacqui Gilchrist, Michele Kristakis, and Corye Bradshaw at ProQuest; and Susan Ciambrano and Amanda Addis at Thomson Reuters for being particularly prompt and/or desirous to help. This time around also required more calls or emails to help desks, and I have nothing but high praise for the help desk staff at EBSCO, OCLC, the Census Bureau, and ABC-CLIO. To a person they were smart, nice, willing to listen, and eager to help, even with the weirdest questions.

Finally, where would we be without our tools and home support? Thanks, fabulous new MacBook Pro and baby sister MacBook Air, for allowing me to work anywhere and making the writing seem fun, and to your big brother with the huge monitor for taking magnificent screen shots. My most heartfelt thanks, however, go to my husband, a walking *Chicago Manual of Style*, who has once again put up with my being totally distracted for weeks on end, who has again patiently read page after page and provided useful editing and reactions, and altogether has been a wonderfully cheerful, supportive, and sustaining presence throughout the process. You are the very best, my dear; I couldn't do it without you.

Preface

Welcome to the wonderful world of database searching! Roy Tennant's (2003) now famous quote that "only librarians like to search; everyone else likes to find" has perhaps been too frequently repeated—but it's hard not to, because it's *true*. There are certain kinds of minds that enjoy solving puzzles and ferreting out information, and the owners of those minds often find a good fit in library careers. Librarians do like to search, although generally we aren't born knowing it: it's a realization that emerges later, with experience or in a class. If you are a researcher or a student in the position of having to search for the information you need, you may also find that there can be some interest and pleasure in the process as well as the product.

If it is true that most people only want to "find," and are perfectly happy with the Google model of one simple search box and long lists of results, one might ask, "Why should I care about learning more sophisticated search techniques? Why should we still teach a course on database searching?" (or "Why should I buy a book on database searching?") "Will there ever be an opportunity to use this information again?"

In offering you this book, I wholeheartedly believe those questions can be answered in the affirmative. Yes, learning about more sophisticated search techniques continues to be helpful, and it will increase your effectiveness in helping others to do research, or your own productivity as a researcher. No matter how simple the initial interface becomes, it still helps to know something about database structure, that is, what is going on under the hood. This is especially helpful for understanding what is *possible* with any given database: what degree of precision in searching you can expect, and thus what you can expect in terms of results. There will continue to be Advanced versions of the interface that will allow experts to do more efficient, targeted, and useful searches. Yes, people will do and are doing more searching on their own: if you are not a librarian and are looking at this book, it will introduce you to resources you might not have been aware of and help you to be more effective. For librarians and library students, searching is a part of our profession, an area in which we need to be ready to offer our users more skills than they have on their own. Indeed, as users do more searching on their own, the questions that they approach librarians with become more difficult. They have taken care of the easy questions; librarians need to be ready for the hard ones. This is still an important part of our skill set.

Most of the techniques and strategies provided in this book are not particularly complex or hard to master, but they need to be stated and learned, because they are not generally how people think. You need to *learn* to parse questions into good search strategies. You need to really internalize how Boolean logic works to understand that when a search returns only a few results, the tactic to take is to use fewer, broader search terms, not add more, and more specific, terms. One of the most essential techniques sounds like the simplest: to use your eyes and truly analyze what is on the screen. This is something that very few people really do, however, so it is also something to learn.

One of the overriding goals in this book is to remain thoroughly grounded in the real world. The examples and exercises involving commercial databases work with ones commonly available at academic and major public libraries. This edition includes more databases that are freely available on the Web, but as in previous editions, all free websites discussed have been carefully chosen for their expected longevity. The emphasis is not on providing every detail of every database presented, but rather how you can use a set of basic concepts ("the Searcher's Toolkit") in order to look at any interface ("use your eyes") and understand what you are seeing ("engage your brain"), so as to use effectively whatever search capabilities are provided. Once you have a basic idea of how databases are put together and have grasped the collection of concepts and techniques this book calls the Searcher's Toolkit, you should be able to plunge into any database that comes along and figure out how it works. In fact, the other main goal for this book is to help you learn to be flexible and adaptable. What more important skill can there be in our rapidly changing world?

This text will expose you to a whole range of databases: multidisciplinary, social science, medicine, science, bibliographic, humanities, and statistical/numeric. You will learn that even when you don't know anything about a subject, using some good, general principles, you should be able to use an unfamiliar database and do a reasonable search. A discussion of information-seeking behaviors and how to do an effective reference interview helps with this. Most important, you shouldn't be *afraid* of any subject area and declare it off-limits. As all of these choices begin to build up, however, the natural question is this: How do you know which database to use? Or should you use the Web? We address these issues as well. Note that although the Web does enter into the discussion from time to time, including a new section on free Web resources in chapter 10, this book does not attempt to teach you to search the Web better. There are already many excellent books on the market to fulfill that purpose. The focus here is on purpose-built, sophisticated databases, both fee-based and some, incredibly, freely available. If you thought searching started and ended with Google, surprise! There's a whole other world waiting for you.

Not only will you learn to search databases, but you'll also learn something about passing your knowledge along: tips and guidance for showing others how to get what they need out of a database. In addition, we'll go over points to consider in evaluating a database for purposes of writing a review, or, for librarians, as part of collection development. With budgets everywhere as tight as they are, librarians are more frequently finding themselves in the position of having to evaluate and choose among current resources.

If you are a library school instructor, you'll find that the chapters after the first three are almost completely freestanding. You can pick and choose, using them in whatever order best suits your needs or teaching style. As in previous editions, exercises using the resources discussed and material that can be used as discussion-starters are included with each chapter, and "Recommended Readings" are provided for selected chapters. New with this edition are "Beyond the Textbook" exercises to get students used to exploring new resources. This edition also offers a new section on Google Scholar and other high quality, free Web databases, along with pointers for finding more, in chapter 10. A final new feature with this edition is a companion website, www.LibrariansGuide.info, which I hope will prove useful to both instructors and students alike. Here you will find short video demos of databases, updates as needed, and the opportunity to leave your comments and suggestions.

A word about vendors, trends, and the Web. Keep in mind that the world of subscription databases is a *business* world: products, units, even whole companies get bought, sold, or merged. Seminal events can occur in government agencies as well. In both cases, the database products produced by these organizations can undergo significant change, and such changes do not occur overnight. This edition of the book reflects the impact of both a major commercial and a major government-sponsored change: you will find the discussion of *Library Literature* and *American FactFinder* are somewhat minimal, as both databases are in a state of profound transition. Should we have waited? Perhaps, but then so much else had already changed that it seemed a disservice not to proceed with the new edition. Having the companion website for the book will be very helpful for these situations, as I will be able to post updates there.

As a business, vendors also keep an eye on each other (and everyone keeps an eye on what Google is doing). Thus, we see trends: the type-ahead suggestion feature pioneered by Google, wherein as you type, searches that others have done or system-controlled suggestions are offered. You will see that in several databases discussed in this book. Quickly learning from each other, vendors now almost universally offer options and opportunities to refine a search on the results page, including having the search interface stay with you on that page. This reduces clicks and makes searching (and thus finding) easier: you keep moving ahead rather than having to go back. To me, this shows recognition that a search doesn't need to be—and probably won't be—perfect the first time, and that it's useful to give users options for fixing a search without having to start over. Does this reduced emphasis on initial search skills mean librarians are out of a job? No, I don't think so, because no matter how easy the vendors try to make it for users, they still can't make people read or see what's on the screen, or grasp quickly and easily what it all means. As trained professionals, we can do all that, and we also have a huge role to play simply in making users aware that the database is there and can help them. Another trend appears to be the development of and emphasis on personalization and customization features: make your own account to hold results from one search session to another, set the number of results you want to see on a page, etc. Finally, some vendors have already come out with versions of their products you can search on your mobile device; many more are working on it (Tenopir, Baker, and Grogg 2010). Undoubtedly mobile searching will soon be a universal feature.

About the Web, I simply wish to state the obvious: we live in the age of the Web, with its incredible capability for change; vendors and nonprofits change the appearance of their interfaces regularly, and it's crucial to be flexible. This book is intended to help you learn to adapt and change, as well as to give you the tools to understand and use what you're looking at, regardless of what the interfaces happen to look like in the future.

Last, a word about the technology known as *metasearch* or *federated search*, which has recently been supplanted by the better idea of *discovery services*. The idea behind both of these technologies can be summarized as a way to search multiple databases through one very simple interface. Federated search systems go out and separately search each database in the specified group at the time the search is entered, and they are notoriously slow. Discovery services preharvest the contents of many databases (and even your online catalog) into one huge index, against which your search is run, and are thus able to execute searches far more quickly. Some academic libraries see this as an answer to getting students to use their subscription databases by providing a familiar, Google-box search interface. Because these types of search systems completely eliminate the vendors' individual interfaces and all their features, they are not a topic for this book. Will discovery services put this book (and one of the most interesting parts of librarians' jobs) out of business? All I can say is that I certainly hope not; I hope we can all keep skillfully searching for years to come. Let's get started—because searching really can be just as rewarding as finding.

1

Database Structure for Everyone: Records, Fields, and Indexes

Whether you are using this book in an upper-level database searching course or an entry-level intro to reference course, it's likely that you have or will have the opportunity to take a true "database" course. This means that some of you may already be familiar with the concepts in this chapter. My goal is to focus on helping you learn and develop strategies to search and interact more effectively with databases rather than getting into the real technology of how databases are built. This chapter provides a very brief and simple introduction to how databases are conceptually put together. In my experience, this is as much as you need to know to apply appropriate search techniques and use the database effectively. There's no point in piling on technical detail if it doesn't further your ultimate goal, which in this case is searching.

It's always interesting to start with a little history, however. Electronic access to information by means of the Web is so pervasive that we take it for granted. You have undoubtedly already used databases somewhere in your academic life. But where did these "databases" come from? Why are they important? What *is* a database, anyway?

Historical Background

Indexing and Abstracting Services

In the Beginning . . .

There was hard copy. Writers wrote, and their works were published in (physical) magazines, journals, newspapers, or conference proceedings. Months

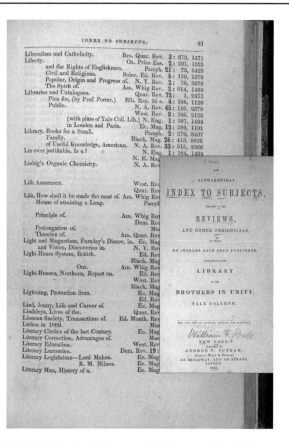

Fig. 1.1. Index listing and title page (*inset*) from Poole's *Index to Periodical Literature.* (Courtesy of the Department of Rare Books and Special Collections, University of Rochester Libraries, Rochester, NY.)

or years afterward, other writers, researchers, and other alert readers wanted to know what was written on a topic. Wouldn't it be useful if there were a way to find everything that had been published on a topic, without having to page through every likely journal, newspaper, and so forth? It certainly would, as various publishing interests demonstrated: as early as 1848, the *Poole's Index to Periodical Literature* provided "An alphabetical index to subjects, treated in the reviews, and other periodicals, to which no indexes have been published; prepared for the library of the Brothers in Unity, Yale college" (Figure 1.1).

Not to be caught napping, the *New York Times* started publishing their *Index* in 1851, and in 1896, taking a page from Poole's, the *Cumulative Index to a Selected List of Periodicals* appeared, which soon (1904) became the canonical *Readers' Guide to Periodical Literature.* Thus, in the mid-19th century, the hard copy Index is born: an alphabetical list of words, representing subjects, and under each word a list of articles deemed to be about that subject. The index is typeset, printed, bound, and sold, and all of this effort is done, slowly and laboriously, by humans.

Given the amount of work involved, and the costs of paper, printing, etc., how many subjects do you think an article would have been listed under?

Every time the article entry is repeated under another subject, it costs the publisher just a little more. Suppose there was an article about a polar expedition, which described the role the sled dogs played, the help provided by the native Inuit, the incompetence on the part of the provisions master, and the fund-raising efforts carried on by the leader's wife back home in England. The publisher really can't afford to list this article in more than one or two places. Under which subject(s) will people interested in this topic be most likely to look? The indexer's career was a continuous series of such difficult choices.

An index, recording that an article exists and where it would be found, was a good start, but one could go a step further. The addition of a couple of sentences (e.g., to give the user an idea of what the article is about) increases the usefulness of the finding tool enormously—although the added information, of course, costs more in terms of space, paper, effort, etc. But some index publishers started adding abstracts, gambling that their customers would pay the higher price (which they did). Thus, we have the advent of *Abstracting and Indexing services* or "A & I," terminology that you can see in the library literature.

The abstracts were all laboriously written by humans. They needed to be skilled, literate humans, and skilled humans are very expensive (even when they're underpaid, they are expensive in commercial terms). Humans are also slow, compared with technology. Paper and publishing are expensive too. Given all this, how many times do you think an entry for an article would be duplicated (appear under multiple subjects) in this situation? The answers are obvious; the point is that the electronic situation we have today is all grounded in a physical reality. Once it was nothing but people and paper.

From Printed Volumes to Databases

Enter the Computer

The very first machines that can really be called *digital computers* were built in the period from 1939 to 1944, culminating in the construction of the ENIAC in 1946 (*Encyclopædia Britannica* 2008). These machines were all part of a long progression of invention to speed up the task of mathematical calculations. After that, inventions and improvements came thick and fast: the 1950s and 1960s were an incredibly innovative time in computing, although probably not in a way that the ordinary person would have noticed. The first machine to be able to store a database, RCA's Bizmac, was developed in 1952 (*Lexikon's History of Computing* 2002). The first instance of an online transaction-processing system, using telephone lines to connect remote users to central mainframe computers, was the airline reservation system known as SABRE, set up by IBM for American Airlines in 1964 (Computer History Museum 2004). Meanwhile, at Lockheed Missile and Space Company, a man named Roger Summit was engaged in projects involving search and retrieval, and management of massive data files. His group's first interactive search-and-retrieval service was demonstrated to the company in 1965; by 1972, it had developed into a new, commercially viable product: Dialog—the "first publicly available online research service" (Dialog 2005).

Thus, in the 1960s and 1970s, when articles were still being produced on typewriters, indexes and abstracts were being produced in hard copy, and very disparate industries were developing information technologies for their own specialized purposes, Summit can be credited with having incredible vision. He asked the right questions:

1. What do people want? Information.

2. Who produces information, and in what form? The government and commercial publishers, in the form of papers, articles, newspapers, etc.

3. What if you could put information *about* all that published material into a machine-readable file: a database—something you could search?

Summit also had the vision to see how the technological elements could be used. The database needed to be made only once, at his firm's headquarters, and trained agents (librarians) could then access it over telephone lines with just some simple, basic equipment. The firm could track usage exactly and charge accordingly. Think of the advantages!

The advantages of an electronic version of an indexing/abstracting system are really revolutionary. In a system no longer bound by the confines of paper, space, and quite so many expensive skilled personnel:

- Articles could be associated with a greater number of terms describing their content, not just one or two (some skilled labor is still required).

- Although material has to be rekeyed (i.e., typed into the database), this doesn't require subject specialists, simply typists (cheap labor).

- Turnaround time is faster: most of your labor force isn't thinking and composing, just typing continuously—the process of adding to the information in the database goes on all the time, making the online product much more current.

- If you choose to provide your index "online only," thus avoiding the time delays and costs of physical publishing, why, you might be able to redirect the funds to expanding your business: offering other indexes (databases) in new subject areas.

As time goes on, this process of "from article to index" gets even faster. When articles are created electronically (e.g., word processing), no rekeying is needed to get the information into your database, just software to convert and rearrange the material to fit your database fields. So, rather than typists, you must pay programmers to write the software, and you still need those humans to analyze the content and assign the subject terms.

In the end, the electronic database is not necessarily cheaper to create; it very likely costs more! The costs have simply shifted. But customers buy it because . . . *it is so much more powerful and efficient*. It is irresistible. Given a choice between a printed index and an electronic version, most people under the age of 60 won't give the printed volume a second glance. The online database is here to stay.

Database Building Blocks

Fields and Records

In essence, databases are made up of fields and records. Fields are like one cell in an Excel spreadsheet: a bit of computer memory dedicated to holding one particular thing, one value (e.g., age) or type of information (e.g., letters, numbers, or an image). A set of fields makes up a record. An analogy would be a row in Excel: one row equals one record. If you prefer a good mental image, think of it as a whole line of shoeboxes with the lids off, and one thing in each box. Every time you add another record to your database, that becomes another line of shoeboxes, into which you put the appropriate bit of information into the box assigned to it (e.g., box 1 is always the number of the row, box 2 is always a last name, box 3 is always the first name, etc.). Each record—each row of shoeboxes—will have the same number of boxes, but you might not have a piece of information for every box; that is, some fields might be blank. Altogether, all the rows (the records) make up the database.

Think about driver's licenses. They all have an ID number, the owner's name, address, date of birth, eye color, a bad photo, etc. I don't know if this is true in all states, but certainly in New York State all of that information resides in a database somewhere. It's easy to imagine the Department of Motor Vehicle's database having fields with names such as Name, Addr, DOB, Eyes, BadPic, etc. Each record represents a person. The fields in each record represent every bit of information that appears on your license, and probably some that aren't actually printed on the license as well. When you send in the paperwork and the check to renew your license, they look your record up in the database, make any changes that you might have indicated in your paperwork (e.g., change the values in your fields), and hit print. Presto, you've gone from being a database entry to being a small card with an unflattering photo.

Decisions, Decisions: Designing the Database

The crucial task in developing a database is deciding what fields the records in your database are going to have, and how big they are going to be, that is, how many characters or numbers they will be able to hold. This "size" represents the computer memory allocated every time a new record is added. (Although memory is cheap now, in a huge project, how much memory will be allocated is still something to consider.) In the best of all possible worlds, a whole design team, including software engineers, subject experts, people from marketing and sales, and potential users, would wrestle with this problem. Nothing might ever get done in such a large and varied group, however, and so probably a more limited team of software engineers and content experts is the norm. The problem is that the design team had better make good choices initially, because it's very difficult, if not impossible, to make significant (if any) changes to the record structure later.[1] This is good and bad. It means there's a certain inherent stability, or at least pressure on these database products not to change too much, but when you wish that they *would* fix something, it can take a long time (if ever) for change to happen. You can take a certain amount of comfort, though, in the knowledge that however much the interface to the database—the way it looks—changes, behind the scenes the same types of information (fields), are probably still there.

Quick Recap

In this section we have described the structure of databases in very simple terms and compared it to the structure of an Excel spreadsheet. The most basic elements of a database are fields and records. A full set of fields makes up a record. Every record in the database has the same set of fields

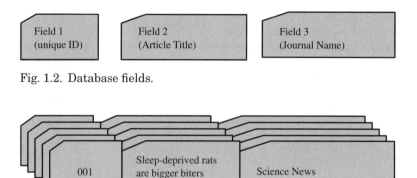

Fig. 1.2. Database fields.

Fig. 1.3. Database records.

(even if, in some records, some fields are blank). All of the records (like the rows in a spreadsheet) together make up the database.

Food for Thought

For an article database, you'd probably have a field for the article title, the name of the journal it appeared in . . . and what else? Think about the other information you would want to capture. Again, the process is something like this:

Define your fields (Figure 1.2):

. . . that make up records (Figure 1.3) . . .

. . . and form the basis of your database.

Beyond Fields and Records

Field Indexes

Fields and records are the basis, the "data" of a database. What makes a database fast, powerful, and efficient are the *indexes* of the fields. It would be very slow if every time you queried the database, it started at field1, record1, and searched sequentially through each field of each record—you might as well go back to hard copy at that rate.

An index, in the sense that we're discussing now, is a list of all the values from a particular field (or multiple fields), with some kind of identifier indicating from which record each value came. This is much like the way the index at the end of a book indicates on which pages a word appears. It becomes part of the database but has a separate existence from the records. An index list can be alphabetized and in various ways optimized for searching. When arranged as a list of locations for a given word, this list is referred to as an *inverted file*. If we continue our very concrete mental image: Picture your rows of shoeboxes lying flat, covering your living room floor. Now imagine copying box 2 from each row, noting on the side of it which row it came from, and stacking those boxes vertically, off to one side. You can arrange that stack anyway you like. Maybe, to return to the driver's license example, that's the field for Last Name. You'd probably want to organize the stack (the index) alphabetically, so that if you wanted to find the record for Smith, John, you could zip to the Ss in the stack, pull out his box, see that it was marked "record no. 3," and run over to the third row of shoeboxes. Thus, the order of the rows in your database, that is, what order you enter your records, doesn't matter at all. You simply build an index and search *that* when you want to find something in your database. Or you can build several indexes; you can make an index of any field you want. However, as always, there are costs and reasons why you might not index every field.[2]

A Very Simple Example

Say we have three articles:

Milky Way's Last Major Merger.

Science News. v. 162 no. 24 p. 376

It's a Dog's Life.

The Economist. December 21, 2002. p. 61

Manhattan Mayhem.

Smithsonian. v. 33 no. 9 p. 44

Let's enhance these just a little by adding a one-line description to each record (so that we have a few more words to search on):

Record 1:

Milky Way's Last Major Merger.

Science News. v. 162 no. 24 p. 376.

New clues about galaxy formation indicate early collision affected Milky Way's shape.

Record 2:

It's a Dog's Life.

The Economist. December 21, 2002. p. 61.

From hard labour to a beauty contest, a history of the work and whims of dog breeding.

Record 3:

Manhattan Mayhem.

Smithsonian. v. 33 no. 9 p. 44

Martin Scorsese's realistic portrayal of pre–Civil War strife—*Gangs of New York*—re-creates the brutal street warfare waged between immigrant groups.

My database will have just four fields (Figure 1.4):

1. Record number (four-number places, e.g., my database will never grow to more than 9,999 articles)
2. Article title

Fig. 1.4. A very simple database record.

  3. Journal name

  4. Abstract

Now we need to index the fields.
  The initial list of words from the Article Title field looks like this:

Milky

Way's

Last

Major

Merger

It's

a

Dog's

Life

Manhattan

Mayhem

More Database Decisions

  There are various things about this list that one might question. What will our indexing program do with those possessives and contractions? Do we want to clog it up with little words like *a*? There are many decisions for database designers to make:

- How will the indexing program handle apostrophes and other punctuation? We take it for granted now that the system will simply preserve it, and users can search for contractions or possessives, but you may still encounter systems that insert a space instead of the apostrophe (dog s), or ignore it and treat the letters as a string (ending up with "dogs" for "dog's").

- What will the indexing program do with the "little words"? That is, words such as *a, an, by, for, from, of, the, to, with,* and so forth, which are usually referred to as *stop words*. These are words that are so common that database designers usually decide they don't want to expend time and space to index them. Indexing programs are programmed with a list of such words and will "stop" indexing when they hit a word on the list. A more descriptive term would be *skip words*, because that is what really happens: the indexing program skips any stop list words and continues to the next word. Almost all databases employ a stop word list, and it can vary greatly from one vendor to the next.

- Should the system be designed to preserve information about capitalization, or to ignore the case of the words? We are so used to systems that do not distinguish upper and lowercase (so that you don't have to worry how you type in your query), but there are times when you would really like the system to know the difference between, say, AIDS (the disease) and aids (the common noun or verb).

Because this is a modern system, we'll decide to preserve the apostrophes and to make *a* one of our stop words, so it won't be included in the index. We can then sort the list alphabetically:

Dog's

It's

Last

Life

Major

Manhattan

Mayhem

Merger

Milky

Way's

Can you see the problem here? We have neglected to include an identifier to show which record a word came from. Let's start over.

Better Field Indexing

Let's make sure that our index list includes the record number and which field the word came from:

0001	Milky	TI
0001	Way's	TI
0001	Last	TI
0001	Major	TI
0001	Merger	TI
0002	It's	TI
0002	Dog's	TI
0002	Life	TI
0003	Manhattan	TI
0003	Mayhem	TI

One more thing: we can include a number representing the *order* of the word within the field (why might this be useful?). We now have something like this:

0001	Milky	TI	01
0001	Way's	TI	02
0001	Last	TI	03

Now we'll sort again.

0002	Dog's	TI	03
0002	It's	TI	01
0001	Last	TI	03
0002	Life	TI	04
0001	Major	TI	04
0003	Manhattan	TI	01
0003	Mayhem	TI	02
0001	Merger	TI	05
0001	Milky	TI	01
0001	Way's	TI	02

Note how even though we deleted the stop word *a* in the title "It's a dog's life," the numerical position of "dog's" reflects that there was an intervening word there: its position is recorded as 3, not 2.

Because people might want to search on the name of the publication, it would be good to index that as well. Our index of the Journal Name field looks something like this:

0002	*Economist*	JN	02
0001	*News*	JN	02
0001	*Science*	JN	01
0001	*Science News*	JN	01, 02
0003	*Smithsonian*	JN	01

Note the multiple indexing of *Science News*. The technical term for this is *double posting*.

To make things even faster and more efficient, after indexing each field, combine the indexes so that you have only one list to search:

0002	Dog's	TI	03
0002	Economist	JN	02
0002	It's	TI	01
0001	Last	TI	03
0002	Life	TI	04
0001	Major	TI	04
0003	Manhattan	TI	01
0003	Mayhem	TI	02
0001	Merger	TI	05
0001	Milky	TI	01
0001	News	JN	02
0001	Science	JN	01
0001	Science News	JN	01, 02
0003	Smithsonian	JN	01
0001	Way's	TI	02

We undoubtedly want to index the content of the one-sentence "abstracts," as well. Here is a list of the words in raw form:

new	beauty	Pre-Civil
clues	contest	War
about	a	strife
galaxy	history	Gangs
formation	of	Of
indicate	the	New
early	work	York
collision	and	Re-creates
affected	whims	The
Milky	of	brutal
Way's	dog	street
Shape	breeding	warfare
From	Martin	waged
hard	Scorsese's	between
labour	realistic	immigrant
to	portrayal	groups
a	of	

Decisions and cleanup are needed on this list of words:

- Stop words—what will they be?

- Hyphenated words—how will they be recorded?

- Proper names—"double post" to include the phrase too?

- Alternative spellings—do we do anything about them or not? (What might you do?)

Luckily, software does almost all of this work for us. You probably will never see any indexes in their raw state. What we've been going over here is in real life very under the hood, often proprietary material for the database vendors. You don't need to know exactly how any particular database works; you simply need to grasp some of the basic principles that govern how databases in general are put together and how they are indexed. This determines how you search them—and what you can expect to get out of them.

Quick Recap

This section discussed the idea of field indexes and the importance of good planning in the design of huge databases. Field indexes refer to the idea that the information contained in a database's fields can be extracted and used to build a list of terms in the database. These lists (the indexes) exist separately from the records in the database, and make rapid, efficient searching of huge databases possible. Much thought goes into the initial database design (i.e., what fields to include, what they are called, how much space to allocate for each one), because the design cannot be easily changed later. Many decisions go into the design of indexes as well, for example, which fields will be indexed, how contractions and possessives will be handled, which words will be treated as stop words, and if and how identification of phrases will be supported.

Examples of Indexes

In the examples that follow, see if you can relate what we've just gone over with the "user's view" of the indexing scheme in these common databases. We'll start with the Subjects index in EBSCO's *MasterFILE Premier*, a multidisciplinary database.

The EBSCO *MasterFILE Premier* Subject Index

Even in a fairly simple display, there is a lot to look at and look for. In this view of the subject index in EBSCO's *MasterFILE Premier* (Figure 1.5), *A* is the area identifying where we are: who is providing the database, which database it is, and which part of the database (e.g., "Subjects") we are in. The last is usefully reiterated in several places.

The *B* section lets us jump around to any point in the index, that is, to the entries on and around whatever word we put in. Note that the results

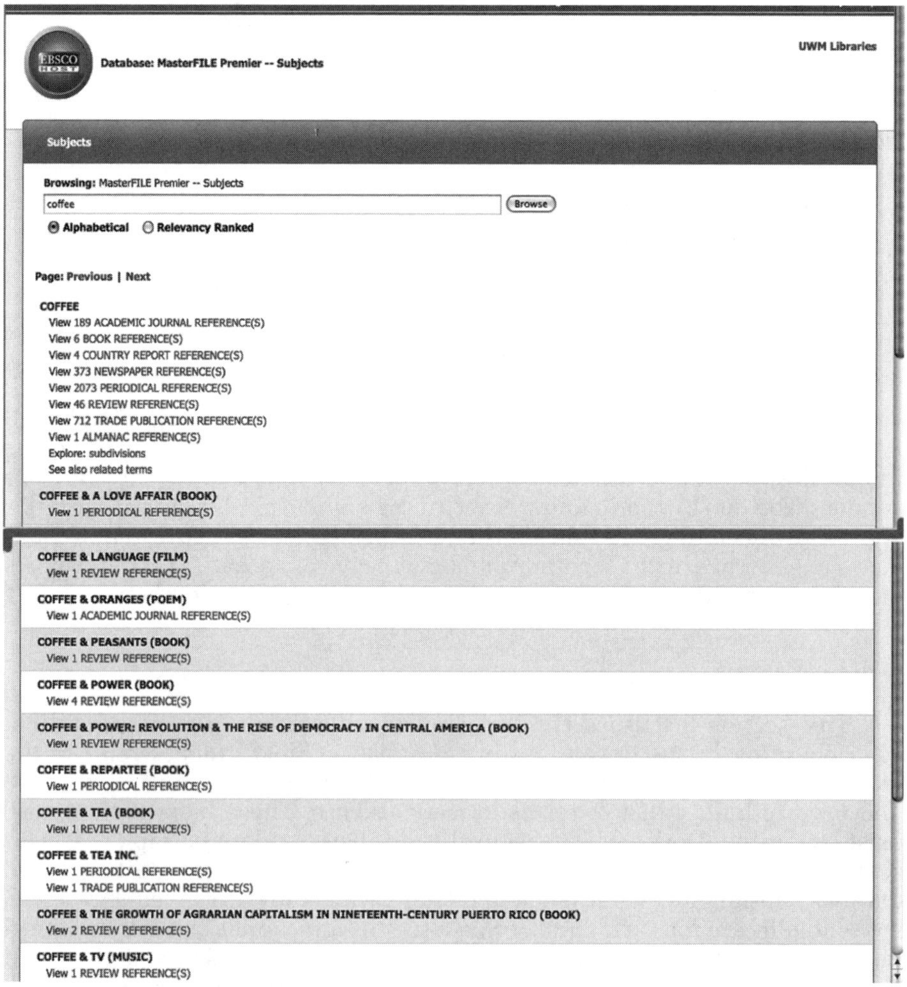

Fig. 1.5. The Subject Index in EBSCO's *MasterFILE Premier*, showing two sections of the "coffee" entries. © 2011 EBSCO Industries, Inc. All rights reserved.

can be returned in alphabetical or in relevancy ranked order: we're seeing the inverted file at work—there are two ways to stack the shoeboxes.

In *C* the actual subject list is provided. The entries in bold and all caps are values from the field designated as *subjects* in this database: words assigned by indexers that capture the essence of the article's content. Note how the entries are a mixture of items: the thing itself (coffee), films, books, poetry, music, company names, and more. The View statements for each entry tell you exactly how many times the term was assigned, and to which type of article (i.e., newspaper, periodical, or review). You can begin to tell what is being captured about each article in this database: subject terms assigned to it and the type of publication it appeared in.

Field Indexes for the WorldCat Database

Moving on to another example, OCLC's WorldCat database (a union catalog of library holdings from around the world) provides examples of the use of *separate* indexes for many fields. In the Browse Index interface, as in EBSCO's Subject list earlier, you have the opportunity to roam around in the indexes, discovering what is there (and thus, what is possible), before committing to a search. There are even multiple indexes for the same fields, because they provide both single-word and phrase indexes for many fields, such as author name (Figure 1.6). The icon for accessing the Browse Index screen is part of the WorldCat Advanced Search interface, discussed in greater detail in Chapter 6. For now, simply observe how it works.

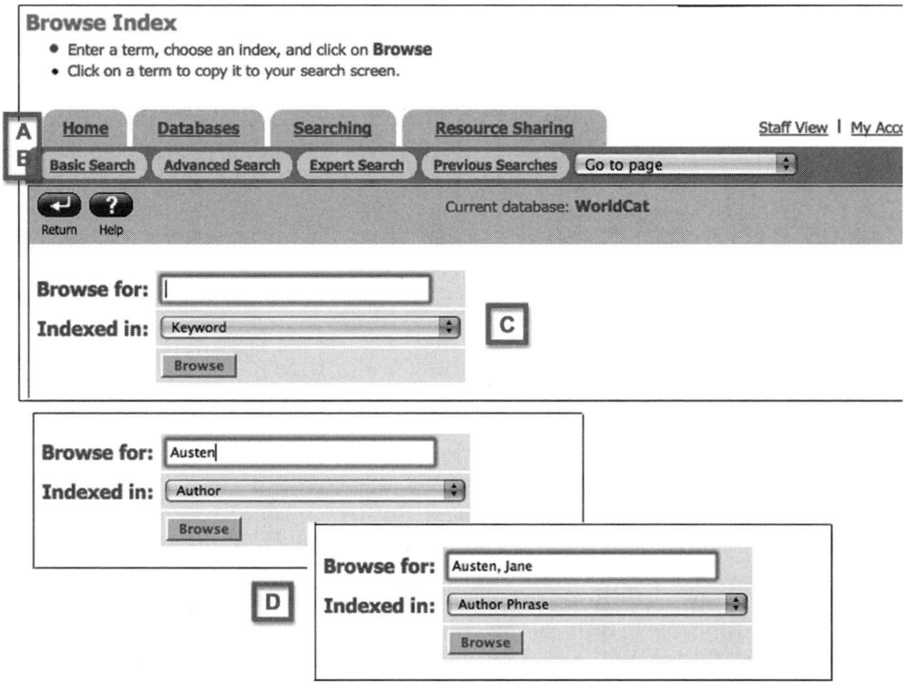

Fig. 1.6. The initial Browse Index screen for the WorldCat® database; examples of single-word and phrase indexes offered for some fields. Screen shots used with the permission of OCLC Online Computer Library Center, Inc. ("OCLC"). FirstSearch® and WorldCat® are registered trademarks/service marks of OCLC.

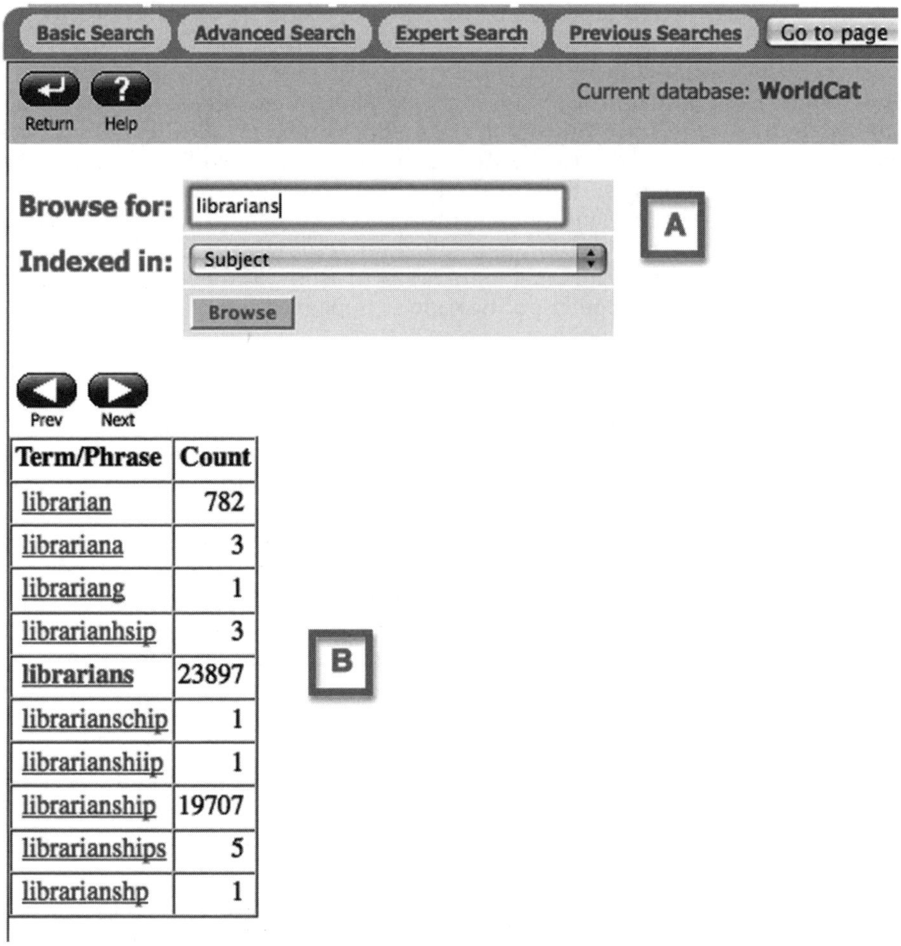

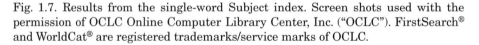

Fig. 1.7. Results from the single-word Subject index. Screen shots used with the permission of OCLC Online Computer Library Center, Inc. ("OCLC"). FirstSearch® and WorldCat® are registered trademarks/service marks of OCLC.

In this case, the *A* area provides four major navigation tabs: you can go Home, change Databases, return to the Searching interface from this Browse Index interface, or log in to participate in Resource Sharing. The *B* area lets you jump directly to one of three search modes, or view the searches you've tried already. Note that the "where am I?" information also appears nearby, that is, the name of the current database. In the *C* area, the index field being searched is set to Keyword. In the screens marked *D*, the drop-down menu has been changed to Author, and then to Author Phrase; an example of the single-word vs. phrase indexes mentioned above. In the Author (single-word) index, you could browse only for an author's last name, for example, Austen. In the Author Phrase, you could browse specifically for Austen, Jane.

Using the Subject Indexes

In Figure 1.7, we have looked up the word *librarians* in the Subject index (A) of the WorldCat database.

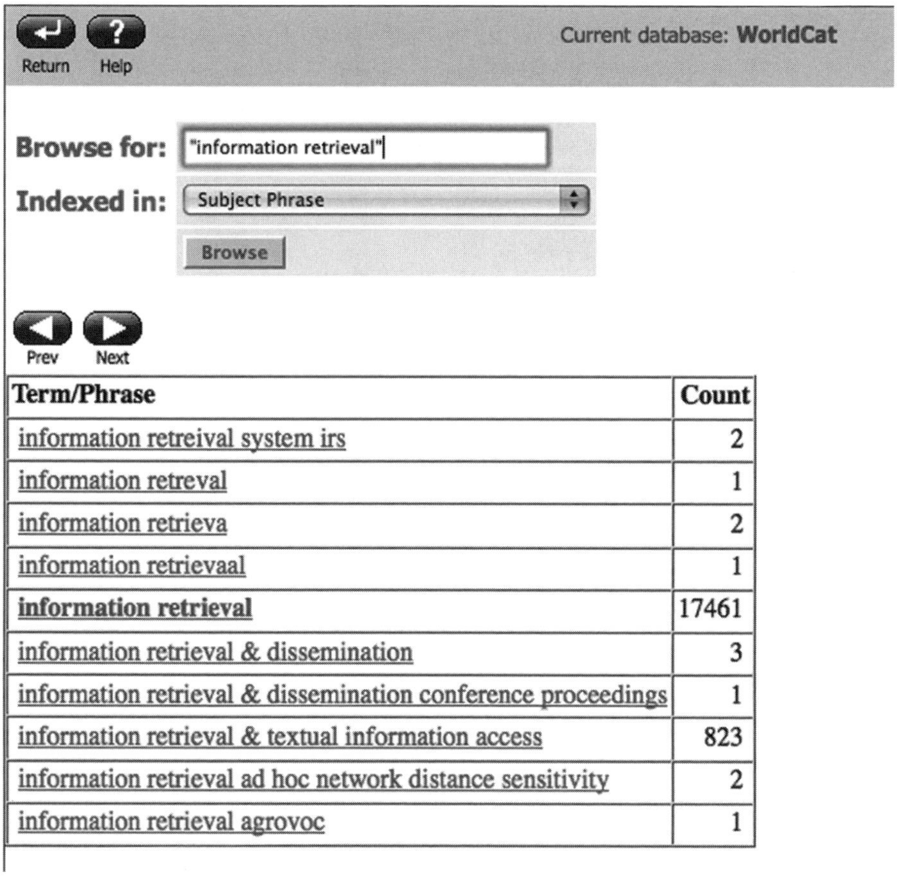

Term/Phrase	Count
information retreival system irs	2
information retreval	1
information retrieva	2
information retrievaal	1
information retrieval	17461
information retrieval & dissemination	3
information retrieval & dissemination conference proceedings	1
information retrieval & textual information access	823
information retrieval ad hoc network distance sensitivity	2
information retrieval agrovoc	1

Fig. 1.8. Results from the multiple-word Subject Phrase index. Screen shots used with the permission of OCLC Online Computer Library Center, Inc. ("OCLC"). FirstSearch® and WorldCat® are registered trademarks/service marks of OCLC.

At *B* in Figure 1.7, we see the results of the search of this index. Note how the term searched on appears in the *middle* of the list, and is in bold. Why do you think the database designers have chosen to display the results this way? Note the terms that only have a count of one. You can tell that the indexing process, that is, the harvesting of terms from the Subject field, is done by a computer program: it simply picks up whatever is there, typos and all. (The errors come from the humans who typed the values into the field. For fallible humans, they are impressively accurate.) The Count field indicates how many items are in the database to which each Subject has been assigned. The numbers tell you something about the overall content of the database, and how useful it might prove for whatever question you're working on. In this case, WorldCat appears to have a wealth of material on librarians (plural) and librarianship, but far fewer entries for "librarian" in the singular.

In Figure 1.8, we see the results of a search for *information retrieval* in the Subject Phrase index; were you to browse forward in this list, you would find literally hundreds of entries beginning with the words: "information retrieval."

WorldCat Detailed Record
- Click on a checkbox to mark a record to be e-mailed or printed in Marked Records.

| Home | Databases | Searching | Results | Resource Sharing | Staff View I My Account I Options I Comments I **Exit** I Hide tips |

| List of Records | Detailed Record | Marked Records | Saved Records | Go to page |

Subjects Libraries E-mail Print Export Help
Bib

WorldCat results for: ti: filter and ti: bubble. Record 1 of 13.

◀ 1 ▶ Mark: ☐
Prev　Next

Detailed Record | Table of Contents | Add/View Comments

The filter bubble :
what the Internet is hiding from you /

Eli Pariser

2011
English ◈ Book 294 p. ; 22 cm.
New York : Penguin Press, ; ISBN: 9781594203008 (hardback) 1594203008 (hardback)

The hidden rise of personalization on the Internet is controlling—and limiting—the information we consume. In 2009, Google began customizing its search results. Instead of giving you the most broadly popular result, Google now tries to predict what you are most likely to click on. According to MoveOn.org board president Eli Pariser, this change is symptomatic of the most significant shift to take place on the Web in recent years—the rise of personalization....

GET THIS ITEM

Access: 🌐 ftp://ppftpuser:welcome@ftp01.penguingroup.com/Booksellers_and_Media/Covers/2008_2009_New_Covers/9781594203008.jpg
Availability: **Check the catalogs in your library.**
- Libraries worldwide that own item: 666
- 🏛 Search the catalog at University of Rochester Libraries

External Resources:
- 📄 Sibley InterLibrary Loan
- 📄 Miner InterLibrary Loan
- 📄 River Campus InterLibrary Loan
- FindIt®
- 📄 Cite This Item

FIND RELATED

More Like This: Search for versions with same title and author I Advanced options ...

Title: **The filter bubble :**
what the Internet is hiding from you /

Author(s): Pariser, Eli.

Publication: New York : Penguin Press,

Year: 2011

Description: 294 p. ; 22 cm.

Language: English

Contents: The race for relevance -- The user is the content -- The Adderall society -- The you loop -- The public is irrelevant -- Hello, world! -- What you want, whether you want it or not -- Escape from the city of ghettos.

Standard No: **ISBN:** 9781594203008 (hardback); 1594203008 (hardback) **LCCN:** 2011-10403

Abstract: The hidden rise of personalization on the Internet is controlling--and limiting--the information we consume. In 2009, Google began customizing its search results. Instead of giving you the most broadly popular result, Google now tries to predict what you are most likely to click on. According to MoveOn.org board president Eli Pariser, this change is symptomatic of the most significant shift to take place on the Web in recent years--the rise of personalization. Though the phenomenon has gone largely undetected until now, personalized filters are sweeping the Web, creating individual universes of information for each of us. Data companies track your personal information to sell to advertisers, from your political leanings to the hiking boots you just browsed on Zappos. In a personalized world, we will increasingly be typed and fed only news that is pleasant, familiar, and confirms our beliefs--and because these filters are invisible, we won't know what is being hidden from us. Our past interests will determine what we are exposed to in the future, leaving less room for the unexpected encounters that spark creativity, innovation, and the democratic exchange of ideas.--From publisher description.

Access: **Materials specified:** Cover image🌐 ftp://ppftpuser:welcome@ftp01.penguingroup.com/Booksellers_and_Media/Covers/2008_2009_New_Covers/9781594203008.jpg

SUBJECT(S)

Descriptor: Invisible Web.
Information organization.
Semantic Web -- Social aspects.
World Wide Web -- Subject access.
Internet -- Censorship.
TECHNOLOGY & ENGINEERING / Telecommunications.
Internet searching.
Information retrieval.

Note(s): Includes bibliographical references and index.

Class Descriptors: **LC:** ZA4237; **Dewey:** 004.67/8

Responsibility: Eli Pariser.

Vendor Info: Baker and Taylor YBP Library Services Blackwell Book Service (BTCP YANK BBUS)

Document Type: Book

Entry: 20110420

Accession No: **OCLC:** 682892628

Database: WorldCat

▶

Subjects Libraries E-mail Print Export Help
Bib

WorldCat results for: ti: filter and ti: bubble. Record 1 of 13.

English I Español I Français I العربية I 日本語 I 한국어 I 中文 (繁體) I 中文 (简体) I Options I Comments I **Exit**

🅒 OCLC © 1992-2011 OCLC
Terms & Conditions

Fig. 1.9. A full record display from the WorldCat database. Screen shots used with the permission of OCLC Online Computer Library Center, Inc. ("OCLC"). FirstSearch® and WorldCat® are registered trademarks/service marks of OCLC.

Record Structure Reflected in Fields Displayed

As a reminder, indexes are built from the fields included in a database record. The fields can be called the *record structure*, and you can get a sense of how simple, or elaborate, a database's record structure is by studying the fields displayed when viewing a record from the database.

The WorldCat database has quite an elaborate record structure; these database designers were making sure that they didn't leave anything out, and that the most complete set of bibliographic information they could assemble would be available to users, as can be seen in a display of a full World-Cat record (Figure 1.9).

The OCLC interface designers are trying to convey a large amount of information here, but they are doing their best to achieve their goal with clarity. Take some time to study the screenshot, noticing how the designers have used different fonts and alignments to convey meaning. If you can, go online and observe the colors used. The field names are lined up on the left, followed by colons. The contents of the fields appear to the right. Under the gray bar marked Subject(s), the terms are labeled Descriptors. Some of the fields probably seem quite mysterious, but think about the purpose of the others, and why the database designers decided to include them. WorldCat has been around since 1967, and it has had to add to its record structure ever since to stay abreast of developments (which can't have been easy). If they had invented the database today, the database designers might have made different choices.

Exercises and Points to Consider

1. What would *your* ideal database record for a journal article look like? Choose any article that interests you, and design a database record for it. What fields will you use? How big will each field be? What will you call the fields? Sketch out what the overall database would be like (and why this article would be included), and justify your choices.

2. Why do you think WorldCat has separate one-word and phrase indexes for the same fields?

3. What is a useful piece of information that is provided when you browse the indexes (in both *MasterFILE* and WorldCat)? How might this affect your search strategy?

4. Go into the *MasterFILE Premier* Subject index, and try looking up *self acceptance*. Page forward a few screens; have you found it yet? Start over at *self*, and page forward until you do find it, noticing as you go how the entries are sorted. (*Hint*: the hyphenated terms file after all the *self* [space] *word* entries.) Finally, look up *self acceptance* again, but this time sort the results by Relevance. Don't be afraid to break away from the straight alphabetical presentation of results if that approach doesn't appear to be working for you.

5. Can you do a field search with Google?

6. People generally think of Google as indexing all the words of all the Web pages that it visits.[3] In some sense, it offers only one huge index labeled "all the text." Why do you think the commercial database

vendors go to so much trouble to provide an elaborate record structure with indexed fields?

7. In the early days of online searching in libraries, only librarians performed searches, after a detailed and careful interview with the patron requesting the search. The librarian would plan the search carefully, and then dial up to connect to the database, using a password and employing a very terse, arcane set of commands to perform the search. Access fees were charged by the minute, with additional charges for records viewed. Try to picture this scenario, and then compare it with the situation today. How do you think the totally open, end-user access has affected databases and their interfaces? Can you think of anything about the current situation that is not an improvement?

Suggested Reading

Tenopir, Carol. 2005. Teaching Student Searchers. *Library Journal* 130 (March 1): 33.

Notes

1. If you're wondering why it would be so hard to change the record structure, remember to think of these databases as huge things: true, adding a new field to a database of just five records would be trivial. But a database of 500,000 records? How are you possibly going to retrospectively fill in the new field for all the existing records?

2. For one thing, the process of initially building the index can take hours. Although this does not mean that it can't be done, remember that every index has to be updated frequently to reflect any changes in your database. It just adds to the complexity of the whole operation.

3. Does Google have stop words, words that it ignores? And does it really index every page all the way to the end? Does this matter?

2
The Searcher's Toolkit: Part 1

In my experience, there are a finite number of concepts, techniques, and strategies for searching databases that make all the difference between aimlessly groping around and efficiently and effectively retrieving useful material. If you spend your whole day searching, then you'll probably discover or develop many more, but for most researchers or reference librarians, the topics in this chapter and the next are most likely all that you will ever need. I've dubbed this set of concepts the *Searcher's Toolkit*. All of them have applications in searching commercial databases, and some can be used with Web search engines (and once you've grasped these concepts, you'll start to see what's missing in the Web search products and understand better why searching the Web is, well, the way it is: sometimes perfect, sometimes very frustrating).

The First Basic Tools

Let us plunge right in with the most fundamental concept of all.

Basic Tool No. 1: Boolean Logic

In fact, this concept is so fundamental that you've probably run into it before, possibly several times through grade school, high school, and college. But do you *really* know what Boolean logic is and how it works? Do you really understand how it will affect your searches? Bear with a discussion of it one more time—you may be surprised!

In the database context, Boolean logic (after a fellow named George Boole [1815–1864][1]) refers to the *logical* (rather than arithmetical) operations on sets. That is, rather than manipulating numbers using symbols for plus,

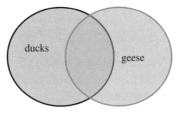

AND

Fig. 2.1. Boolean AND: Ducks
AND Geese.

minus, multiply, or divide, Boolean logic controls what happens to sets of things when acted on by *logical operators*. The Boolean operators used in database searching are:

AND

OR

AND NOT (frequently expressed simply as *NOT*; more on this later.)

Venn Diagrams

Arithmetical expressions (e.g., 2+2) result in some value (i.e., 4). Boolean expressions result in either a sub- or superset of the original sets; rather than producing a specific value, logical operators have an *effect* on the sets, producing a different output set. The effects of Boolean expressions are traditionally illustrated with drawings called *Venn diagrams*. Venn diagrams are always done with circles and shadings as in Figure 2.1, which keeps them nicely abstract. Feel free to start thinking of the terminology "sets," and these circle illustrations as "sets of database records," to make the concept more concrete. With just one operator in effect, Venn diagrams are quite simple to draw and to understand what the operator's effect is.

Boolean AND

In Figure 2.1, the circle on the left represents the set of all the database records that include the word *ducks*, a few of which also include the word *geese*. The circle on the right represents all records that include the word *geese*, a few of which also include the word *ducks*. A search for *ducks AND geese* retrieves only those records that mention *both* terms, represented by the smaller, overlapping section. It is easy to get confused here, because our regular use of the word *and* is additive, that is, it produces more (e.g., "two scoops, and sprinkles, and some whipped cream, please"), but a Boolean AND is very different: an AND operator will always, in practice, return a set that is *smaller* than either of the original sets. Theoretically, the largest set it could return would still be only of equal size to the smaller of the original sets. For example, at one point in time, the ProQuest Research database contained 456 records that contained *Obama, Michelle* in a field called Person, and 19,853 records containing *Obesity* in a field called Subject. A search on

Obama, Michelle in the Person field,

AND

Obesity in the Subject field

produced 29 records.

Notice how even when the initial sets are quite large, the combined, "ANDed" set is considerably smaller. When one of the initial sets is much smaller than the other, as is the case here, the resulting set is affected even more.

AND says that *all* criteria must be met for an indicated action to happen (usually retrieval of a record). What the Boolean operators are really doing is evaluating true or false. The computer's thought process goes something like this:

If (ducks) is true (e.g., present in the record)

AND (at the same time, in the same record)

If (geese) is true

Retrieve the record.

So, to reiterate: the number of records meeting multiple conditions is, in practice, always smaller than the set of records meeting just one condition, and it is usually significantly smaller. The more conditions (criteria, terms) that you set, the smaller the number of records that will be retrieved: there will be fewer documents about ducks AND geese AND loons than there are about just ducks AND geese. If one of the initial sets is very small, ANDing it with some other term is likely to reduce the results to zero. But our next operator, OR, is here to help with that potential problem.

Boolean OR

In Figure 2.2, the circle on the left represents all the database records that include the word *banana*, and the circle on the right represents all the database records that include the word *orange*. In this case, we don't care what other words they contain, or how much they overlap. Thinking of this as a search, the OR retrieves *all* the bananas records, plus *all* the oranges records (including records mentioning both), for a total of a LOT of records! Again, our common parlance can make this confusing: usually we use the word *or* to mean "either one or the other"—"I'll have the banana *or* the orange." We wouldn't expect to be handed both fruits in response to that statement. But in Boolean logic, OR means "either the one, or the other, or

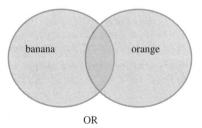

OR

Fig. 2.2. Boolean OR: Banana OR Orange.

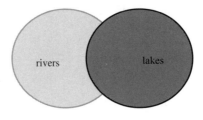

NOT

Fig. 2.3. Boolean NOT: Rivers NOT Lakes.

both." Either of the criteria can be met for the computer to retrieve the record:

If (banana) is true (e.g., present in a record)

OR

If (orange) is true (present in a record)

Retrieve the record.

Think of it this way: in practice, Boolean OR is (practically) always more. By employing a judicious combination of Boolean AND and OR operators, you can "grow" small results sets in a controlled fashion, as we'll see later in this chapter.

Boolean NOT

Finally, Figure 2.3 represents the Boolean exclusion operator, which you'll see expressed as AND NOT and simply NOT with almost equal frequency. For our purposes, the terms are interchangeable, and this text will generally use simply NOT to make the operators as distinguishable as possible.[2] If this feels confusing, take comfort that at least the effects of this operator are more in line with our common usage of *not*: rivers NOT lakes retrieves records that include the term *rivers*, as long as they do NOT also contain the word lakes. Both criteria must be met, in the sense that the first term must be present, and the second term must *not* be present, for a record to be retrieved. The set of records retrieved can be thought of as just the lighter area of the *rivers* circle; anything from the darker *lakes* circle would not be in the results set. Note how the syntax is subtly different (which is further proof that even when a database vendor just uses NOT, what is really going on is AND NOT):

If (rivers) is true (present in a record)

And

If (lakes) is NOT true (not present in the record)

Retrieve the record.

As you would expect, like AND, NOT almost always reduces the number of records retrieved. In general usage, you'll find that you don't often use the NOT operator in commercial databases: the possibility of missing useful records just because they happened to include the "NOTed" out term is too risky.

If too many results are coming back, the better strategy is almost always to AND in another term, rather than to NOT out a term.

Order of Boolean Operations

A statement using just one Boolean operator—ducks OR geese—is straightforward. But just as you can write arithmetical expressions with several operators (2+2–3*9), you can write Boolean expressions with multiple operators. You will encounter plenty of searches that require more complexity than simply (word) AND (word). Again, just as in the arithmetical statements, the Boolean operators have very specific effects, and the order in which they are processed has a powerful effect on what ends up in the results set. When there is more than one operator in a search statement, they are generally evaluated in this order:

- NOT operations are performed first.
- Then AND operations are evaluated.
- Finally, OR operations are performed.

This is called the *order of operation*. This is the standard order for processing Boolean operators, but some systems simply evaluate statements left to right, the way you read. The results could be very different, depending on which order is used. Although it's important to be aware of the idea of order of operation, luckily you don't have to figure out what it is on each system you use. There is a simple way to take control and bend the order of operation to your will.

The Power of Parentheses

To control the order of operation, many systems allow you to group your ANDs, ORs, and NOTs with parentheses: ( ). Just as in arithmetic statements, the use of parentheses is helpful either to make the order of operation explicit, or to override it. What happens is that the expression in parentheses will be evaluated first, and then the order of operation (standard or left to right) will take over.[3] Throwing parentheses into the mix can dramatically change the way the system interprets the search. For example, the statement

ducks NOT migration OR geese

produces the same result set as

(ducks NOT migration) OR geese

because in this case, putting the parentheses around the NOT statement (causing it to be executed first) is exactly the same as what happens in the standard order of operation (NOT first, OR last). The set of documents retrieved would be fairly large, and it would contain records for ducks (as long as those records didn't mention migration) and any records mentioning geese—even records that discuss geese and migration. OR really opens the door to let things back in, sometimes in surprising ways.

Represented as a Venn diagram, the statement (ducks NOT migration) OR geese looks like Figure 2.4.

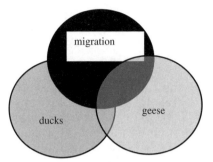

Fig. 2.4. (Ducks NOT Migration) OR Geese.

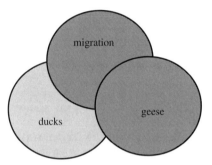

Fig. 2.5. Ducks NOT (Migration OR Geese).

The results of this search would include all the records except those represented by the visible dark area of the "migration" circle. Note that records about geese that mention migration *would* be included in the results; the NOT only affects the duck records. However, writing the search statement as

ducks NOT (migration OR geese)

will produce quite a different result set, much smaller and more focused. These would be records that mention ducks, and only those duck records that don't mention either migration or geese—the lightest area in Figure 2.5. The Venn diagram for this statement is shown in Figure 2.5.

Quick Recap

This section introduced the first and most fundamental tool in the Searcher's Toolkit, Boolean logic. The Boolean logical operators are AND, OR, NOT (also expressed AND NOT). Adding terms to a search with AND will reduce the number of results, as will "NOTing" out a term. "ORing" more terms into a search will increase the number of results. Boolean expressions are often represented graphically with Venn diagrams. The standard order of operations for Boolean statements is to evaluate any NOT statements first, followed by AND statements, and finally by OR statements. Putting part of the statement in parentheses changes the order of operations, because the parenthesized section will be evaluated first.

Basic Tool No. 2: Controlled Vocabulary

The conundrum of online searching is that "We want to look for concepts, but we are forced to search for words" (Walker and Janes 1999). Think about it: if you wanted an *overview* of some topic, or a *discussion* of the pros and cons of some action, or especially *one good article on* . . . how do you express these squishy notions to a digital search engine? Even if you can search the full text, the item you want might not include in its text "this is an overview" or "here is a discussion" and certainly not "here is the latest best article" on topic xyz. All that you can do, in each of these cases, is to search on words that represent the topic. In the world of commercial, subscription databases, there is an additional, powerful option: the provision of *controlled vocabulary*, also known as *subject headings*, a *thesaurus*,[4] *descriptors*,[5] or *authority control*.[6] Controlled vocabulary is one of the added extras, one of the contributions of the companies that put together the databases, and one of the reasons they charge a subscription fee to access them. Remember the indexers from chapter 1? You are paying for a bit of human analysis on each entry in the database. If done well, this analysis is worth the price of admission for the efficiency that it provides.

Advantages of Controlled Vocabulary

Why is controlled vocabulary so valuable?

- Controlled vocabulary saves you from having to come up with, and then search for, every possible synonym (or alternative spelling) for a term. For example, if all of the articles discussing various kinds of clothing are assigned a subject heading of "clothing," you don't have to worry about looking for all the possible ways clothing might be expressed, for example: dress, raiment, drapery, costume, attire, habiliment, vesture, vestment, garment, garb, apparel, wardrobe, wearing apparel, clothes, outfit, trousseau, suit, trappings, togs, day wear, night wear, zoot suit . . .[7]

  - *Note*: Don't let your synonym neurons atrophy completely, though, because if you try a term in a subject or thesaurus search and get no results, not even a "see" reference, you'll need to think of another term with which to start. And, of course, there is no controlled vocabulary on the Web.

- Theoretically, the use of controlled vocabulary should make your search more complete: if the indexers at the database company have reliably assigned a subject heading of *waterfowl* every time an article mentions geese or goose, duck or ducks, loon or loons, or any other waterbird, it should only be necessary to search on *waterfowl* as a Subject to retrieve everything.

- It can be used to disambiguate words that have several meanings (e.g., mercury—a planet, a car, a god, or a metal?), aiding in the precision of your search results. (*Precision*, in searching, is an important technical term, rather than just descriptive. See "Searching Lexicon 3: Recall versus Precision" later in this chapter). For author names, *authority control* provides *one* way to look up an author known by more than one name (e.g., Mark Twain/Samuel Clemens).

- It provides a safe and helpful entry point into an unfamiliar subject area. Even if you know nothing about the subject, you have the assurance that the terms in the subject list are correct and appropriate. By browsing in the list and getting a sense of the terms (especially if there are "see" or "see also" references), you can often get ideas and develop or refine a search strategy.

Expressing these points in more formal terms (Walker and Janes 1999), controlled vocabularies:

- Facilitate the *gathering of like items*
- Help with *comprehensiveness* of results
- Help with *precision* of results
- Help *broaden understanding* of a topic in an unfamiliar subject area

Basic Tool No. 3: Field Searching

This tool harks back to the discussion of database structure in Chapter 1: how records in databases consist of a series of fields, each designated to hold a particular value. *Field searching* simply means the ability to restrict your search to a specific field, for example, to search just the *author* field for a particular value (a name). Most databases offer some kind of default set of fields that are searched, so if you're unsure, in a hurry, or just getting a sense of what the database might contain, you can always throw a word or phrase into the first available search box and hit search, just like you usually do on the Web. Taking a few moments to determine what fields are available for searching can be very valuable, however. Field searching focuses your search, and usually makes it more efficient. For example, say that you wanted to search a database of English literature for works by an author named—English! Just searching on the keyword "English" without limiting to the author field would result in hundreds of irrelevant results, because a great many of the records undoubtedly mention the word in a title or abstract, or English might appear in a Language field that gets included in a Default Fields search. The database designers spent all that time deciding what fields to have—so definitely exploit this feature if it is available.

Combining Field Searching and Controlled Vocabulary

The combination of field searching with controlled vocabulary is especially effective; for example, find an appropriate term in the list of subject terms and then search on it, restricting your search to the Subject Terms field. Of course, you will often construct searches combining all three of these initial tools, to produce a search such as

Hanushek → in the → Author field

AND

Education → in the → Subject Terms field

AND

2000–2011 → in the → Date field

You can even make use of Boolean operators *within* the same text entry field. Remember the Michelle Obama example from earlier in the chapter that only produced 29 results? We could increase the number of results in a controlled, efficient way by ORing in related terms for one of the concepts, like this:

Obama, Michelle → in the → Person field

AND

Obesity OR weight control OR nutrition → in the → Subject field

This search produces 44 results. Can you explain in your own words what is happening in this search? This is a very important and useful concept; we will visit it again before leaving this chapter.

There are more tools for your Searcher's Toolkit waiting in Chapter 3. Before going on, however, there are some terms in what we'll call the Searching Lexicon that, while they may not make you a better searcher, are useful to know because they give you a way to describe or better understand your search results.

Terms in the Searching Lexicon

Searching Lexicon 1: False Drops

A *false drop* is a document that is retrieved by your search terms, but the terms in the document are not used in the sense you intended, for example, a search on "employment or jobs or careers" that retrieves articles about Steve Jobs. False drops epitomize the problem of wanting to search for concepts but only being able to search for words! They are not *wrong* in a technical sense: the words in the records match the words you typed in— they just aren't being used to express the meaning you had in mind. (To make up for the inconvenience, such results are often quite humorous, if not downright bizarre.) When you get what appears to be a completely off-the-wall result, don't immediately assume that the system is defective or that something is wrong. Now you have a term for such a result; it might simply be a false drop.

Controlled vocabulary and field searching can help avoid the false-drop problem, although even those tools may not make it go away completely. Systems that search large quantities of full text are especially prone to the false-drop problem.

Searching Lexicon 2: Stop Words

Stop words were mentioned in Chapter 1 but are worth revisiting here. Stop words, aka *noise words*, are those little words that most systems (commercial database or Web search) do not index. Typical choices for a stop-word list could include *an, by, for, from, of, the, to, with, be, where, how, it, he, my, his, when, there, is, are, so, she,* and *her*. There is no standard list of stop words that all databases adhere to, which is good in a way, because it allows for the possibility of a database having a relatively short list of stop words, or possibly even none at all. This means, however (if you determine that stop words might be interfering with your search results), that you'll have to dig around in the database's help files and hope that the list of stop words is documented somewhere. There will be occasions where the words that a database or search engine has chosen *not* to index are very important, and you'll need to come up with creative ways to get around the problem. (One of the most famous examples is a search on that famous line, "to be or not to be"—can it be done?)

Searching Lexicon 3: Recall versus Precision

Recall and precision have to do with the number and quality of the results retrieved by your search:

- *Recall* refers to retrieving more results—spreading your net as wide as possible, and probably picking up a number of less relevant results along with the good results. *High recall* means that you are unlikely to miss any relevant items.

- *Precision* refers to focusing your search down, retrieving fewer, but more perfectly on-target and relevant results. *High precision* means that you are unlikely to retrieve very many, if any, irrelevant results (no false drops).

What might be the pros and cons of each?

- With greater recall the chances are better that you won't miss any relevant materials, but you'll invest more time going through your results, reviewing them after the fact to filter out the irrelevant items (in other words, you might have to wade through an awful lot of junk to find the gems).

- The more precise your search is, the more likely it is that you'll miss some things. There will be items in the database that might well meet your needs, but that your search didn't pick up because your choice of terminology or fields or limits was just a little *too* specific.

Google provides a great example of both ends of the recall–precision spectrum: ultimate *recall* is all the matches to a simple search. Ultimate *precision* is represented by the "I'm Feeling Lucky" search button, which takes you to just one (theoretically ideal) result.

Should I Aim for Recall or Precision?

Neither one—recall or precision—is intrinsically good or bad; they simply describe an outcome. But recall and precision also provide a useful a way to think about your search, to guide how you go about it: what database or search engine you use, and what search techniques you employ. The outcome desired dictates the search style employed: someone who is testing a choice of PhD thesis topic wants to spread the net as wide as possible to make sure that no one has looked at their particular problem before. For that situation, high recall is crucial. Similarly, if you believe you're looking for an obscure topic, but you want absolutely everything and anything that can be found about it, you'll want to try for maximum recall. You might start with a Web search, or in an appropriate database, enter a very simple style of search (e.g., no controlled vocabulary, not limited to any specific field). An undergraduate writing a short paper or a community hobbyist investigating a new topic, however, may be perfectly served by a high-precision search that identifies a few recent, relevant articles, even though many more related, or equally relevant, articles remain behind in the database. In that case, choose an appropriate database, check for subject terms, perhaps combine two or more with Boolean operators, and use some field searching.

Quick Recap

This section of the chapter has introduced two more tools in the Searcher's Toolkit, as well as three terms in the Searching Lexicon. You now have these major tools in your search arsenal:

1. The concept of Boolean logic for combining terms: the operators AND, OR, and NOT, and the use of parentheses to affect the order in which the Boolean operators are processed.

2. The concept of controlled vocabulary: terms that the vendor has applied to help you get all the articles on a topic without having to keyword search every variation or synonym, and to disambiguate among various meanings.

3. The concept of field searching: restricting your search to specified fields to make it more precise and efficient.

You also now know that database indexing programs have lists of certain words they do *not* index, known as *stop words*. In addition, you have some new language to describe the results of your searches:

• False drops

• Recall

• Precision

Applying the Tools

Let's look at EBSCO's *MasterFILE Premier*, a multidisciplinary database, and see how these tools apply there.

MasterFILE Premier: Notes and Search Examples

The first challenge with any database is to be able to look at and interpret what is presented in the interface. We're so used to looking at busy Web pages that we look—but we don't really *see*. To turn yourself into a more efficient and effective searcher, however, it is important to be able to look over an interface and quickly translate what's there into the tools you are looking for:

• Does it use Boolean operators for combining terms?

• Is it possible to search in specific fields, and if yes, which ones?

• Is any kind of controlled vocabulary available? (Can you browse it?)

Determining Availability of Search Tools

Most databases offer two search modes: *Basic* and *Advanced*. Usually the previous questions won't be answered by looking at the Basic search

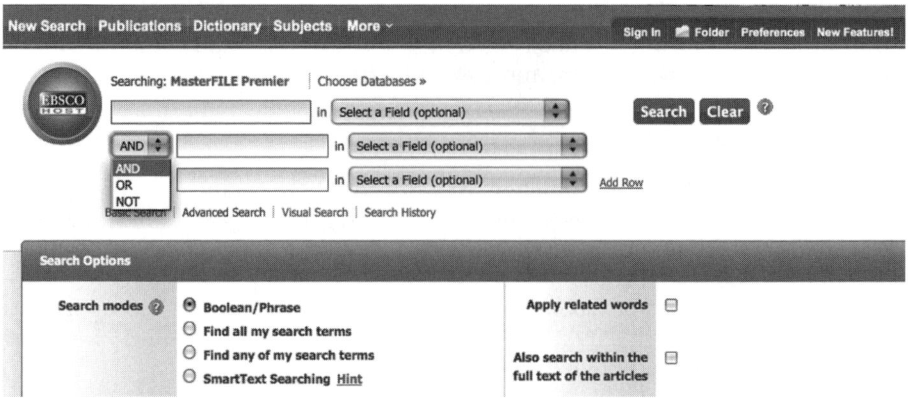

Fig. 2.6. Advanced Search interface, showing Boolean operators, in *MasterFILE Premier*. © 2011 EBSCO Industries, Inc. All rights reserved.

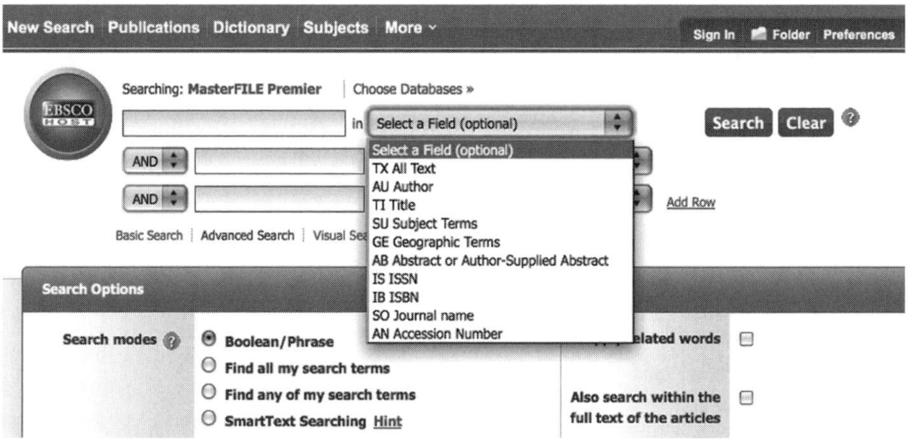

Fig. 2.7. Fields available for searching in *MasterFILE Premier*. © 2011 EBSCO Industries, Inc. All rights reserved.

interface, but there should be good information in the Advanced screen. Figure 2.6 shows the Advanced Search interface in *MasterFILE Premier*. What do you see? Are your first three tools available?

Check: Boolean operators work here. In fact, there appears to be an alternative way to achieve a Boolean effect: note the *Search modes* area, and the *"Find all ..."* and *"Find any ..."* options. (You will explore the SmartText option in one of the Exercises at the end of the chapter.) The whole lower area of the screen is devoted to *Limit* options, but we haven't talked about limits yet, so we won't go into those.

Now take a look at Figure 2.7: do we have the option of restricting our search to certain fields?

Check: there are fields available for searching. The list of fields gives a clue, reinforced by the top bar in the interface, that some kind of controlled vocabulary might be available, and that it can be browsed. See the word *Subjects* in the bar across the top?

Controlled Vocabulary: The Subjects List

Some databases offer separate lists of the terms that have been indexed from various fields (as in the WorldCat screenshots in Chapter 1, where there were separate lists of terms for the Subject and the Subject Phrase fields). The *MasterFILE Premier* Subjects list is an all-in-one affair: it includes terms from many fields, not just "subjects" per se. You can use it to identify controlled vocabulary, as well as to identify titles of books, poems, companies, places, and people—proper names of all kinds. The *MasterFILE Premier* Subjects list also provides some nice value-added information: each entry includes the article publication type(s), and how many of each, available for that heading. Sections of the entries starting at the Subject "Mars" demonstrate this well (Figure 2.8a and 2.8b):

The *MasterFILE* Subjects list is useful if you are looking for one thing (a person, place, book review, company, etc.) from one sort of publication, for example, academic journal references to Mars (the planet). It makes it very easy to connect directly to the results you intended (minimizing false drops). It does not, however, offer any way to construct a multiple-term search, or to view all the articles on a topic, regardless of type of publication.

Multiple Field Searches in MasterFILE

To set up a Boolean search and use known values in specific fields in *MasterFILE Premier*, the best approach is to check the Subjects list, determine the correct form of the terms you want to use, then click on Advanced Search and type the terms in yourself, setting the field to be searched to Subject (or Author, etc.). One cautionary note: do not include the parentheses on the terms that have been glossed to distinguish their meaning, for example, Mars (Planet) has to be entered Mars Planet.

Search Example 1

A patron approaches and says: "I want to find some articles about the Mars lunar lander." Something about this doesn't sound quite right to you, but the patron insists on that terminology.

The most simple, literal approach (besides going to the Web) might be to go to *MasterFILE Premier*, and simply type in "mars lunar lander," as shown in the upper part of Figure 2.9.

This produces only one result (Figure 2.9)—and a very odd one, at that! (Would you call this a false drop?) You were right to think there was something wrong with the patron's terminology; however, it's always worth taking a look to figure out why you got something. In this case, you can see that one of the subject headings in this odd result is *space probes*, indicated by the arrow in Figure 2.9. Aha! That sounds good. From Figure 2.8b we know there should be lots of entries for the planet Mars. Because the Advanced search screen is right here for us above the results, we can reformulate our search immediately by filling in these two known subject headings and setting their fields to Subject Terms (reflected in the results screen in Figure 2.10).

The results of this search are now on target, and the first results of many are shown in Figure 2.10 (note that these results are in *relevance* order; there are more recent results). If you scrolled down a bit, the additional suggested subject headings on the left would confirm that we're on the right track and would offer ways to focus the search further. (The patron must

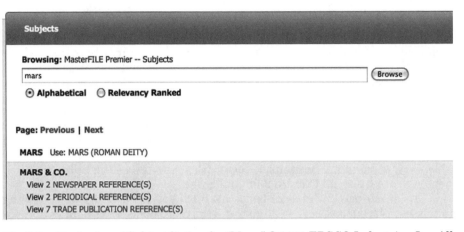

Fig. 2.8a. Beginning of Subject listing for "Mars." © 2011 EBSCO Industries, Inc. All rights reserved.

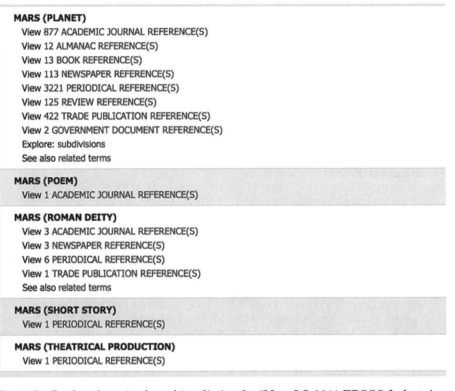

Fig. 2.8b. Farther down in the subject listing for "Mars." © 2011 EBSCO Industries, Inc. All rights reserved.

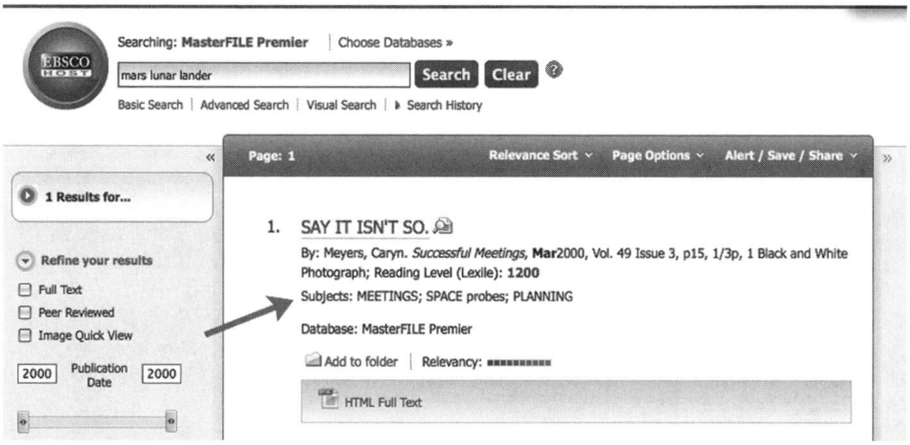

Fig. 2.9. Search for "mars lunar lander," showing a single result and its subject headings. © 2011 EBSCO Industries, Inc. All rights reserved.

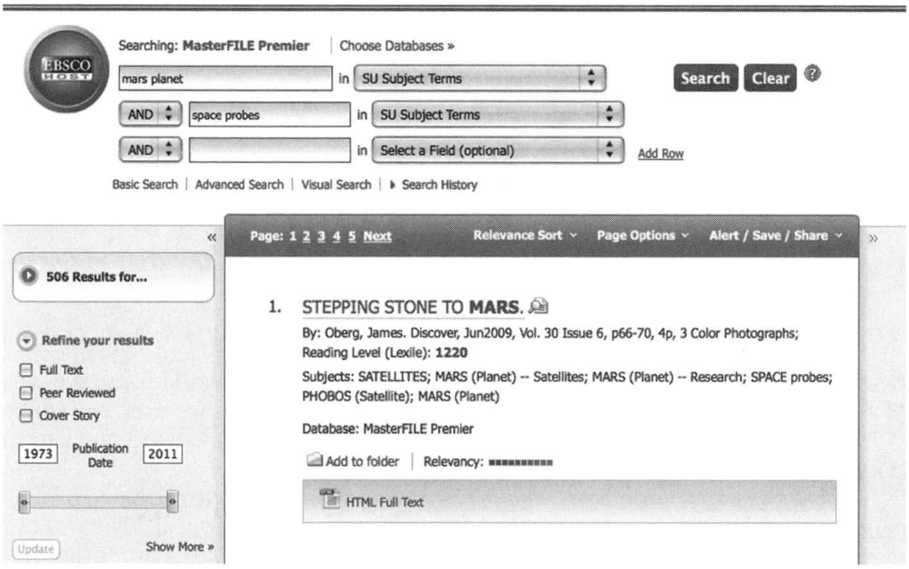

Fig. 2.10. Better results from search strategy using subject terms. © 2011 EBSCO Industries, Inc. All rights reserved.

have been thinking of a Mars Lander or Rover—the "lunar" part was misremembered.) We will be seeing EBSCO's interface again in chapter 7, where we will go into more of its features in detail.

Boolean Logic: Advanced Search versus Basic Search

As a final note to this chapter, unfortunately we have to reveal that there are no comfortable absolutes in this business. The Advanced Search screen may not always be the best answer, as shown in the following two screenshots. In Figure 2.11, a Boolean search was set up in the Advanced

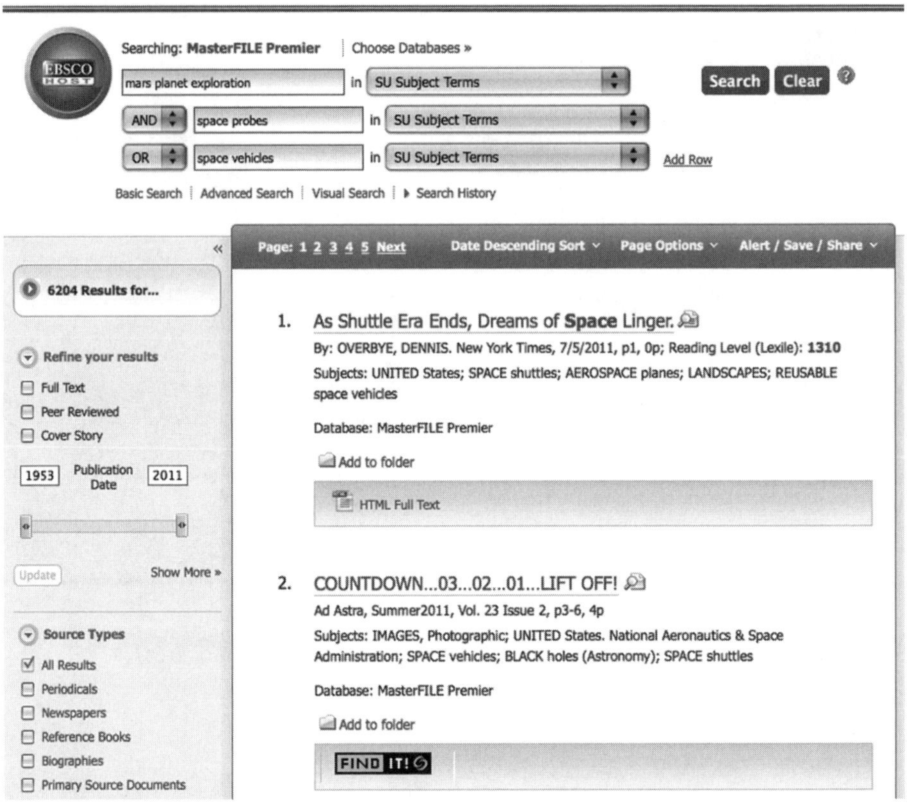

Fig. 2.11. Boolean logic pitfalls in the Advanced Search screen. © 2011 EBSCO Industries, Inc. All rights reserved.

Search screen, using the operators in the drop-down menus. The huge number of results (6,204) and the presence of only one of our search terms (space vehicles) in the most recent result should set off alarm bells in your mind. Something has gone awry.

What the searcher *meant* was Mars planet exploration and (space probes or space vehicles), that is, anything about the exploration of Mars using mechanisms sent there. If the searcher thought to type "Mars planet exploration" in the first field, and to AND that with "Space probes OR Space vehicles" *all in the second search field*, the search would work the way it was intended (Figure 2.12) and would produce 585 on-target results. The interface structure doesn't lead you to think of doing it this way, however, and so the results of the Figure 2.11 search are full of false drops (unless you choose the "sort by relevance" option, and then they are old).

In the Basic screen, however, it's a snap to do it right, using those powerful parentheses (Figure 2.13). You can immediately tell your search is right by the titles in the results and the suggested subject headings on the left.

This is a point to keep in mind: *basic* doesn't necessarily need to mean simplistic. Because you are now a master of Boolean operators and parentheses, it can be *easier* to do some searches in the Basic mode. (There are even ways to indicate what field to search in the Basic mode, but that can wait.) For quick iterations of a search, testing various terms and combinations, the Basic search box is very useful.

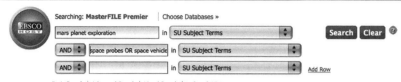

Fig. 2.12. Use of Boolean operator *within* a search field to achieve the desired results. © 2011 EBSCO Industries, Inc. All rights reserved.

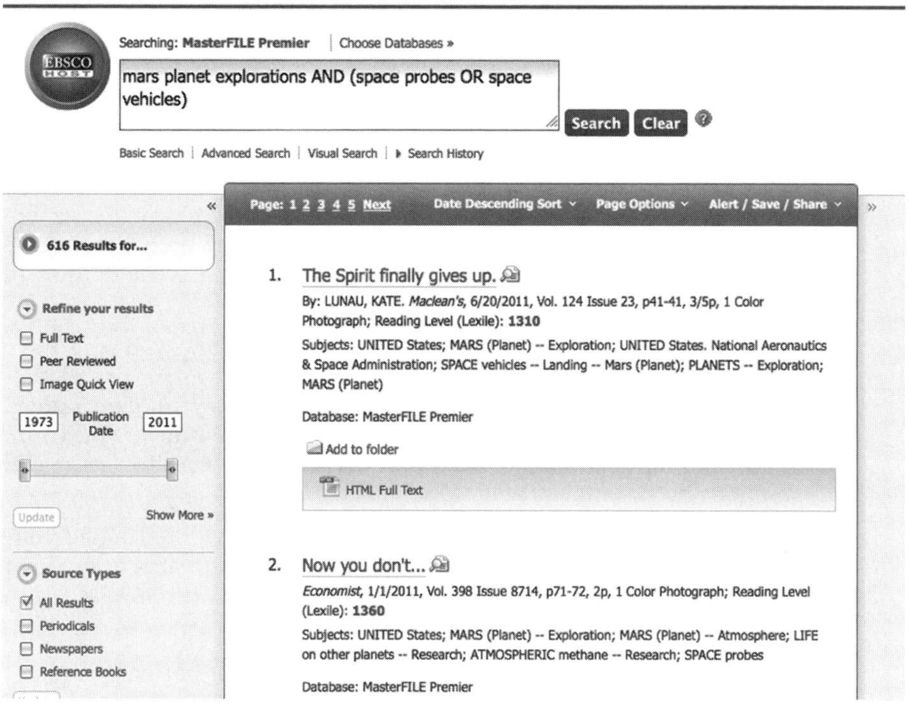

Fig. 2.13. Successful Boolean search statement and results in Basic mode. © 2011 EBSCO Industries, Inc. All rights reserved.

Exercises and Points to Consider

1. Consider these statements:

   ducks OR geese NOT migration

   (ducks OR geese) NOT migration

   (ducks AND geese) OR loons

   ducks AND (geese OR loons)

   (ducks OR geese) AND migration

   (ducks OR geese) NOT migration

   (ducks OR (geese NOT migration)) AND lakes

   Try drawing Venn diagrams for the paired statements to see how (or if) they differ. Then try describing in words what the content of the documents retrieved by these statements would be. Test out the statements in the Basic search mode of any multidisciplinary database similar to *MasterFILE* (look for names such as *ProQuest Research*, *OmniFile*, or *Academic Search Complete*, or a group called "multidisciplinary" or "general" in the guide to databases on your institution's library website).

2. Pick three terms relating to a subject that interests you, and explore searching them in various ways in the database you chose in question 1. Try a number of Boolean combinations in Basic search mode, try setting up similar searches in Advanced mode, and see if your terms appear in the Subjects list. Even though we didn't discuss them, experiment with the various limits options, both in the search screen and in the results screen.

3. In the *MasterFILE* Advanced Search, try the "mars lunar lander" search again, but this time set the Search mode to SmartText Searching. The results will be very different. In fact, you might not ever realize that there's no such thing as a Mars lunar lander, because the results are so appropriate. Experiment with the SmartText mode for a while. Would you want to set this as the default in your library? Why or why not?

4. In describing the benefits of controlled vocabulary, you will have noticed a consistent use of terms such as *should*, as in "use of subject headings *should* ensure that you retrieve everything on a given topic," rather than the more certain term *will*. What do you think might prevent controlled vocabulary from being a perfect retrieval panacea?

5. Say you set up a search and set the field drop-down for one of your terms to Subject—but you didn't check the Subjects index list first—you're just taking a shot in the dark. Your search results are zero. Why?

6. If you had part of a citation and were trying to find the rest of the information (a *known item search*), what type of search would you probably try first, one that had high recall or one that had high precision? Based on your answer, what type of resource (commercial database or Web search) and techniques would you use? What if your first approach didn't work?

Sidebar 2.1. Analyzing Recall versus Precision

Say that there are N relevant items out there. You have a search engine that retrieves items based on a query. We can make a chart that describes the efficacy of the search in terms of the four possible types of results (Table 2.1). You can think of actual numbers being substituted for all the types of results.

True positives are search results that indeed are relevant items. You can clearly count these.

False negatives are failures of the search: relevant items that are out there but are not retrieved. If you know there are N relevant items altogether, then this number is N – (true positives). This is called a *Type II* error in statistical hypothesis testing (the test wrongly reports that a true hypothesis is false).

False positives are search results that are useless and irrelevant. You can count these because you're looking at them. This is called a *Type I* error in statistical hypothesis testing (the test wrongly reports that a false hypothesis is true).

True negatives are all of those items not found that indeed you don't care about because they are irrelevant. There are presumably a great many of these unless something is really off in the system. We don't usually use this number.

Considering the *numbers* of these types of results, we can define the following:

Recall: the number of relevant items found divided by the number of relevant items out there (N):

Recall = (True positives)/[(True positives) + (False negatives)] = (True positives) / N.

Precision: the number of relevant items found divided by the number of items found (relevant and irrelevant):

Precision = (True positives) / [(True positives) + (False positives)].

One error measure is the number of false results divided by the number of relevant items out there (N):

Error rate = [(False positives) + (False negatives)] / [(True positives) + (False negatives)]

= [(False positives) + (False negatives)] / N.

So if you have good recall (near 1), you don't wind up with lots of missed but relevant items, but your results could be diluted by lots of false positives, or items that are wrongly retrieved as being relevant when they are not.

If you have good precision, on the other hand, you can be more sure that your results are actually relevant, but you might be missing a lot of other relevant items in your search (you could have a large number of false negatives). Error rate is just the proportion of both types of errors to the total number of relevant items you ideally would like to retrieve.

Self Test

You're looking for information on a guitar maker called David Daily.

Google finds 4,130,000 hits on "Daily Guitars," two of which (the first two, not surprisingly, as this is Google) are relevant. You have reason to know that there are actually two relevant websites out there. What are the recall, precision, and error rate for this search?

Google finds 31,500 hits on *hog farm waste runoff problems* (entered without double quotation marks), of which we will declare that 2,600 are relevant. The authoritative document you are consulting says there are "several thousand" relevant items on the Web. What are reasonable ranges for the values of recall, precision, and error rate for this search?

Sidebar Table 2.1. Retrieval versus relevancy chart.

Actual Items	Retrieved Items	
	Relevant	Irrelevant
Relevant	True positives	False negatives
Irrelevant	False positives	True negatives

Notes

1. Boole was a British mathematician and philosopher. "As the inventor of Boolean algebra, the basis of all modern computer arithmetic, Boole is regarded as one of the founders of the field of computer science." This and more details about George Boole are available from *Wikipedia*, the free online encyclopedia, http://en.wikipedia.org /wiki/George_Boole (accessed June 14, 2011).

2. Strictly speaking, in mathematical logic the terms NOT and AND NOT are different. NOT is a unary operator, that is, it can take just one argument: NOT argyle, for example, if you were offered a world of socks and were willing to take anything but argyle. AND NOT is a binary operator, that is, it takes two arguments: pie AND NOT banana cream—you must provide a first set, and then a second set that you wish to exclude. Databases and Web search engines, even when they express the operator as NOT, mean AND NOT. This is subtly conveyed in the advanced search interfaces of databases: the "AND OR NOT" options don't start until *after* the first text input field.

3. You can have multiple levels of parenthetical expressions, a syntax known as *nesting* or *nested statements*, in which case the most deeply nested statement will be evaluated first, followed by the parenthetical expression around it, and so forth. You may very seldom, if ever, need to construct a nested statement, but it's interesting to know that you can.

4. Thesaurus, plural thesauri. A formal term for a particular variety of controlled vocabulary. When used in the context of bibliographic databases, a thesaurus may provide the list of subject headings in a hierarchical fashion, showing relationships between the terms (broader, narrower, related), and it may provide pointers to the best terms to use.

5. Certain databases use the term *descriptors* for subject headings.

6. Most often associated with library catalogs, *authority control* refers to a system of controlled vocabulary specifically for author names.

7. With thanks to the *ARTFL Project: Roget's Thesaurus, 1911*, http://machaut.uchicago .edu/?action=search&resource=Roget%27s&word=clothing&searchtype=headword.

3

The Searcher's Toolkit: Part 2

The tools covered in chapter 2, Boolean operators, controlled vocabulary, and field searching, are the most fundamental. The tools that we'll add here are further refinements: additional search functions; a simple search strategy that can be used in any situation, which will enable you to execute ever more sophisticated searches; and finally a list of "mental tools." The intent is always to enable you to get the information that you're after more efficiently and effectively.

Completing the Toolkit: Basic Tools 4–7

Basic Tool No. 4: Proximity Searching

In addition to allowing you to specify that your search results must include certain terms (Boolean AND: ducks AND geese AND loons), most of the subscription database systems also allow you to set up an even more sophisticated search, in which you set a rule for the relationship between those terms. That is, you can state how close to each other, and sometimes in what order, they must appear in the text to qualify for retrieval. This is known as *proximity* searching.

Proximity searching allows you to specify that termA appears within so many words of termB. For example, if you were trying to discover names of consulting firms that work with the food and beverage industry, it's quite possible that such a thing would only be mentioned as an aside—neither concept would be enough to merit a subject heading. Searching "consulting AND (food OR beverage)" would probably result in a large number of false drops, because the words could occur in the documents but have nothing to do with each other (e.g., consulting could show up in the first paragraph and food or beverage in the last paragraph, in a totally different context). The only way that you're going to have any chance of getting something meaningful is if the terms are somewhat close to each other: at least within the same paragraph, and even better, within the same sentence, within five to ten words of each other. There's also nothing to prevent you from combining the two approaches: termA within five words of (termB or termC).

When your search topic falls below the radar of subject headings (controlled vocabulary), and you have some text to work with (at least an abstract, if not full text), proximity searching is a wonderful way to get greater precision in your results. You will still get false drops, but not nearly as many as you would using only Boolean operators.

Proximity Searching Strategy

In setting up a proximity search, start by trying to envision how the writer might have expressed what you're looking for: in this case, it might be phrases such as "consultants to the consumer packaged goods, personal care, and food and beverage industries . . ." or "a leading food industry consultant . . ." or "has chosen ABC, a Boston consulting firm, for their new beverage marketing campaign . . ." This helps you to decide whether to set the proximity number lower (4 or 5), or higher (8 or 10). In this case it would be good to set it higher, because it's possible that the writer might have listed several industries, as in the first phrase example. Obviously, this presupposes that you are fairly familiar with the literature of the topic at hand. What if you aren't? In that case, simply experiment: start with a proximity of five words, and (as described in "pearl growing," below) learn from the results, increasing or decreasing the proximity number as seems appropriate.[1] There's no rule that you have to get it exactly right the first time!

Proximity Operators

Like a Boolean search, a proximity search is expressed with special operators. Unfortunately, unlike the universal and easily recognized AND, OR, NOT (AND NOT) used for Boolean expressions, proximity operators vary from system to system, so it's harder to produce a nice neat list to memorize. Even the syntax—the operators—can be mysterious looking, using simply N (for *near*) or W (for *within*), and a number to indicate the number of possible intervening words. Some systems, such as EBSCO, even offer two flavors of proximity operators: one for specifying just proximity, the other for dictating both proximity and word order (termA must occur within so many words, and *before* termB). Let's look at some examples.

Proximity Search Examples

ProQuest

ProQuest offers two types of proximity, NEAR and PRE, which can be shortened to N and P (capitalization is not required; I am simply using it for clarity). The NEAR command only requires that your search terms be within <number> words of each other. The PRE command specifies that the first term must appear within so many words of the second term, *in that order*. The syntax for these commands is N/<number> and P/<number>. An example of the first type of proximity search would be:

homeless n/4 teenagers

In response to this search, the ProQuest system will return records where the word *homeless* appears within four words of *teenagers*, regardless of word order. All of the following phrases would meet the search criteria:

teenagers who have been homeless for more than . . .

Chicago district ponders residential program for homeless teens . . .

those involving teenagers, prostitutes, and the homeless . . .

even teenagers who are not homeless . . .

has been homeless ever since he was a teenager . . .

EBSCO

EBSCO also has two proximity operators, but its syntax is slightly different: N<number> and W<number> (note there is no slash between the operator and the number). They are used as follows:

Near

teenagers N5 homeless

That is, the word *teenagers* must appear from zero to five words away from *homeless* in the text for a document to be retrieved. The terms can be in any order: teenagers first, or homeless first.

Within

homeless W3 teenagers

This means that the word *homeless* must appear within three words of *teenagers*, *in that order* (homeless first), to be retrieved. In a ProQuest database you would express this as homeless P/3 teenagers. These subtle variations are the norm, so be prepared to be flexible and to take a quick glance at each database's Help file for guidance.

Factiva

In another variation on this theme, in *Factiva* you spell out *near* and append a number, such as near5, to set the parameters for your proximity search. If you were looking for information about gourmet or specialty pickles, you'd probably be interested in an article that mentions "the specialty market now extends to pickles, teas . . ." The search

specialty near5 pickles

would pick up this article. The pickle reference is so casual that the subject headings for the whole article give no clue that it might mention pickles. (And trust me: if you are trying to find information about the specialty pickle market without spending a fortune for a market research report, you'll take any reference, no matter how casual.)

Factiva also provides a conceptual rather than numerically bound operator with "same" to specify "in the same paragraph." For example, "Merck same research" retrieves articles in which Merck and research occur in the same paragraph, in any order.

Determining Proximity Operators

Unlike Boolean operators, proximity operators usually don't appear as drop-down menu choices in the database interface. While the use of N or near, and W or within, is fairly standard, the way they are interpreted and the use (or not) of additional characters such as a slash mark make each database just a bit different. Given that there are several subtle variations that might be used, it's best not to just guess. To find out whether a database provides proximity searching and what syntax to use, you'll need to explore files such as Help or Examples.

Importance of Proximity Searching in Full-Text Databases

Proximity, although requiring a bit more effort to discover, is becoming an ever more valuable function as vendors strive to provide more and more searchable full text. A database that is just an electronic version of an index simply doesn't offer that many words to search on. The text fields (i.e., author, title, journal name, and abstract) aren't that big, so the use of Boolean operators in that situation is usually fine (using proximity in such a situation might well reduce your results to zero, in fact). Matches on termA AND termB in the limited realm of index fields are likely to be relevant because the terms are, in a sense, by definition close to each other. In a full-text situation you could certainly still restrict your search to just subject headings (if they are available), or a field such as title, and use Boolean operators, but by searching the full text you have the opportunity to get at more deeply buried aspects of an article, to tweeze out nuances and secondary topics that cannot possibly be covered by a few, necessarily broad, subject headings. The more searchable full text a database has, the more important the ability to do proximity searching becomes, because it is the only useful way to really mine all that text for everything it has to offer.

Really Close Proximity: Phrase Searching

Searching on exact phrases can be extremely important in some cases, and the inability of some databases to do this (easily) can really inhibit how effectively you can search. In the commercial database world, the way you indicate to the system "this is a phrase search" can vary considerably.

EBSCO databases and *Factiva* perform phrase searches without quotation marks or indicators of any kind: their search functions assume multiple word entries in the search box should be searched as a phrase. ProQuest, LexisNexis, and the Web of Science databases work as the Web search engines do: enclose the terms to be searched as a phrase in double quotes. (ProQuest's Help says it treats two-word queries as a phrase by default, but using the quote marks never hurts.)

Uses for Phrase Searching

Phrase searching is useful any time you're searching for things such as the name of a place or an organization (especially if the name is made up of common words) or a multiword concept or topic (latch key children, gourmet pickles, missile defense shield), or—especially on the Web—if you're tracking down more complete information from incomplete fragments. Problems such as the rest of the lyrics, or indeed the real title, of a song whose only line you can remember is "is the moon out tonight?" can be quickly resolved and put in context (and possibly bar bets won) by plunking the quote-bound phrase into Google. In a more academic scenario, say you have a bad or incomplete reference to a thesis or a journal article. If it is available to you, head for a database such as *Dissertation Abstracts*, or an appropriate subject database, and try a partial phrase from the title, or the author's name and a word from the title, depending on what information you (seem) to have.[2] (If that doesn't work, try only the most distinct words as a title field search, and if that doesn't work, go to the Web. You might not find the actual item, but at least you might find a more accurate, complete reference to it from someone else's bibliography.)

Proximity and phrase searching are useful for reducing and focusing your results; they tend to increase the precision of the search. The next tool takes us back the other way, providing a way to broaden the search net (to increase recall).

Basic Tool No. 5: Truncation

"Truncation" is an efficient way of extending your search to pick up many variations on a word without having to (1) think of all the possible variants or (2) input them with endless "ORs". Truncation allows you to search on a word stem and retrieve any word beginning with those letters, for example,

harmon*

to retrieve harmony, harmonious, harmonica, etc.

In another database, the syntax and results for the truncation function might be

employ$

to retrieve employ, employs, employee, employment, employer, employed, etc.

Note that when the stem (the letters being truncated) is a word in its own right, that word will be included in the search results. Truncation generally means the word stem, and any number of characters following, from zero on up.

Using Truncation

Truncation is a tool that is equally useful in field searching and in full-text searches in commercial databases. In a field search, for example, truncation is a wonderfully efficient way to pick up several related subject headings at once (searching poet* to pick up poet, poetics, poetry) or variations on author names (with and without a middle initial, for instance, or even with or without a first name being spelled out: Adams, J!). In a full-text search, obviously, truncation greatly increases the number of documents that are eligible for retrieval. When you are fishing around for a concept or topic that you think might be rather rare, and that isn't expressed with any set phrases or words, the combination of truncation and a proximity search can be invaluable. The earlier example of trying to identify any articles mentioning companies that act as consultants to the food and beverage industry is a prime candidate for this technique:

Consultan* near10 (food or beverage*)

to retrieve consultant, consultants, or consultancy, within a 10-word radius of food or beverage or beverages.

Common Truncation Symbols

Truncation symbols vary somewhat from database to database, but the ones most frequently used are:

- ' * '
- ' ! '
- ' ? '

Factiva uses the symbol "$," which is more unusual, but always strikes me as appropriate for this resource from the financially focused Dow Jones company.

Determining Truncation Symbols

As is the case with the other tools in this chapter, there is likely to be nothing in the initial search interface to indicate whether truncation is supported and, if so, which symbol to use. There are databases that don't offer a true truncation function, but simply search on a limited set of variants (e.g., plural forms) automatically. Some information is supplied in Table 3.1, but if the database in question is not listed, or if you want to check the most current usage (it could change), look for links to "Help" or "Examples" to determine how the database at hand handles truncation.

Table 3.1. Truncation and wildcard symbols used by various vendors.

Vendor	Truncation Symbol	Wildcard: 1 for 1 match[a] Symbol	Wildcard: 0 to 1 match[b] Symbol
EBSCO	*[c]	?	#
Endeavor (OPAC)	?	N/A[d]	N/A
Gale	*	?	!
LexisNexis	!	*	N/A
ProQuest	*[e]	?	N/A
Web of Science[f]	*	?	$

[a] Replaces characters on a one-for-one basis: wom?n to retrieve woman or women
[b] Replaces zero to one character; useful for picking up American and British spellings: colo!r to pick up color or colour
[c] May also be used between two other words in a phrase to replace any whole word, for example, type * diabetes retrieves type 1 diabetes or type II diabetes
[d] Not available
[e] To specify an upper limit for the number of truncated characters, use the syntax: $n. For example, nutr$5 retrieves nutrition, nutrient, nutrients.
[f] All symbols in WoS may be used for both right- *and* left-hand truncation

Wildcards

Closely related to truncation are *wildcard* symbols, in the sense that a symbol is used in place of letters. Whereas truncation symbols represent any number of characters, wildcards are used to substitute for characters on a one-to-one basis. Be prepared for confusion: the symbols used for wildcards are the same as those used for truncation, but the effect changes, depending on the vendor. That is, one vendor may use "!" for truncation and "*" for a wildcard, while another exactly reverses those two meanings. For example, LexisNexis uses "*" as its wildcard (one-to-one replacement) symbol and "!" as its truncation symbol. In EBSCO, ProQuest, and the *Web of Science*, "*" is used as the truncation symbol (for any number of characters at the end of a word) and "?" is used as the wildcard symbol, replacing characters on a one-to-one basis. These vendors also offer additional wildcard symbols that substitute for exactly zero-to-one character for situations in which you want to pick up alternative spellings (most commonly, US/UK variants). The symbol used is different in each case; see Table 3.1 or check the database Help for the most up-to-date information.

Using Wildcards

Wildcards are probably most frequently used to replace just one letter, for example:

wom?n

retrieves woman, women, womyn. Multiple wildcards can be used to substitute for an equal number of characters, for example,

manufactur??

will retrieve manufacture, manufactured, or manufactures, but not manufacturing.

As noted earlier, a search situation in which the zero-to-one character wildcard symbol can be very helpful is for picking up US/UK alternative spellings, such as

labo$r   to get either labor or labour

globali#ation   to get either globalisation or globalization

If you were searching a database that included British publications, and you wanted to be sure you picked up relevant material from them, this use of wildcarding could be very important.

Truncation/Wildcard Symbols Reality Check

Some information on common truncation and wildcard symbols used by different vendors is supplied in Table 3.1, but you are always encouraged to consult the database's Help file for the most up-to-date information on what functionalities the database supports and the appropriate symbols to use.

This probably strikes you as a fairly esoteric capability, and perhaps you won't need to use such functionality very often. In real life, you're much more likely to stick a truncation symbol on the end of "manufactur" and be done with it. But knowledge is power!

Sidebar 3.1: Department of Confusing Things

In everyday speech, the term *wildcard* is often used to mean truncation. For example, you'll hear the symbol used at the end of a word to retrieve multiple endings expressed as a wildcard. I'm quite guilty of this myself: when working with a student who has never heard of truncation, the easiest course of action is to call the odd thing being demonstrated a wildcard, because almost everyone immediately grasps the sense of that notion. If you are getting serious enough about searching that you're looking at the Help files, however, you should know the technical terms used in the business and understand that different symbols can have different effects (one replaces only one character, while another is used to replace any number of characters).

Quick Recap

This part of the chapter has introduced Tools 4 and 5, proximity searching (which tends to reduce the number of results) and truncation and wildcards (which increase the result set). Proximity searching allows you to search for documents containing terms within a given number of words of each other. Proximity searching is particularly valuable for searching full text. Phrase searching is the closest form of proximity searching and can be very important for retrieving accurate results. Truncation refers to the use of a symbol to substitute for 0 to N characters at the *end* of a word. Wildcards are symbols used to substitute on a one-to-one basis for characters *within* a word. Proximity and phrase searches tend to narrow and focus results; truncation and wildcards help to increase the potential set of results. To determine the symbols or syntax to use, in all cases consult the database's Help or Examples files.

Basic Tool No. 6: Limits to Constrain Your Search

Limits or *Limiters* are preset options in the search interface that can be used to further define your search. They are described here as *preset options* to distinguish them from the words or subject terms that you have to come up with and type in. Limits make use of fields in the database record that are used to store attributes of the record rather than conceptual content: you could say limit fields are about the article, not what the article is about. Limiters usually appear as check boxes or drop-down menus. Typical Limit choices include the following:

- Scholarly (or *peer reviewed*)
- Publication or article type (book, conference proceeding, review, editorial, etc.)
- Language
- Full text (e.g., in a database that offers some records with full text and some without, this limit will constrain the search to retrieve only matching records offering full text)[3]
- Date

The Date Limit

The Date Limit is a bit of an anomaly. In the context of a known citation, you would consider it a "content" field: the date would be part of the unique information identifying that citation (Joe Blogg's 2001 article is not Joe Blogg's 2006 article). However, if you are searching for material published before or after a certain date, or in a particular date range, the date information becomes an attribute used to limit your search results. The way the date option is displayed in the search interface is frequently hybrid as well, offering both a drop-down menu of preset choices and fields for specifying a specific date (or date range).

Basic Tool No. 7: "Pearl Growing," A Useful Search Strategy

This charming expression[4] refers to the process of doing a very simple search first, with the intent of achieving high recall, and then examining the results to find appropriate subject headings or to discover further or alternative terms to search on from the most on-target hits. You then add one or more of these terms to your search strategy, or replace your previous terms with the new ones, to produce a more precise list of results. This is very useful when you are venturing into a new database or unfamiliar subject matter, or when you simply don't have the time or inclination to do formal preparatory work by hunting around in the subject indexes.

A Search Example Using Pearl Growing

For example, let us say that you're an engineer, and you are tired of your straight engineering job. A colleague suggests that you look into jobs in engineering sales. Whenever you're working with someone and doing this sort of career exploration—What is the work like? How is the pay? Are there openings, or is it a stagnant market?—a good first thing to check is the *Occupational Outlook Handbook* (OOH).[5] If you had come to see me, we'd start there. At the OOH, a keyword search for "engineering sales" (with the quotes) produces just one result, for Public Relations Specialists. Huh? Browsing the index under *E* doesn't help either. A search on just "sales" finally does it, and we find that such people are referred to as "sales engineers." This is useful. Let's move on to a database and try for some articles about sales engineers.

Going to a database of business articles, ProQuest's *ABI/Inform*, we can start by seeing if, by chance, "sales engineer" is a subject term. It's not. So then we can try the quick-and-dirty approach: simply searching "sales engineers" in the citation and abstract, hoping to pearl grow from the results. We can prescreen the results a bit by choosing the "Scholarly journals" limit. Among the results is an article titled "Control and autonomy among knowledge workers in sales: An employee perspective." Despite the "knowledge workers" in the title, the abstract is full of the phrase "sales engineers." This looks useful! From the subject headings—Employee Attitude, Control, Sales, Studies, and Human Resource Management—we decide that the subject term Sales could be useful. Examining some of the other results, we notice that Salespeople is also a subject term. We go back to the search interface and try:

Sales OR Salespeople—in Subject

AND

Engineers—in Abstract,

which nets us 36 results.

The ProQuest system also automatically provides helpful, usually in-sightful search suggestions in the results interface, in this case:

Engineers AND Polls & surveys (both terms will be searched as subjects).

Engineers AND Personal profiles (both terms will be searched as subjects).

To reiterate, the strategy in pearl growing is to start with a fairly simple, broad search, examine the most likely results, and learn to refine or improve the search based on subject headings or other terminology used in the on-target results. This technique is really only useful in the structured, subject-headings world of commercial databases. On the Web, you may encounter links in search results saying "More like this," which are trying to do the same thing. How well they do it, and what they are basing the similarity on, are open questions.

Quick Recap

This section of the chapter completed our survey of the seven tools in the Searcher's Toolkit: number 6, Limits, and number 7, the pearl-growing strategy. Limits are preset options built into a search interface that enable you to search by document attributes such as language, article or document type, peer reviewed, and date. Pearl growing refers to a strategy of starting with a very simple keyword search, examining the results, and discovering useful subject headings or additional terms to search on from the most on-target records.

Your Mental Toolkit

Understanding and being able to use concepts such as Boolean logic, controlled vocabulary, proximity searching, and limits will definitely go a long way toward making you a more effective searcher. In addition, there are certain mental attitudes that will help you a great deal as well. Of course, there are some aspects of mind or personality that you either have or you don't: general curiosity, interest and enjoyment in puzzles, and an ability to think out of the box, that is, to make connections or have ideas (lightbulb moments) *beyond* the research request as it is explicitly stated. But there are three important mental tools that you don't have to be born with; rather, you can make a conscious effort to develop them. These are tools to employ in any search, which can be just as important in your success as a searcher as your knowledge of search functions.

The mental toolkit:

- *A healthy skepticism*: Do not trust anything someone tells you that "they remember," or even anything that is printed in a bibliography.

- *Willingness to let go*: Someone may offer a great deal of information, but if the results keep coming up zero, or wrong, *let go* and drop pieces of information, one at a time.

- *Maintain mental clarity and patience*: Be systematic about your searching; don't just thrash around rapidly trying this and that. It may seem to take longer to stop and think and try one change at a time, but in the end it will save time.

To emphasize the second point: one of the biggest pitfalls in searching is not being willing to *not* look for a part of the information provided. In general: be flexible, not fixated.

Summary and Advice

And that's your toolkit. You now have some concepts, some tools that you'll use over and over, in various combinations, and some attitudinal tools to use as well. My advice for how to employ this information to the best advantage is fairly simple:

1. Master the concepts.
2. Do not attempt to memorize exactly which databases offer which capabilities. Instead . . .
3. Train your eyes!

Learn to scan an interface quickly. Look for *Help* or *Search Guides*. (Actually read them, although be prepared: sometimes the *Help* is not updated as quickly as changes are made to the database.) You now know *what* to look for,[6] so simply look for it. Nothing on that screen should be "noise" or ignored. This is the most important thing you can do: LOOK with your trained eyes. Why? Because

Things can change at any time—and they will change!

Especially now that database vendors have moved their products to the Web, their interfaces have become more fluid. They are more stable than most Web pages, but still, the lure and the ability to change things so easily is hard to resist. Indeed, by the time you see this book, the interfaces shown in the figures here may have already changed anywhere from a little to a lot. You need to be flexible, and able to relearn continually as the interface designers move things around and change their terminology. Let me assure you that you will become good at it, but you need to be alert and ready for change ("oh, now that tab is orange, and they've changed the name Advanced Search to More Options. Same thing. OK."). I cannot emphasize this enough:

USE YOUR EYES. They are the best tool that you have.[7]

Exercises and Points to Consider

1. Consider again this search: homeless N/4 teenagers, which produced this result:

   has been homeless ever since he was a teenager . . .

   Count the words between *homeless* and *teenager*. Why would the article containing this phrase be retrieved by this search?
2. What do you think would be the best way to search for a personal name, especially if you wanted any article that made any mention

of the person? Would you use a phrase or proximity search? What are the pros and cons of each method?

3. Consider again this search: Consultan* near10 (food or beverage*). How might you alter this slightly to make even more documents eligible for retrieval? What might be the pros and cons of doing that?

4. Going back to ProQuest's suggestions when we did the "sales engineers" search:

   Engineers AND Personal profiles (searched as Subjects)

   Engineers AND Polls & surveys (searched as Subjects)

   What would be an elegant way to accomplish both of these searches at once?

5. One major vendor whose syntax wasn't addressed in detail in this chapter is Gale. Go to a Gale database, and see if you can find out the following: Does it support proximity searching, and what is the syntax, if so? Phrase searching? What about truncation and wildcards?

Suggested Reading

Tenopir, Carol. "Are You a Super Searcher?" *Library Journal* (March 1, 2000): 36, 38. The date might look old, but the discussion of characteristics of what makes a good searcher are just as relevant today as when this article first appeared.

Notes

1. When dealing with a totally unfamiliar subject area, it's also very useful to do a Google or Google Scholar search, just to get a sense of how people write about the topic.

2. Bell's Reference Desk Rule No. 1: citations almost always have a mistake in them somewhere.

3. Beware, though, that if the database is enabled with a technology for linking to full text in other databases to which the library subscribes, turning on the full-text limit could eliminate potentially useful results.

4. Why "pearl growing"? Well, you throw out a small bit (one or two words, say), a seed. Then from all the results, you add layers, the way a pearl adds layers of nacre around a grain of sand. I guess you could call it "onion growing," but it doesn't sound quite so nice! To be honest, this is one of my favorite and most frequently used techniques.

5. Available at the U.S. Bureau of Labor's website (http://www.bls.gov/oco/).

6. Just in case you had a momentary mental lapse, "what to look for" is Boolean operators, controlled vocabulary, fields you can search, proximity operators, truncation and wildcard symbols, and limits that you can set.

7. Well, they need to be connected to your brain, of course . . .

4
Social Science Databases

Introduction to Subject Databases

Before plunging directly into the nuts and bolts of the following databases, let's pause for a moment to think about the whole idea of subject-specific databases. The following statement might fall into the "duh" category, but sometimes it's good to start with the absolute basics: a subject-specific database is a searchable, electronic resource devoted to a particular topic. It focuses on a subject area by including only the journals, books, conferences, or other published materials in that discipline. Naturally, there are journals that are useful and interesting to more than one subject area, and you will discover that some journals are indexed in several different databases. In general, however, if you are doing research that falls into an identifiable subject area, working with the appropriate subject databases is the most efficient and effective way to pursue that research. Why is a subject database better than a Web search in this case? A Web search is just that: it will find *Web pages* and various other media that are freely available on the Web, but it is not an organized, structured index of commercially published material (Google Scholar muddies the waters here; more on that in chapter 10). A Web search is by definition "all subjects"—it's anything the search engine's indexing program has picked up. A Web search may well find someone's paper, if they have put it on the Web, or a reference to a paper within another paper that someone put on her website. But it is *not* a complete, orderly scan of all the appropriate journals and other published materials in a subject area. That kind of organized, thorough, ongoing effort implies an organization, staff, and money, and it is not something anyone is going to give away for free. They are each very powerful in their way, but subject databases and Web search engines are very different animals.

How do you know what databases there are for your subject? Go to the website of any major university, find the university library page, and look for links such as "databases," "electronic resources," "subject guides," or "resources by subject." Almost all institutions of higher education will have enough of these databases that they will offer a list of them by subject. Simply scanning the alphabetical list, you will probably be amazed at the number and variety of different databases that are out there.

The number and variety of databases on the market is remarkable. But who knew? Why don't at least some of these databases have the name recognition of Google? Is it simply the difference between free and fee? Access to the subject databases is almost all by subscription, but you certainly get value for money. Yet compared with Web search engines, subject databases are almost unknown among the general public, and this is a shame, because they are so good at what they do.

This chapter looks at three databases that support research in the social sciences. There are many more, of course, but these three represent the key resource in their respective subjects, and focusing on these three will give us exposure to a familiar and two new interfaces.

Library Literature & Information Science

Background and Coverage

Since many readers of this book probably are librarians or library school students, it seems only right to start with the original database of librarianship: *Library Literature & Information Science*. Started as a print index in 1921 by the H.W. Wilson Company, *Library Literature* has been available online for many years, first through Dialog, then via Wilson's own WilsonWeb, and now, after the merger of Wilson with EBSCO in 2011, through the EBSCO interface. The *Library Literature* database provides indexing for materials back to the early 1980s and full text dating from 1997. Although there are two other library science–specific databases (LISA—*Library & Information Science Abstracts*, and LISTA—*Library, Information Science & Technology Abstracts*, which we will touch on again later) and other databases that index some library journals, *Library Literature* has historically stood out for "its high-quality indexing, full text, complete coverage of the journals that are indexed, and participation of an advisory committee for journal title selection" (Tenopir 2003). In addition to journal and review articles, *Library Literature* has records for books, book chapters, conference proceedings, library school theses, and pamphlets. Coverage is international.

Notes and Search Examples

As alluded to earlier, the H.W. Wilson Company merged with EBSCO Publishing on June 1, 2011. At the time of this writing, all of the Wilson databases are in the process of being transitioned to the EBSCO platform, and unfortunately, the process is not scheduled for completion until early 2012—too late for this book's publishing deadlines. EBSCO has been wonderful about answering my questions, so although I cannot provide any screenshots of *Library Literature* in the EBSCO interface, I feel comfortable describing what to look for and providing some searches to try. There is also the advantage that EBSCO has offered the LISTA database[1] for several years, and my EBSCO sources say that the new *Library Literature* will be like LISTA but with the *Library Literature* content. (I expect we may see some wonderful synergies as a result of having these two excellent library databases under one umbrella in the not-too-distant future.) You have seen a bit of the EBSCO interface in chapter 2, and you will get more in chapter 7, so learning about *Library Literature* should simply be a matter of mapping this particular content onto an interface with which you are already familiar.

Advanced Search Interface

Go to *Library Literature*, and take a look at the Advanced Search interface. As we saw in the introduction to the EBSCO interface in chapter 2, Boolean operators are available, and we can search in specific fields. Which fields are available? Take a moment to open another EBSCO database in another window or tab, and compare the fields and field names in *Library Literature* to the other database: Are they the same? Different? Now examine (and compare) the options available in the "Limit your results" area: Are there any features specific to this database within the basic EBSCO format? Last, and most important, take a look at the "tool bar area," the blue bar across the top of the interface, and examine all the options available to you. Is there a link called "More"? If there is, be sure to see what it offers: if the options to browse the indexes of certain fields and/or do a cited reference search are offered, this is probably where you will access those features. In particular, you should see a link for *Thesaurus* in the blue tool bar area.

Library Literature Thesaurus

One of the great strengths of the *Library Literature* database has always been its Thesaurus; a hierarchical guide to the subject headings of this database. In a sense, this is a guide to the language of librarianship. The Thesaurus will do its best to guide you to the correct controlled vocabulary to use (via *Used for* terms), show you how terms interact hierarchically (which ones are *Broader*, *Narrower*, or *Related*), and explain how each term is intended to be interpreted (in the *scope note*).

When you access the Thesaurus using the link at the top of the screen, you should get an interface that looks like Figure 4.1. (This screenshot was taken from EBSCO's LISTA database, which also uses a Thesaurus; the *Library Literature* implementation should be the same.) Notice particularly the radio buttons below the search box: if you are not certain that what you're looking up is an exact subject, the *Term Contains* or *Relevancy Ranked* options are much better than the *Term Begins With* option. The risk of the Term Begins With option is that if your term isn't a Subject or even a *Used for* term, you are likely to get a "your term would be here" message, which might be frustrating.

Try looking up OPAC, the acronym for Online Public Access Catalog, first as a Term Contains, then as a Relevancy Ranked search. You should discover that you are directed instead to *Use* the term Online Catalogs. A couple of clicks in, you should be looking at the full record for Online Catalogs, which tells you what it means (the scope note), along with Broader and Used for terms. *Online Catalogs* is the term that the Thesaurus designers have decided will be the subject heading assigned to all articles on this topic, no matter how it is referred to in the article itself. Thus, theoretically, if you searched for Online Catalogs as a subject, your results should include every relevant record in the database. ("Theoretically" because even indexers have bad days: there might be articles that are mis-indexed.)

The *Used for* terms represent many possible ways that people might look for this idea, as we just did. How many *Used for* terms have been assigned

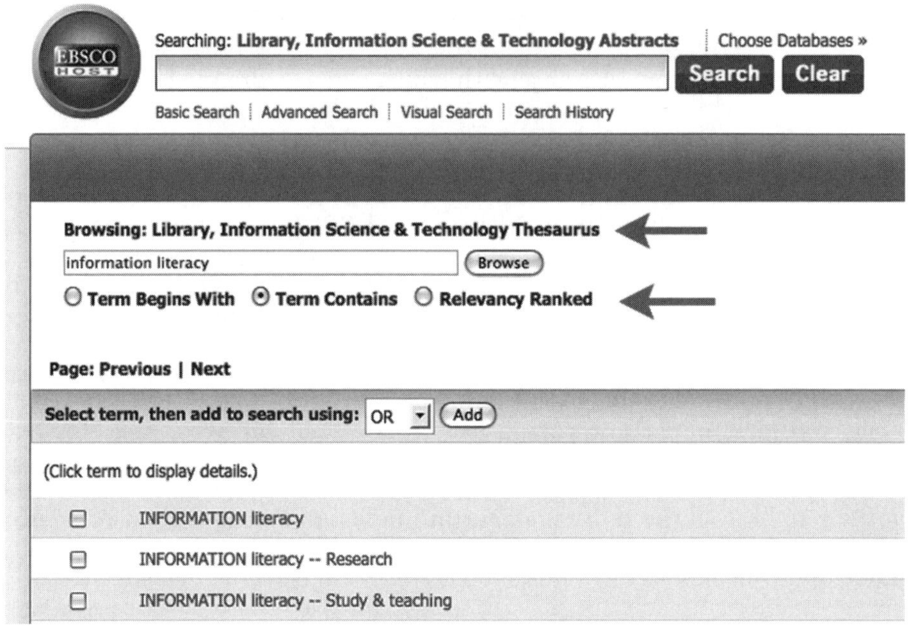

Searching: **Library, Information Science & Technology Abstracts**   ⋮ Choose Databases »

EBSCO
HOST

Search   Clear

Basic Search ⋮ Advanced Search ⋮ Visual Search ⋮ Search History

Browsing: Library, Information Science & Technology Thesaurus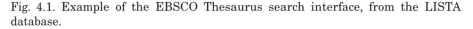

information literacy   (Browse)

○ **Term Begins With**   ⊙ **Term Contains**   ○ **Relevancy Ranked**

Page: Previous | Next

Select term, then add to search using: OR ▾ (Add)

(Click term to display details.)

☐   INFORMATION literacy

☐   INFORMATION literacy -- Research

☐   INFORMATION literacy -- Study & teaching

Fig. 4.1. Example of the EBSCO Thesaurus search interface, from the LISTA database.

to Online Catalogs? (Count them.) This means we have that many opportunities to be guided to the correct term in the Thesaurus, and to access relevant results in the main database even if we don't search on the preferred term. As noted before in discussing controlled vocabulary, otherwise we might have to think of all these variations and search them all. A good set of subject headings, consistently applied, makes searching so efficient.

Search Example 1: Identifying Terms Using the Thesaurus

We'd like to find articles on how library school curriculum is changing in response to advances in information technology (IT).

Since we know that this database is already focused on libraries and librarians, do we need to include the "library school" part? See what you get if you only type in curriculum (and choose the Relevancy Ranked option). You might want to change your search to

library school curriculum

This should guide you to the entry for "Library schools/Curriculum." Take a look at the full record display for that term. Where does it fall in the Thesaurus hierarchy, that is, are there any Broader terms? How about Narrower, Related, or Used for terms? How many of each are there? The next thing to evaluate is what you can do with this information. Again, my understanding is that the *Library Literature* Thesaurus implementation will resemble that for the LISTA database. In that case, the terms should have check boxes so that you can select more than one, and then you add them to your search with a choice of Boolean operators: a really handy facility not previously possible. If this is the case, select two of the headings that look interesting and pertinent to you, and add them to your search using OR. This operation will be reflected in the search box at the top of the same page (also handy). Add parentheses around those two ORed terms, and add the following to that search statement: AND "information technology" (with the quotes). Run that search.

The Results screen should look familiar: as in other EBSCO databases, the search interface is available above the results list, and the usual (very useful) "Refine" tools are all there on the left side. Check the terms listed under Subjects in the Refine panel to see what else you can learn about terminology surrounding this topic.

Search Example 2: Guiding Your Search with Related Thesaurus Terms

You want to find some information on chat services as part of reference. You start by looking up "reference chat" in the Thesaurus (using the Relevancy Ranked option). You should not get an exact match, but see if you get a list that includes such entries as: "Reference Services — Automation" and/or "Instant messaging (Internet)" among other things. Although an entry called "Instant messaging" sounds much more on target, the somewhat clunky Reference services — Automation term came up for a reason. Take a couple of moments and try this search in a couple of ways.

Select the "Reference Services — Automation" entry and add it to your search, then add "chat" as a keyword. Scan your results. How many are there in all? Roughly how many are on target (try to estimate from the first couple of screens)? How recent are they, and how quickly do the dates start to get old?

Now go to the Advanced Search screen, and set up this search:

Reference Services — Automation OR Instant Messaging — *in* SU Subject

AND chat *in* Select a Field (optional)

Again, how many results do you get, how on target (precise) are they, and how current? Which set of results do you feel would work better for you if you were writing a paper on this topic? (There is no right or wrong answer to that question!)

Working with Results

No matter how good your search skills are, there are bound to be items in your results that are not as useful as the others. The database vendors understand this, and therefore generally offer a way to collect selected records. EBSCO databases use a folder analogy: for any records you want to output, click the associated Add to Folder link. (Another common implementation you will see in other databases is for each record to have a check box for marking or collecting it.) Typical output options are to print, save, email (send records and/or full text to yourself or someone else), and export to a citation manager program, all of which are offered by EBSCO databases. The folder and output options will be discussed in more detail in chapter 7 when we look at *America: History and Life*, another EBSCO database.

Quick Recap

In this section we looked at *Library Literature & Information Science*, the oldest and longest-running index devoted to the library field. *Library Literature* indexes journal articles, books, book chapters, conference proceedings, library school theses, and pamphlets. Materials are mainly in English, but coverage is international, and a number of other languages are represented. The *Library Literature* Thesaurus is custom built for this database, and it is an important tool for discovering subject headings and relationships between headings. Discussion and examples in this section were briefer than usual, because at the time of writing *Library Literature* was in the process of moving from the H.W. Wilson platform to the EBSCO platform (which already provides another library database, LISTA). In a sense, this major change will allow us all to rediscover this well-known database of librarianship, making it fresh and new for instructors and students alike.

ERIC on the Web

Background and Coverage

ERIC, the Education Resources Information Center, is another database with a long history of excellence, but it has gone through some significant changes in its lifetime. ERIC was a "born digital" effort: in 1966, the Department of Education established 16 clearinghouses, each with its own educational subject specialty, to "gather, index, and input bibliographic information" (Tenopir 2004) for journal articles and documents known as *grey literature*. Grey literature is material that has not been commercially published, but that has scholarly value: papers presented at conferences, progress reports, working papers, technical reports, lab notebooks, student papers, curriculum guides, etc. One of the great contributions of the ERIC database was the amount of effort put into gathering, evaluating, indexing, inputting, and making available (through a microfiche distribution program, and now directly in PDF format) a huge amount of otherwise unpublished and inaccessible, but valuable, grey literature. At more than 1 million records, the ERIC database is now the largest and foremost subject resource for education.

But what the government creates, the government can also change. Starting with the Education Sciences Reform Act of 2002, the ERIC effort began to change. In December 2003, the 16 clearinghouses were closed, "as part of an effort to revamp, streamline, and centralize" the system (Viadero 2004). The Education Department's goals were laudable: one centralized, easy-to-use resource with more full text. What followed, however, was a period of interregnum: the database and the materials already indexed continued to be available, but no new material was being added, even though production continued apace. In March 2004, the Department of Education awarded the contract for their new vision of the ERIC system to Computer Sciences Corporation (CSC), and by June 2005 the loading of new materials had resumed. The library community closely followed all of these changes. Members of the Education and Behavioral Sciences Section of the Association of College Research Libraries/American Library Association and the Education Division of the Special Libraries Association continue to monitor what is happening with the database and to communicate with CSC, providing a useful outside oversight for this important resource. The latest news of

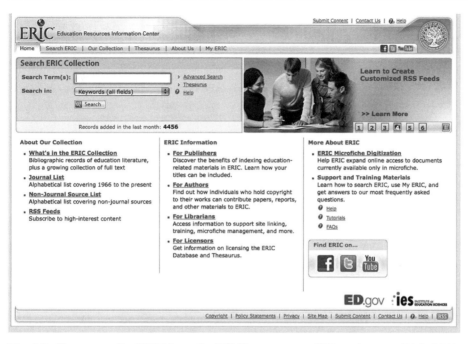

Fig. 4.2. Home page for ERIC from the U.S. Department of Education, as of July 2011.

interest to librarians is available at the ERIC website; see the "For Librarians" link in Figure 4.2.

Luckily, even when there were 16 clearinghouses offering various services in support of their educational topic area, there was still only one ERIC database to which they all contributed records. A variety of vendors contract with the CSC to obtain the ERIC data, and each vendor then offers the database through its own search interface. In addition to these choices, the Department of Education also provides free access to ERIC on the Web, and it is this version we will work with here.

Notes and Search Examples

Home Page: News and Social Media

The ERIC database on the Web is available at http://www.eric.ed.gov. Take a look at Figure 4.2: notice how much more chatty the page is than you typically find in a commercial database. Take a moment to look around; what are all the things they are trying to communicate here?[2]

The ERIC presence on YouTube is a collection of video tutorials; you will find them quite useful and brief. We will go into more detail here. As is typical, we have a "Basic" search box right on the home page, with a couple of ways to get into other search modes: "Search ERIC" next to the "Home" tab and a link to Advanced Search. Let's go see how advanced a free version of a database can be.

Advanced Search Interface: Functions and Fields

What do we have here in Figure 4.3? The most important parts of the site are provided as navigation tabs just under the ERIC logo, marked "A" in

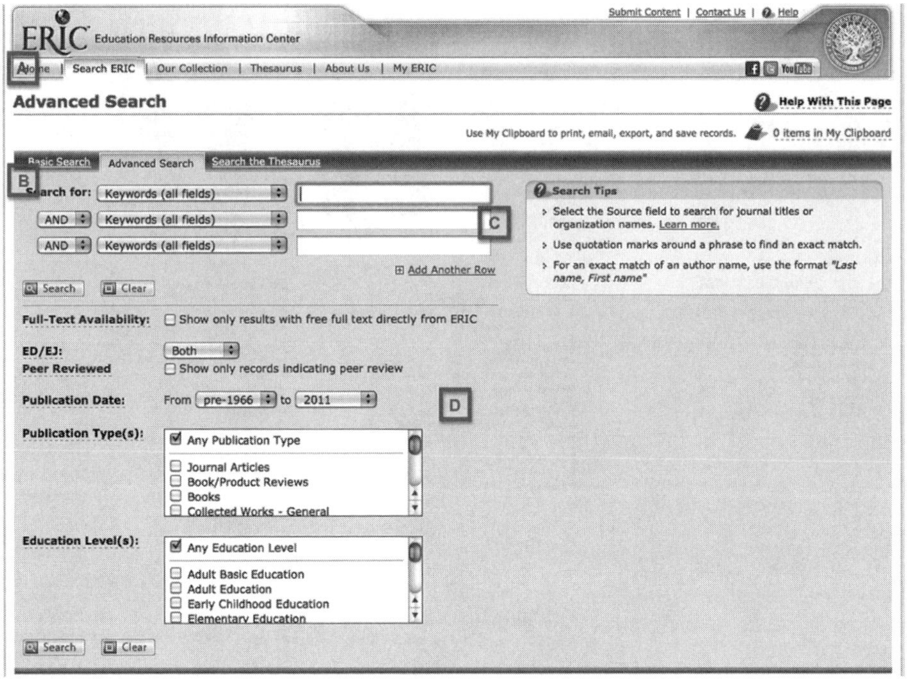

Fig. 4.3. ERIC Advanced Search screen, as of July 2011.

the screenshot. In the bar marked "B" we have links for two search modes (Basic or Advanced) and a link to "Search the Thesaurus." (Your brain should be going "Ping! Controlled vocabulary available!"). Notice too the emphasis on the Thesaurus: it is available in two places even though the locations are close together on the screen. Then there is a typical set of entry boxes for your search, really quite like EBSCO's advanced search interface: three boxes for text entry, drop-downs with Boolean connectors, and drop-downs to indicate which field you want the term to be searched against ("C"). But there's one interesting difference: the drop-downs for the fields to be searched *precede* the text-entry boxes. Do you think this helps you to notice them?

If you take a look at the list of fields available for searching, the list isn't very long, and it includes a mixture of the very familiar and the somewhat arcane. Title, Author, Descriptors (e.g., subjects), Source (e.g., name of a journal), and Publisher are recognizable, and are things you might know off the top of your head (or could look up using the Thesaurus). The ISBN and ISSN should be familiar ideas, but you might or might not have these numbers at your fingertips. Slightly more unusual is the emphasis on the organization producing the work: Institution (which we will see again in the *Web of Science*) and Sponsoring Agency. At the arcane end of the spectrum, for those unfamiliar with ERIC, is the field "ERIC #" and a field called "Identifiers." The ERIC # is a unique identifying letter–number combination assigned to each item as it is added to the database. Anything that appeared in a journal has a number preceded by EJ (for *ERIC Journal*); all of the unpublished documents are coded ED (for *ERIC Document*; the grey literature mentioned previously in the Background section). According to the ERIC Help, Identifiers are terms "that provide specific identifying information in a category:

geographic names, laws and legislation, or tests and testing." If you were looking for material relating to a specific law, for example, the Childrens Online Privacy Protection Act, searching a word or phrase from the name of the law in this field could be helpful.

Last, in the upper part of the screen, don't skip over the Search Tips box (to the right of "C")—the hints are actually useful, and only take a second to read.

Limits

Below the search input area at "D" we have limits, again, some familiar, and some unique to this database:

Full Text: self-explanatory

ED/EJ: allows you to limit your results only to published journal articles (EJ), or only to unpublished, grey literature (ED). The default is to retrieve Both.

Peer Reviewed: self-explanatory

Publication Date: somewhat oddly, the most granular you can get is by year, which isn't very granular. This is rather unusual for a date limiter.

Publication Types: self-explanatory

Education Level(s): the level of education discussed in the document or article. This field provides an excellent example of why it's worth using a subject-specific database; educators will almost always be looking for information aimed at a particular grade or group of people, and this specialized field allows them to filter their results by exactly that aspect.

Search Example 1: Using the ERIC Thesaurus

The search example that we'll use for our tour of the ERIC database is to find material on training teachers of deaf students.

Let's start by using the Thesaurus to find the right Descriptors (or subject terms) we might use for this search. We could Search the Thesaurus from the link in the blue bar, but remember, there is also access to the Thesaurus in the tabs just above the words "Advanced Search." Using the Thesaurus tab, we find we can browse as well as search the Thesaurus, and we can even browse by category. Figure 4.4 shows this multifaceted access.

Browsing in the "Ds" we get to entries starting with "Deaf (1966–1980)" and continuing through the term "Deafness." Searching on the term "Deaf" returns 10 Thesaurus entries that include the word deaf anywhere in the entry—but the search results do *not* include the term "deafness," which we will discover is the current, correct subject heading. Figure 4.5 shows both sets of results.

We are very, very oriented toward *searching*—but browsing has value as well: it eliminates the possibility of typos, it allows you to see all the variations on a term (in alphabetical order), and it shows you the context, the terms immediately around the term you had in mind. That might not always matter, but it could. In this case, the power of searching the Thesaurus is that it provides entries that don't necessarily *start* with the term you entered. Both approaches are useful.

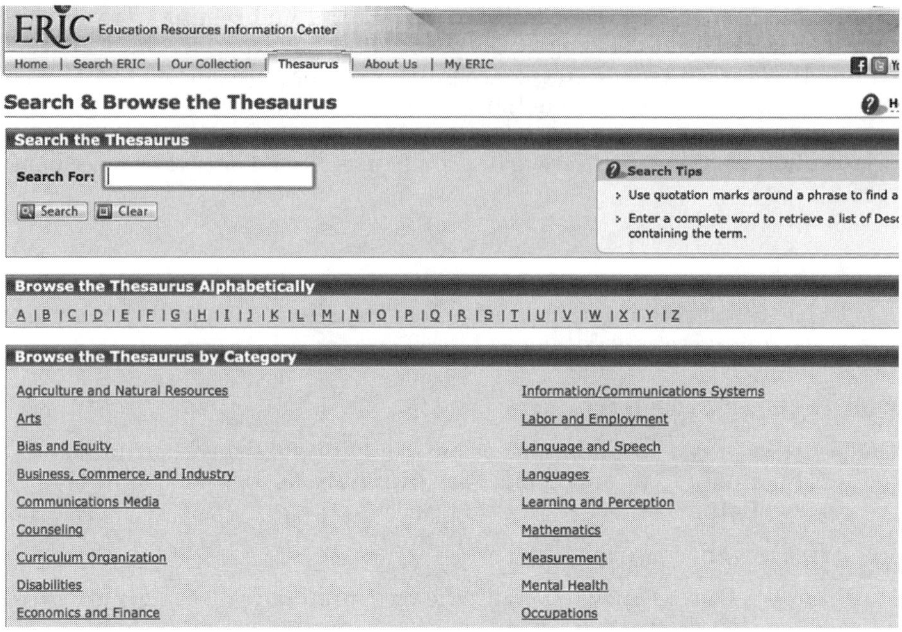

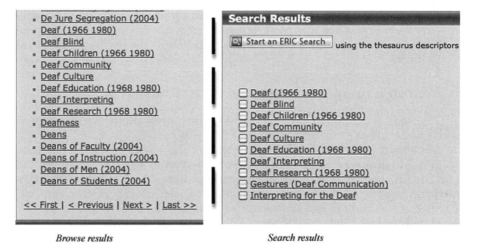

Fig. 4.4. ERIC Thesaurus search, browse, or browse by category options, as of July 2011.

Browse results   Search results

Fig. 4.5. ERIC Thesaurus browse versus search results, as of July 2011.

ERIC Thesaurus

As noted earlier, the term "Deaf" has a year range associated with it— 1966–1980. This is an indication that the term is no longer used; they changed the descriptor to something else. But what? Clicking on the entry for Deaf (1966–1980) gives you a screen telling you to "Use Term: Deafness" —with Deafness conveniently linked. Clicking that, we now get a full Thesaurus record (Figure 4.6).

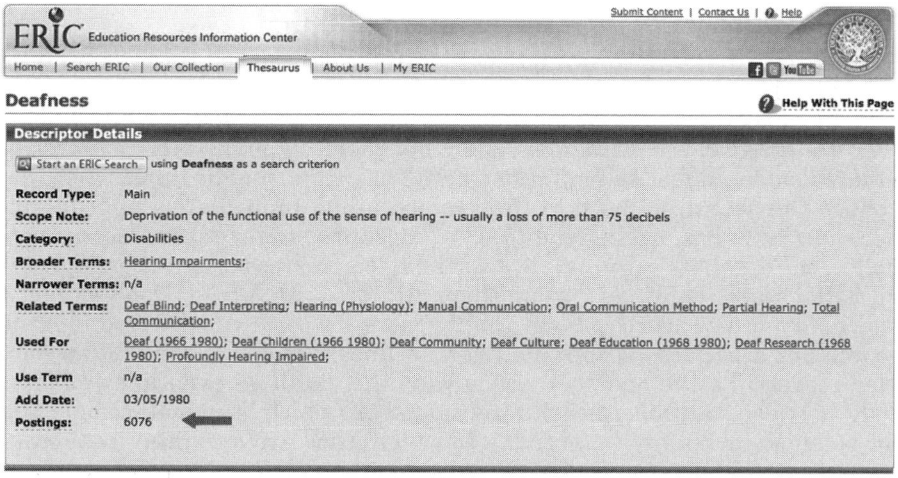

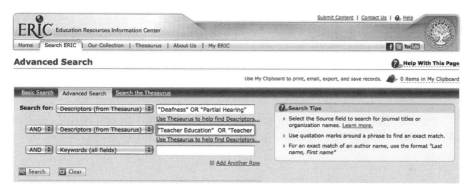

Fig. 4.6. Full ERIC Thesaurus record for "Deafness," as of July 2011.

Fig. 4.7. Search strategy for training of teachers of deaf students, as of July 2011.

This is informative and very useful: now I know all the terms *not* to use, broader terms and related terms—including one that I like: "Partial Hearing." That could be useful in this search. We also finally find out how many records have been assigned this Descriptor/Thesaurus term (see Postings: at the bottom). We could start a search right from here (see the button?), but we haven't finished discovering the rest of our search terms.

Use the Thesaurus tab to return to Search & Browse Thesaurus. Try searching for: teacher. How many Thesaurus Descriptors does this term retrieve? (It is the education database after all.) Let's do a more specific search. How many Thesaurus terms are retrieved when you search for teacher education? Yes, quite a few, but two of them look particularly useful. Let's construct a beautiful search (Figure 4.7):

Descriptors field: "Deafness" OR "Partial Hearing"

AND

Descriptors field: "Teacher Education" OR "Teacher Education Programs"

No limits applied. How many results does it produce?

Caveat Inquisitor[3]

Searcher beware. Notice how very carefully I entered those Thesaurus terms in the search fields: all the double quotes and precise capitalization. There is a very good reason for that: *you must enter the terms EXACTLY as they are listed in the Thesaurus, AND put them all, even single word ones, in double quotes, for the search to work.* You will also notice that when you change the field drop-down to Descriptors, a link immediately appears under the search box, urging you to "Use Thesaurus to help find Descriptors." Follow the database's urging: click the link, look up terms, and use the "Start an ERIC search" button to paste them into the search field. Don't worry: it won't start a new search; it will simply paste the term you selected into the search box associated with that "Use Thesaurus" link. You can build a complex search like the one shown this way; the database even knows to put "OR" between multiple terms in the same box (which is a small consolation for being so incredibly unforgiving in every other way). In other databases it's almost always so much looser: you can put any part of a subject heading in, even truncate it, set the field to "Subjects," and it will happily go search and produce results. Here that is not true. If you set the search field to Descriptors, they have to be entered perfectly or you get zero results. You would think that having made such an important database available for free on the Web, it would have been designed to be more forgiving. They've provided a very useful tool, and then made one of the most important parts of it hard to use. It's unfortunate.

Results

At the time of this writing, there are 123 citations in the results list, of which only the first is visible in the screenshot (Figure 4.8). Spend some

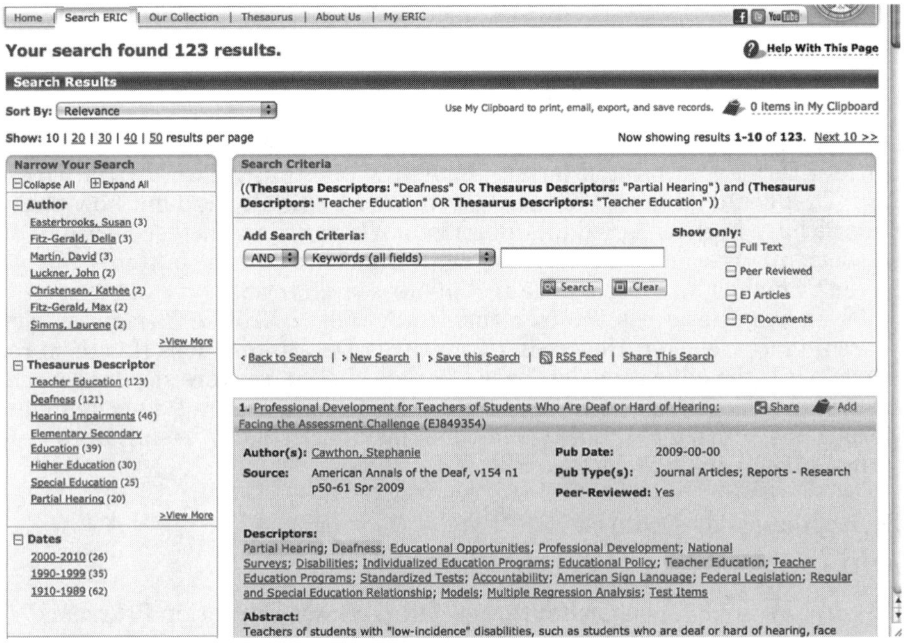

Fig. 4.8. ERIC Results page, as of July 2011.

time on the results page; it's rather busy, but everything there is very useful. You can sort your results by Relevance (the default), or in a host of other ways; your search is echoed back to you ("Search Criteria"); you can adjust your search by adding "Search Criteria" or any of the four most frequently used limits. The "Search Criteria" box also offers links to go Back to Search, start a New Search, Save this Search, Share it, or create an RSS feed for the search: it's quite impressive. Take a moment to remind yourself that this is not a commercial vendor's product; this is coming to you for free (well, for those of us in the United States—"your tax dollars at work"). The way the results are displayed is in line with what appears to me to be a trend of providing more information for each record up front (in this case, the full set of Descriptors and the beginning of the abstract), rather than requiring you to click into the record.[4] The panel on the left side provides a rich set of ways to "Narrow Your Search." Simply by observing the titles listed under Source (visible further down the page) you learn quite a bit about the journals in this topic area. Note too the very small icons labeled "Share" (via a host of social media websites) and "Add." The latter icon is a clipboard, and it represents the way to collect selected items from your results set for printing or other forms of output.

Search Example 2: Keywords and Pearl-Growing Strategy

Sometimes (in fact, most of the time), you don't have time for a very structured approach, where you carefully check the indexes and thesaurus entries before deciding on your search terms and setting up the strategy. When a busy graduate student is at the desk asking for resources on corrective feedback in second language acquisition (SLA), you are absolutely allowed to go to ERIC and simply type in what she's told you, as shown in Figure 4.9.

Keywords: corrective feedback

AND

Keywords: second language acquisition or SLA

This strategy seems to work quite well: certainly the first page of results looks good, and the student is particularly interested in an article titled "Second Language Writing Research and Written Corrective Feedback in SLA:

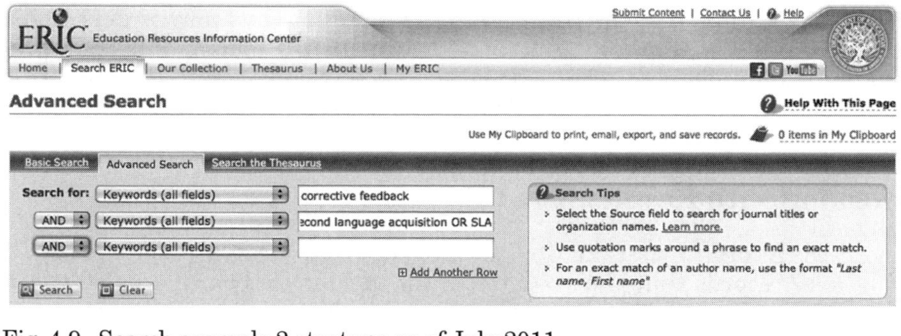

Fig. 4.9. Search example 2 strategy, as of July 2011.

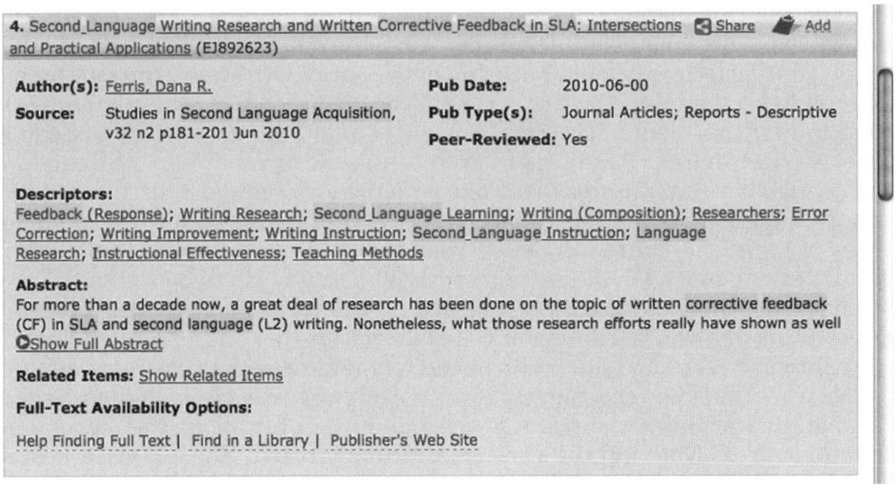

Fig. 4.10. "Ideal" result record, providing ideas for Descriptors to search, as of July 2011.

Intersections and Practical Applications." You might be concerned, however, that the "exact match" of a keyword search might have caused the search to miss a quantity of useful material. But here is a great tip: remember the pearl-growing strategy introduced in chapter 3? Well, it's not just for focusing or reducing results; it can also be used to grow results from a perhaps overly specific search. Thus, immediately on hearing the patron's expressions of interest about that "ideal" record, you should take a good look at the descriptors, which are pictured in Figure 4.10.

Ah! Second Language Learning—or Second Language Instruction! They both look like perfect headings. Be aware, however, that although it's very tempting to click on a linked subject heading, if you do you'll get *all* the records with that heading—but the rest of the context of your current search (the "corrective feedback" part) will be left behind. To use this information, you'll need to return to the Advanced Search interface, change the dropdown for the second search box to Descriptors, and make use of the "Use Thesaurus to help find Descriptors . . ." link. Searching on second language will produce both terms you want to use; select them both and use the Start an ERIC Search button to paste them into your search (Figure 4.11).

This search strategy yields a larger set of results, while remaining nicely on target.

One additional caveat: the "Show Related Items" link may or may not be useful to you. It appears to perform an enormous OR search, because it produces huge numbers of results. If viewed in relevancy order, this might be useful, but generally my advice would be to learn from an initial search, and then construct a better search yourself.

Working with Results: The Clipboard

Each record in your results list has a clipboard icon associated with it. You "add" records that you wish to output to your clipboard; a master icon above the search results reflects the "# items in My Clipboard" (Figure 4.12). This is similar to EBSCO's folder analogy for these functions.

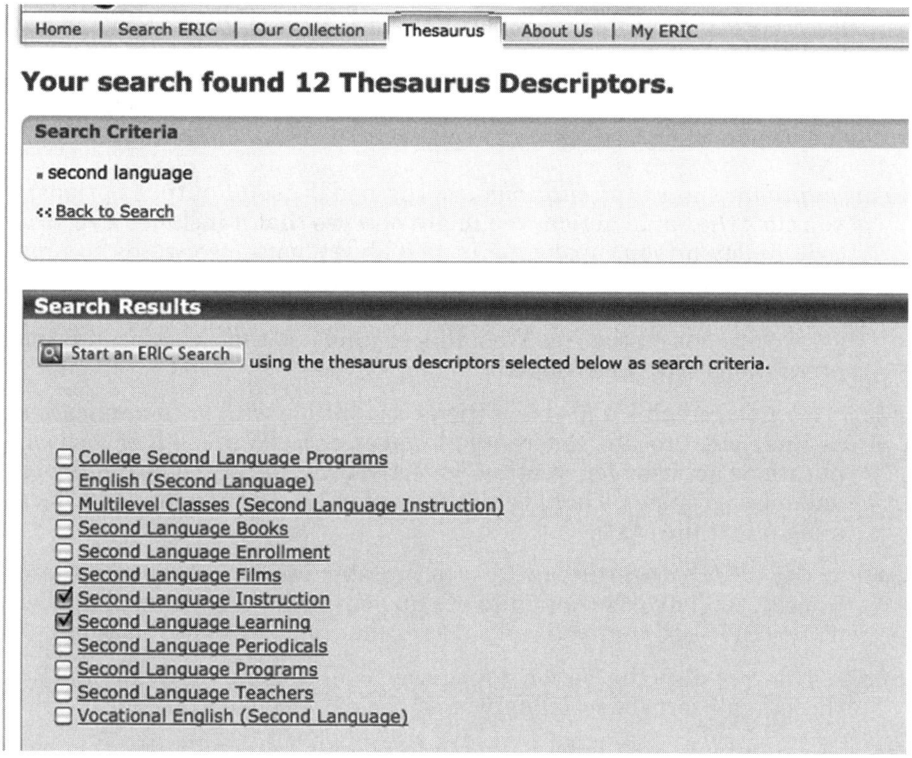

Fig. 4.11. Choosing Descriptors from the Thesaurus to paste into a search, as of July 2011.

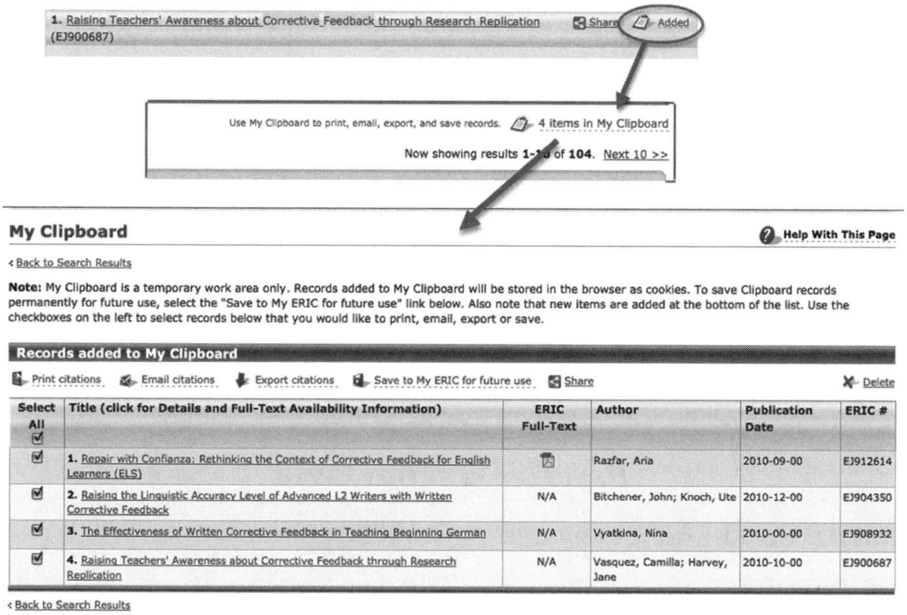

Fig. 4.12. The ERIC Clipboard: icon in a record, keeping track in the interface, and the My Clipboard screen, as of July 2011.

My Clipboard Page: Email, Print, Export, Save, Share, and Help

A variety of output functions are available in the My Clipboard display, included as part of Figure 4.12.

Print citations and *email citations* are the usual useful output options; if you click the email option, you might observe that it includes a security code function (you must type in two blurry nonsense words to prove you aren't a robot). The experience so far has been so similar to what you would experience with a commercial database that one might forget we are out on the free Web: this reminds us that we are, and some precautions have been added.

Export citations creates a file of citations compatible with such applications as EndNote, ProCite, Reference Manager, or RefWorks. All of these applications are used for creating correctly formatted footnotes, endnotes, and bibliographies. There is also the option to output your citations as a plain text file (.txt).

Save to My ERIC for future use. If you are starting an extended research project, you have the option to set up your own personal account here ("My ERIC"), so that you can save results from session to session.

Share. There is also the option to "Share" one or more of these citations through all sorts of social networking sites: very Web 2.0.

Help is ubiquitous: each label is linked to pop-up help and more; this page and all others have a context-sensitive Help With This Page link.

Quick Recap

We have just looked at the free Web version of ERIC, the Education Resources Information Center, the premier database for education. ERIC is produced under the aegis of the US Department of Education and dates back to 1966. The ERIC database is offered by many different vendors and is freely available at the Department of Education's website. ERIC indexes journal articles and *grey literature*—scholarly works that have not been commercially published. The free version offers search features as sophisticated as those found in any commercial database, including an Advanced Search offering Boolean operators, field searching, controlled vocabulary (called Descriptors), and limits. There is a strong emphasis on use of the ERIC Thesaurus, but Thesaurus terms must be entered according to strict conventions. Use of the links provided to look up and paste terms to your search eliminates pitfalls in use of Thesaurus terms. A "Clipboard" analogy is used for selecting and outputting multiple records.

PsycINFO from Ovid

Background and Coverage

PsycINFO is the online version of the American Psychological Association's venerable *Psychological Abstracts*, a print abstracting and indexing service dating from 1927. At more than 3 million records as of May 2011, *PsycINFO* is the largest, and most well known, index of the literature of psychology and the behavioral sciences. In addition to journal articles, document types indexed in the database include books and book chapters, dissertations, and electronic collections. The American Psychological Association (APA) draws on international sources, with journals in more than 29 languages, and English-language books and book chapters from all over the world. The full list of facts and statistics for *PsycINFO* is very impressive (American Psychological Association 2011). The Thesaurus terms (subject headings) used to index entries in the *PsycINFO* database are developed and applied by APA indexers.

One of the truly remarkable features of *PsycINFO* is the range of time it covers. *PsycINFO* has abstracts of books and journal articles dating from as early as 1806, although most journals are from the 1880s to the present, and most of the books are from 1987 to the present. The database is updated weekly, and the latest updated week is reflected in the search interface (Figure 4.13). Also notable is the profoundly scholarly nature of the material indexed: as noted in the APA's *PsycINFO Facts* (2011), of the "more than 2,450" journals covered, "99%" are peer reviewed.

Like ERIC, the *PsycINFO* online database is available from quite a few different vendors. Depending on which vendor and what backfile option your institution has chosen to subscribe to, you may have access to the complete file in one database, or the file may be divided in various ways, and you may have access to all or only to the most recent file.

Extensive Set of Search Fields

Another aspect of the *PsycINFO* database that demonstrates what an expertly crafted product it is (and it is, literally, crafted by experts in the field) is the set search fields used in the record structure. As of May 2010, the APA Field Guide included 39 fields, from Unique Identifier to a field for Correction Update Record (to hold the date a record was corrected, if correction was necessary). The APA appears to be fearless about making changes in the field structure, field names, and field content values, something that, as we've indicated in this book, is not a task to be taken lightly. The list of fields changed significantly from the first to the second edition of this book; now, rather than trying to reproduce a list here, I feel the best thing is to refer you to the online Field Guide at the APA website—it contains the most up-to-date and complete information: http://www.apa.org/pubs/databases/training/field-guide.aspx (as of December 2011). The list includes searchable and display-only fields (indicated with an asterisk), and it provides helpful information about what the field is used for: content or possible values.

Some of the fields listed in the online table deserve to be highlighted here:

- Cited references (the article's bibliography; this is very important in tracing the development of research)

- Auxiliary material (indicates that there is additional material, such as audio, video, websites, tables, data sets, etc., separate from the source document)

- DOI (Digital Object Identifier, to help users link to full text and provide a stable URL for the item)

- Methodology (a field indicating what kind of study, e.g., clinical, field, qualitative, quantitative, is discussed. This would be of great interest to psychological researchers)

Why Look at Ovid's *PsycINFO*

We're going to take a look at *PsycINFO* as offered by the database vendor Ovid. The Ovid interface differs from the ones that we have seen so far in a couple of interesting and, to me, quite useful ways:

- It has a built-in map-to-subject-heading feature that tries to offer you the best subject heading choices based on the terms you type in.

- It encourages you to build your search one concept at a time, which turns out to be very handy because when you have all the conceptual pieces, it is then very easy to experiment with putting them together in different combinations.

Notes and Search Examples

It's time to jump in and see what the Ovid interface is like. As you should be beginning to expect, we will go directly to the Advanced Search interface—after all, we are not Basic searchers.

Advanced Search Interface

What do you notice about the interface shown in Figure 4.13? The first thing that registers for me is the emphasis on the Search History area: my eyes see that first. Then note: we are in Advanced Search mode, but there is only one text-entry box. There are links for several other search options (Find Citation, Search Tools, etc.), which are obvious enough but not intru-

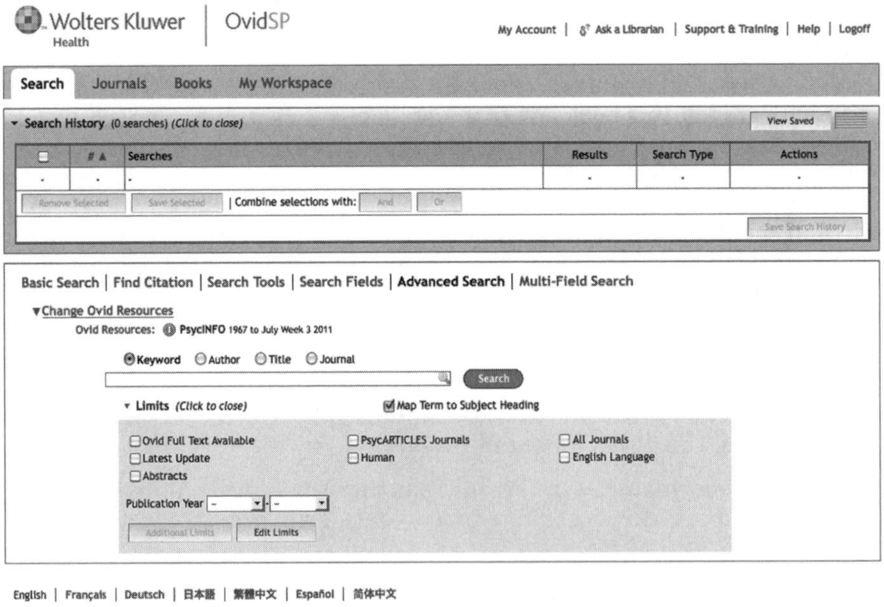

Fig. 4.13. *PsycINFO* Advanced Search interface. The PsycINFO® screenshots are reproduced with permission of the American Psychological Association, publisher of the PsycINFO® Database, all rights reserved. Copyright © 2000–2011 Ovid Technologies, Inc.

sive. Also clear but not distracting is the link to "Change Ovid Resources" (to change to another Ovid-provided database, a typical option with vendors that offer many databases) and information about the Resource you are now in—*PsycINFO*—with the date coverage available in this institution's subscription. The four types of searches possible in the current Advanced Search mode are cleanly and efficiently presented: four radio buttons above the search box, with check boxes for the most frequently used Limits immediately below the box. In all, it is an elegant and useful presentation.

Here are some additional notes about this interface.

As mentioned previously, the most effective way to use this database is to build your search one step at a time, with the results of each step recorded in the Search History. Thus, putting the Search History table first and foremost in the display makes sense, because it becomes very important as you work in this database. The individual searches can then be quickly and flexibly combined and reused, as we shall see.

When the text-entry field is set to "Keywords," the "Map Term to Subject Heading" option is turned on by default, which is important: this is one of the special powers of the Ovid interface, that it gets you from Keywords to Subject Headings as an integral part of the search process.

In a quick description of the other search-mode links, Find Citation provides a set of fields in which you can enter whatever parts of a citation you have in order to complete the citation and see if there is a record for that work in the database. The Search Tools link allows you to search supporting materials, such as the Map Terms list, Thesaurus, Permuted Index, or Scope Notes (definitions of subject headings), which govern the content of *PsycINFO*. If you know that you want to search just within a certain field or fields, the Search Fields tab[5] takes you to a screen where you enter your term in a search box; you can restrict your search to a particular field by clicking its check box. (This is quite different from the drop-down menu approach.)

As mentioned earlier, the most frequently used limits are available directly below the search box area. Once a search has been performed, an "Additional Limits" button becomes visible and offers other, more detailed limits. Note that a standard limit in this subject area is "Human" (to rule out articles about tests or studies on animals).

Here is what the Ovid interface is like to use.

Search Example 1: Building Your Search Concept by Concept

We'd like to search the psychological literature for material on the "effect of peer pressure on self esteem." We'll start by typing the following into the search box:

peer pressure

Then press return. This brings up the "Mapping Display" screen, shown in Figure 4.14.

The Mapping Display

Because the "Map Term to Subject Heading" feature was turned on, the system automatically tries to match, or "map," what you type in against its Thesaurus, the hierarchical list of subject headings for *PsycINFO*. The results can be quite fascinating, because even in the case of an exact match (as

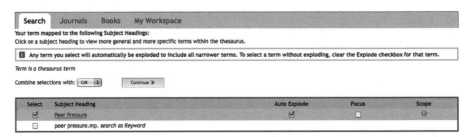

Fig. 4.14. *PsycINFO* Mapping Display for peer pressure. The PsycINFO® screenshots are reproduced with permission of the American Psychological Association, publisher of the PsycINFO® Database, all rights reserved. Copyright © 2000–2011 Ovid Technologies, Inc.

we have here: Peer Pressure is a subject heading), the system also offers all the other headings that have a Thesaurus relationship to this heading, that is, they are broader, narrower, or "related." The immense amount of thought that the Thesaurus designers put into their product can make your searching life so much easier, by suggesting relationships and lines of thought that might not have occurred to you.

Each heading has two options: *Auto-Explode* (if you scroll down, the interface explains that this will pick up the heading and any narrower headings, ones indented below it in the hierarchy) and *Focus*. *Focus* means that the indexers decided that the heading was a main aspect, or focus, of the article. Only a few of the subject headings assigned to an article will be designated as a Focus, so you may want to use this option sparingly in the initial phases of your search.

For the current search, we'll leave Auto-Explode on, but we won't check Focus—we'll leave it a little more open. Clicking the Continue button returns us to the main search page, which now displays our search history, the interface to start another search, and the beginning of our results list, as shown in Figure 4.15.

Building the Search

Now to add the second concept of our search, by typing

self esteem

into the search box. Again, this maps exactly to a subject heading.

As shown in Figure 4.16, this time we'll click the Focus box, because we really want the main theme of these articles to be about self-esteem. There should be more than 14,000 results for this search.

Combining Search History Sets

Now we will combine the results of these two searches. In the Search History box, we could check off both searches and use the "Combine Selections with" AND button. Note, however, that each search in your history is numbered: an insider's shortcut is that you can simply type

1 and 2

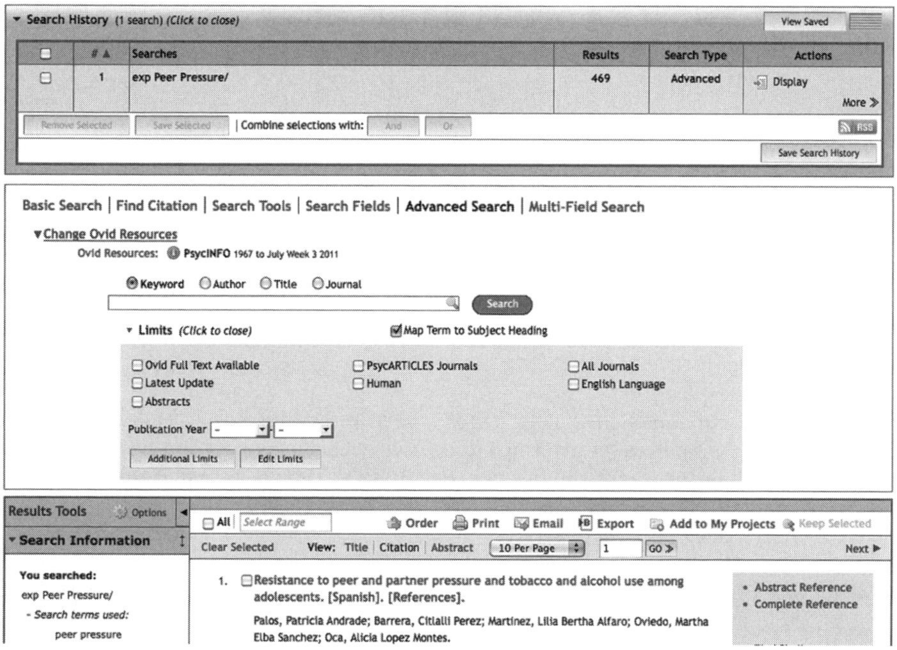

Fig. 4.15. *PsycINFO* initial results screen. The PsycINFO® screenshots are reproduced with permission of the American Psychological Association, publisher of the PsycINFO® Database, all rights reserved. Copyright © 2000–2011 Ovid Technologies, Inc.

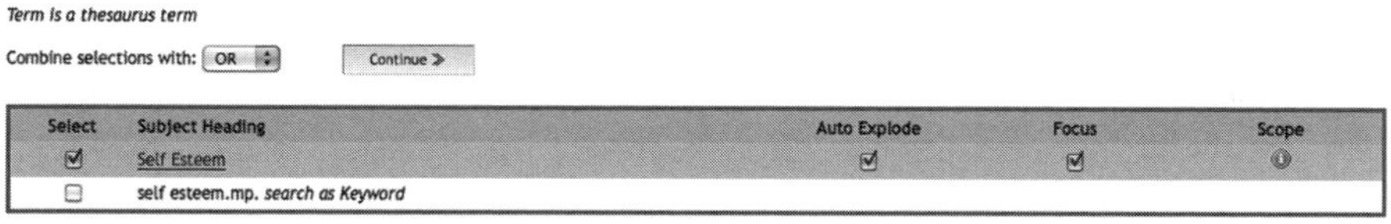

Fig. 4.16. Checking Focus on the Mapping Display. The PsycINFO® screenshots are reproduced with permission of the American Psychological Association, publisher of the PsycINFO® Database, all rights reserved. Copyright © 2000–2011 Ovid Technologies, Inc.

into the search box, as shown in Figure 4.17 (or whatever numbers correspond to the searches in your search history that you wish to combine.)

You can use any of the Boolean operators, and parentheses for making nested statements, to combine Search History set numbers in this way. Each variation will, of course, produce a set of results that differs to a greater or lesser extent. If you have built up a series of searches, this is a very fast and easy way to experiment with them to arrive at an optimal set of results.

Results

Presto: our combined sets result in 12 articles, as indicated both in the Search History display and at the beginning of the results list, shown in Figure 4.18. A useful feature of the Ovid interface is that allows us to see the search history, search interface, and results all on the same page. These results seem on target, but 12 isn't a lot. How might we get more?

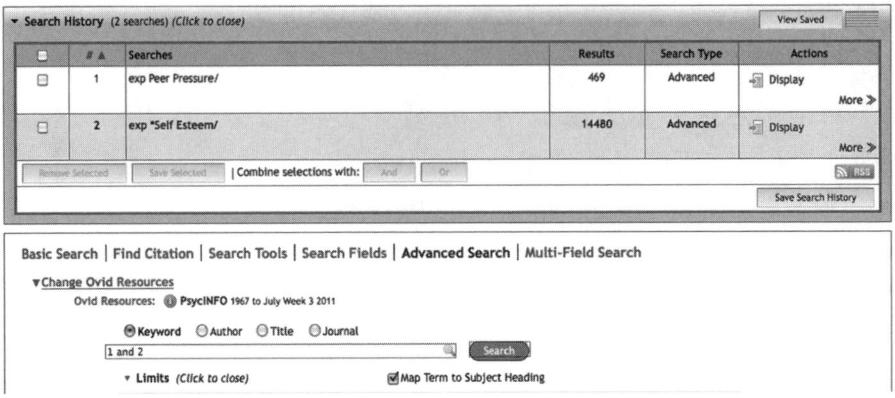

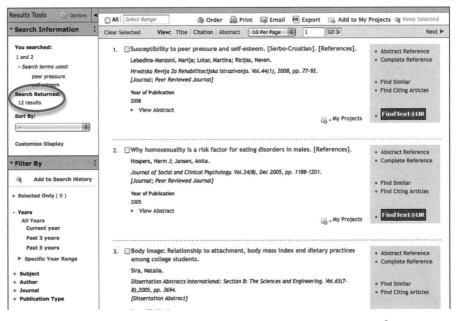

Fig. 4.17. Shortcut: combining sets using search numbers and a Boolean operator. The PsycINFO® screenshots are reproduced with permission of the American Psychological Association, publisher of the PsycINFO® Database, all rights reserved. Copyright © 2000–2011 Ovid Technologies, Inc.

Fig. 4.18. Result of combining sets 1 and 2: 12 articles. The PsycINFO® screenshots are reproduced with permission of the American Psychological Association, publisher of the PsycINFO® Database, all rights reserved. Copyright © 2000–2011 Ovid Technologies, Inc.

Search Example 1 Redone: Getting More with OR

Let's do this search again. This time, to *avoid* mapping directly to a term, type "pressure from peers" into the search box. This causes the Mapping Display to show us a whole list of possible subject headings, from which we can select several terms in addition to Peer Pressure. Note the "Combine selections with" drop-down at the top of the page. It's set to OR, which is

Select	Subject Heading	Auto Explode	Focus
☑	Peer Pressure	☑	☐
☑	Peer Relations	☑	☐
☑	Social Influences	☑	☐
☐	Tobacco Smoking	☐	☐
☐	Peers	☐	☐
☐	Drug Abuse	☐	☐
☐	College Students	☐	☐
☐	Human Sex Differences	☐	☐
☑	Interpersonal Influences	☑	☐
☐	Body Image	☐	☐
☐	Age Differences	☐	☐
☐	Cross Cultural Differences	☐	☐

Fig. 4.19. Selecting several subject headings related to peer pressure. The PsycINFO® screenshots are reproduced with permission of the American Psychological Association, publisher of the PsycINFO® Database, all rights reserved. Copyright © 2000–2011 Ovid Technologies, Inc.

what we want (Figure 4.19). After picking several headings and ORing them together, yes, the number of results is enormous: more than 45,000.

Don't panic.

Combining from the Search History

There were LOTS of hits for self esteem when we searched it before, so let's reuse that search, and combine it with our new set of "peer" topics (here is the beauty of being able to quickly and easily reuse previous sets). Simply type the numbers of the sets that you want to combine into the search box, in this case: 2 and 4.

Applying Limits

OK, it's still a fairly big set of records, but still, don't panic. Let's make use of some of those limits that are so easily provided in the interface: English Language and Publication Year. If the results list still seems daunting, there are a couple of options. You could try another limit: Ovid Full Text Available. Simply select the Limits that you want to use, and click the Search button. It feels odd, because there is nothing in the input field next to the Search button, but the system understands that you are applying limits. There are also options to "Filter" (e.g., narrow) your results in the panel to the left of the results list, as shown in Figure 4.20. The lists for each Filter (Subject, Author, Journal, Publication Type) represent the most frequently occurring entries from the total results list; thus, you might decide to look only at the articles from the journal that had the most articles on this topic, or articles by an author who publishes on the topic frequently. There's also an interesting feature I haven't encountered before: the Search Information, Filter by, and My Projects parts of the left-hand panel are "floating" lists; you can simply click and drag their headers to arrange them in the order you want (or have them not appear at all, using the "Options" link next to the words Results Tools). This is an unusual example of the trend toward personalization in databases.

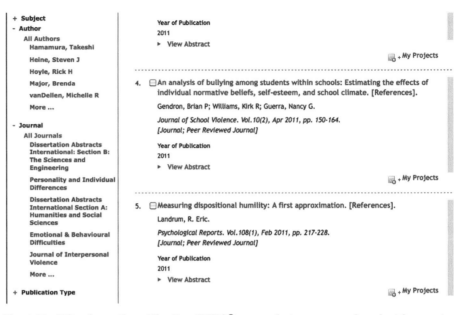

Fig. 4.20. Filter by options. The PsycINFO® screenshots are reproduced with permission of the American Psychological Association, publisher of the PsycINFO® Database, all rights reserved. Copyright © 2000–2011 Ovid Technologies, Inc.

	# ▲	Searches	Results	Search Type	Actions
☐	3	1 and 2	12	Advanced	🗐 Display More ≫
☐	4	exp Interpersonal Influences/ or exp Peer Relations/ or exp Peer Pressure/ or exp Social Influences/	45085	Advanced	🗐 Display More ≫
☐	5	2 and 4	649	Advanced	🗐 Display More ≫
☐	6	limit 5 to (english language and yr="2007 -Current")	66	Advanced	🗐 Display More ≫

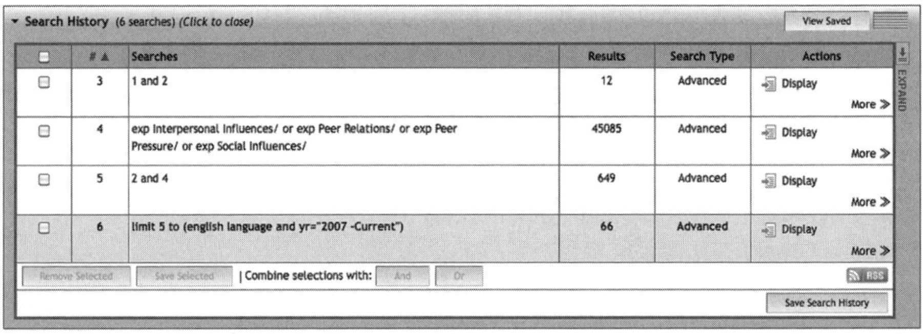

Fig. 4.21. Limits applied to reduce the number of results. The PsycINFO® screenshots are reproduced with permission of the American Psychological Association, publisher of the PsycINFO® Database, all rights reserved. Copyright © 2000–2011 Ovid Technologies, Inc.

Using just the check-box limits, we whittle down the results to 66, a manageable set of results (Figure 4.21).

More Search History Advantages

The Ovid piece-by-piece approach to searching is also helpful if you decide to change direction as you're working. If you get a new idea, you simply start that new thread, and then experiment with combining it with previous searches. You can delete searches if you're really sure they aren't useful (using the Remove Selected button in the Search History box), but you can also just keep adding new ones. Although the interface will default to showing

☐	# ▲	Searches	Results	Search Type	Actions	
☐	1	exp Peer Pressure/	469	Advanced	⬚ Display More ≫	CONTRACT
☐	2	exp *Self Esteem/	14480	Advanced	⬚ Display More ≫	
☐	3	1 and 2	12	Advanced	⬚ Display More ≫	
☐	4	exp Interpersonal Influences/ or exp Peer Relations/ or exp Peer Pressure/ or exp Social Influences/	45085	Advanced	⬚ Display More ≫	
☐	5	2 and 4	649	Advanced	⬚ Display More ≫	
☐	6	limit 5 to (english language and yr="2007 -Current")	66	Advanced	⬚ Display More ≫	
☐	7	exp Body Image/	7856	Advanced	⬚ Display More ≫	
☐	8	exp Television Advertising/ or exp Advertising/	7506	Advanced	⬚ Display More ≫	
☐	9	6 and 8	1	Advanced	⬚ Display More ≫	
☐	10	2 or 7	21712	Advanced	⬚ Display More ≫	
☐	11	8 and 10	98	Advanced	⬚ Display More ≫	

Remove Selected   Save Selected | Combine selections with: And   Or   ⬚ RSS

Save Search History

Fig. 4.22. More search history combinations. The PsycINFO® screenshots are reproduced with permission of the American Psychological Association, publisher of the PsycINFO® Database, all rights reserved. Copyright © 2000–2011 Ovid Technologies, Inc.

you only the four most recent searches, the small Expand tab on the upper right of the Search History table will reveal them all.

Figure 4.22 shows an example of the results you get when you add two new searches (for material about body image and about advertising) and combine them with previous searches. We find that the new search set 8 produces only one result when ANDed with search set 6, so we might simply try combining set 8 with the large set on self esteem, set 2. This combination results in 26 citations (not pictured in the screenshot), perhaps not enough, so we OR set 7, about Body Image, with set 2, and then AND that with the advertising set to get a substantial set of 98 records—all with a few flicks of the keys.

Working with Results

The first 10 results of the latest search are always listed on the main search page, starting below the Search interface (see Figure 4.15). As with many databases, you select citations of interest by clicking their check boxes. Just above the results, the "Results Tools" (Figure 4.23) offer options for handling your results: marked items can be printed, emailed, saved, or exported to a bibliographic software application. You can choose exactly which fields to include, which citation style you want them formatted in, and whether or not to include your search history. The "Order" feature ties in with the subscribing institution's Interlibrary Loan system, allowing quick and easy ordering of documents not locally available. "My Projects" is similar to ERIC's "My Clipboard"—if you are engaged in a long-term research project, you can create your own personal account in the system to store results over

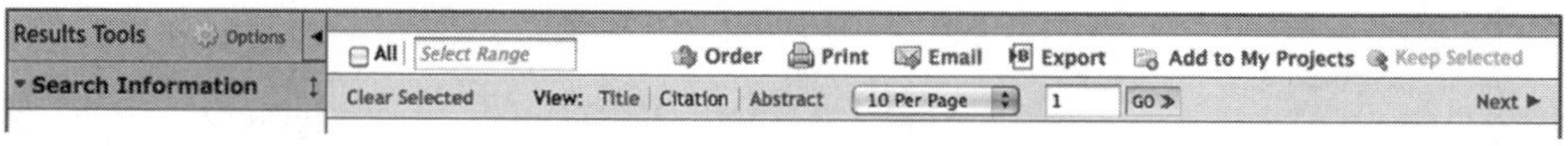

Fig. 4.23. The "Results Tools." The PsycINFO® screenshots are reproduced with permission of the American Psychological Association, publisher of the PsycINFO® Database, all rights reserved. Copyright © 2000–2011 Ovid Technologies, Inc.

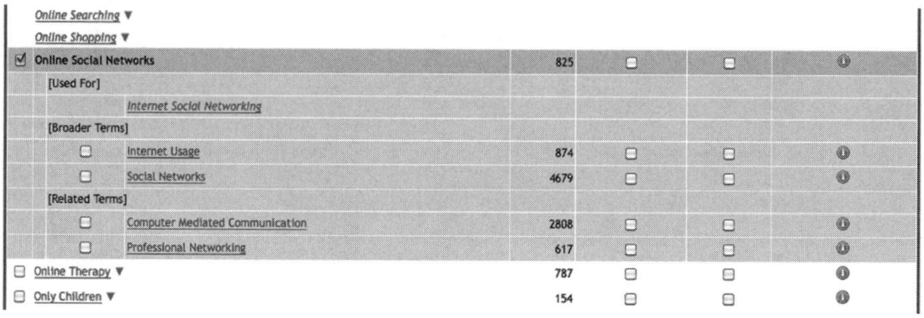

Fig. 4.24. *PsycINFO* Thesaurus of Psychological Index Terms, 11th edition, at the term "Online social networks." The PsycINFO® screenshots are reproduced with permission of the American Psychological Association, publisher of the PsycINFO® Database, all rights reserved. Copyright © 2000–2011 Ovid Technologies, Inc.

time. There are also various customization features provided in this area: you can choose how much of the results you want to view (perhaps just Titles initially), or how many results to display per page.

Additional Feature: The *PsycINFO* Thesaurus

You can directly access the *PsycINFO* Thesaurus by going to the Search Tools tab, selecting Thesaurus from the drop-down menu, and entering a term. You can also access it from the Mapping Display screen in the course of a search by clicking on any of the linked subject headings. (Figure 4.19 shows a good example of a list of linked subject headings in a Mapping Display.) In either case, you'll get taken to the Thesaurus display for that term. This allows you to see how the term fits into the hierarchy, what narrower terms will be included if you leave the Auto-Explode box checked, what terms are broader, and what terms are related, as indicated in Figure 4.24. It can be quite interesting to wander around in the Thesaurus for a bit.

Quick Recap

PsycINFO is the preeminent index to psychology literature, and is produced by the American Psychological Association. The complete version of the online database provides journal indexing back to 1806 and covers journals, books, book chapters, technical reports, dissertations, published conference papers, bibliographies, and more. Sources are international. Using *PsycINFO* through the Ovid interface takes advantage of the Ovid "Map to Subject Heading" functionality, which automatically provides a list of suggested terms from the *PsycINFO* Thesaurus for any word or phrase typed into the search field. Specialized functions in the Subject Heading Mapping Display are Auto-Explode, that is, automatically search the indicated term and all narrower subject headings, and Focus, that is, restrict the search to records in which the indicated term is a major aspect (or focus) of the article. The optimal search style to use in the Ovid interface is to build a search one concept at a time, and then combine sets from the search history. This is very different from the other databases considered so far. The most commonly used Limits appear in the Advanced Search interface, and many more are accessible by means of the Additional Limits button. In addition, options for filtering a search by Subject, Author, Journal, or Publication Type are available in the results interface. The Ovid interface offers a number of customization and personalization features.

Exercises and Points to Consider

Check the book companion website, www.LibrariansGuide.info, for supplementary materials.

1. I've heard that there's a bibliography of movies that had librarians in them—surely *Library Literature* would be the place to find out? Try going to the Thesaurus and searching for "librarians in film." What do you get? Is "librarians in movies" any better? If neither of these seems to lead you to the right subject heading, fall back to the quick-and-dirty approach: do a keyword search on "librarians in movies" and then see what subjects are associated with the results. How many results do you get for the keyword search? How many results do you get when you do a new search by the right subject heading? (Although they are getting rather old, take a look at the article titles—some of them are rather amusing.)

2. Search example 2 in *Library Literature* was about chat services as part of the Reference function. Go to the database, reproduce the suggested searches, then compare the results with what you get by simply typing in Reference chat as a keyword search and, if you want, applying one or more Subjects that you discover in the Refine panel. To take a devil's advocate role here: aren't these results just as good as those that we retrieved with a much more elaborate search? Carefully compare the results—are there any records not found in the last set (the keyword search here) that really would have been bad to miss? Not to undermine the more sophisticated techniques that this text has been encouraging you to learn, but the reality is that most people simply do a keyword search, and in some—perhaps many—cases, that approach does the job. When it doesn't work, you need to be ready with better techniques. Message: Don't get rigid, either about what you're seeing, or what you're doing.

3. Say that you want to catch up on what's being written about information literacy classes in college or school libraries (whichever you are more interested in). Rather than using the Thesaurus, you simply do an Advanced search on "information literacy" in Keyword, AND "college" [or "school"] in Subject, and let *Library Literature* do the work of informing you about appropriate subject headings by

observing what comes up under Subject in the left panel of the Results screen. What is the Thesaurus term for this kind of teaching? Pick a subject heading under the Subject suggestions and see how it affects the number of results. Try adding a keyword, such as "evaluation," to your last search. Finally, go into the Thesaurus and look up "information literacy." What can you learn about this term?

4. One last quick search in *Library Literature*: the latest hot idea in database searching is known as "discovery services." A vast improvement over "federated searching," discovery services build a giant index of the contents of many databases, plus your catalog records, which you can then search all at once through one Google-box interface and get results fast. (The federated search systems queried each database at the time of the search, and they were agonizingly slow.) See what *Library Literature* has to offer on "discovery services." Is there a subject heading for this kind of thing yet?

5. In the first Search Example for ERIC, we used a very structured approach, carefully checking the Thesaurus before deciding on our search terms and setting up the strategy. Compare that with the following much less structured approach. Try simply searching:

    Teaching the deaf—as Keywords.

    This search results in a great many more records (more than 1,500). Look over the results; some of the results are on target, but others probably aren't (sort them by date to make this more apparent). Although our search recall has gone up, the precision of our search has gone down. If you had started with this search, what would you immediately start doing to cut down and focus the results?

6. It is likely that your school has access to ERIC via a commercial vendor. Repeat all the example searches in that version, observing the differences between the free and the fee versions. Leaving aside any familiarity and comfort-level issues you may have with the commercial version's interface, how do the search experiences compare? Do you get the same results sets? How easy is it to work with results, or to get to full text?

7. (Questions 7 and 8 are designed for use with *PsycINFO* from Ovid; if your access is via another vendor, try executing similar searches in that version.) Your sister recently had a baby, and is upset because the baby's sleep patterns aren't settling down at all. She wonders if the baby has some kind of sleep disorder, and if it's going to affect her (the baby's, not the mother's!) development.

    You start by going to *PsycINFO* and typing in "sleep disorders."

    That maps directly to a subject heading, but you're curious about what might be included "under" it, or near it in the Thesaurus list. Click the subject heading to find out.

    Now look down through the list. Hmm—"Sleep Onset"—that's kind of the problem. What lies beyond that in the list? Oh look! "Sleep Wake Cycle"! That sounds good. Select that, and click its Explode box. Click the Continue button.

    Next term: type "infants" in the search box, and see what comes up on the Mapping Display.

    "Infant Development"—that looks good. Select that and Continue.

Now combine those two searches by ANDing their search set numbers together.

Do you like the results?

8. A friend has a child with Aspergers syndrome (a form of autism) and is worried about how this could affect his verbal and writing skills, that is, his language development. In *PsycINFO*, what happens if you search and then combine Aspergers Syndrome (this is how the term appears in *PsycINFO*) and Language Development? (You don't get very many.) Maybe we could "widen our net" on the "Language" aspect of the search. Type in the broad term Language, and see if the Mapping Display offers more subject headings that we could use. Choose several. Now combine this new (very large!) set with the Aspergers Syndrome set. It should result in more results than before.

9. As you compare what is discussed about these databases with what you see on your screen, you will undoubtedly spot additional features or functionality not mentioned here. Figure out what these other features or functions do, and ask yourself why they were included. Think about which users would most benefit from [feature X], and how you might market it to them (i.e., get them to use it). Discussing this as a class or in small groups will help to generate more ideas as you bounce ideas off one another. Consider doing this Exercise for every chapter that discusses specific databases in this book.

Beyond the Textbook Exercises

Exercises requiring other Social Science databases

1. A student needs some recent articles from business journals about how J.P. Morgan Bank is doing in recovering from the subprime mortgage crisis.

2. An undergraduate in an anthropology class wants to write a paper about the origins of socioeconomic class, for example, when did social classes first emerge? Are they really ancient—were there social classes among the cavemen? (What would be a more scholarly expression for humans of that era?) Another phrase that emerges in discussing the topic with the undergraduate is "social stratification." Consult your school's lists of databases by subject (two of the subjects are mentioned here, but if there is a list for Sociology, check that too), choose some appropriate databases and search strategies for this topic, and try them. Record your search process, especially search terms as you discover new ones, and make notes about your results.

3. An economics PhD student calls my office at 5:05 on Friday afternoon. He's out of town, and is calling because he knows the title and author of a paper—how can he get it? My first question: do you mean a journal article? Answer: yes, but he doesn't know which journal. The article title is "Ability Sorting and the Returns to College Major" and the author's last name is Arcidiacono. What journal (volume, issue, year, pages) did this appear in? Can you determine if your institution has access to this online?

Notes

1. This will come up again in chapter 10 when we talk about free resources, but it would be a disservice not to mention it now: EBSCO provides the LISTA database *for free* at www.libraryresearch.com. Thank you EBSCO!

2. The note about the ERIC Microfiche Digitation project is worth reading: they have digitized the entire collection, spanning 1966–2004, and have made approximately 65 percent of it available. The rest is waiting for permission from authors, which they are trying to obtain through their online form. This is wonderful news for researchers, and for university libraries, many of which have acres of fiche cabinets full of ERIC microfiche. If only all that film were no longer needed.

3. This is one of several choices for equivalent Latin terms produced by searching for "searcher" at the English-to-Latin Word Search Results section of the Perseus Library at Tufts University (http://www.perseus.tufts.edu/hopper/definitionlookup?lang =Latin). Another was "indagatrix" (she who investigates, a searcher), which I would love to put on my business cards.

4. This is useful to the user, but frustrating to a taker of screenshots because one can no longer provide an overall sense of the results in one image.

5. If you do this in the Ovid interface, you'll find that the list of fields is far longer than the list referred to at the beginning of the discussion of *PsycINFO*. This list represents the searchable field structure devised by Ovid; to be totally honest, I can only make a reasonable guess that a mapping process must take place to make the data supplied by the APA work with this structure.

5
Databases for Science and Medicine

The databases in this chapter, besides being intrinsically interesting and well-crafted systems, provide a view into their respective disciplines that goes beyond their content. Obviously, medical databases index medical material, and science databases index scientific publications. But the two subject databases considered here are functionally quite different, and I believe the difference reflects a basic tenet of each discipline.

Every discipline or profession has its own language: a specialized vocabulary is one of the things that unites and defines a profession (think of all the jargon we use in libraries). In almost no area is this truer than in medicine: a major part of the study of medicine is mastery of its language. The language is crucial, and *the* medical database, PubMed, reflects this. One of the key components of PubMed are MEDLINE records, which are distinguished by their detailed system of subject headings and subheadings for *terms*, painstakingly applied by trained professionals. We will see in PubMed that the system will do its best to translate whatever terminology you enter into subject terms, as well as search your terms simply as words. Consider this as you experiment with PubMed, and see if you agree: the basic tenet here is a focus on "*what*." Medical terms represent "*what*": what organ, what condition, what symptoms, what drugs, and what outcome.

In contrast, the approach taken by the scientist who developed the *Science Citation Index* (and later similar indexes for the other disciplines) was that the *citations* were of paramount importance: the references associated with scientific papers. To me, this represents *who*. Who was cited? Who was citing? Although it is used in other organizations, the *Science Citation Index* is a very *academic* product, and in academia, a great deal rides on who you are (which you establish by publishing your work) and who has recognized your work (by citing it). You will find that the *Web of Science* citation indexes do not use subject headings (in the sense that we've seen so far) at all.

Another way this difference in emphasis (what versus who) is reflected in the functionality of each database is the way they arrive at "Related records." In PubMed, an algorithm based on words (what) identifies related records. In the citation indexes, shared citations (who) identify related records.

As you work through this chapter and become familiar with these databases, keep this idea in the back of your mind: that medicine is focused on what (terms) and the citation indexes are focused on who. See if you can spot additional aspects of the databases' functionality to support it.

PubMed and MEDLINE

It's easy to know where to start a consideration of medical databases: it has to be PubMed, the über medical database available to all on the Internet. PubMed is developed and maintained by the National Center for Biotechnology Information (NCBI), at the U.S. National Library of Medicine (NLM), which is part of the National Institutes of Health (NIH). The difficulty is knowing where to stop: the major component of PubMed is MEDLINE, a huge, immensely detailed, highly specific, and sophisticated resource for an elite professional field, and PubMed extends this resource to be even larger and richer in its content. Let me declare right here: this text is not going to attempt to teach you to be a medical researcher. If you get a job in a medical library, you will receive thorough training from professionals in the field. Instead, in the spirit that you can achieve *something* reasonable, no matter what the subject area, by employing the same basic strategy (i.e., engaging in a reference interview, using your searching techniques, and keeping your eyes open), what follows will be a demystifying look at doing medical literature searching through PubMed. This is similar to how we looked at ERIC: many commercial database vendors offer the content, but the government also provides it freely to everyone who can get online. Quite staggering when you consider the quality and quantity of the content.

We will start with some information about the MEDLINE database specifically, so that you have a better understanding of the main content you are interacting with before starting to search it through PubMed.

About MEDLINE

MEDLINE (Medical Literature Analysis and Retrieval System Online) is a product of the NLM, which describes it as their "premier bibliographic database" containing "over 18 million references to journal articles" in the life sciences, with a focus on biomedicine. Date coverage for the MEDLINE database as offered through commercial vendors is generally from 1966 to the present, but PubMed includes material back to 1945 and even older. MEDLINE is a journal citation database (many citations offer links to full text, but the database itself does not contain full text), and it is international in scope: it selectively covers "approximately 5,516" journals from all over the world, in 39 languages. The NLM enhances records from non–English-language journals by supplying translated article titles, and "about 83%" of those records include abstracts in English. The database is updated daily, from Tuesday through Saturday, with the addition of "2,000–4,000" new citations each day. (Additions "each day" does not mean, however, that the contents of a journal published yesterday will be indexed and added today. The kind of detailed processing required to create full MEDLINE records takes time.) In 2010 alone, "nearly 700,000" references were added to the database. This phenomenal effort is the result of a distribution of labor among the NLM, its international partners, and collaborating institutions (U.S. National Library of Medicine 2011b).

A key distinguishing feature of MEDLINE is its carefully crafted thesaurus, known as *MeSH*, for *Medical Subject Headings*. (Think of it as the Library of Congress Subject Headings for the medical world.) This highly developed, hierarchical system of subject headings is also the work of the NLM, which has a whole branch devoted to continuous maintenance, revision, and updating of the MeSH vocabulary,[1] The impression one gets is that this is a dynamic system, continually growing and changing in response to developments in scientific and medical research and practice. Statistics about MeSH are impressive: the 2011 MeSH contained 26,142 subject headings ("descriptors") augmented with more than 177,000 other "entry terms" (U.S. National Library of Medicine 2011a). An entry term is like a *see* reference: if you search the MeSH database for Vitamin C, it brings up the record for Ascorbic Acid, the official heading. Vitamin C is just one of seven such "entry terms" for this common chemical, which helps to explain the huge number of entry terms versus actual subject headings.

As with any thesaurus, of course, these terms are then employed by highly trained indexers to describe and provide entry points for each article. As a user of this database, one important thing for you to remember is that indexers are instructed always to choose the most specific terms available. Although the MeSH system is hierarchical (to 11 levels of specificity . . .), with such broad terms as "Digestive System Diseases" at the most general level, if an article is discussing a specific malady, such as Crohn Disease, *only the more specific term* will be applied as a heading. All the layers of headings between Digestive System Diseases and Crohn Disease (e.g., Gastrointestinal Diseases, Gastroenteritis, and Inflammatory Bowel Diseases) would *not* appear as additional subject headings. So you have full permission to enter very specific terms here.

PubMed: More than MEDLINE

And now for PubMed (http://pubmed.gov). As a database of medical citations, you could think of PubMed as what you'd get if databases were like hamburgers: "Give me MEDLINE—and super size it!" MEDLINE is the main component of PubMed, but PubMed offers a number of groups of additional material:

- Newer material: in-process citations are records that have not yet been indexed with MeSH; they represent the very latest in the literature.

- Older material: citations from 1946 to 1965, known as OLDMEDLINE, and publisher-supplied citations that precede the date that a journal was selected for indexing in MEDLINE.

- Additional material:
  - Citations for articles in MEDLINE journals that were not selected for the MEDLINE database because of their non–life sciences content.
  - Citations to some additional life science journals that submit full text to PubMedCentral®.

- Citations to author manuscripts of articles published by NIH-funded researchers.

- Citations for both the entire work and each chapter of a subset of ebooks available on the NCBI Bookshelf.

(U.S. National Library of Medicine 2010).

Overall, be aware that PubMed is going in both directions, backward and forward. There are citations in PubMed from as early as 1809, and there are publisher-supplied citations to the latest literature (tagged "Epub ahead of print"). PubMed is much more than a super-sized database of medical citations, however. It is a portal to databases from the NCBI—of gene sequences, molecular structures, etc.—to "Services" such as citation matchers and a special interface for clinical queries, and to "Related Resources" such as Clinical Trials and Consumer Health information. It's huge, first-class, professional information, and it is freely available on the Web. I'm afraid we won't do more than touch the surface of the possibilities here, but at least you'll now know that it exists, and you can explore further when and if the need should arise.

Introduction to the PubMed Interface

Let's take a look (Figure 5.1): http://www.pubmed.gov. What a clean, neatly laid out page! One Google-box search field, descriptive information about what PubMed is, and three categories of links below. I can highly recommend the tutorial links under Using PubMed in the first list; one of our search examples will make use of the citation matcher function in the second list, and if you are interested in searching the MeSH database, it's first in the More Resources list. Go online where you can see it better, and notice that there is a "Limits" link just above the search box, and in the upper right corner there is "My NCBI Sign In"—again, you are being offered a personalized experience and a way to carry results over from one search session to another.

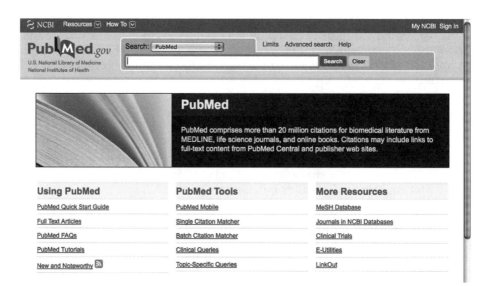

Fig. 5.1. PubMed home interface, as of July 2011.

Sidebar 5.1

Beware the trap of expectation that because PubMed is a free Web resource and is apparently easy to use that somehow the content will be "easier." Not in the slightest. As noted in the opening discussion of this section, PubMed contains the highly sophisticated MEDLINE database content, plus additional material not indexed by MEDLINE, and links to advanced scientific resources such as the NCBI genome databases. In other words, despite the fact that this is a free Web resource that is open to the world, this may not be the place for the average mortal to try and find an answer to a medical question. If you are working with a health professional, researcher, or student in the health sciences, yes, this is the place. If you want to help your mom or your neighbor find some health information, go to MedlinePlus.gov.

Notes and Search Examples

This section will take you through four types of searches: a topic search, a simple field codes search, a known item search, and an author-subject search.

Search Example 1: A Topic Search

Our first search in PubMed is looking for material on heart failure in middle-aged women: a "topic" search. (Note: this condition, also known as congestive heart failure, is common in much older women but unusual in middle-aged women.) Starting from a very simple keyword search, we will learn some ways to focus our results using the Search details information and Limits.

As we start typing the word: heart in the search box, the system starts offering us "suggestions," as shown in Figure 5.2. (Note that although I use the term "suggestions," these are really just things other people have searched for: they are not recommendations or in any sense better. They can be handy, and they might give you ideas, but don't feel as if you have to choose any of them over your own terminology. If you find the suggestions distracting, you can turn them off.) The suggestions include "congenital

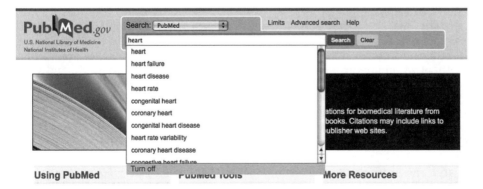

Fig. 5.2. The PubMed search box "suggestions" based on entering 'heart' in the search box, as of July 2011.

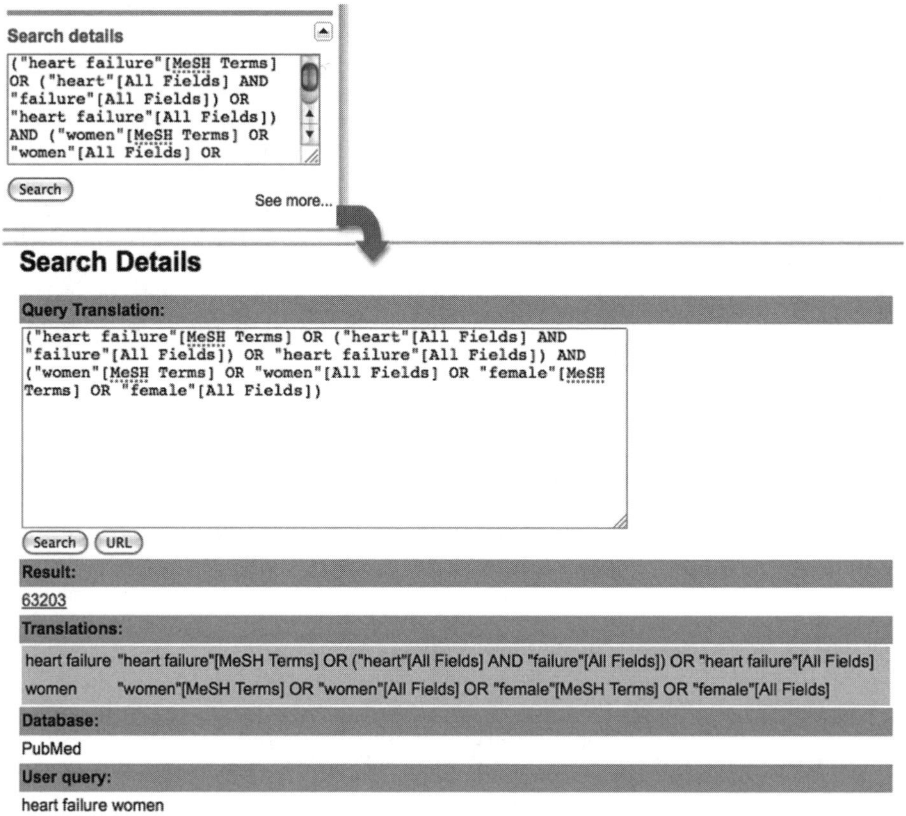

Search details

("heart failure"[MeSH Terms]
OR ("heart"[All Fields] AND
"failure"[All Fields]) OR
"heart failure"[All Fields])
AND ("women"[MeSH Terms] OR
"women"[All Fields] OR

(Search)   See more...

Search Details

Query Translation:

("heart failure"[MeSH Terms] OR ("heart"[All Fields] AND
"failure"[All Fields]) OR "heart failure"[All Fields]) AND
("women"[MeSH Terms] OR "women"[All Fields] OR "female"[MeSH
Terms] OR "female"[All Fields])

(Search) (URL)

Result:

63203

Translations:

| heart failure | "heart failure"[MeSH Terms] OR ("heart"[All Fields] AND "failure"[All Fields]) OR "heart failure"[All Fields] |
| women | "women"[MeSH Terms] OR "women"[All Fields] OR "female"[MeSH Terms] OR "female"[All Fields] |

Database:

PubMed

User query:

heart failure women

Fig. 5.3. Search details "portlet" and full screen, as of July 2011.

heart disease" and "congestive heart failure" among others. We will just type our concepts, however: heart failure women.

This produces a daunting set of results (more than 63,000 at the time of writing), but fear not. We will learn why there are so many, and how to bring the number down to something more manageable (and on target). Look down the results screen and find the Search Details "portlet" shown in Figure 5.3. The system is telling you how it interpreted your search. Clicking the "See more . . ." link produces a full interface to this information, also shown in Figure 5.3.

The Search Details screen provides a full Query Translation, the total number of results, the Translations for each phrase or single word (amazing; how does it know?), which database was searched (because there are a number of other biomedical databases available here besides PubMed), and your original "User query." Both "translation" areas show us immediately why there are so many results: the terms were searched as subject headings (since they happen to exactly match some headings), plus they have been searched simply as words in "All Fields," and the appropriate variants have been ORed together. (It's really an *amazingly* smart system.) We can start learning from this information and focusing our results right here. We could search the appropriate terms only as MeSH Terms—but then we are losing out on all the extras, all the newer material available in PubMed.[2] So let's not do that. We'll just create a new search query that is slightly smarter than our first one (and incorporates the useful idea that the system supplied, i.e., that "female" is a synonym for "women"). Note that the Boolean operators are always entered in caps:

"heart failure" AND (women OR female)

We click the Search button and our results are reduced somewhat. Now to apply some Limits.

The Limits link in the search interface area (the upper part of Figure 5.4) provides access to a full screen of Limit options, as shown in the lower part of Figure 5.4. For this search, we are choosing to limit by Dates—Published in the Last: 5 years; Species: Human (can't hurt to be specific); Language: English; Sex: Female (can't hurt to reiterate), and Ages: Middle Aged: 45–64 years. This reduces our results to ~8,000, which of course is a still a great many, but if the patron wasn't able to come up with additional aspects (what *about* heart failure in middle-aged women—the effects of exercise? diet? simply the incidence?) to plug into the search, I would feel comfortable having the person start to review the results for additional ideas.

The initial results are shown in Figure 5.5. Note that the default sort order for displaying the results is by "recently added," which is *the date the citation was added to the database*, **not** the publication date. In this case, I have left it at the default, but don't hesitate to open the Display Settings and change the order to Pub Date. It can make a difference in the initial results.

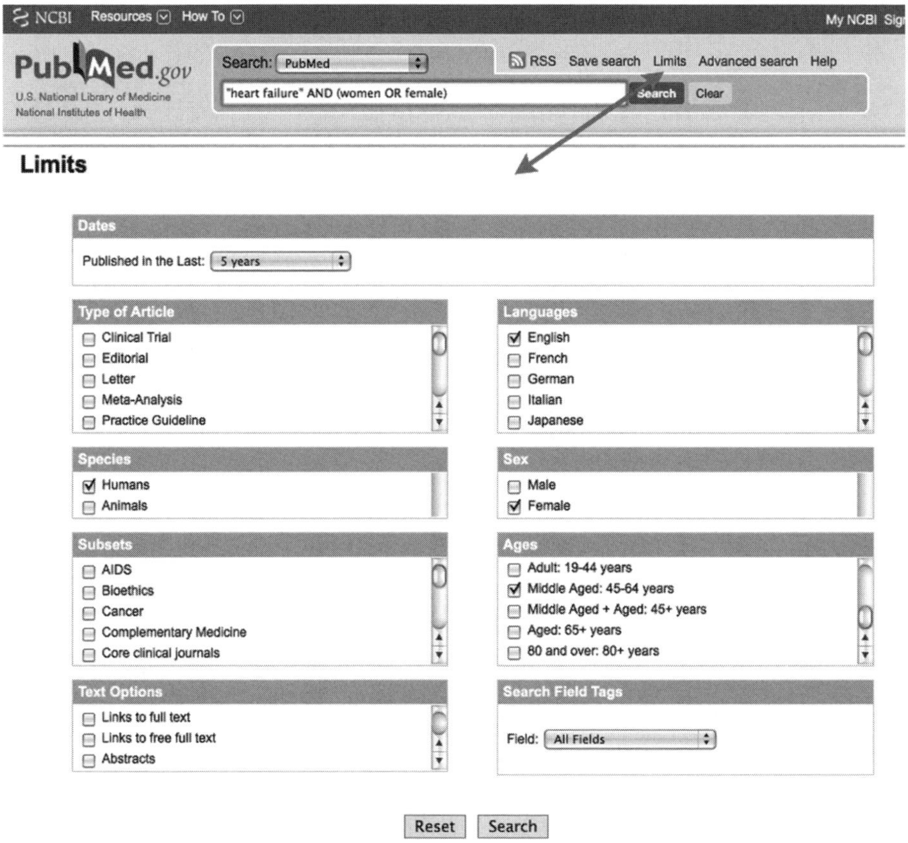

Fig. 5.4. Applying limits, as of July 2011.

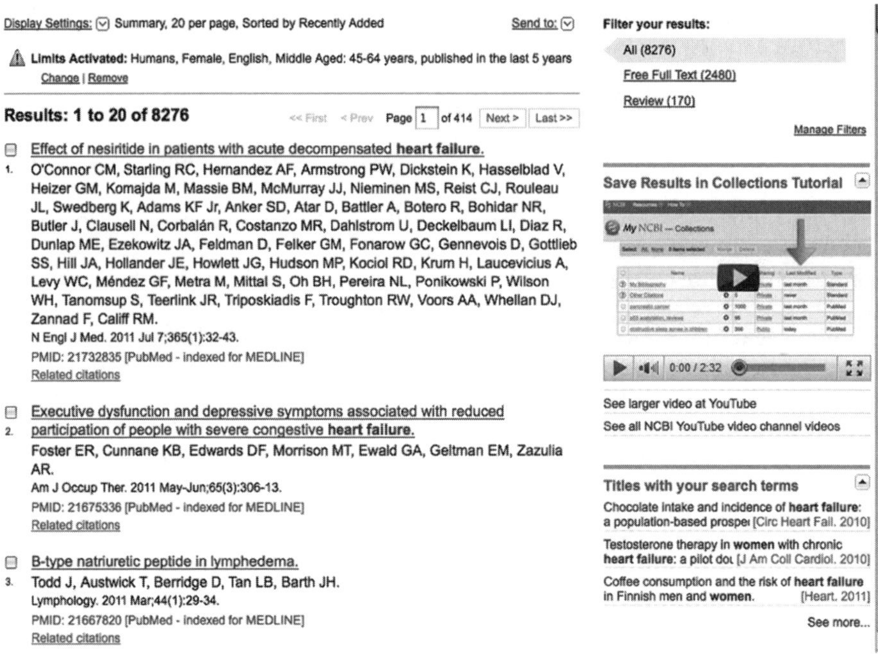

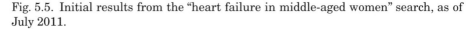

Fig. 5.5. Initial results from the "heart failure in middle-aged women" search, as of July 2011.

The titles look on target, and in addition to the Search Details box, PubMed provides a number of other useful features on the right side of the screen (rather than the left, as in most of the databases we've seen so far). A quick video tutorial on how to save your results in "Collections" was featured at the time of this writing. This is followed by an area highlighting "Titles with your search terms," which is one of the best ways to zoom in on articles on your topic that you can mine for additional search terms, no matter what their publication date (e.g., "Chocolate intake and incidence of heart failure: a population-based prospective study of middle-aged and elderly women" from 2010. It's worth looking at.) The system tells you how many of the titles in the results are available for free from PubMed Central, and every step of your "Recent activity" is listed, allowing you to jump back to a previous search or activity if desired.

As noted previously, this could be a reasonable point at which to start looking at records in the results (or just jump into the "titles with your search terms") to come up with additional terms to add to and focus the results.

Search Example 2: Searching with Field Codes

Search 1 was all very well, but what if you wanted just a quick and dirty way to get a few on-target results? Rather than figuring out ways to focus a huge set of results, you could then take the approach of "pearl growing" from the best items in a small set to learn headings or other terms so you can create a new strategy that retrieves more, but still on-target, items. Our second search example will demonstrate the use of the title field code in a PubMed search string to specify that terms be searched only in the title field. Using field codes is like setting a drop-down menu to a particular field.

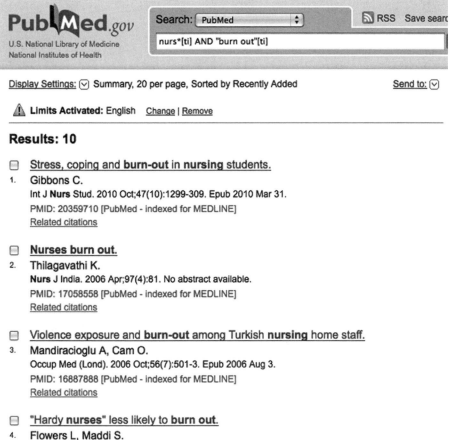

Fig. 5.6. Results from search example 2, on burnout in the nursing profession, limited to English, as of July 2011.

Field codes are always encased in square brackets, and the field code for the title field is pretty obvious: [title]. You can spell it out, or use the two-letter version (and look extra-cool to your friends): [ti]. You can use truncation and other search operators (parentheses, Boolean, phrase quotes) with field codes. To look for articles on burnout in the nursing profession, we might enter this search:

nurs*[ti] AND "burn out"[ti]

in the PubMed search box. As of July 2011, this produced just 17 results, in quite an array of languages: German, French, Italian, and Spanish in addition to English (this is a worldwide issue, obviously). Limiting to English, we get just 10 results, as shown in Figure 5.6.

We pick the result titled "'Hardy nurses' less likely to burn out" (because in the back of our mind is really how to prevent burnout) and learn a lot from this record's MeSH headings, which are shown in Figure 5.7.

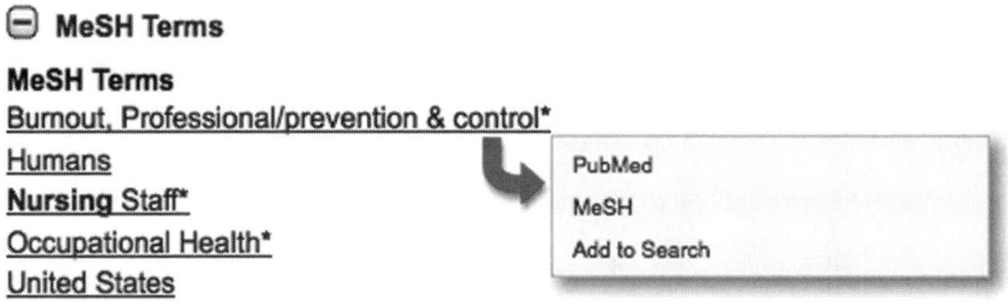

Fig. 5.7. MeSH Terms in the "Hardy nurses" record; mini-menu options, as of July 2011.

Burnout is such a common phenomenon that it has its own subject heading. Nurses are "Nursing Staff," and, aha, there *is* a good way to specify that we want material specific to the United States. Clicking these headings in a record brings up a tiny menu with the options to (start a new search in) PubMed, (look this term up in the) MeSH (database), or Add (the term) to Search, as shown in the right side of Figure 5.7.

We might use the mini-menu to Add the Burnout, Nursing Staff, and United States MeSH headings to our Search—but that might be just a tad restrictive. Instead, let's just copy and paste the terms we want to use (you don't need to include the asterisks), AND them together, and put double quotes only around the "United States" phrase, for example:

Burnout, Professional/prevention & control AND Nursing Staff AND "United States"

which produces a beautiful set of 77. This approach takes advantage of the fact that PubMed will always try to search terms as MeSH headings *and* as keywords: it gives you both good precision and more recall without a lot of fussing around or missing out on any very recent citations that have not had MeSH indexing applied yet.

Our next example is a common type of search: for a known (or half known) item that might turn into a topic search.

Search Example 3: Known Item Search

Clicking the PubMed.gov logo always returns us to the home screen (Figure 5.1). In this search example we will use the Single Citation Matcher link to look up a known item. In this case, we are working with a person who has partial "known" information: she remembers that the title of the article mentioned tamoxifen and singing, and that it appeared in one of the PLoS (Public Library of Science) journals. Figure 5.8 shows this search ready to run; carefully note how the journal title has been entered: PLoS[space]* (wildcard), indicating any of the PLoS [Word] journal titles. Entering this as PLoS* (no space between PLoS and the asterisk) will not work.

The result is what the person remembered (Figure 5.9), and because it is a PLoS journal the full text is freely available, but she didn't realize it was only a comment on another article (indicated at "A" in Figure 5.9). She could follow the link to the original article, or this might be the time to look at the MeSH Terms for this article, which include Voice/drug effects. Perfect!

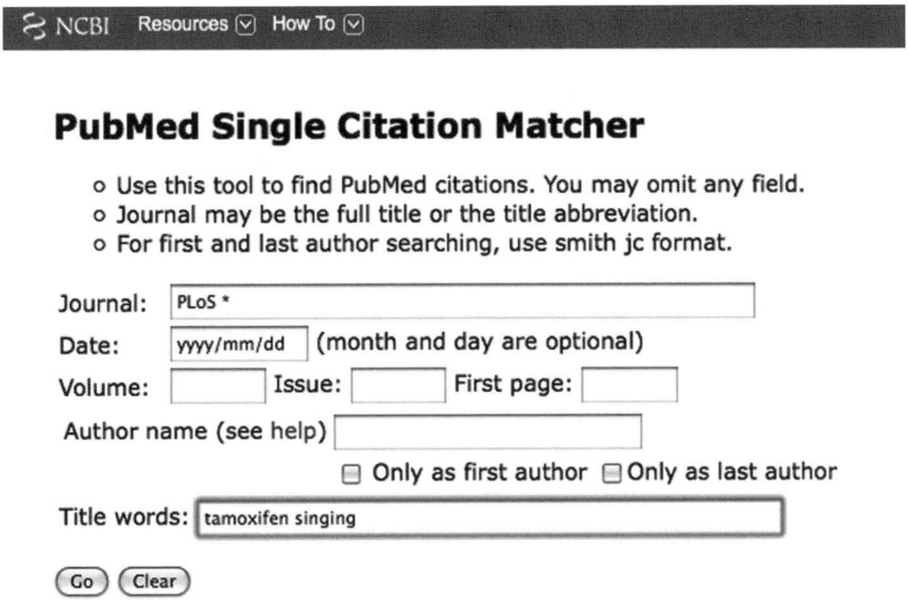

PubMed Single Citation Matcher

- Use this tool to find PubMed citations. You may omit any field.
- Journal may be the full title or the title abbreviation.
- For first and last author searching, use smith jc format.

Journal: PLoS *

Date: yyyy/mm/dd   (month and day are optional)

Volume: Issue: First page:

Author name (see help)

☐ Only as first author ☐ Only as last author

Title words: tamoxifen singing

(Go) (Clear)

Fig. 5.8. Using the Single Citation Matcher to find a known item, as of July 2011.

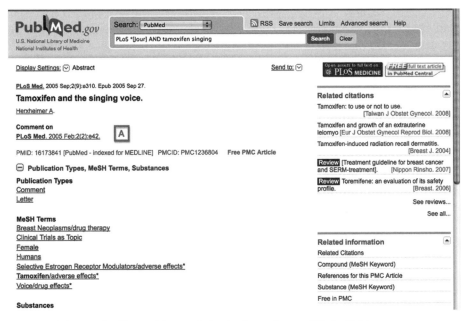

Fig. 5.9. The single "Tamoxifen and singing" result, as of July 2011.

Running a new PubMed search for Voice/drug effects is definitely the thing to do now; the patron could then add the name of a drug or a substance to the search box to focus the results. For example:

"Voice/drug effects"[MAJR] AND (estrogen OR "oral contraceptives").

Search Example 4: An Author-Topic Search

Our final search example is a type of search frequently done in medical research: an author-topic search. With the knowledge that author names are entered lastname[space]firstinitial (or two initials), and that the field code for author is [au], you can execute this type of search very easily and efficiently. For example, to find a set of articles that Mary Story, PhD, RD, authored (alone or with others) on the topic of obesity, we simply enter

Story M[au] AND obesity

This produces a set of 136 articles as of July 2011—prolific author, Mary Story!

Now you have several strategies for searching in PubMed. It's time we took a good look at a complete record from PubMed, which will lead us into our last topics: outputting citations and getting to the full text.

A PubMed Record

Figures 5.10a and 5.10b provide a complete view of a PubMed record. You'll find it easier to see everything if you get online and look up this record yourself: simply search "chocolate intake and incidence of heart failure" as a phrase in PubMed. The original article appeared in Circulation: Heart Failure (abbreviated Circ Heart Fail) in September 2010.

In the upper portion of the record, represented by Figure 5.10a, notice first that your search interface stays with you, even at the record level. To me, this is part of a trend to reduce clicks, to help you keep searching (and thus finding), to keep moving ahead rather than having to go back. Below that, looking across from left to right, you can control how the record is displayed (Display Settings), choose output options (Send to), and (perhaps) access the full text via the publisher's button. (More on this under Output.) Just below that are listed Related citations, which are related based on terminology. (Examine these, and store your impressions away, to compare with the "related results" you get from the *Web of Science* later in this chapter, where relatedness is based on shared citations in the papers' bibliographies.) Below that, you find that this article has been cited by "1 PubMed Central article"—again, something to tuck away: the citation indexes in the *Web of Science* used to be the only game in town in terms of tracking who is citing whom. Back on the left, the bulk of the record consists of familiar things: the full citation and a detailed abstract. But you also find out that this article has been "Commented" on by a later article, which is treated differently from a citing article. Give and take at work in scholarly discourse!

In the lower portion of the record, represented by Figure 5.10b, the two sections "Publication Types, MeSH Terms, Grant Support," and "LinkOut— more resources" are shown open (the default when initially viewing a record is that these are both closed). The incredibly detailed work of the NLM indexers is shown in the full list of MeSH Terms applied to this record, and note the inclusion of the list of grants that supported this research. The LinkOut section provides links to known sources of full text, and note especially the link under the word Medical that goes to MedlinePlus Health Information. This is the stepping stone from the professional world of medicine (where the air may be a bit thin for us mere mortals) to information that is authoritative yet accessible. It's a very nice touch, I think.

Display Settings: ⊙ Abstract   Send to: ⊙

Circ Heart Fail. 2010 Sep 1;3(5):612-6. Epub 2010 Aug 16.

Chocolate intake and incidence of heart failure: a population-based prospective study of middle-aged and elderly women.

Mostofsky E, Levitan EB, Wolk A, Mittleman MA.

Cardiovascular Epidemiology Research Unit, Department of Medicine, Beth Israel Deaconess Medical Center, Harvard Medical School, Boston, Mass 02115, USA.

Abstract

BACKGROUND: Randomized clinical trials have shown that **chocolate intake** reduces systolic and diastolic blood pressure, and observational studies have found an inverse association between **chocolate intake** and cardiovascular disease. The aim of this study was to investigate the association between **chocolate intake** and incidence of heart failure (HF).

METHODS AND RESULTS: We conducted a prospective cohort study of 31,823 women aged 48 to 83 years without baseline diabetes or a history of HF or myocardial infarction who were participants in the Swedish Mammography Cohort. In addition to answering health and lifestyle questions, participants completed a food-frequency questionnaire. Women were followed from January 1, 1998, through December 31, 2006, for HF hospitalization or death through the Swedish inpatient and cause-of-death registers. Over 9 years of follow-up, 419 women were hospitalized for incident HF (n=379) or died of HF (n=40). Compared with no regular **chocolate intake**, the multivariable-adjusted rate ratio of HF was 0.74 (95% CI, 0.58 to 0.95) for women consuming 1 to 3 servings of chocolate per month, 0.68 (95% CI, 0.50 to 0.93) for those consuming 1 to 2 servings per week, 1.09 (95% CI, 0.74 to 1.62) for those consuming 3 to 6 servings per week, and 1.23 (95% CI, 0.73 to 2.08) for those consuming ≥1 servings per day (P=0.0005 for quadratic trend).

CONCLUSIONS: In this population, moderate habitual **chocolate intake** was associated with a lower rate of HF hospitalization or death, but the protective association was not observed with intake of ≥1 servings per day.

Comment in
Circ Heart Fail. 2011 Jan 1;4(1):e5; author reply e6.

PMID: 20713904 [PubMed - indexed for MEDLINE]   PMCID: PMC3052999 [Available on 2011/9/1]

Final Version
Circ Heart Fail

Related citations
Letter by Marcadenti and Oliveira de Abreu Silva regarding article, "Chocolat [Circ Heart Fail. 2011]

Chocolate consumption and mortality following a first acute myocardial infarctii [J Intern Med. 2009]

Consistency with the DASH diet and incidence of heart failure.   [Arch Intern Med. 2009]

Review Incidence and epidemiology of heart failure.   [Heart Fail Rev. 2000]

Review Prevention of heart failure.
[J Card Fail. 2002]

See reviews...

See all...

Cited by 1 PubMed Central article
Chocolate: (un)healthy source of polyphenols?
[Genes Nutr. 2011]

Related information
Related Citations
Cited in PMC

Fig. 5.10a. Full record from PubMed, upper portion, as of July 2011.

⊖ **Publication Types, MeSH Terms, Grant Support**

Publication Types
Research Support, N.I.H., Extramural
Research Support, Non-U.S. Gov't

MeSH Terms
Aged
Aged, 80 and over
Analysis of Variance
Cacao*
Chi-Square Distribution
Female
Heart Failure/epidemiology*
Heart Failure/prevention & control
Humans
Incidence
Middle Aged
Monte Carlo Method
Proportional Hazards Models
Prospective Studies
Questionnaires
Registries
Sweden/epidemiology

Grant Support
F32 HL091683/HL/NHLBI NIH HHS/United States
F32 HL091683-02/HL/NHLBI NIH HHS/United States
T32 AI007535-11/PHS HHS/United States
T32 AI007535-11A1/AI/NIAID NIH HHS/United States

⊖ **LinkOut - more resources**

Full Text Sources
HighWire Press
Ovid Technologies, Inc.
Swets Information Services

Medical
Heart Failure - MedlinePlus Health Information

Fig. 5.10b. Full record from PubMed, lower portion, as of July 2011.

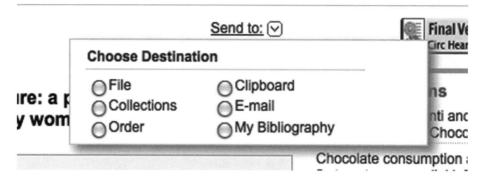

Fig. 5.11. The *Send to* menu options, as of July 2011.

Output in PubMed

The *Send to* link at the top of the record display offers a brief, tele-graphic menu of choices, as shown in Figure 5.11. *File* is analogous to "save" in many other databases: it will simply download and save the current record as a text file. *Clipboard* is just like My Clipboard in ERIC, or the Folder in an EBSCO database: the place to store records during the course of a session, to be emailed or otherwise output en masse. The e-mail option is self-evident. *Collections* and *My Bibliography* are options available to those who create their own account in PubMed (known as "My NCBI" after the parent organization): again, the emphasis on personalized access, and long-term research projects. *Order* will be addressed in the next section, Getting to the Full Text.

Getting to the Full Text

Accessing full text in PubMed can present issues in certain situations. PubMed provides as many links as it can to full text, some of which are free (titles in the collection called PubMed Central and other open access journals), and others that are subscription based. If subscription based, PubMed will link directly to the publisher's website and to any other sources, as described earlier. If the local library has a subscription to one of those sources, and the user is onsite, access from the library or organization is thus "recognized" by the external subscription site, and the user will get the article he or she needs. If the user is offsite, but using something like virtual private networking (VPN) that makes them appear to be within the IP range of the organization, again, the user will connect seamlessly to the desired full-text article. The organization can also set up a customized access link to PubMed, which requires users to authenticate but then can offer them access to the local link resolver service for getting to full text (or requesting an Interlibrary loan). However, when a user is offsite, has not used the institution's special link to PubMed, and is *not* running VPN—then things get complicated. In that case, the subscription site will not recognize the user, and he or she will be presented with a screen asking him or her to pay for access. The user would have to know to go back to the library's website, and either start the session again using the customized access link, or look up the journal name to see if the library has paid for electronic access, follow links from there into the journal, the right volume, issue, etc. It's much more complicated than most users are willing to master, remember, or put up with. Librarians are naturally bothered by the idea that their users are not getting to material that is actually available to them under the right circumstances. It can be very hard to train people to use a special link—after all, it's so easy to simply type "pubmed.gov."

Of course, libraries can't afford to subscribe to every journal, so there will be plenty of cases where the subscription sites would ask a user to pay no matter what the circumstances were. This is what Interlibrary Loan (ILL) is for. But in PubMed ILL also becomes complicated.

Order

As mentioned earlier, there is an option called *Order* in the Send to menu. The Order function in this case will take the user to an NLM function known as Loansome Doc (cute or what?), which has nothing to do with the local library and will charge the user for document delivery. *Only* if an offsite user has accessed PubMed by way of the local, customized access link, and he clicks the icon for the link resolver service, will he get link(s) to the local ILL system. It makes life—tricky.

However, in both cases (full text that actually *is* available or redirection to the local ILL service) human nature works in our favor. Most people will balk at having to pay, and instead may well ask the library: "How can I get this?" It's a perfect opportunity for the librarian to either direct them to the local ILL service, or to make their day by informing them "we have this, and here it is."

Quick Recap

This part of the chapter has provided an introduction to the pre-eminent database of medical literature citations, PubMed. PubMed is part of a portal to scientific databases provided by the National Center for Biotechnology Information (NCBI), all of which are freely accessible online. The primary component of PubMed is MEDLINE, but PubMed also includes additional material: items older, newer, and beyond the scope of MEDLINE. Things to remember about MEDLINE are that it is the product of the U.S. National Library of Medicine (NLM), and it is an index to medical journals from around the world. A defining feature of MEDLINE is its thesaurus, known as "MeSH" (*Me*dical *S*ubject *H*eadings). The search examples in this section demonstrated four ways to search PubMed. First, you can simply enter terms in the search box and then refine the results using information in the Search details page, applying limits, looking at the suggested Titles with your search terms, and learning from those records, etc. Second, you can specifically search for words in article titles using the field code for title: [ti]. Third, author-subject searches can be constructed similarly, using the author's name (in the form: lastname initial[s]) and the author field code: Smith JL[au] with a word or phrase indicating the subject. Last, the Single Citation Matcher interface is useful for looking up known, or partially remembered, items. Overall, keep in mind that the PubMed search box accepts Boolean operators, parentheses for nesting statements, double quotes for phrases, and truncation. Remember to put Boolean operators in all caps (AND, OR, NOT).

PubMed provides links to full text whenever possible, to either free or fee-based resources. Users can encounter difficulties accessing full text from subscription services when they are using PubMed from outside their institution. It is possible to customize PubMed so that it provides linking services to local resources, but users must then access PubMed using a special, institutional link, which can be hard to train users to do.

The *Web of Science* and the Citation Indexes

Now we're going to take off the stethoscope and get into the mind-set of the scholarly academic researcher. Think of yourself as Joe(sephine) Bloggs, PhD. When you write a scholarly paper, it almost always involves a literature review, or at least a process of consulting previous articles that you can quote to support various points throughout your paper. You are drawing on past knowledge in this way, building on the ideas of previous researchers and taking them further, or moving tangentially. If we look at your list of references, we can trace the lineage of your ideas back in time. For J. Bloggs, undergraduate, this is still a common and accepted way to get started writing a paper: to find a recent work that is related to what you want to write about and trace its references. This is fairly easily done, because the references provide the information about the other articles (accurately, you hope). However . . . there are works in every field that achieve the status of classic papers, that are cited by subsequent authors over and over again. What if you wanted to trace that evolution, that is, all the people who had *cited* a particular paper or book? A professor could hand you a classic work from 1965 and tell you: "that's the authoritative work in this area." What do you do with that? A place to start would be to see who has cited that work recently, and in what context. You want to trace the evolution of those ideas *forward* in time. How in the world could you do that?

History of the Citation Indexes

The concept of tracking and indexing not just articles, but the references associated with those articles, was the brainchild of Dr. Eugene Garfield, founder of the Institute for Scientific Information (ISI). From a concept first outlined in a 1955 article in the journal *Science*, the oversize, print, multivolume sets known as the *Science Citation Index* (1963–), the *Social Science Citation Index* (1965–), and the *Arts & Humanities Citation Index* (1976–) have been providing researchers with a unique and powerful way to trace the evolution and impact of ideas over time. As Carol Tenopir (2001) put it: "The power of citation searching lies in the capacity to take a seminal article and uncover who the author was influenced by (who was cited) and go forward in time to discover how that seminal research affected newer works (who is citing it)." Now it was possible, albeit somewhat physically challenging (because of the size of the volumes—huge—and the size of the print—tiny) to trace "who is citing whom." As technology progressed, the Citation Indexes moved to CD-ROM, and then to the Web. If ever a tool benefited from going electronic, it is this one. The whole concept of what a citation index allows one to do seems much easier to grasp and to explain to others in an online realization. It also makes possible many enhanced features, which we'll explore as we work through the database functionality.

Citation Indexes in the *Web of Science*

In 1992, ISI was acquired by the Thomson Corporation, which has continued to take the citation index concept from strength to strength. The Science, Social Science, and Arts and Humanities Citation Indexes are now all part of the *Web of Science*, which itself is one element in an overall *ISI Web of Knowledge*—the total suite of research tools offered by Thomson Reuters.

Web of Science Content

In all, the *Web of Science* indexing and abstracting tools cover more than 10,000 of the "highest impact journals" from around the world (Thomson Reuters 2011). More and more years of back files have been added to the database, steadily expanding coverage back in time, as well as forward, with weekly updates. Depending on the subscription package, coverage can go back as early as 1900 for the Science Citation Index and 1956 for the Social Sciences. The institutions in my purview have opted for the "1973 to the present" package. What this date cutoff refers to is how far back the records for the *journal articles* go; under a "1973 to the present" subscription, you can still search a *cited reference* from any time period, but you will only be allowed to see records for articles citing that reference that were published from 1973 to the present. Keep reminding yourself that this database has a dual nature: the cited references records, which can be from any date, and the journal article records, which are restricted depending on the subscription.

As you might imagine (if you haven't, you should), an undertaking of this size and complexity involves thousands of workers, incredible feats of programming, etc. It is big, and frankly, it's expensive. You are likely to find it only at major research libraries, but it's worth being aware of as part of your overall understanding of how research works, and how our current knowledge builds on past work. If you work in an academic environment, this is part of understanding the scholarly animal.

An Index Focused on Citations

The unique feature that the citation indexes introduced was that each bibliographic record (author, title, journal, year, etc.) also included the list of cited references—the bibliography—for that article. The cited references are associated with their articles, but each reference is also recorded in the database as an independent, "cited reference" record, which can be searched and used in various ways. Note too that although the type of source material indexed in the *Web of Science* databases is only journal articles (i.e., no books, technical reports, etc.), the references associated with a source article can be any type of material, and thus cited reference records can be not only articles but also books, reports, unpublished papers, or whatever the author has cited. (If your brain is starting to hurt, don't despair: it's actually surprisingly clear and easy once you get into the database.) Again, note the dual nature of this database: source records, which are *only* journal articles and cited reference records, one for each item in the bibliography of each source article, which can be any type of document. What can you do with all this information?

Regular Topic Searches; Tracing *Back* by Means of Citations

You can use the *Web of Science* databases just like any other indexing and abstracting product: to perform a keyword search to find articles on a particular topic, to find articles by a particular author, or to track down a specific article when you have only partial information. The added twist is that having identified one or more articles, you can also see the list of references from each article, and by looking at this bibliography, you can, if the items are linked (to other journal article records in the database), immediately start tracking the ideas in a current article *back* in time.

Tracing Forward and Tracking Citations for Tenure

Because you can search cited references, you can see which subsequent articles have cited a particular work. As mentioned previously, you can track the development and influence of an idea from when it was first published to now—a way to bring research forward, from old to new. In addition to helping students and scholars in the process of writing papers, citation indexes also provide important—even crucial—functionality. Researchers can use this database to find out who is citing their work, and in what context. The crucial element is that in the "publish-or-perish" scramble for academic tenure in the United States, faculty who are up for tenure can use these databases to show how many times their papers have been cited by others, which can be a key factor in proving their eligibility for tenure.

Relating Records by Citations

As mentioned previously, in electronic form, the data captured by the citation indexes can be exploited in new and useful ways that were impossible in the print version. The *Web of Science* databases have a feature called *Related Records*. Related records are articles that have at least one cited reference in common. Articles that share four, five, or more references are likely to be discussing the same topics. This is a completely different way to locate relevant papers on a topic that might not have been found with a traditional author or subject search. Think of it this way: this is about as close to "searching by concept" as opposed to "searching by words" as you can get. True, you start with a word search (to produce the initial results), but then, based on shared references—shared *concepts*—you can move into related intellectual territory. This is a powerful concept and tool.

Additional Differences in Available Fields

Present: The Address Field

The article records in the *Web of Science* databases also include an Address field, used to record where each author works. This is useful in several ways. From a librarian's perspective, it provides a quick way to get a sense of the total output of a particular department or person (if they publish in journals covered by the *Web of Science*) and what sorts of things they write about. Used in conjunction with the Analyze function (discussed as an advanced feature at the end of this chapter), it can be used to determine where your institution's faculty publish most frequently, and thus, which journals to lobby hardest for during a serials review. It allows an academic or corporate researcher to track what a colleague (or a competitor!) at a specific institution is publishing. The researcher could search on just author name, or author name combined with address (to disambiguate common names), to track known people. Using a keyword(s) and address search, the researcher could track the output of a department or unit at another institution, without knowing any specific names at all.

Absent: Subject Headings Fields

Finally, there is one thing that hasn't been mentioned about these re-markable databases. Did you notice? Having just discussed MEDLINE, where subject headings are crucial and heavily emphasized, here at the *Web of Science* we haven't mentioned them at all, because . . . the citation indexes don't use subject headings! Yes, it's true. All the databases we've looked at up to this point have used some kind of subject indexing, and I've made a big point of emphasizing it. Now we come to a set of databases that don't use added subject terms at all, but that are every bit as powerful and compelling (if not more so) than the previous databases. The determination not to employ subject indexing was another part of Dr. Garfield's vision. The labor- and thought-intensive process of having humans analyze each article and apply subject terms slowed down the production of the indexes too much for the needs of the scientific research community. Such indexing also tends to be very subject specific, trapping work within one discipline. Using citations as retrieval terms "integrated the data by taking an interdisciplinary approach. Researchers in one field often create work relevant to researchers in an-other" (Thomson Reuters 2005). (There is also an advantage that in the sci-ences, paper titles tend to be more descriptive and express the true content of the work, thus providing a richer source of keywords for searching.) So, you will not find indexer-applied subject headings here. But I can almost guarantee you won't miss it. Let's take a look.

Searching the *Web of Science*: Main Search Interface

Figure 5.12 shows the initial search screen for the *Web of Science* data-bases (the details will depend on your subscription, but this should be close).

By now this type of search interface should seem fairly familiar: three text-entry boxes joined with Boolean menus (Basic Tool #1) and typical de-faults showing in the drop-down menus, which offer many other choices of fields to search (Basic Tool #3). The area below, labeled Current Limits, ac-tually represents two limits and two customizations. The true limits (Basic Tool #6) are Timespan, and which of the Citation Databases you wish to search (i.e., one, two, or all three). When you get to the Results pages, you'll find many additional limits you can apply to "Refine" your results. The other two features here are part of the version 5 release of the *Web of Knowledge*: one to adjust how your search is executed and one allowing you to adjust the results display to your liking. The search feature is called "Lemmatization," and having it on allows your search to automatically retrieve spelling vari-ants (such as U.S.–U.K. differences) and alternative forms of the search terms, for example, plurals, including irregular plurals such as mouse and mice. The display options allow you to change the number of results per page, how they are sorted (a plethora of options), and whether or not to show the Refine panel. My advice would be to always keep the Refine panel showing; it's im-mensely useful.

I've noted several of the Searcher's Toolkit items in the discussion of the search interface earlier; see the Sidebar for additional information. Remem-ber, though, there will be no Basic Tool #2 in this database: no controlled vocabulary. In studying this page, also notice the emphasis on customiza-tion: there are four sorts of "My . . . x" and "My . . . y" in the links across the very top and an invitation to "Customize Your Experience" by creating a personal account in the text panel on the right side. Thomson Reuters did a lot of user research and determined that personalizing the search experience

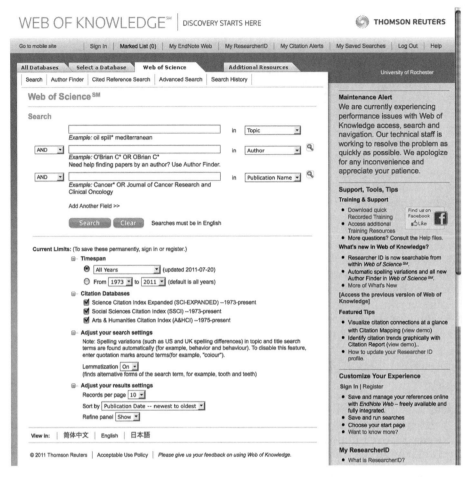

Fig. 5.12. The *Web of Science* initial search screen. Web of Science^{SM} from Thomson Reuters Web of Knowledge^{SM}.

as much as possible might be the answer to meeting the needs of their very diverse universe of users.

We're going to start with a search on a scientific topic, so we'll leave only the *Science Citation Index Expanded* checked under the Citation Databases limit. We'll leave Lemmatization on, and use the default sort order (Publication date—newest to oldest) for the results.

Search Example 1: A Topic Search

We'll get our feet wet with a simple search (Figure 5.13):

"acid rain" AND forest* —as Topic.

Set the second text box drop-down menu to Document Type, and then choose Article from the list that appears where the text box was.

Sidebar 5.2

Here's an inventory of your Searcher's Toolkit for the Citation databases:

- Boolean operators: AND, OR, NOT
- Proximity operators: SAME, NEAR/#
- Order of precedence: NEAR/#, SAME, NOT, AND, OR
- No stop words: you can search for phrases such as "Vitamin A"
- Enclose phrases in double quotes.
- Truncation/wildcards:
  - *—zero to "many" characters, can be used at the end *or the beginning* of a term (left-hand truncation). Note: This cannot be used on a publication year search, for example, 200* does not work.
  - ?—substitutes for characters on a one-to-one basis, for example, ? = one character, ?? = two characters, etc. Can be used within a word or at the end of a word.
  - $—zero or one character only, for example, labo$r to get labor or labour
- Limits for Language, Document Type, and many more fields are available in the search box drop-down menus. (*You can even search by funding agency or grant number.*)

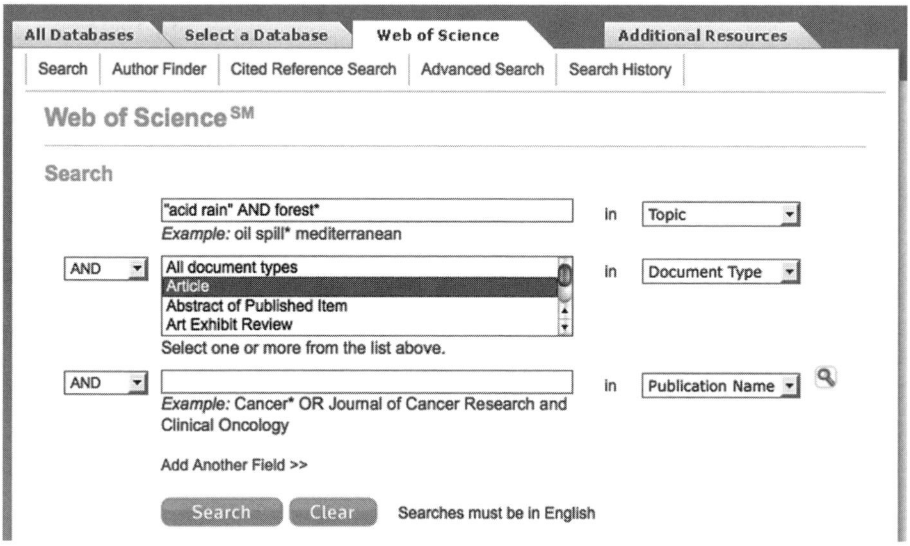

Fig. 5.13. A first, simple topic search. Web of Science[SM] from Thomson Reuters Web of Knowledge[SM].

Search Results

The initial results for this search are shown in Figure 5.14. The *Web of Science* results screen is incredibly powerful and informative, thanks to the Refine Results panel. Not only does it provide a chance to immediately refine your results by applying any of the limits listed, but by providing the hit counts for each one, you also get a sense of who writes on this topic most frequently, which journals are most important, and which institutions are most interested in this area. You don't need to know which limits you might want to use up front; you can decide afterward and can easily choose the ones that seem most promising (this is pearl growing at its finest). You can also immediately Analyze the results, or create a Citation Report (the icons and links at "A" in Figure 5.14). With this database's emphasis on citations, it's no surprise to see that each result record includes a line for Times Cited ("B" in Figure 5.14), so you can see immediately what kind of impact the papers are having on their field. (There hasn't been time for the newest articles to get cited, obviously.) This is no ordinary results screen: it's a powerhouse.

This is a lot of results, however, and really what we had in mind was material about acid rain and forests in the United States. Nothing could be easier: examining the Refine Results panel, we find we can limit by Countries/Territories, as shown in Figure 5.15.[3] (Another approach that might not have immediately occurred to you would be to limit by the institution the authors are associated with: in this case, one might try the top two insti-

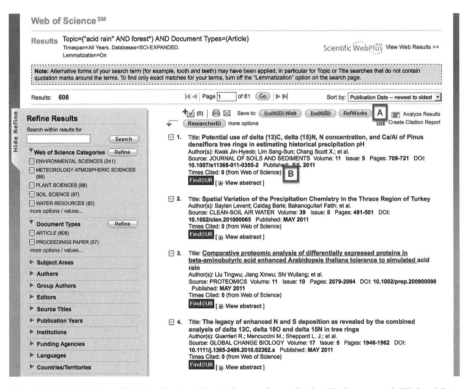

Fig. 5.14. Initial results for the "acid rain" search, with the Refine panel. Web of Science[SM] from Thomson Reuters Web of Knowledge[SM].

Fig. 5.15. Refining the results by country. Web of Science^SM from Thomson Reuters Web of Knowledge^SM.

tutions listed, the U.S. Forest Service and Cornell University.) We will check USA and click the Refine button. As promised by the record count associated with "USA," we are now looking at a more manageable 192 results.

A section of the first page of results is shown in Figure 5.16; these are papers that have had time to be cited. Especially take note of record 5: in only 11 months since publication in August 2010, this article has been cited—by articles in other journals indexed by the *Web of Science*—five times. This paper is making an impact. Note too that records 5 and 6 have the same author: Likens Gene E.[4] If you were to check the list of names under Author in the Refine panel, you would find that Likens leads the list: he is the most prolific author in this set of 192 records (at least, as of this writing).[5] This is the kind of thing I mean when I say you can learn a lot about a topic simply by observing the information on the *Web of Science* results display.

Another new feature in the *Web of Knowledge* version 5 interface is the ability to take a look at the abstract of any record, without leaving the results list, by using the View abstract link ("A" in Figure 5.16). After reading the abstract for record 6, we decide this is a good one, and we go into the full record display, as shown in Figure 5.17.

A lot of information is being presented here (and the highlighting of our search terms is rather distracting), but let us focus on the citation information being presented. Of first importance is obviously the Times Cited number: this information is given in the body of the record (third line down) and prominently displayed in the panel on the right—along with the beginning

☐ 5. Title: **The role of science in decision making: does evidence-based science drive environmental policy?**
Author(s): Likens Gene E.
Source: FRONTIERS IN ECOLOGY AND THE ENVIRONMENT Volume: **8** Issue: **6** Pages: **E1-E9** DOI: **10.1890/090132**
Published: **AUG 2010**
Times Cited: **5** (from Web of Science)
Find@UR [⊞ View abstract]

☐ 6. Title: **Ecosystem Thinking in the Northern Forest-and Beyond**
Author(s): Likens Gene E.; Franklin Jerry F.
Source: BIOSCIENCE Volume: **59** Issue: **6** Pages: **511-513** DOI: **10.1525/bio.2009.59.6.9** Published: **JUN 2009**
Times Cited: **5** (from Web of Science)
Find@UR [⊞ View abstract] **A**

☐ 7. Title: **Analysis of cloud and precipitation chemistry at Whiteface Mountain, NY**
Author(s): Aleksic Nenad; Roy K.; Sistla G.; et al.
Source: ATMOSPHERIC ENVIRONMENT Volume: **43** Issue: **17** Pages: **2709-2716** DOI: **10.1016/j.atmosenv.2009.02.053**
Published: **JUN 2009**
Times Cited: **5** (from Web of Science)
Find@UR [⊞ View abstract]

☐ 8. Title: **Phytolacca americana from Contaminated and Noncontaminated Soils of South Korea: Effects of Elevated Temperature, CO_2 and Simulated Acid Rain on Plant Growth Response**
Author(s): Kim Yong Ok; Rodriguez Rusty J.; Lee Eun Ju; et al.
Source: JOURNAL OF CHEMICAL ECOLOGY Volume: **34** Issue: **11** Pages: **1501-1509** DOI: **10.1007/s10886-008-9552-x**
Published: **NOV 2008**
Times Cited: **1** (from Web of Science)
Find@UR [⊞ View abstract]

☐ 9. Title: **Avian population trends in the vulnerable montane forests of the Northern Appalachians, USA**
Author(s): King David I.; Lambert J. Daniel; Buonaccorsi John P.; et al.
Source: BIODIVERSITY AND CONSERVATION Volume: **17** Issue: **11** Pages: **2691-2700** DOI: **10.1007/s10531-007-9244-9**
Published: **OCT 2008**
Times Cited: **1** (from Web of Science)
Find@UR [⊞ View abstract]

☐ 10. Title: **Atmospheric SO2 emissions since the late 1800s change organic sulfur forms in humic substance extracts of soils**
Author(s): Lehmann Johannes; Solomon Dawit; Zhao Fang-Jie; et al.
Source: ENVIRONMENTAL SCIENCE & TECHNOLOGY Volume: **42** Issue: **10** Pages: **3550-3555** DOI: **10.1021/es702315g**
Published: **MAY 15 2008**
Times Cited: **4** (from Web of Science)
Find@UR [⊞ View abstract]

Fig. 5.16. Results after refining by country, showing records 5–10. Web of Science[SM] from Thomson Reuters Web of Knowledge[SM].

of the list of the citing articles. The fourth line down in the body of the record is the count and link to the list of Cited References, along with a link to "view related records." Both of these options are repeated in the panel on the right.

Take a look at the Related Records (Figure 5.18). Do they seem related or useful to you? Notice that the first two in the list are also by Likens—he is citing his own work and reusing many sources, both quite typical practices in scholarly publishing. And again, you can refine these results.

Search Example 2: An Author Search

Here's another example: say that you are familiar with Stephen Hawking's books but want a list of journal articles by him. We'll set the search field to Author, and, as the interface indicates, enter the name as Hawking S* (no comma, and do not spell out the first name).[6] How many S Hawkings can there be? But we can add Cambridge and set the search field to Address to be sure that it's the one that we want (Figure 5.19).

The results for this search indicate that Stephen Hawking is a prolific author, and that almost all of his articles are frequently cited, as well. If you can access this database, note too that there is great variation in how his name is listed: Hawking S. W., Hawking Stephen, Hawking S, and Hawking SW. By entering just his first initial with the truncation symbol we easily retrieved all the variations.

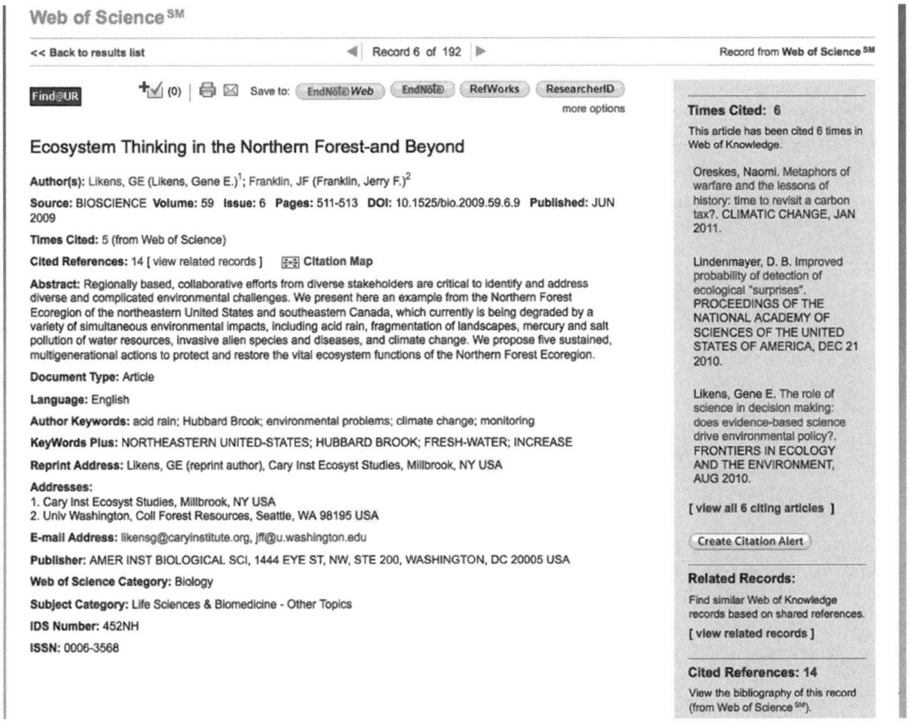

Fig. 5.17. Full record from the "acid rain" search results. Web of Science[SM] from Thomson Reuters Web of Knowledge[SM].

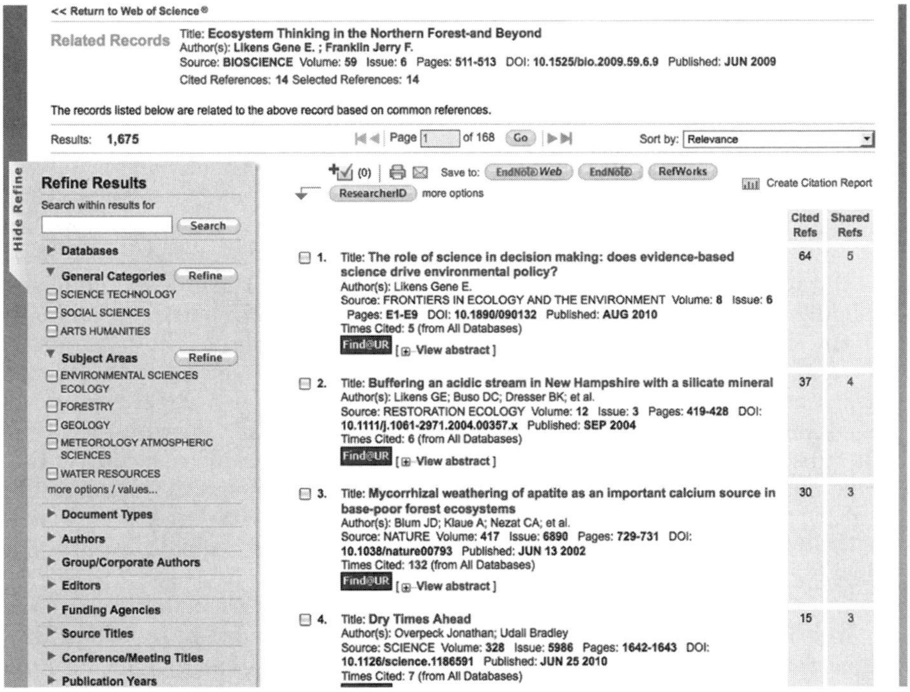

Fig. 5.18. Related Records, based on shared citations, for the 2009 Likens article. Web of Science[SM] from Thomson Reuters Web of Knowledge[SM].

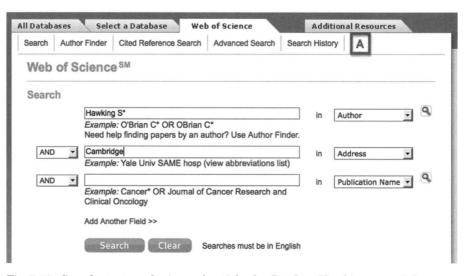

Fig. 5.19. Search strategy for journal articles by Stephen Hawking—partial screen. Web of Science^SM from Thomson Reuters Web of Knowledge^SM.

Cited Reference Searching

Let's move on to the special functionality of this database: searching a *Cited Reference*. Wherever you are in the database, notice that the search function links stay with you, allowing you to change direction at any time ("A" in Figure 5.19). To change search modes, click the Cited Reference Search link.

Cited Reference Search Example 1: Finding Articles that Cite a Book

Now let us say that you are interested in the classic book by James Watson, *The Double Helix*, in which he described the discovery of DNA. How many times has it been cited? Is it still being cited by current authors? In what contexts? As mentioned in the introductory notes for the *Web of Science* databases, here is an interesting thing: we can perform a search based on something that is both outside the year coverage (1973–current), and outside the material type (book rather than journal article) of the main database, and find articles that have cited that work. You can do a cited reference search on really ancient material, of any document type, and get results, as long as someone has cited it in a journal article since 1973 (or whatever year your subscription coverage begins). Ponder that for a couple of minutes: this can be difficult to get straight in your mind. We're not used to working with material that is outside of the stated year span of the database.

Cited Reference Search Input

In this case, we will make use of all the fields provided in the Cited Reference Search screen and boldly type in the information as given. Later on, we'll work on an example that isn't as tidy or straightforward. (You might note that there is link to a Cited Reference Search tutorial handily placed in the interface; this link will follow you through the process.)

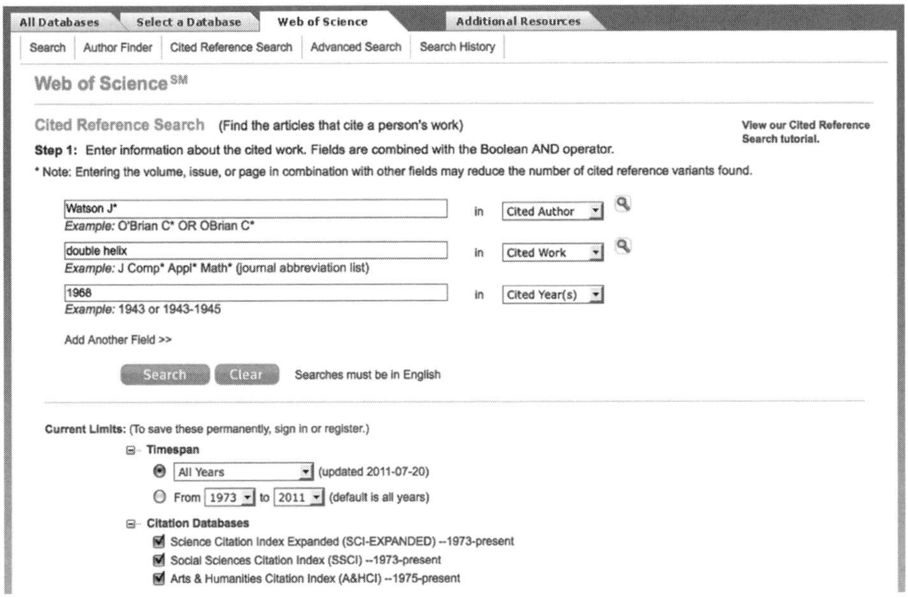

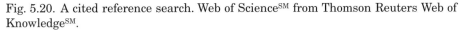

Fig. 5.20. A cited reference search. Web of Science^{SM} from Thomson Reuters Web of Knowledge^{SM}.

As shown in Figure 5.20 type in:

Cited Author: Watson J*

Cited Work: double helix

Cited Year(s): 1968

In the Limits area, select all the databases: *Science, Social Science*, and *Arts and Humanities*.

This produces a list from the Cited Reference Index, as shown in Figure 5.21.

Cited Reference Index Results

Yikes! A million variations! Is this all the same thing? Unfortunately, yes. This represents all the ways that people have cited this work in their bibliographies. Every time somebody writes a reference a little differently (or even incorrectly!), that reference gets its own entry (note the "Hint" in the instructions just above the results). Although Thomson does do a lot of cleanup and normalization of references, it would be impossible to check and fix every reference for every article and still maintain the rate at which new material is added to the databases to keep them current. As a result, materials that are frequently cited produce results lists like this one. Don't panic; now you know why.

Getting to the Articles Doing the Citing

Luckily, 30 variations is no problem: we can simply click the Select All* button to grab them all, and then click the Finish Search button. Now we are

Cited Reference Search   (Find the articles that cite a person's work)

Step 2: Select cited references and click "Finish Search."

Hint: Look for cited reference variants (sometimes different pages of the same article are cited or papers are cited incorrectly).

CITED REFERENCE INDEX
References: **1 - 30 of   30**

|◄ ◄| Page 1   of 1 (Go) |► ►|

(Select Page) (Select All*) (Clear All)   **Finish Search**

Select References	Cited Author	Cited Work [SHOW EXPANDED TITLES]	Year	Volume	Page	Article ID	Citing Articles **	View Record
☐	WATSON J	DOUBLE HELIX	1968		123		1	
☐	WATSON J	DOUBLE HELIX	1968		183		1	
☐	WATSON J	DOUBLE HELIX	1968		212		1	
☐	WATSON J	DOUBLE HELIX	1968		222		2	
☐	WATSON J	DOUBLE HELIX	1968		35		1	
☐	WATSON J	DOUBLE HELIX	1968		38		1	
☐	WATSON J	DOUBLE HELIX	1968		5		1	
☐	WATSON J	DOUBLE HELIX	1968		77		3	
☐	WATSON J	DOUBLE HELIX	1968		CH16		1	
☐	WATSON JD	DOUBLE HELIX	1968				583	
☐	WATSON JD	DOUBLE HELIX	1968		107		1	

Fig. 5.21. Beginning of the Cited Reference Index list produced by the cited reference search. Web of Science[SM] from Thomson Reuters Web of Knowledge[SM].

presented with the articles that have cited this classic work (over 500 of them), with the most recent ones listed first.

Amazing! What an array: subject areas from Acoustics to Zoology (literally: click the "more options/values . . ." for Subject Areas in the Refine Results panel, and then sort the list alphabetically). Here are six articles selected from the first two pages of results that demonstrate the range of disciplines referring to this work, and the international scope of the journal list.

- When Is a Molecule Three Dimensional? A Task-Specific Role for Imagistic Reasoning in Advanced Chemistry
  Stieff, Mike
  SCIENCE EDUCATION, 95(2): 310–336 MAR 2011

- Life Forms: Elizabeth Bishop in "Sestina" and DNA Structure
  Rogers, Janine
  MOSAIC—A JOURNAL FOR THE INTERDISCIPLINARY STUDY OF LITERATURE, 43(1): 93–109 MAR 2010

- High Local Concentration: A Fundamental Strategy of Life
  Oehler, Stefan; Mueller-Hill, Benno
  JOURNAL OF MOLECULAR BIOLOGY, 395(2): 242–253 JAN 15 2010

- Expert Algorithmic and Imagistic Problem Solving Strategies in Advanced Chemistry
  Stieff, Mike; Raje, Sonali
  SPATIAL COGNITION AND COMPUTATION, 10(1): 53–81 2010

- Research Education Shaped by Musical Sensibilities
  Bresler, Liora
  BRITISH JOURNAL OF MUSIC EDUCATION, 26(1): 7–25 MAR 2009

- The Nobel Prize of Physiology and Medicine 2008: undoing the Gordian knot. The Nobel Prize in Chemistry 2008: another genetic tool at the service of science
Lacadena, Calero Juan-Ramon
ANALES DE LA REAL ACADEMIA NACIONAL DE FARMACIA, 75(1): 65–76 2009

On to one more cited reference challenge . . .

Cited Reference Search Example 2: Using the Cited Work Index

Getting back to Stephen Hawking, say that you'd like to see who has been citing his book *A Brief History of Time* recently. (The book was published in 1988.) This is basically like the previous cited reference search. We would start at the Cited Reference search screen and enter the author's name, in the correct way, and the year the work was published (Figure 5.22):

Title Abbreviations and the Cited Work Index

Now you might be wondering why the Cited Work field was left blank. In the previous example we put it in (*Double Helix*). Why not here? The book is called *A Brief History of Time*, right? Well, yes, and it also has a subtitle: *From the Big Bang to Black Holes*. The issue here is that we have a Work title that is potentially many words longer, and this database is very big on abbreviations. Very big. They have to be, to fit all the information in. The point is that almost every cited reference title will be abbreviated in some way, and it's a very, very bad idea to try to *guess* the abbreviation. (Although you might use truncation successfully.) Note the helpful links associated with the Cited Work field: to the journal abbreviation list and to the magnifying glass icon at the end of the input field that lets you "select terms from the index." This is the access point for Browsing all the values in the Cited Work List. We know that this is not a journal, so we'll use the cited work index. Because I know how this story comes out, here is a hint: the favorite way to abbreviate History in this case is "Hist." The Cited Work Index very nicely allows us to type in the beginning of what we're looking for and jump to it in the list. If we jump in the index to "brief hist time" (because there are

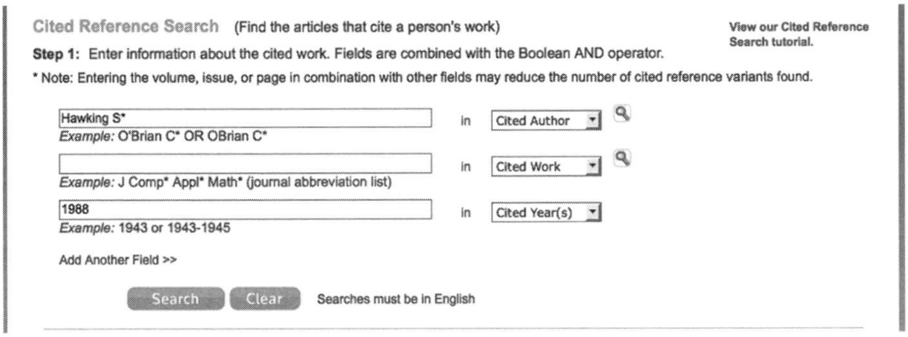

Fig. 5.22. Cited reference search for Stephen Hawking's book published in 1988. Web of Science[SM] from Thomson Reuters Web of Knowledge[SM].

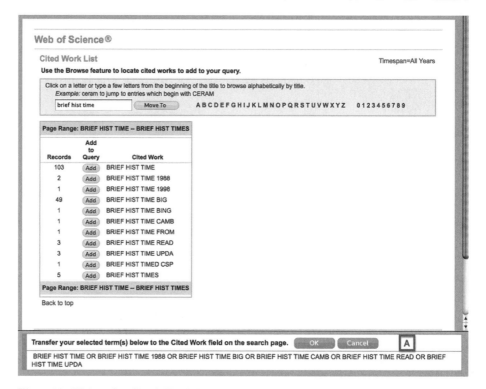

Fig. 5.23. Using the Cited Work List to select variants on a title. Web of Science^{SM} from Thomson Reuters Web of Knowledge^{SM}.

a great many other "brief hists," as it happens) we find the list pictured in Figure 5.23.

We'll choose all the variations[7] up to the last two, which look like they might be referring to something else. What a handy system this is: we can simply click the ADD button for each one, and it appears in the selection field below, intelligently ORed together ("A" in Figure 5.23). A click of the OK button inserts this whole string into the appropriate field in the search screen. Performing the search now results in another amazing list of variations on a theme, as indicated by the set of snippets from two screens of results in Figure 5.24. Observe the progression: Hawking S Brief Hist Time, then Hawking S Brief Hist Time Big, then the Hawking SW Brief Hist Time entries, then Hawking SW Brief Hist Time Big, and so on—single initial entries first, with title variants, followed by the two initial entries and their title variants.

Results: Example 2

In addition to name and title variations, new entries are created in the database every time someone includes the chapter or page number in his or her citation for this work. As mentioned before, basically what appears at the end of an author's article is what goes into the database. Remember Reference Desk Rule No. 1: citations are *never* quite accurate. If you don't believe that yet, try this: look up Hawking S* as a cited author (without any other fields filled in). Browse forward through the screens, noticing that some peo-

CITED REFERENCE INDEX
References: 1 - 50 of 69

|◀ ◀ | Page 1   of 2 Go |▶ ▶|

Select Page   Select All*   Clear All   **Finish Search**

Select References	Cited Author	Cited Work [SHOW EXPANDED TITLES]	Year	Volume	Page	Article ID	Citing Articles **	View Record
☐	HAWKING S	BRIEF HIST TIME	1988		117		1	
☐	HAWKING S	BRIEF HIST TIME	1988		121		1	
☐	HAWKING S	BRIEF HIST TIME	1988		65		1	
☐	HAWKING S	BRIEF HIST TIME	1988		8		1	
☐	HAWKING S	BRIEF HIST TIME	1988		CH8		2	
☐	HAWKING S	BRIEF HIST TIME	1988				372	
☐	HAWKING SW	BRIEF HIST TIME	1988		10		1	
☐	HAWKING SW	BRIEF HIST TIME	1988		CH9		1	
☐	HAWKING SW	BRIEF HIST TIME BIG	1988				228	
☐	HAWKING SW	BRIEF HIST TIME BIG	1988		104		1	

Fig. 5.24. Selections from the Cited Reference Index list for Hawking's *Brief History of Time*. Web of Science℠ from Thomson Reuters Web of Knowledge℠.

ple referred to the book by versions of its subtitle (Big Bang, Black Holes), to the entries beginning *Breve Hist Temps* (aha—this book was translated into French—and *Brevisima*—Italian!) and beyond. Note the many variations in titles and year (probably different editions), and this is only the Hawking S section of the list! Imagine what might be waiting when you get to the two-initial part of the list.

Pause and Think

Again, take a moment to ponder this: all of these entries represent articles that *cited* this book. There is no general record for this book in this database, because it doesn't index books. There is no record for the thing itself, but endless records that refer to it. Isn't that rather interesting? Exploring the world of scholarship is lovely, but ultimately, of course, you want to identify some records and do something with them. On to output options.

E-mail, Print, Save, or Export Results

Marking and Outputting

The process for outputting records from the *Web of Science* is similar in many ways to the process for other databases that we've looked at so far, but with some twists. If you can determine which records you want to print, email, or export to bibliographic management software from the information given in the results list, you simply check-box those records, and then choose what to do with them using buttons at the top of the screen (to the left of "A" in Figure 5.14), or the quick Output Records panel at the bottom of each result screen (Figure 5.25).

Should you move off that results screen by going to the next page of results or by looking at a full record, the system will retain any records you have check-boxed so far by adding them to the Marked List. Such records

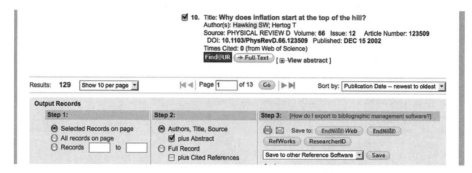

Fig. 5.25. The Output Records panel. Web of Science^{SM} from Thomson Reuters Web of Knowledge^{SM}.

will then appear with a new icon (a red check mark) in the results list, and they are no longer "recognized" by the Output Records panel: if you choose the Print or E-mail buttons, for example, the system will tell you that you have to select at least one record using the check boxes. If you've been marking things and moving from screen to screen of your results, you must go into the Marked List to output them. (When viewing a full record, the only option for marking it is to use the "Add to Marked List" button; therefore, you have to go into the Marked List to work with records selected in that way.)

Output From the Marked List Screen

The link to the Marked List appears at the top of the screen with the links to Sign in, My EndNote Web, My ResearcherID, etc., as shown in Figure 5.26.

The Marked List screen shown in Figure 5.27 is rather busy because it is offering you as many options as possible for handling your output. Even though you are in your Marked List, you still get the options to output "All records in this list," "All records on page," or "records #-#." You can indicate exactly which fields to include in the output from an extensive list of choices, and the function buttons (Print, E-mail, and Save to various citation management programs) from the Output Records panel are repeated here. The list of marked articles begins at the bottom of the screen.

The email function is good: it lets you put in your address for return address and add a note to explain why you're sending the information. If you are sending results to someone else, being able to have your email address appear as the sender rather than a strange system-generated email address from the vendor makes the message look less like spam.

Advanced Features: Advanced Search and Analyze

Advanced Search

The Advanced Search screen (Figure 5.28) offers options for you real search hackers out there: searching with field codes and detailed syntax, or manipulating sets from your search history—somewhat like the experience we had in Ovid's version of PsycINFO. (Specific access to the search history

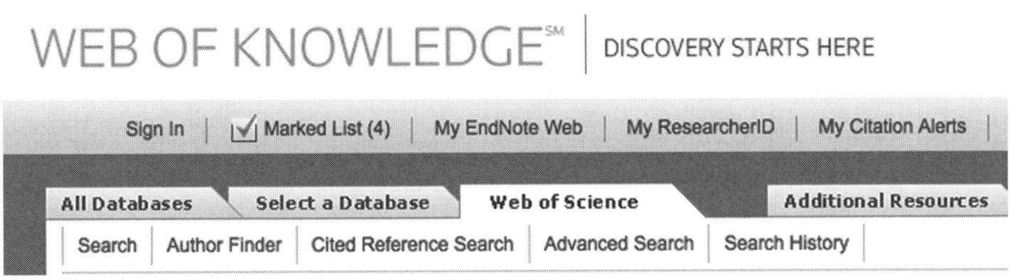

WEB OF KNOWLEDGE℠ | DISCOVERY STARTS HERE

Sign In | ✓ Marked List (4) | My EndNote Web | My ResearcherID | My Citation Alerts

All Databases | Select a Database | Web of Science | Additional Resources

Search | Author Finder | Cited Reference Search | Advanced Search | Search History

Fig. 5.26. Access to the Marked List. Web of Science℠ from Thomson Reuters Web of Knowledge℠.

Marked List (4 records)

<< Exit Marked List

Your marked list contains records from 1 database(s).
You can output summary data for all records using the "total records" view, or output more product-specific data from each listed database.

4 total records on the Marked List
    Output author, title, source, abstract, and times cited for all records in the Marked List.

4 records from **Web of Science℠**   X Clear Marked List
    Output complete data from this product for these records.

Output Records   [⊟ Hide Output Options]

Step 1:   **Step 2:**   **Step 3:**   [How do I export to bibliographic management software?]
                            Select from the
● All records in this list (up to 500)   fields below: 🖨 ✉ Save to: (EndNote Web) (EndNote) (RefWorks)
○ All records on page   ResearcherID
○ Records [   ] to [   ]
                                                      [Save to other Reference Software ▾] (Save)

☑ **Author(s) /**   ☑ **Title**   ☑ **Source**   ☑ **Conference**
  Editor(s)

☐ Abstract*   ☐ Cited References*   ☐ Document Type   ☐ Conference
                                                                       Sponsor(s)

☐ Addresses   ☑ **Times Cited**   ☐ Keywords   ☐ Publisher
                                                                       Information

☑ **ISSN / ISBN**   ☐ Cited Reference   ☐ Source Abbrev.   ☐ Page Count
                          Count

☐ IDS Number   ☐ Language   ☐ Web of Science   ☐ Subject Category
                                                 Category

☐ Funding
  Information
*Selecting these items will increase the processing time.
[Reset]

Records: **4** |◀ ◀ Page [1] of 1 (Go) ▶ ▶| Sort by: [Publication Date -- newest to oldest ▾]

                                                                     📃 Analyze Results
                                                                     📊 Create Citation Report

⊗ 1. Title: **Local Observation in Eternal Inflation**
       Author(s): Hartle James; Hawking S. W.; Hertog Thomas
       Source: PHYSICAL REVIEW LETTERS Volume: **106** Issue: **14**   Article Number: **141302** DOI: **10.1103/PhysRevLett.106.141302**

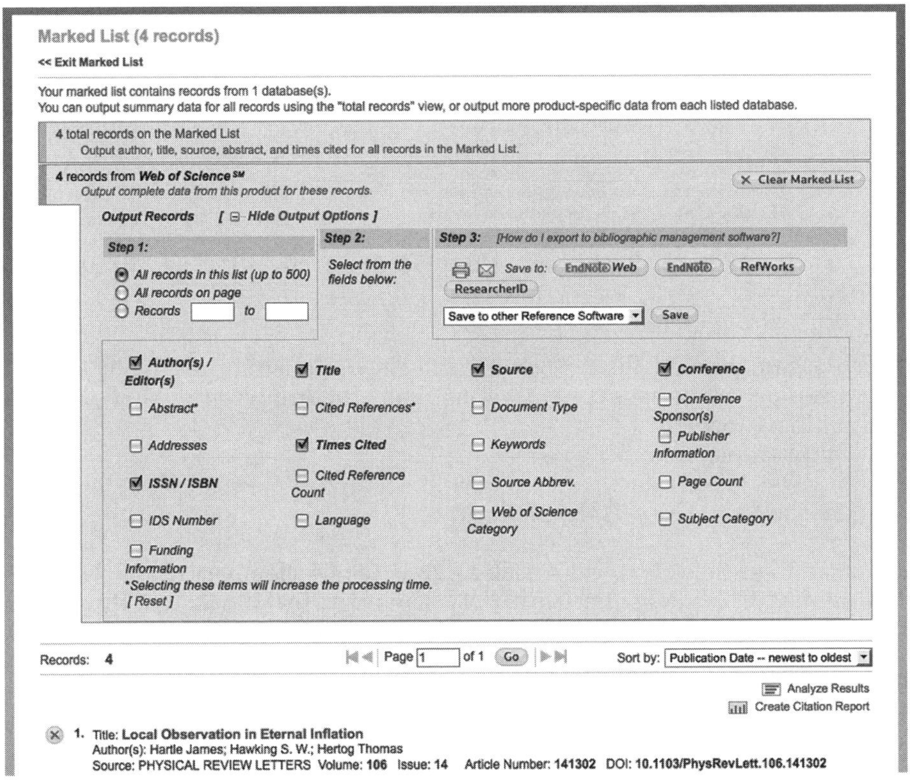

Fig. 5.27. The Marked List screen. Web of Science℠ from Thomson Reuters Web of Knowledge℠.

is also available in the series of search function links across the upper part of the interface.)

Analyze Results

In everyday usage of searching for articles and tracing citations, you probably won't find yourself using the Analyze Results feature that frequently. However, for tracking publication patterns or doing general research on scholarship (e.g., Who is doing it? Where—in what countries, by

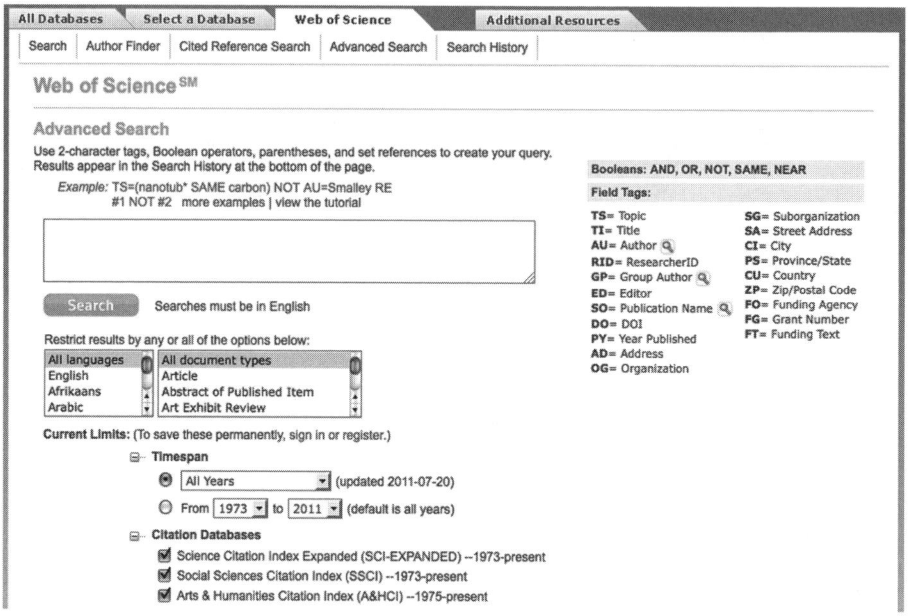

Fig. 5.28. The Advanced Search screen. Web of Science^SM from Thomson Reuters Web of Knowledge^SM.

which organizations? What journals are they publishing in? What subject categories does this department publish in?), the Analyze function provides a fascinating tool.

For example, searching for:

informat* studies SAME Milwaukee

in the address field retrieves articles published by members of the School of Information Studies at the University of Wisconsin-Milwaukee. If we Analyze these results by Subject Area, the majority are, as we might expect, classed as Information Science/Library Science. But other subjects are represented too, particularly Computer Science, which is quite interesting (Figure 5.29).

Quick Recap

In the second half of this chapter, we looked at the *Web of Science* databases: three citation indexes representing science, social science, and arts and humanities. The driving idea behind these databases is that *citations*, both articles cited and citing articles, are an efficient and effective way of doing research and seeing how various lines of research relate to and build on each other. Unlike every other database considered in this textbook, the three citation indexes making up the *Web of Science* have no human-applied controlled vocabulary.

The *Web of Science* databases have a dual nature. One aspect is an article database, which you access through the main search page. This database of journal articles can be searched by topic (keyword searches), or by author, journal title, the author's address, or several other field choices. Records produced by such searches include both the list of all works cited by the

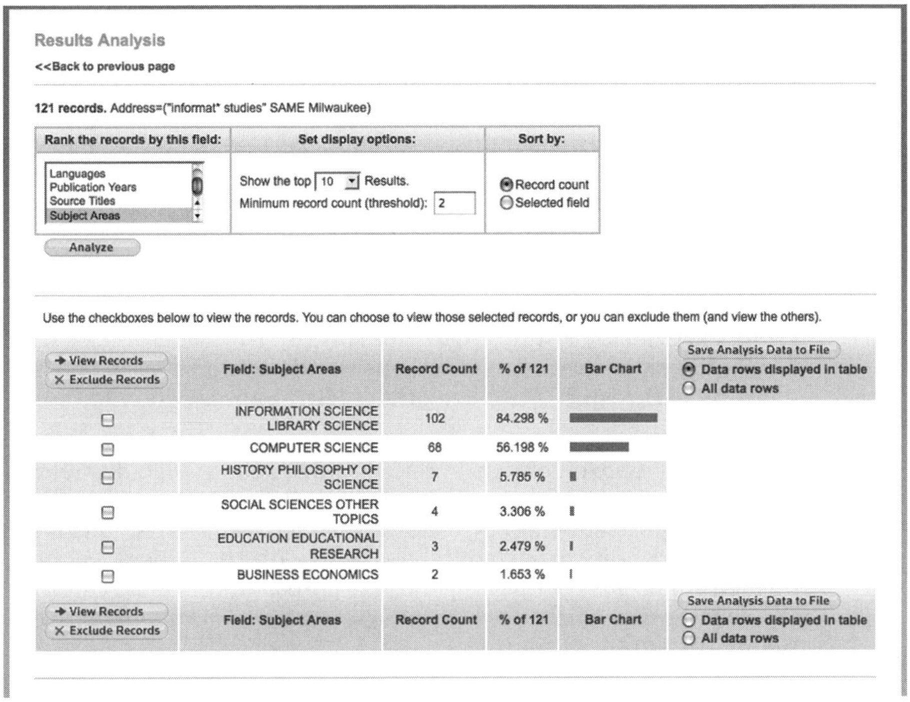

Fig. 5.29. The Results Analysis interface and output. Web of Science^SM from Thomson Reuters Web of Knowledge^SM.

article (its bibliography, in highly abbreviated form), and links to more recent articles that have cited that article. Each article record also has a link to related records, which are identified based on the number of cited references they share.

The other side of the dual nature is a database of records representing every cited reference from the records in the article database. This set of records is accessed using the Cited Reference search, which allows you to search for current articles that have *cited* a particular work from the past. The original cited work can be any material type, not just journal articles, and it can be from any date. Since the titles of the works in these citations are stored in a highly abbreviated format, it is important to use the built-in lookup indexes to pull up citations (and variations) correctly.

Altogether, the *Web of Science* databases are a quintessentially academic product, reflecting the importance of citing the work of others, publishing in the "highest impact" journals, and most importantly, getting cited. Tenure cases—and thus an assistant professor's whole future—often depend on the latter two items; this is serious business.

Exercises and Points to Consider

Check the book companion website, www.LibrariansGuide.info, for supplementary materials.

1. In PubMed, start typing in male pattern baldness. Something that other people have searched seems to be male pattern baldness

treatment. Choose that suggestion. Your result set should be more than 8,800 records. Come up with some strategies for focusing and refining this search.

2. In PubMed, try searching for: trigger finger guitar*. How many results do you get? How might you find some more on this topic?

3. While you're searching in PubMed, try some of the Related citations links. If you have access to the *Web of Science*, do a search there, and take a look at some Related Records links. Going solely by the titles produced in each case, what is your impression of how well the different databases' "relatedness" function works? PubMed relates articles by a word algorithm, and *Web of Science* does it by number of shared citations. Does either approach seem to produce more related results than the other? (Gut impression only; no research required.)

4. For fun and amazement: at PubMed, change the search drop-down from PubMed to All Databases. Put in any term you want (diseases are good, as are substances: chocolate, coffee, wine, beer). You'll see the number of hits in each database for your term. Even if you have no idea what most of these resources represent, this is fascinating! (You can always click the "?" to get a fairly understandable description of the database content.)

5. A search scenario: You are applying for the position of librarian for physics and astronomy at the (name of university here). You want to make points when you meet the astronomy faculty, and a good way to do that is to find out what they've been writing about. In the *Web of Science* you search for:

    Topic: galax*

    Address: (part of school name) SAME astron* (SAME state abbreviation, if needed to distinguish). How many results do you get? Which people are publishing most frequently? Try changing the Topic word (e.g., planet* OR "deep space") and searching again. Can you put together a picture of these faculty members and their research from your efforts?

6. In the *Web of Science*, look up Hawking S* as cited author again. Note the remarkable number of variations—lots of different years, in French, etc. Select only those entries where the citation seems to be odd or incorrect in some way, then "Finish" the search and look at the articles produced—interesting titles!

7. Do a search on an author with a fairly common name, such as Brown C*. Then use the Refine options in the results screen to differentiate the results by subject area, by name, etc. Experiment and familiarize yourself with all the possible options.

8. Now that you've finished this chapter, what do you think about the opening premise: that the medical database is about *what*, and the science database is about *who*. Do you find this valid? Did you see further evidence to support this theory?

Beyond the Textbook Exercises

1. On the PubMed homepage, click the MeSH Database link under More Resources (you can also search the MeSH database of terms by changing the drop-down in the search interface, but you should visit this page). On the MeSH home page, now enter tendonitis in the search box. What is the official MeSH term for tendonitis? When did this term start being used? What was the former term? Now, see if you can figure out how to construct a search that will find articles on the causes (hint: etiology) or diagnosis of this condition, and ways it can be treated, using nothing but the check boxes and buttons supplied in the page. Then use the Search PubMed button to run it.

2. Start in the *Web of Science*, using just the Science Citation Index Expanded. Do a search on "black holes" AND "Large Hadron Collider" as a Topic. Limit the years to be searched to 2001 to [the current year]. How many results do you get? Notice that sometimes Large Hadron Collider is referred to by its acronym. Go back to the search interface and revise your search to retrieve either the spelled-out phrase or the acronym (still ANDed with "black holes"). How many results now?

   Now use the Analyze Results feature to find which authors have published most frequently on this topic. (Yes, you could also find this out simply by looking under Authors in the Refine Results panel, but this is a good excuse to use another feature.) At the time of this writing, CAVAGLIA, M and GINGRICH, DM led the pack with nine papers each. Armed with these names, now go to www.arXiv.org, an open-access source for a number of disciplines but which is mainly known as an e-print archive for Physics. The number and detail of the topics for Physics on the arXiv home page are a strong indicator of the primacy of Physics here. (arXiv—pronounced "archive"[8]—is to physicists what ERIC is to the education community: *the* database.) Look around on the home page, noticing how different this site is from the commercial databases.

   Search for each of these names as Authors in arXiv. (If the names have changed, i.e., if different people are now the most frequent authors, search for those names.) Where can you perform this search? Is there an Advanced Search? What can you learn from that page? Does it seem to matter how you enter an Author name (e.g., Cavaglia M or M Cavaglia)? On how many papers is M Cavaglia listed as an author? Notice how many authors are often listed on these papers, and the frequent notation "et al. (### additional authors not shown.)". What happens when you search Gingrich with his initials? Figure out a solution to that problem; Gingrich does have papers in arXiv (how many?). What is the title of the paper that Gingrich contributed to that has 2549 "additional authors not shown"? (Fancy searching is not required; just use your eyes on your results.)

   It doesn't matter if you haven't a clue what these papers are about: given a name, part of a title, or some keywords, and your knowledge of the Searcher's Toolkit, you can execute a perfectly respectable search (and get results) on a site like arXiv.

Notes

1. In June 2011, the MeSH home page (http://www.nlm.nih.gov/mesh/meshhome .html) was quite "homey"—they were still celebrating the 50th birthday of MeSH; there was a photo of 11 members of the MeSH Staff, with a link to their biographies; and vocabulary suggestions were actively invited. Indeed, everything you could possibly want to know about MeSH is there—including a link to download an electronic copy of the whole database!

2. Among other reasons for not limiting yourself to just MEDLINE citations, this can make a big difference depending on where you are in the calendar year. The NLM stops adding records to MEDLINE during November and December, while maintenance is done on the database. During that time, and at the beginning of the new year while they race to catch up, you'd miss out on a potentially significant body of literature.

3. Alert readers who notice in Figure 5.15 a field called Keywords Plus and a Subject Category may wonder why earlier we said there were no indexer-applied subject headings in this database. Does this mean the *Web of Science* is getting into subject headings? In a word, no. Keywords Plus terms are automatically generated terms, representing words or phrases that show up most frequently in the titles of an article's *references*. Subject Category is the subject category of the *journal* that the article appeared in, a value decided once and then applied automatically every time a record is added from that journal. Finally, in other records you may notice "Author Keywords." These are exactly that: author-supplied terms, a useful addition, but the addition of these terms did not slow down the process of getting the record into the database, and there is no controlled schema for them—they are simply whatever the author provided.

4. This looks totally normal, but the spelling out of the author's first name is another new development with *Web of Knowledge* version 5. Historically, these citation indexes have only stored initials for author names, for example, Smith P or Smith PE.

5. Just for curiosity's sake, I used the Citation Report function to see which article in this set of results had been cited most often. It turns out to be our man Likens GE again, with Driscoll CT and Buso DC. "Long-term effects of acid rain: Response and recovery of a forest ecosystem." Science 272 (5259): 244–246. April 12 1996. As of December 2011, it had been cited 445 times! Likens is obviously "the man" in this field.

6. You don't *have* to use the wildcard; you can also use initials for both first and middle names, if you're sure that the author always uses the middle initial. While *Web of Science* is beginning to add spelled out first names, you are still better off using the FirstInitial* form, to ensure that you retrieve older and newer records. Not sure what Hawking's middle name is? Google for "Stephen * Hawking"—you'll be able to verify his name (and anything else about him) in no time.

7. My favorite is "Brief Hist Time Bing" . . .

8. The X in the name is the Greek letter X, pronounced "chi," thus: "archive."

6
Bibliographic Databases

From the beginning of this book, we have been focusing on "article" databases that serve an abstracting and indexing (A&I) function: databases that provide a means to identify (and often to supply) articles from periodical publications. In this chapter, our focus shifts to "bibliographic" databases, which we define as resources that provide information (mainly) about books. While A&I databases provide information about the contents of journals, and may include book chapters, conference papers, or other materials, bibliographic databases provide information about the contents of a particular library, or many libraries, or any collection of book titles (e.g., *Books in Print*, Amazon.com). Put another way, an A&I database is like being *inside* a collection of journals or books, seeing all the contents, while a bibliographic database is like being on the *outside*, running your eyes down the spine titles of everything (book, bound journal, video, etc.) sitting on the shelves of a library or other collection.

You have undoubtedly used a bibliographic database many times already as a student or as a regular library user: every library's online catalog is a bibliographic database. The Online Public Access Catalog (OPAC) is how you find out about the contents of that particular library. If you think about it for any time at all, it's easy in today's networked, everything-is-on-the-Web world to see that it would be even more interesting if you could find out about the contents of other libraries without having to go to each of their catalogs and search. It would be incredibly useful to gather the records from many libraries and provide them as one massive "union" catalog. Such things were at one time published in hard copy, but an electronic database version would obviously be far more powerful and useful. It would provide all the contents of all the libraries, searchable through one interface. This sounds like a totally natural idea now—but can you imagine having this vision in 1967? That is when Frederick G. Kilgour and university presidents in Ohio founded the *Ohio College Library Center* (Jordan 2003) in order to "share library resources and reduce costs by using computers and technology" (Helfer

2002). The original idea was to establish an online shared cataloging system, which OCLC introduced in 1971, and an Interlibrary Loan system, which was introduced in 1979 (Helfer 2002). OCLC introduced the FirstSearch interface and access to several databases, including the union catalog, dubbed WorldCat, for use as a reference tool in 1991 (Hogan 1991). OCLC (the acronym now stands for *Online Computer* Library Center) was a brilliant idea, way ahead of its time.

Most of this chapter is devoted to an exploration of WorldCat and to its free Web version, WorldCat.org. We'll conclude with some suggestions and reminders about what to look for in your own local catalog.

WorldCat: The "OPAC of OPACs"

In the online Help for WorldCat, OCLC rather modestly describes its product as a catalog of books and other materials in libraries worldwide. WorldCat is far beyond just a union catalog, however. The OCLC website pulls no punches, describing it as a "the world's largest and most comprehensive catalog" (OCLC 2011a). As of December 2011, over 72,000 libraries were contributing to the database, representing 170 countries (OCLC 2011b). How was it, and is it, possible to put together and maintain such an enormous resource?

Background and Coverage

Note: in the following discussion, although it is always the same body of information being referring to, *how* it is referred to differs depending on the library context. To Cataloging and Interlibrary Loan (ILL) departments, this database is usually known simply as OCLC. To librarians and library users, the database information is presented via WorldCat. (The cataloging and ILL interfaces and programs for interacting with the database are very different from those in WorldCat.) When the discussion concerns Cataloging or ILL, the text refers to this resource as the OCLC database. In the context of a database used by reference librarians and patrons, it is referred to as WorldCat. Again, it is all the same body of information.

Part of the brilliance of OCLC's vision for creating this far-reaching union catalog was to make it a distributed, cooperative effort, and one that had immediate benefit for those supplying the effort. The business model here is that libraries pay annual fees to be members of OCLC, as well as activity fees to search the database and download records for use in the library's local catalog. However, whenever a cataloger at a member library contributes a new record or improves an existing record, the library receives *credits*. The more the library contributes, the more credits it receives.[1] While an actively contributing library is usually also an actively "using" library (thus incurring more service fees), receiving the credits does help to keep the financial relationship from being entirely one sided. OCLC manages the contributed data and provides many services and benefits based on the database information. Thus, the OCLC database is built by catalogers at member libraries, already experts in their field, who would need to create records for their library's holdings anyway. By contributing their work, these member library catalogers offset the costs of searching and downloading records supplied by *other* member libraries. Everyone benefits in terms of time, effort, and efficiency. One of the great benefits is that this huge bibliographic collection is made available as a sophisticated database to reference librarians and patrons in the form of WorldCat, and it is freely available to the world in the form of the simpler WorldCat.org.

The scope of WorldCat is dazzling: as of this writing, the number of records in WorldCat has passed the 250 million mark, representing works dating from before 1000 BC to the present, in nearly 500 languages. As a collaborative, contributed effort, the database is updated constantly: according to the OCLC website, on average a new record is added to WorldCat every 10 seconds.[2] The records in WorldCat represent the whole gamut of material types, everything that the contributing libraries have cataloged: books, serials, manuscripts, musical scores, audiovisual materials (i.e., videos, DVDs, audiotapes, and other "sound recordings"), maps, and electronic resources (i.e., websites, electronic journals, e-books, etc.), and these are just the common formats. There is, literally, everything from stone tablets to electronic books, and more.

A Tool for Many Parts of the Library

The OCLC database is both a creation and a tool of the *cataloging* department. Original catalogers create new records that get added to the local OPAC and to the OCLC database, while copy catalogers download preexisting records for the local OPAC and add the local library's holdings to existing OCLC records (a process known as *tagging*). As you might imagine, the OCLC database is also integral to the Interlibrary Loan function. OCLC supplies several services that help to speed and streamline resource sharing by ILL departments.

As a *reference* and *collection development* tool, librarians can use WorldCat to

- Explore new or unfamiliar topics presented in reference questions to get a sense of what is available in a subject area.

- Find resources in an area that their library is limited in.

- Find resources in a particular format.

- Find everything written by a particular author.

- Test the waters before encouraging a patron to request an ILL by seeing how many libraries own the item, and where those libraries are located.

- Identify government documents.

- Verify citations (for titles of books, journals, etc.), check publication dates, serial start dates, etc.

- Provide an interim solution if the local catalog is down (but the holdings are in WorldCat).

- Develop a collection by seeing what's out there on a topic, what other libraries own, and what they might want to buy.

Note that records for serial publications in WorldCat can include holdings records, that is, the dates of the journal run owned by the library. It has always been possible to use WorldCat to see if another library owned a particular journal, but until holdings records were added to the WorldCat records, there was no way to tell if that subscription was current or had stopped, say, in 1964. This is very useful for ILL staff, as well as those at the Reference Desk.

Notes and Search Examples

Let's get into the database, start looking for our Searcher's Toolkit items, and get a sense of how this database differs from the article databases. We have several lighthearted searches to try here in WorldCat. We'll go straight to the Advanced Search screen (Figure 6.1) to begin.

Advanced Search Screen

The WorldCat interface includes several features that are different from what you typically encounter in an article database, which reflect its role as an access point to the contents of libraries. The immediately visible differences have to do with Limits and Ranking possibilities. We can limit by the fairly typical Year and Language, but here is a brand new limit: Number of Libraries, that is, how many libraries own the item. The choices are 5 or more, 50 or more, or 500 or more. (Think about this one for a moment: What is the implication here? Why might you want to use this limit?) Rather than a drop-down menu of document types common in article databases, we have a whole section of the screen devoted to choosing *material* types (Books, Serials, Archival Materials, etc.). We can choose to limit our search only to the

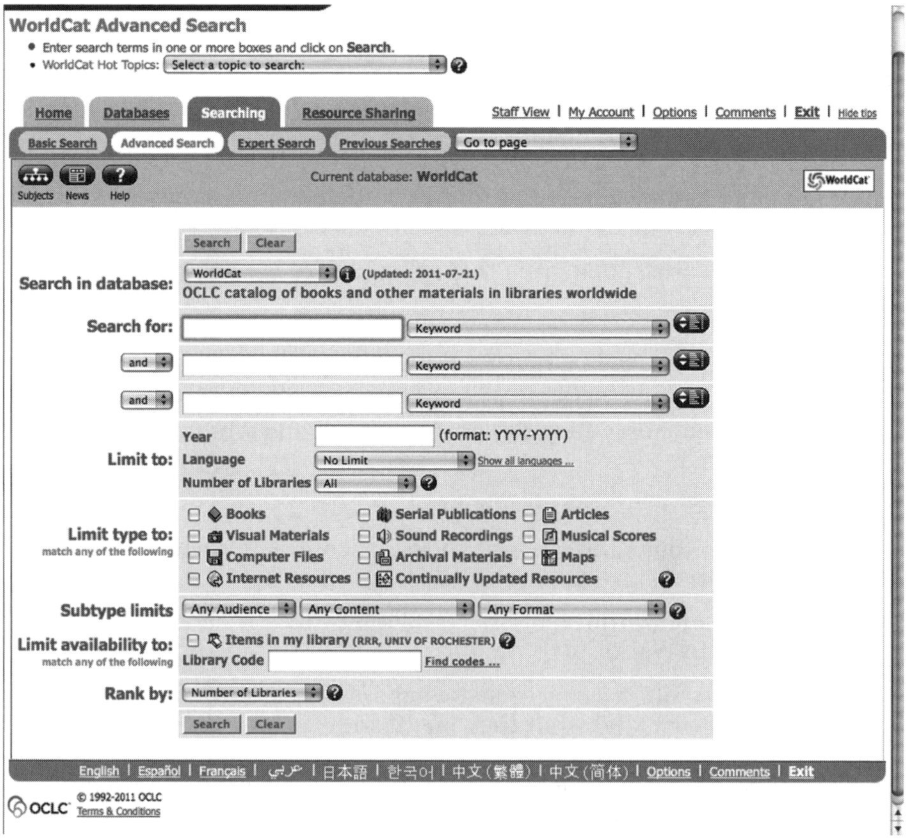

Fig. 6.1. WorldCat® Advanced Search screen. Screen shots used with the permission of OCLC Online Computer Library Center, Inc. ("OCLC"). FirstSearch® and WorldCat® are registered trademarks/service marks of OCLC.

holdings of a particular library (i.e., the library that you are in, or another library that you indicate by an alpha code) using the options in the "Limit availability to:" area.

We also have new *Subtype limits* to define our audience, content, and format. Under audience, we can specify Juvenile or not Juvenile. Under content, we have options for Fiction, not Fiction, Biography, Thesis/dissertation, Musical recording, or Non-musical recording. The format options are Large print, Braille, Manuscript, Microform, not Microform, CD audio, Cassette recording, LP recording, VHS tape/Videocassette, and DVD Video/Videodisc. These "subtypes" say a lot about WorldCat as both a reflection of the content and a tool for *public* libraries, which also distinguishes this database from the article databases in this book. Not that academia doesn't use World-Cat constantly; it does. But WorldCat is equally useful in any other kind of library too: it's a database of all the libraries, for all the people. Quite an achievement!

Last in the display is a "Rank by" setting. The "Rank by" options are Number of Libraries (the default), Relevance, Date, or Accession Number. The Rank by options, especially the default (Number of Libraries), are another reminder that this database is all about the holdings of many libraries.

More differences become apparent when we compare the fields available for searching (the drop-down menus associated with the three text-input fields in the "Search for" section). The searchable fields in WorldCat are all about identifying books and other complete items that you would find on library shelves or, increasingly, digital items owned by libraries. There are many variations on Author (nicely gathered together and indented under *Author*), along with Publisher and Publisher Location, and specific Standard Number choices: ISBN and ISSN. We have an opportunity to search by Material Type in more detail (e.g., "book not URL"), or types of Musical Compositions (overtures, part-songs, etc., or phrases such as folk music, gospel music, etc.). WorldCat certainly has subject-related search fields, but subjects here are rather different: in addition to Subject, Subject Phrase, and Descriptor, we have Genre/Form, Geographic Coverage, Named Corporation and Conference, and Named Person.

"Subject" is an excellent way to start exploring WorldCat, however, in conjunction with some limits.

Search Examples

Search Example 1: Finding Materials in Other Languages

You'd like to find some cookbooks for your friend's Korean mother, who doesn't speak English. Take a quick browse of the Subject index (available by clicking the black and white "up/down" button following the drop-down menus) to see the number of times each of the following has been applied as a subject: cooking, cookbooks, and cookery. You'll find that "cooking" has been applied in the overwhelming majority of cases. To be comprehensive, let's search for either cooking or cookbooks in the Subject field. We can then use our Language limit to limit to materials about Cooking in Korean.

Notice the tabs above the results list, shown in Figure 6.2, indicating the number of results for each type of media. Note too that there are over 2,200 records for cookbooks in *Korean*—isn't that incredible? (In case you're curious, the Sound file is an instructional cassette tape.) Remember that the results are sorted, or ranked, by the number of libraries that own the item.

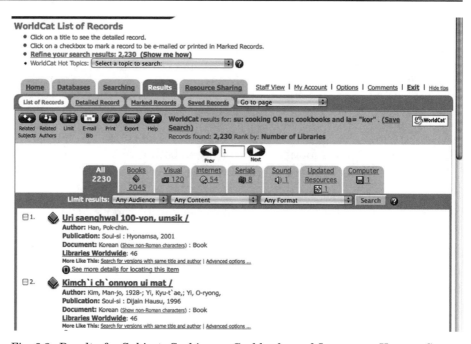

Fig. 6.2. Results for Subject: Cooking or Cookbooks and Language: Korean. Screen shots used with the permission of OCLC Online Computer Library Center, Inc. ("OCLC"). FirstSearch® and WorldCat® are registered trademarks/service marks of OCLC.

Search Example 2: Finding Materials for a Specific Audience

Your kids are beginning to show an interest in cooking, and you'd like to see if there are some cookbooks written for children.

Returning to the Search screen (the Searching tab is a good way to do this), we already have our Subjects in place. Any limits that you set previously will also still be in effect, so remember to change the language back to English. This is the perfect occasion to use that first Subtype limit, audience, to specify that we want materials for a "Juvenile" audience. Figure 6.3 shows this search ready to be run.

There are plenty of options to explore, as indicated by the number and variety of formats shown in the Results screen in Figure 6.4.

Note that there is even one entry on the "Musical Scores" tab—how peculiar! Whenever you see an odd result, don't immediately assume that it's a mistake. Take a good look at the record and find out why it's there. In a carefully crafted database like this one, where your search has been set up only in terms of subjects and field search values (rather than as a keyword search), it is highly unlikely that an odd result will be a false drop. By looking and figuring out why it's there, you'll add to your understanding of database lore in general, and you'll discover interesting and bizarre things that may bring a smile to your face (and remind you why this profession is so much fun).

Here is why our search retrieved this "Musical Score." It's a book of children's songs and activities, including recipes, for Halloween. See the Descriptors and Notes fields in Figure 6.5.

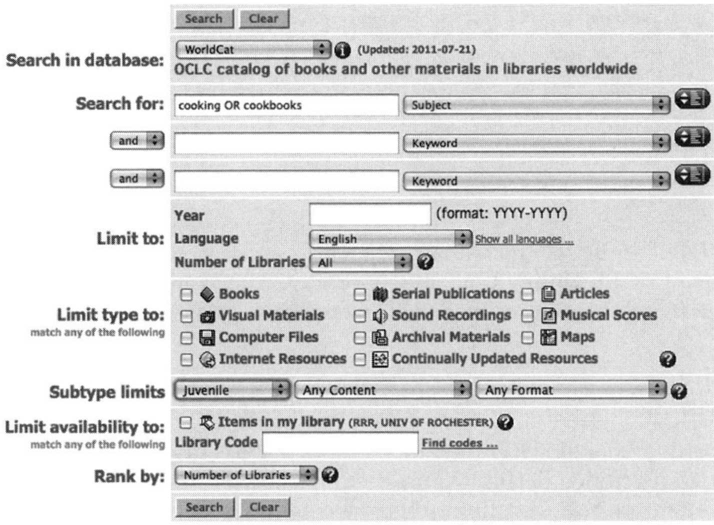

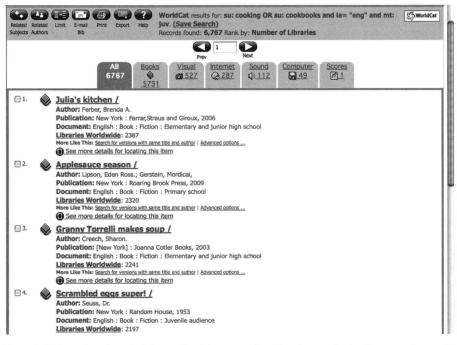

Fig. 6.3. Cookbooks for kids search strategy. Screen shots used with the permission of OCLC Online Computer Library Center, Inc. ("OCLC"). FirstSearch® and WorldCat® are registered trademarks/service marks of OCLC.

Fig. 6.4. Results for Subject: Cooking or Cookbooks and Audience: Juvenile ("cookbooks for kids"). Screen shots used with the permission of OCLC Online Computer Library Center, Inc. ("OCLC"). FirstSearch® and WorldCat® are registered trademarks/service marks of OCLC.

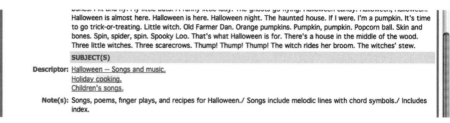

Fig. 6.5. Explanation of the "Musical Scores" result. Screen shots used with the permission of OCLC Online Computer Library Center, Inc. ("OCLC"). FirstSearch® and WorldCat® are registered trademarks/service marks of OCLC.

Search Example 3: Finding Materials by Genre

Switching to a slightly darker vein, now we'd like to find some mystery novels with a science fiction theme.

We'll change the first field where we searched "cooking" as a Subject to the phrase "science fiction" and search that as a Subject Phrase. Then we'll add another field search to find materials with "mystery" in the Genre/Form field (Genre/Form is part of the indented list under Subject in the drop-down menu). Any limits that you set previously will also still be in effect, so remember to change the Subtype back to Any Audience.

Figures 6.6a and 6.6b give us a view into a full record: note the Amazon .com-like feature of providing the book cover and a brief blurb. In fact, the one record is really being offered two ways: the upper, generally eye-catching, easy-to-grasp-quickly section (Figure 6.6a), and then the lower, nitty-gritty, all-the-details section (Figure 6.6b). Even when an image of the cover art is not provided, the basic citation information is set off in this upper section.

Search Example 4: Finding Materials on a Current Topic

Now for something a bit more serious: let's look for non-fiction materials on global warming that have been published recently. Checking the Subject Phrase index, we find that global warming is indeed a subject. For the Year limit, we'll look for the years 2008–2012. Finally, we'll set the Subtype limit to "not Fiction" to rule out science fiction horror stories. The complete strategy is represented in Figure 6.7.

The results are a dazzling array, as indicated by the tabs in Figure 6.8. At the time this search was run, there were 955 items classified as Internet; these are ebooks, and the huge number shows how prevalent this format is becoming. (And note: here is another search with one musical score in the results—take a look, it's rather amusing.)

Using WorldCat for Citation Verification

WorldCat is also invaluable for resolving citation problems, such as determining what the *real* title of a work is, or its publication year, author, etc. You can use it to fill in information on books and other formats, or to determine what material type a title really is (i.e., a monographic series? A conference report? A serial publication?). WorldCat can be particularly useful for resolving questions about serial publications, especially esoteric titles or titles that have ceased publication (and that don't appear in a periodicals directory). If we know that something existed at some time, then it is likely

Fig. 6.6a. Upper part of a full record display. Screen shots used with the permission of OCLC Online Computer Library Center, Inc. ("OCLC"). FirstSearch® and WorldCat® are registered trademarks/service marks of OCLC.

FIND RELATED	
More Like This:	Search for versions with same title and author I Advanced options ...
Title:	**Ashes of the earth :** **a mystery of post-apocalyptic America /**
Author(s):	Pattison, Eliot.
Publication:	Berkeley, CA : Counterpoint : Distributed by Publishers Group West,
Year:	2011
Description:	359 p. ; 24 cm.
Language:	English
Standard No:	**ISBN:** 9781582436449 (hbk.); 1582436444 (hbk.) **LCCN:** 2011-2167
Abstract:	In a post-apocalyptic world, Hadrian Boone, a fallen founder of the colony of Carthage, joins forces with a policewoman to investigate the camps of outcasts in the hopes of discovering who murdered the colony's leading scientist.
SUBJECT(S)	
Descriptor:	End of the world -- Fiction. Armageddon -- Fiction.
Genre/Form:	Science fiction Mystery fiction
Class Descriptors:	**LC:** PS3566.A82497; **Dewey:** 813/.54
Responsibility:	Eliot Pattison.
Vendor Info:	Ingram Baker and Taylor YBP Library Services Blackwell Book Service (INGR BTCP YANK BBUS)
Material Type:	Fiction (fic)
Document Type:	Book
Entry:	20110118
Update:	20110426
Accession No:	**OCLC:** 663952958
Database:	WorldCat

Fig. 6.6b. Lower part of a full record display. Screen shots used with the permission of OCLC Online Computer Library Center, Inc. ("OCLC"). FirstSearch® and WorldCat® are registered trademarks/service marks of OCLC.

that *some* library, somewhere, owns it, and chances are good that that library also contributes records to WorldCat.

Search Example 5: Finding Materials in Other Libraries

A student comes to the Reference Desk and says: "My professor said I should look at some journal—it's the British journal of clinical something or other, I can't remember . . . but she said she knows the library at SUNY Buffalo gets it . . ."

Fig. 6.7. Global warming search strategy. Screen shots used with the permission of OCLC Online Computer Library Center, Inc. ("OCLC"). FirstSearch® and WorldCat® are registered trademarks/service marks of OCLC.

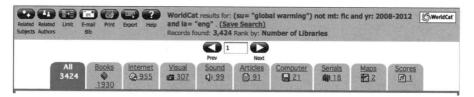

Fig. 6.8. Tabs showing the range of results for the global warming search. Screen shots used with the permission of OCLC Online Computer Library Center, Inc. ("OCLC"). FirstSearch® and WorldCat® are registered trademarks/service marks of OCLC.

In doing any kind of citation verification or completion in WorldCat (or in an article database), the Searcher's Toolkit tools that you'll want to make good use of are the field indexes and truncation symbols. If at all possible, especially in tracking down journals, try to come up with the ISSN for the publication (or ISBN for books). Words are fuzzy and easily mistaken, but numbers don't lie. There is only one identifying number for every publication (exceptions exist, of course, but as a general principle you can depend on this). It's much more efficient and accurate to search by number than by name.

However, because we are unsure of the journal name, we can't determine an ISSN and look it up that way. Checking the Title Phrase field index for "British journal of clinical" we find the following (Figure 6.9).

Since there are obviously quite a few *British Journal of Clinical . . .* titles, and since the student isn't sure, rather than trying to choose anything from the index list, we'll simply return to the Advanced Search screen and get ready to search: British journal of clinical* as a Title Phrase.

The patron has also told us that this journal is available at the "library at SUNY Buffalo." (SUNY stands for State University of New York, the large system of colleges and universities in New York State.) We could refine our

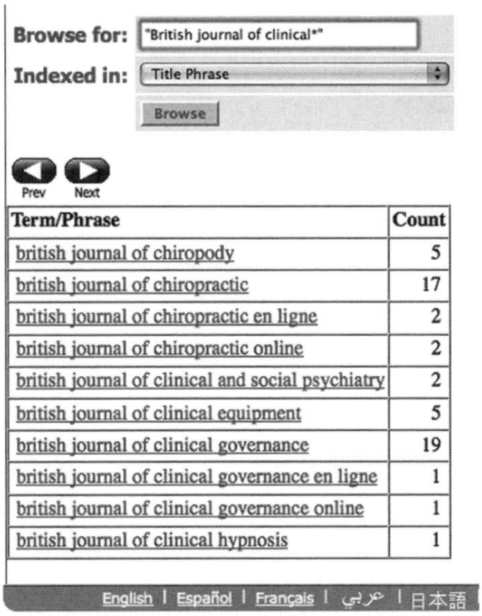

Fig. 6.9. Browsing the Title Phrase field index. Screen shots used with the permission of OCLC Online Computer Library Center, Inc. ("OCLC"). FirstSearch® and WorldCat® are registered trademarks/service marks of OCLC.

search by finding the "Library Code" for the library at Buffalo and entering it in the "Limit availability to" section (see Figure 6.1). Clicking the "Find codes . . ." link opens the "Find an OCLC Library" search in a new window. Since we're not sure if the library at SUNY Buffalo has a specific name, we'll play it very safe, and simply search Buffalo as the City, and "SUNY" in the name of the Institution.

This search gives us four results, but now we have a new dilemma: there appear to be two entries that are exactly the same except for their symbols, which appear in the first column of the table (Figure 6.10). One is BUF and the other is SBS—which is it?

There is no need to agonize while we have Boolean operators at hand—we'll simply try them both, using OR. Back on the search screen, our mystery journal search is now ready to run using just the first text input field and the Library Code field:

British journal of clinical* → Title Phrase

Library Code: BUF or SBS

Upon seeing the results (Figure 6.11), the student decides it must be the first title, because it's for a psych class.

The student might also want to know "is SUNY Buffalo's subscription current?" And it would be even more convenient if the journal were here, at the University of Rochester, so she wouldn't need to drive to Buffalo—or best of all, if she could simply access it online. There is an immediate tip-off here in the results screen: the *The British Journal of Clinical Psychology* entry

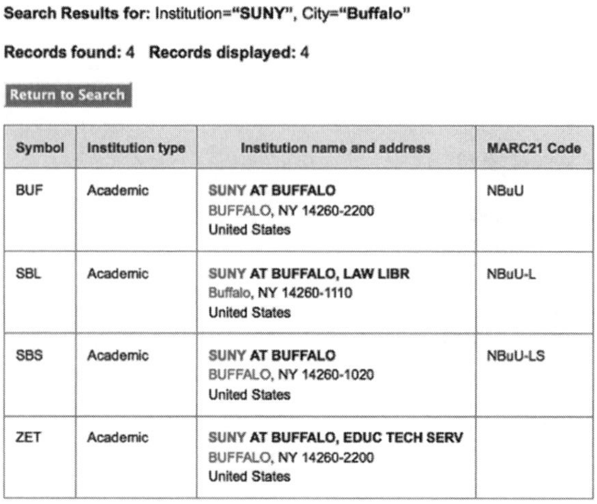

Search Results for: Institution="SUNY", City="Buffalo"

Records found: 4   Records displayed: 4

Return to Search

Symbol	Institution type	Institution name and address	MARC21 Code
BUF	Academic	SUNY **AT BUFFALO** BUFFALO, NY 14260-2200 United States	NBuU
SBL	Academic	SUNY **AT BUFFALO, LAW LIBR** Buffalo, NY 14260-1110 United States	NBuU-L
SBS	Academic	SUNY **AT BUFFALO** BUFFALO, NY 14260-1020 United States	NBuU-LS
ZET	Academic	SUNY **AT BUFFALO, EDUC TECH SERV** BUFFALO, NY 14260-2200 United States	

Fig. 6.10. "Find an OCLC Library" search results. Screen shots used with the permission of OCLC Online Computer Library Center, Inc. ("OCLC"). First-Search® and WorldCat® are registered trademarks/service marks of OCLC.

Fig. 6.11. Results for the *British Journal of Clinical** search. Screen shots used with the permission of OCLC Online Computer Library Center, Inc. ("OCLC"). FirstSearch® and WorldCat® are registered trademarks/service marks of OCLC.

includes a small icon with the notation "Univ of Rochester," indicating that the title *is* held locally. But are the local holdings up to date? Clicking the "Libraries worldwide" link for any of these records reveals a very useful feature noted earlier, in the "A Tool for Many Parts of the Library" section. Many serial records in WorldCat now include holdings information, that is, in addition to indicating which libraries own the title, the years and volumes

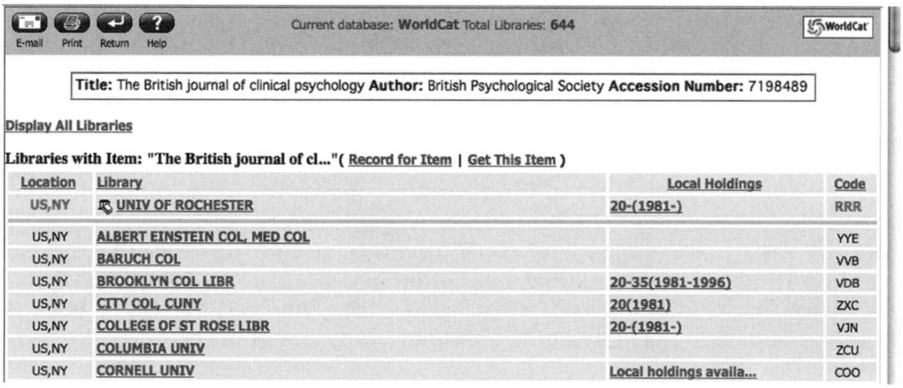

Fig. 6.12. Holdings information screen. Screen shots used with the permission of OCLC Online Computer Library Center, Inc. ("OCLC"). FirstSearch® and WorldCat® are registered trademarks/service marks of OCLC.

owned are available as well (Figure 6.12). The local holding library is helpfully listed first.

This is all very nice, but what really catches the student's eye is the link to an electronic version, which is available both from the record for the print version and from the e-journal record (the third one in Figure 6.11). That will probably be her preferred way to look at the journal.

Quick Recap

The first half of this chapter has looked at the subscription version of WorldCat, a bibliographic database that is different from all the other databases in this book. Rather than being an index to journal articles or statistical publications, it is a database of the contents of all kinds of libraries: public, academic, and corporate. The range of materials included and the audiences that might be served by the information contained here are thus incredibly broad.

WorldCat is the largest union catalog in the world, comprising records for books and many other material types from thousands of member libraries. The database is a distributed effort, built by catalogers at contributing libraries. As a reference tool, WorldCat can be used in many ways, such as for exploring topics or doing collection development, finding resources in a particular format, verifying citations for books or other materials, or discovering where materials that your library does not own are available (e.g., which other libraries own them). The WorldCat Advanced Search interface has many Limits (for material types) and Subtype limits (for audience, content, and formats) not found in other databases. The Results screen is tabbed to allow users to see all the results, or to view records by material type (serials, Internet resources, maps, etc.). Every record includes a "Libraries worldwide" link to view the list of libraries that own the item. One can also restrict a search to a particular library.

WorldCat.org

When the National Library of Medicine provides the entire contents of MEDLINE (and more) for free on the Internet in the form of PubMed or, similarly, when the Department of Education gives us ERIC, it's wonderful; it's amazing. But after all, these are government-produced resources: in the United States, these are our tax dollars at work. So while these are very important additions in terms of information sharing, they aren't *completely* unexpected. In contrast, when OCLC, a private, for-profit organization, decided to provide the WorldCat database for free on the Internet as WorldCat .org, it was, to me at least, a breathtaking move. WorldCat had only ever been offered through OCLC's FirstSearch platform (which makes sense); it was the result of thousands of contributing member libraries' efforts, and building it had involved a great deal of money sloshing back and forth over the years. To decide to "give it away" must have involved meetings and discussions and struggles beyond the powers of my imagination.

Background: The Path to WorldCat.org

OCLC didn't immediately produce the current WorldCat.org: starting in December 2004, OCLC first experimented with a program dubbed Open WorldCat, which only inserted "Find in a Library" pages into the results from Google and other search engines. Open WorldCat also let the search engines have access only to certain subsets of the total WorldCat database, and it operated under a number of other constraints as well (Hane 2006). Although limited in many ways, Open WorldCat evidently convinced OCLC that they should go further, and the appearance in August 2006 of WorldCat.org, a "destination website," was greeted very positively by librarians (Flagg 2006; Hane 2006). At last, anyone who could get online could search the entire WorldCat database, using a simple, friendly interface. Each search result is linked to a "Find in a Library" information page, where the user can enter his or her zip code and receive a list of nearby WorldCat-participating libraries that own the item. Users can also link right to a library's online catalog record to check circulation status or access electronic content directly ("OCLC Launches" 2006).

Developments and Change

Since its launch, WorldCat.org has been enthusiastically adding both technical and social features to appeal to all sorts of audiences. Since 2006, it has been possible to add a WorldCat.org search box to your personal or institutional Web pages or download Web toolbars or plug-ins for your favorite browser. RSS feeds from WorldCat.org were also part of the launch, as was the ability to add reviews and notes on individual items ("OCLC Launches" 2006). By early 2007, WorldCat.org records offered links out to related "Web Resources," faceted browsing, a Chinese-language interface, and automatic geographic location sensing based on IP address ("WorldCat .org Adds New Features" 2007). By August 2007, WorldCat.org was offering personalization with "My WorldCat" accounts, allowing users to build and share lists of materials as well as a personal profile ("WorldCat.org Adds List-Building" 2007). Since then, OCLC has added the ability to limit results by format and to be kept up to date on the contents of other people's (public) lists by means of RSS feeds. To aid students and other writers in their quest for easier bibliography creation, WorldCat.org can format citations in any of five common styles (APA, Chicago, Harvard, MLA, Turabian), and lets you export them to RefWorks, EndNote, or other bibliographic management software. (Want to learn how to do it? The tutorial is a video, only 1:47 minutes long, on YouTube.) And what would modern life be without Facebook and

Google? To further its intention to be where the users are, OCLC provided code to Facebook to allow users to add WorldCat.org as an application there, so that you can have a WorldCat.org search box on your Facebook page. OCLC's relations with Google Books, a strong emphasis circa 2008, appear to have cooled somewhat: WorldCat.org results limited to Format eBook appear to provide links to Google Books only when there is no other ebook source. On the Google Books end, a quiet link to "Find in a library," without the WorldCat logo, appears below all the purchasing options in the "Get this book" list. WorldCat.org has its own blog, where you can keep up on the latest features, among other things. There are apps so you can use WorldCat .org on your mobile phone. You can tag WorldCat records, follow it on Twitter, or watch tutorials or "why I love WorldCat" videos on its YouTube channel. Where the trends go, WorldCat.org is right there with them.

Notes and Search Examples

As of July 2011, the WorldCat.org home screen shown in Figure 6.13 offered one search box, five tabs, and various announcements and invitations to log in (two places marked "A"). If you want to search "everything," you can, and then refine your results afterward. Or, if you know you're looking for a DVD to while away the evening, this search screen lets you specify that, or one of the other most common formats people tend to search for.

Note that this screen is "home" for WorldCat.org. The Search link just above the logo ("B" in Figure 6.13) offers the options to Search for Library

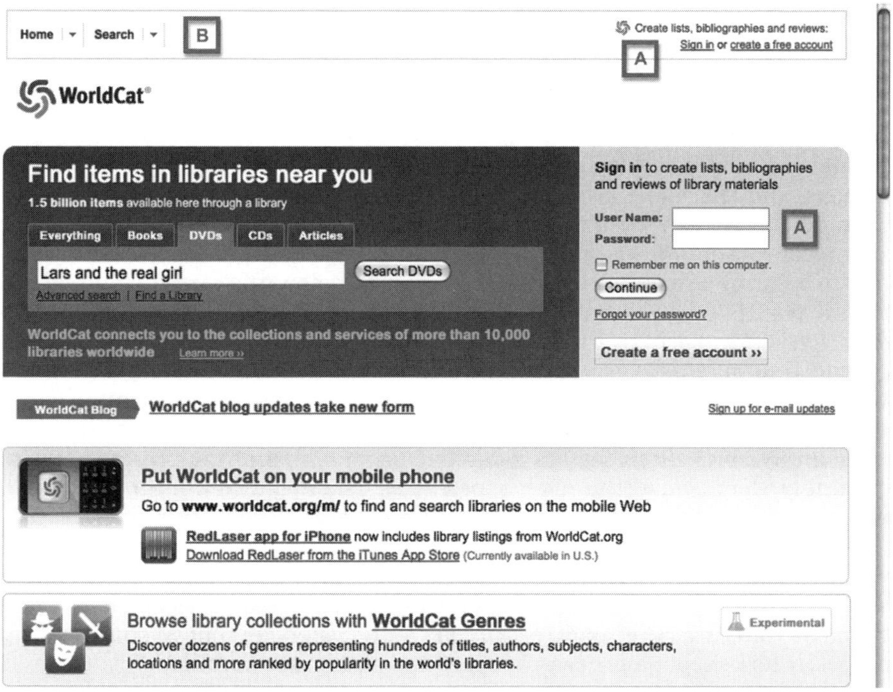

Fig. 6.13. WorldCat.org home screen set to search for a DVD, as of July 2011. Screen shots used with the permission of OCLC Online Computer Library Center, Inc. ("OCLC"). FirstSearch® and WorldCat® are registered trademarks/service marks of OCLC.

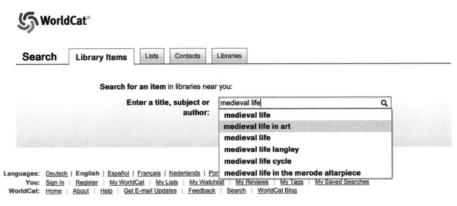

Fig. 6.14. WorldCat.org "basic" search screen set up for search example 1, as of July 2011. Screen shots used with the permission of OCLC Online Computer Library Center, Inc. ("OCLC"). FirstSearch® and WorldCat® are registered trademarks/ service marks of OCLC.

Items, Search for Lists, Search for Contacts, or Search for a Library. You might expect that Search for Library Items interface would be the same as on the home screen, but it turns out to be even more minimalistic (Figure 6.14). Let's think of it as the basic search. Note the "intelligent search box" that offers suggestions as you type, just as PubMed does (we will see this again, in a more sophisticated implementation, in *Statistical Insight* in chapter 8). Google started it, and produced another trend.

Both the home and the basic search screens also link to an Advanced search (Figure 6.15), which provides just enough additional sophistication to make it efficient but not overwhelming. This interface offers a very clean and easy to use set of useful options. (An aside: I also find it interesting how this interface has changed in three years. In 2008, the "Enter your search terms" area consisted of five text input boxes, labeled Keyword, Title, Author, Subject, and ISBN or ISSN or OCLC Number. That has now changed to three drop-down menus whose default settings are probably the types of information most commonly searched for: Keyword, Title, and Author [the content of all three drop-downs is the same]. The area below that used to be labeled "Limit results by [optional]." It offered the same options it does now, but *in a different order*: Format, Publication Date, Content, Audience, and Language. At the time of this writing, this area is labeled "Narrow your search [optional]," and the order of the limits is Year {rather than Publication Date], Audience, Content, Format, and Language. Obviously, some department is busy analyzing search logs to see what people do, and making changes accordingly to optimize the user experience. The evolution of an interface is really quite fascinating.)

As you work through the examples, note that every results page and record display page includes a search box, along with a link to the Advanced search, at the top of the page. This is very useful for adding terms to an existing search or changing direction on the fly: there's no need to return to a search interface page unless you need the extra functionality.

Search Examples

Here are just a few ideas for getting into WorldCat.org and exploring its features. Since it is freely available and also very likely to keep chang-

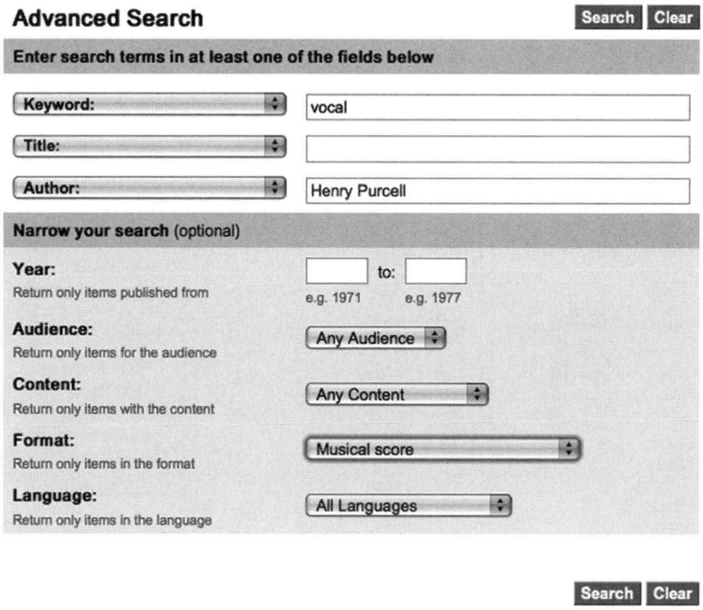

Advanced Search
 Search   Clear

Enter search terms in at least one of the fields below

Keyword: vocal

Title:

Author: Henry Purcell

Narrow your search (optional)

Year:
Return only items published from   to:
                                        e.g. 1971   e.g. 1977

Audience: Any Audience
Return only items for the audience

Content: Any Content
Return only items with the content

Format: Musical score
Return only items in the format

Language: All Languages
Return only items in the language

 Search   Clear

Fig. 6.15. WorldCat.org Advanced search screen set up for search example 2, as of July 2011. Screen shots used with the permission of OCLC Online Computer Library Center, Inc. ("OCLC"). First-Search® and WorldCat® are registered trademarks/service marks of OCLC.

ing, screenshots here are kept to a minimum, but features to look for are described.

Search Example 1: Using the Refine Panel to Focus a Broad Search

Say that you are a student taking a course on medieval history, and you have to write a paper on some aspect of the period that interests you. A pretty broad mandate, and frankly, you're not sure if you're that interested in *any* aspect of medieval times, at least not enough to write a paper on it! Maybe if you could see a lot of results, however, something will get your attention. At the Home screen or the "basic" interface, you type in

 Medieval life

as shown in Figure 6.14. Wow! Plenty of results—and observe, a feature that has become ubiquitous: the panel on the left offering a host of ways to limit or Refine your search. First and foremost are the Format options; this placement is unusual and, thus, interesting. In Figure 6.16, this long narrow area has been broken into three columns to use the space more efficiently.

Note the marvelous detail in the Format listing: there are eBooks, which we would expect, but there are also such things as Continually updated resource, Downloadable image, eVideo, Blu-ray—and if that's not enough, evidently there are more to choose from, indicated by the "Show more . . ." link. If one of the titles in the results list doesn't catch your eye immediately, the most helpful way to "Refine" your search in this case might be the last option, by Topic.[3] Clicking "Show more . . ." in this case reveals a fascinating list of topical areas for "medieval life," and surely one of them will be interesting

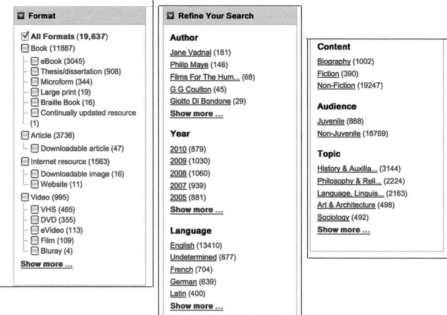

Fig. 6.16. Refining panel for the "medieval life" search, arranged to save space, as of July 2011. Screen shots used with the permission of OCLC Online Computer Library Center, Inc. ("OCLC"). FirstSearch® and WorldCat® are registered trademarks/ service marks of OCLC.

enough for a whole paper's worth of writing (there's even a Library Science topic area for medieval life).

Search Example 2: Using WorldCat.org to Find Musical Scores

A student working on a Master's in vocal performance is home on break and preparing for a midyear vocal recital. She wants to do an all-Purcell program, but knows that her school's library isn't strong on that period. Going to WorldCat.org, she simply types in

Purcell music

and is stunned at the number of results; what a jumble of types and authors are represented. Sadly, she misses the "Refine Your Search" area on the left, but does notice the Advanced Search link at the top, just below the search box that is echoing back her initial search. In the Advanced Search screen, she knows that her Author is Henry Purcell, and after looking at the Format drop-down for a moment, she recognizes just what she wants: "Musical score," as shown in Figure 6.15. At the last minute, she adds "vocal" as a Keyword, having noticed material on "keyboard" compositions in the earlier results. Ah! These results are more manageable. In fact, now that she's not so overwhelmed by the results, she notices the panel on the left side, spotting the Format option: Downloadable musical score. Talk about score! She mines that list, then returns to the list of all Musical scores simply by clicking that box again in the left panel. Going through those results, the material only available in print from various libraries, she creates an account and starts putting together a list to follow up on later.

Search Example 3: Finding Materials Based on Partial Information

The year is 2008, and a friend mentions to you that she was reading a great mystery novel, set in Victorian times, that really conveyed what daily life was like then (and made her awfully glad not to have had to live through the Victorian era). Of course, she told you the title, but a couple of weeks pass, and this is all you can remember about it. You could email her and admit that you have no short-term memory, or you could see if WorldCat.org could provide any ideas. In the Advanced screen, you set up a search as in Figure 6.17.

Specifying "Subject—mystery" and "Content—fiction" seems rather redundant, but because this is all you have to focus your search, you do it anyway. Amazingly, you spot two likely possibilities right away in the results list: Kept, a Victorian Mystery and The Worcester Whisperers: a Victorian Crime Story. Blood Orange Brewing might be possible, too. (The cheerful coloration in the cover of the Death on the Lizard[4] book rules it out immediately. Perhaps we shouldn't judge a book by its cover, but we invariably do.) Going into the full records for each of the likely ones, the abstracts in every record, and comments from other WorldCat users, help to narrow the field quickly. Kept appears to be the most in-depth and Dickensian of the possibilities. That could well be it!

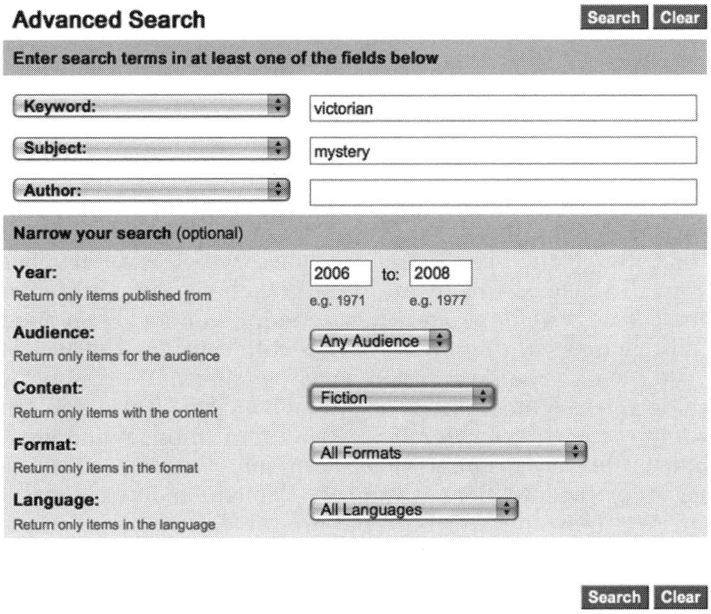

Fig. 6.17. WorldCat.org Advanced search screen set up for search example 3, as of July 2011. Screen shots used with the permission of OCLC Online Computer Library Center, Inc. ("OCLC"). FirstSearch® and WorldCat® are registered trademarks/service marks of OCLC.

WorldCat.org: A Bold Stroke in the Case for Libraries

Librarians are increasingly anxious that their profession and their institutions will be made redundant by products such as Google, but with WorldCat.org, OCLC is making a resounding counterattack. Their stated goal in providing WorldCat.org is to "make library resources more visible to Web users and to increase awareness of libraries as a primary source of reliable information" (Flagg 2006). The methodology is direct: put the content of the WorldCat database directly into the hands of everyone online, at a brief, easy-to-remember Web address, and let the site grow and participate in whatever new Web developments come along. It's a breathtaking concept!

Quick Recap

WorldCat.org provides free access on the Web to the entire contents of the WorldCat database, with the aim of helping users discover and use library content. It is designed for easy use by any Web user, in both the "one search box" versions on the home page and the "Search for Library Items" page, and the easy-to-use Advanced search page. The extensive options that appear in the left-side panel on the Results page provide many ways to focus a search, and they are particularly valuable for broad keyword searches. When a record for an item is displayed, WorldCat.org displays a list of libraries that own the item, geographically arranged from nearest to farthest. The geographical detection is done either automatically based on the IP address of the user, or by the user's entering a zip code. WorldCat.org offers features for personalization (e.g., personal accounts to create a public profile, lists, and bibliographies, or to add notes, tags, or reviews to a record), alerting (email updates and RSS feeds), and citation management (e.g., create bibliographies or export records to RefWorks and EndNote).

Revisiting Your Local OPAC

Even though WorldCat is a (huge) union *catalog*, I always think of it as a *database*. On the other hand, I always think of my institution's online catalog as—a catalog, not a database. Now, why is that? Is it because WorldCat comes to us through the FirstSearch interface (which is an article database model) or, in the case of WorldCat.org, in a Web search-engine model, and our library catalogs come from other vendors, vendors who specialize in online public access *catalogs* that have a different kind of look and feel? Whether you have the same reaction or not, go now and revisit whatever library catalog you use most often. Try to look at it as if it were a new database. Examine it with the Searcher's Toolkit in mind: What fields does it offer? What limits? Does it offer a basic and an advanced search mode? Are there even other modes? Does it support Boolean searching, wildcards, or truncation? Are there stop words? What are the default search settings? Are there any special features that have been customized for *your* library?

Now compare searching your OPAC with searching WorldCat and with WorldCat.org. Does one seem more transparent (in terms of how it works) than the other? Look up an item owned by your library, and then find the record for it in WorldCat,[5] and in WorldCat.org. How do the record displays compare? Think about what factors might be driving the needs of a remote, *union* catalog as opposed to the local catalog for one library (or library system). WorldCat.org figures somewhere in the middle of the two: it is the huge WorldCat catalog, but it is also trying very hard to be local. How well does it succeed?

In general, you may find it easy to fall into using the local OPAC just as a title look-up device, forgetting what a sophisticated search engine it really is (or, perhaps, it isn't). It's worth taking a few moments and reacquainting yourself with this local resource, which you probably think you know so well.

Exercises and Points to Consider

Check the book companion website, www.LibrariansGuide.info, for supplementary materials.

1. In the section called "A Tool for Many Parts of the Library," we mentioned a couple of ways you might use WorldCat at the Reference Desk. What other uses can you think of?

2. Find some books on fast food (what's the best way—that is, what's a good subject heading—to get books that are really on "fast food," and not about food you can prepare fast?)

3. Half-remembered reference problem: a patron comes in trying to describe some books she has enjoyed. She remembers the author's name was "something-something Smith," and the books are mysteries, about a female detective in Africa somewhere. Try just searching the author field for Smith, and the Genre/Form field for mystery, and see if you can identify this series of books.

4. If you have a favorite author or genre, see if you can use WorldCat to find all the records for those works in your local public library branch. (Tip: use the code look-up screen.)

5. You're at the Reference Desk on the weekend, and some junior high school kids come in looking for information about corsets and bloomers for a project. A social history type of encyclopedia might really be best; otherwise, books would be a better way to go than articles for this age group. Try searching your local catalog and see what you can find; then try the subscription WorldCat database (unless your local catalog has a "Juvenile audience" limiter, which would be unusual) and see if you can find more materials or get some additional ideas that way.

6. WorldCat claims to have records for everything from clay tablets to electronic books. See if you can find examples of both ends of this spectrum. Hints: in each case, use a combination of keywords and Limits. For the clay tablets, note that such things would normally be housed in an Archive, thus making them—what kind of materials? Learn from your results what a more formal term for clay tablets is, that you might add as an alternate term to your search. For electronic books, try your favorite author and the "Internet Resources" Limit. Hint: Look up your author in the Author Phrase index, last name first, to find how his or her name is most commonly entered.

7. WorldCat results are sorted, or ranked, by the number of libraries that own the item. There are three other options, but ranking is often set as the default. Why do you think that is? What would be the advantages and disadvantages of other results display options?

8. Now try the searches in exercises 2 to 5 in WorldCat.org. What are the advantages and disadvantages of searching using the First-Search interface versus the WorldCat.org interface?

Beyond the Textbook Exercise

In the case of WorldCat, it really isn't possible to go "beyond the textbook," because there is literally nothing like it. However, we can look at a different way to use this resource. Think about the following approach to cultural research, introduced to me by a faculty member in anthropology. You can use WorldCat to track longitudinally how new concepts emerge and grow, as reflected in their publication counts. Try this: In WorldCat.org, search globali#ation (you won't find a peep about something as geeky as the wildcard symbol for one internal letter in the WorldCat.org Help, but anything you can do in the subscription version, you can do here) to pick up both the U.S. and U.K. spellings of the term. Now go to the Year option in the Refine Your Search panel, and click the "Show more . . ." link once, or even twice, to show publishing volume for materials with this keyword year by year (once you click "Show more" the list appears in straight chronological order, with counts by year). You'll see that, barring a couple of anomalous years (1900 and 1970), in 1986, this term starts appearing with ever-increasing frequency, up to the watershed year of 2009, after which its appearance seems to be tapering off somewhat. Try this for other topics (such as global warming) and see what you can find out.

Notes

1. Not all member libraries can or do contribute records, of course. Many small libraries simply pay to be able to search and download records for their local catalog, as it is still more efficient and economical than employing cataloging staff.

2. Visit the "Watch WorldCat grow" page at http://www.oclc.org/worldcat/newgrow .htm. It is absolutely fascinating.

3. In the image of the Refine list, you might wonder about the initial list of years provided to refine by: it might make you think nothing was published about medieval life in 2006, because the list goes from 2010 in consecutive order down to 2005, but skips 2006. Clicking "Show more . . ." explains it, however: there are materials published on this topic every year, but just by happenstance, it turns out that 2010–2007 and 2005 simply had the highest hit counts, and thus were the system's choice of Years for display in the initial Refine panel. Once you click Show more, the list is presented in straight chronological order, with hit counts for each year.

4. The "Lizard" refers to the southernmost tip of Cornwall, in England.

5. Check the "Items in my library" box to make sure that you get the version of the record with which your library is associated. Although the ideal might be one record per title in WorldCat, the reality is that there are often several records for the same title, because participating libraries have cataloged the item slightly differently.

7
Humanities Databases

Although people come to librarianship with all kinds of different backgrounds and with many different undergraduate degrees, from purely anecdotal evidence it seems to me that there is still a preponderance of people with undergraduate degrees in the humanities who enter the library field (or am I imagining that large sigh of relief among you readers, now that we've arrived at the humanities chapter?). In any event, it's likely you'll find the two databases considered here, *America: History and Life*,[1] and the *MLA International Bibliography*, to be interesting, easy to use, and a fascinating window into their respective disciplines.

As with MEDLINE and the *Web of Science* in chapter 5, in *MLA* we have an excellent example of a database structured specifically for its subject matter. What is uniquely important to *MLA* and its users are attributes of written (and other forms of) communication: genres, themes, influences, etc., all of which are supported in *MLA* records, and very clearly reflected in the version of the *MLA* database described here. In *America: History and Life*, we have an excellent example of a familiar interface (EBSCO) that has been customized just enough to take advantage of the unique content and fields available in this particular database.

We will observe some disciplinary differences between the two resources in their approach to languages and dates. In the history database, it is sufficient to have the usual single field for language of publication. In the literature database, however, language of publication and language as the *subject* of the publication are equally important and are supported by two distinct fields. For historians, this kind of distinction arises around dates: *when* something happened is part of a publication's content and needs to be distinguished from when the item was published. Thus, two fields: one, a special-purpose field to specify the historical period discussed in the publication, and the other, the usual date-of-publication limit field. The *MLA International Bibliography* also has the usual publication date limit field and a separate field for the period being discussed, but their set of "Period" values (a browsable index list) reveals a rather different mind-set about dates. As in chapter 5, while we work through these two resources, in addition to absorbing information about functionality and content, try to be alert to aspects of each database that seem specially designed to support its subject discipline.

America: History and Life

Background and Coverage

America: History and Life (AHL), and its complement, *Historical Abstracts* for world history, were the flagship products of ABC-CLIO, originally a family-owned company devoted to history and social studies reference products. In 2007, these two databases were acquired by EBSCO, and by July 2008 were available solely through that interface. Gail Golderman, writing for *Library Journal* in November 2008, described AHL as "the definitive bibliographic reference covering the history, culture, area studies, and current affairs literature of the United States and Canada, from prehistory to the present" whose content and functionality "has only gotten better since being acquired by EBSCO" (Golderman 2008). The introduction of *America: History and Life Full Text* in 2010 provides continuing evidence that this is so.

In terms of scope and coverage, the journal list for AHL included 1,825 titles as of June 2011. Analysis of the list shows that coverage for a few journals extends back into the 1800s and early 1900s, with the majority of the coverage starting in the 1950s and beyond. In addition to articles, book and media reviews, relevant dissertations, and, most recently, eBooks, discussing any period of American and Canadian history from prehistory to the present, are eligible for inclusion. The database is updated monthly, and approximately 16,000 entries are added per year.

Although EBSCO also offers a full-text version of AHL, we will be working with the A&I (abstracting and indexing) version of the database: it contains citations, most with abstracts that are written by staff members or supplied by authors, and some full text. As with most database products, there is an increasing emphasis on adding as much full text as possible (even in a version not specifically named "Full Text"), so we will see records offering HTML or PDF full text. EBSCO is able to do this by drawing full text from its other databases (if you also subscribe to those databases) and by working with JSTOR. The database can also be configured to help users get to other sources of full text via linking systems. A combination of these history indexes, a subscription to the full-text journal archive service JSTOR, and a linking technology would be very powerful and convenient for users.

Notes and Search Examples

If you subscribe to both *America: History and Life* and *Historical Abstracts*, you can configure your EBSCO links to search both databases at once, or each one separately. The following scenarios are based on searching AHL by itself.

Advanced Search Interface

The Advanced Search screen (Figure 7.1) should look familiar, because it is similar to the interface for *MasterFILE Premier* introduced in chapter 2. Running through our usual mental checklist of the Searcher's Toolkit, it's easy

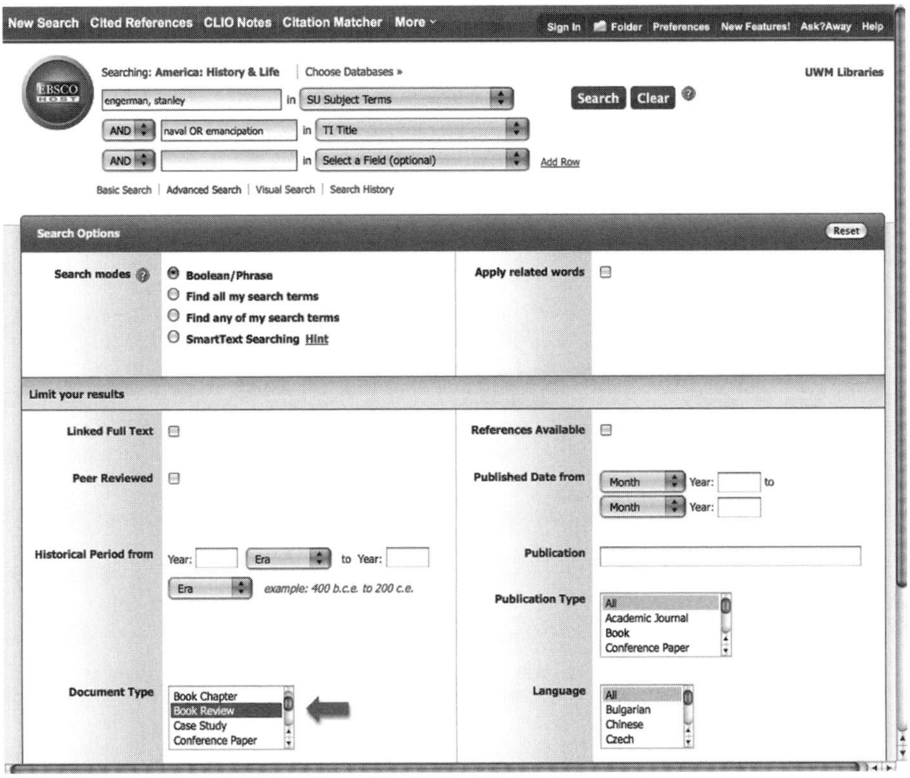

Fig. 7.1. Advanced Search screen, showing search strategy to find book reviews. ©
2011 EBSCO Industries, Inc. All rights reserved.

to see we have field searching, Boolean operators, and limits—including several special-purpose limits we didn't see in the *MasterFILE* interface. Looking back up at the very top of the screen, rather than one combined list of
Subjects, as in *MasterFILE*, in this database we have access to Indexes. We
can infer that we will be able to browse the values for several distinct fields,
as in WorldCat. (We will address the two other interesting options, Cited
References and CLIO Notes, a little later in this section.) Figure 7.1 shows
the screen set up to run a search that demonstrates one of the common uses
of this database.

Search Example 1: Finding Book Reviews

In this search example, we'd like to find reviews of two of Stanley Engerman's books, *Naval Blockades in Peace and War* and *Slavery, Emancipation,
and Freedom*. Since we are looking for material that is, in a sense, *about* this
person, we enter his name directory style (last name, first name) in the Subject Terms field, enter keywords from the two titles we are interested in
(ORed together) in the Title field, and select "Book Review" as our document
type from the Limits area (see arrow in the figure). Our search is ready, as
shown in Figure 7.1.

Our results appear to be right on target, judging by the first three records shown in Figure 7.2 (the left- and right-side result screen panels have
been closed in this shot to fit more records into one image).

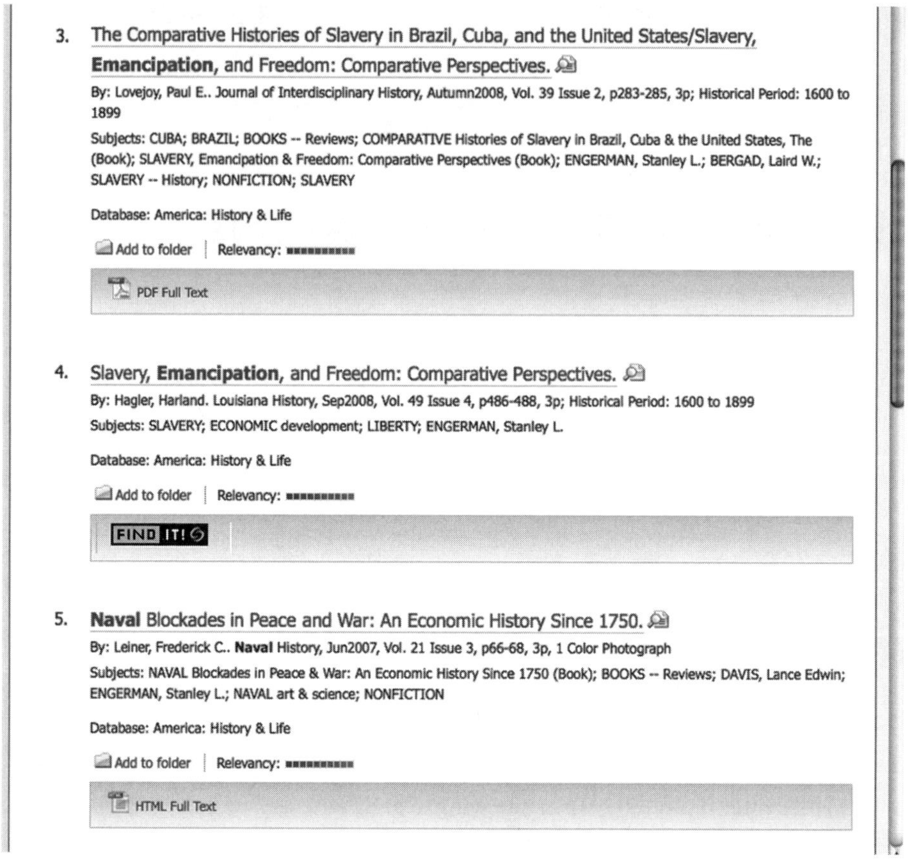

Fig. 7.2. Initial results for book review search (partial screen). © 2011 EBSCO Industries, Inc. All rights reserved.

There are some things to understand about this search: in the case of a book review, since the title of the book being reviewed almost always appears as at least part of the title of the review article, you can specify that your keywords (from the title of the book or books you are interested in) be searched in the Title field. (You can, of course, also search them simply as keywords, e.g., do not select a field.) But the *author* of the books must be searched as a Subject, not as an Author. If I wanted to find book reviews *by* Professor Engerman (and he is a prolific reviewer), then I would search his name, again directory style, against the Author field and simply apply the Book Review document-type limit. Try that and see how many you get.

Search Example 2: Finding Material about a Topic in a Particular Period

In this search, we want to produce a list of references to works about organized crime during Prohibition, that is, the period from 1920 to 1933 when the Volstead Act was in effect. Now we get to use the Historical Period limit field, with its "Era" drop-down menu for specifying "b.c.e. (BC)" or "c.e. (AD)."[2] Figure 7.3 shows relevant parts of the search screen set up for this search.

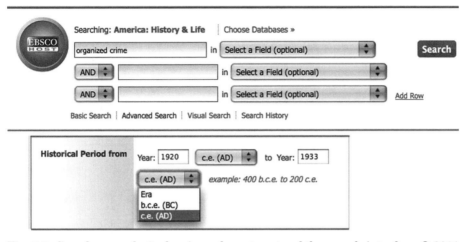

Fig. 7.3. Search example 2, showing relevant parts of the search interface. © 2011 EBSCO Industries, Inc. All rights reserved.

In the results screen for this search (pictured in Figure 7.4A and B), we have many options for further adjusting our results. The search interface stays with us, which is always useful for adding more terms or changing a search without having to go back to a search screen. On the left side, we have the (by now) familiar "Refine your results"[3] panel full of handy options and information. We could immediately limit these results to just those with full text, those that have a list of references included, or those that are peer reviewed. Using the input fields or the slider bar, we could limit just to records with a more recent Publication Date. Just below that, the "Show more>>" link would superimpose the full limit interface over the current screen (a functionality known as an Ajax window), so we never need to fully leave the current screen.

Scrolling down to see the rest of the Refine panel (Figure 7.4B), we find options to limit by Source Type, such as Academic Journals, and/or by adding a Subject heading to the original search (it turns out that "Organized crime" is actually a subject heading. Good!). Clicking any of the options in the Refine panel brings up an Ajax window to put the change into effect, as shown by the second window in the Figure 7.4B screenshot.

In all cases, if you don't like the new results, it's very easy to get back to your original list: All the limits you've chosen are listed at the top of the Refine panel. They can be removed from the search criteria by just clicking the X icon associated with them (Figure 7.5).

Figure 7.6 shows the top of the list of results, where you will find more options for customizing how you want to view your records ("A"). There are choices for Sorting, how many records are displayed on a Page, and a whole set of options under Alert / Save / Share, as shown in the figure. Most of the records provide an abstract, and all provide their Subjects, right on the results screen. This causes the display to be longer but reduces the number of clicks needed to decide whether a result is relevant or not (as well as providing many more opportunities to learn new terms you might employ in your search). If available, article results include the number of Cited References in the article ("B" in Figure 7.6); clicking the linked number displays the references (shades of the *Web of Science*!).

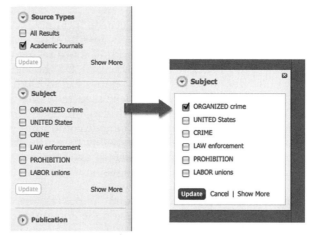

Fig. 7.4a. Initial results screen for search example 2. © 2011 EBSCO Industries, Inc. All rights reserved.

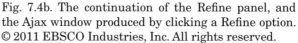

Fig. 7.4b. The continuation of the Refine panel, and the Ajax window produced by clicking a Refine option. © 2011 EBSCO Industries, Inc. All rights reserved.

Search Example 3: Searching Cited References

The ability to search cited references ("Who has cited Joe Blogg's classic paper/book lately?") is new with EBSCO's hosting of AHL. Citations are as important to historians as to the scientists in Thompson Reuter's *Web of Science*, and it's exciting to see another database vendor tackling this labor-intensive issue.

Here's our example for this search: We'd like to see publications that have cited Doris Kearns Goodwin's *No Ordinary Time: Franklin and Eleanor Roosevelt: The Home Front in World War II*, published in 1994. Clicking Cited References in the top bar, we get the search interface shown in Figure 7.7. The interface is set up to run our cited reference search with Goodwin, Doris Kearns in the Cited Author field, and the beginning of her book's

Fig. 7.5. Top of the Refine panel, showing limits applied. Clicking the X icon removes the limit. © 2011 EBSCO Industries, Inc. All rights reserved.

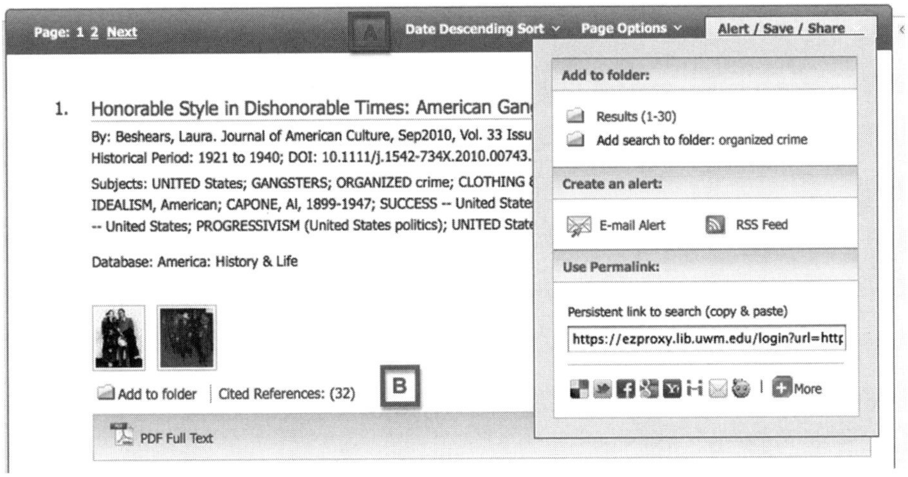

Fig. 7.6. More results list features. © 2011 EBSCO Industries, Inc. All rights reserved.

title in the Cited Title field. (Why no year? Well, the hardcover appeared in 1994, the paperback edition appeared in 1995, followed by audio and Kindle editions—we don't really care which edition, so we'll leave it open.)

This search already feels very different from the Cited Reference searching in the *Web of Science*—no constraints on how the name is entered, no agonizing about how a title (referring to a book or an article title) or a Source (which could again be a book title or the name of a journal) are abbreviated or entered: simply enter the initial words, or even a keyword. Now look at the results screen; the first three records are pictured in Figure 7.8.

We can enter full words because the citation records contain full words.[4] Amazing!

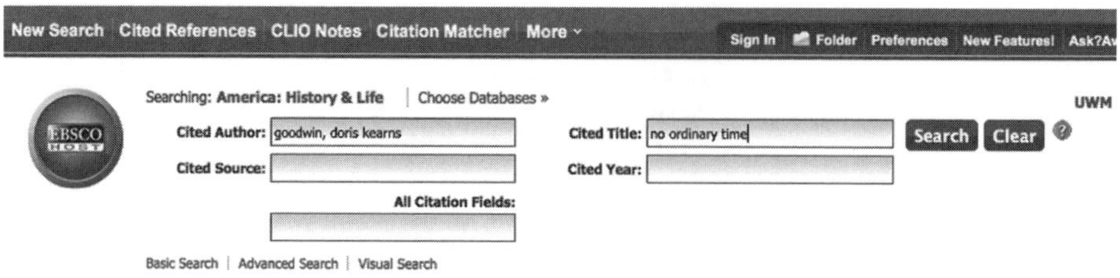

Fig. 7.7. Cited reference search interface, set to run search example 3. © 2011 EBSCO Industries, Inc. All rights reserved.

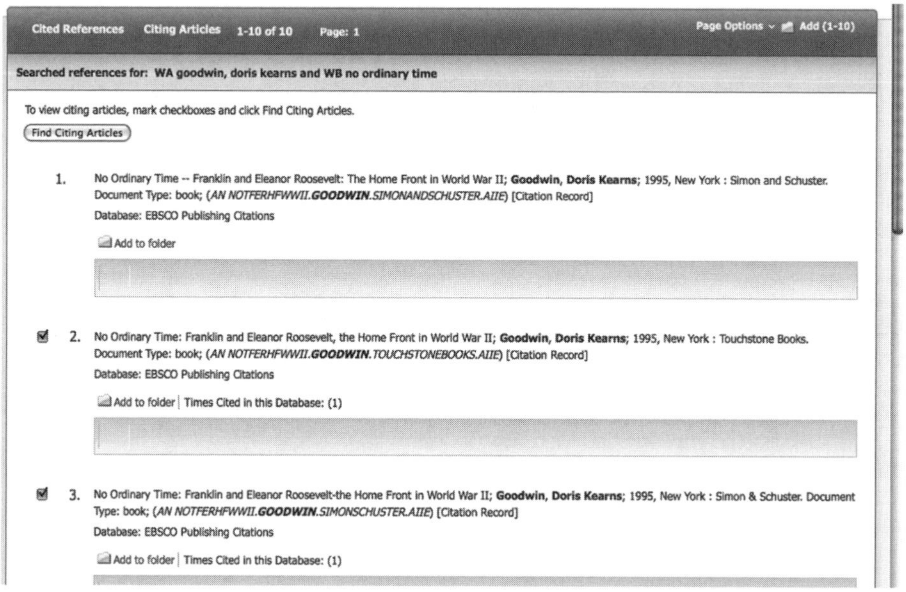

Fig. 7.8. Cited References search results display. © 2011 EBSCO Industries, Inc. All rights reserved.

Using the check boxes to select all the records that have citing articles, we click the Find Citing Articles button and arrive at a screen of seven results. The top of this screen is shown in Figure 7.9. We are reminded of how the whole process started by the presence of the search interface at the top of the screen, and the reminder just above the records: "These records cite: WA goodwin, doris kearns and WB no ordinary time." (WA and WB are field codes.) We can toggle between the Cited References and the Citing Articles using the links in the bar between the search interface and the results list.

Now that the results include the abstract and the Subject terms, the display is too long to show in one screenshot, but I cannot resist giving you a sense of the fascinating, scholarly material available in this database. Here are the other titles in this set of seven, followed by the number of cited references each one has in parentheses:

1. "The Guiding Spirit": Philip Loeb, The Battle for Television Jurisdiction, and the Broadcasting Industry Blacklist. (126)

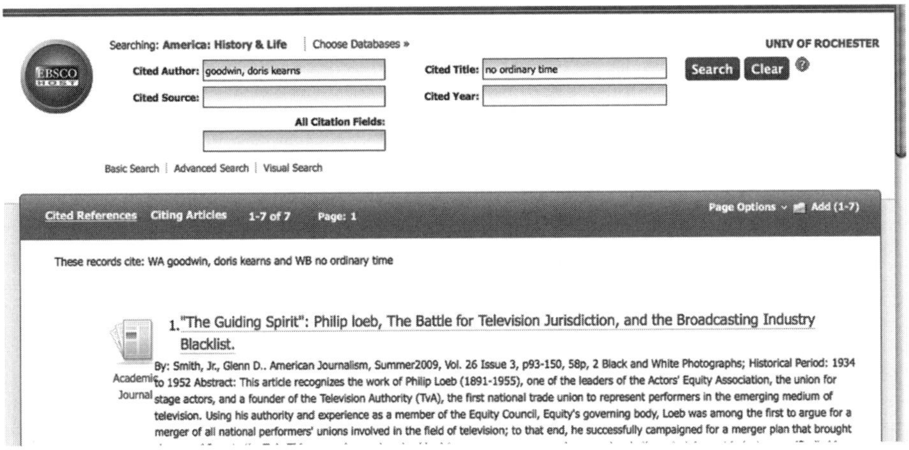

Fig. 7.9. The beginning of the Citing Articles for search example 3. © 2011 EBSCO Industries, Inc. All rights reserved.

2. Westbrook Pegler, Eleanor Roosevelt, and the FBI. (60)

3. Broken Circle: The Isolation of Franklin D. Roosevelt in World War II. (95)

4. Preparing for a National Emergency: The Committee on Conservation of Cultural Resources, 1939–1944. (44)

5. Queer Hoover: Sex, Lies, and Political History. (109)

6. Race, Roosevelt, and Wartime Production: Fair Employment in World War II Labor Markets. (30)

7. Oral history and the story of America and World War II. (30)

Using just two bits of information about a work, we have found seven newer articles in this database that are related (and yet going in interesting new research directions), all of very high scholarship judging by the number of cited references (one of which is, of course, to Goodwin's book). To me, there is nothing quite like cited reference searching for producing intriguing and unexpected results.

It's time we stopped to look at a full citation, to see how to collect and output records for our own research and bibliographies.

Many Tools: Folder, Output Options, and More

The Records Folder

A full record display is shown in Figure 7.10. In addition to the detailed record itself, you can see that the left- and right-side panels offer a wealth of options. On the left, in this case we do get a link to the PDF of the full text, a link to the Cited References, and the option to "Find Similar Results" using SmartText searching.[5] In the right panel you have a plethora of tools for outputting, citing, and reusing this record, discussed in more detail later.

In EBSCO databases, you collect the records that you're interested in by adding them to a "folder." Your opportunities for adding items to this folder

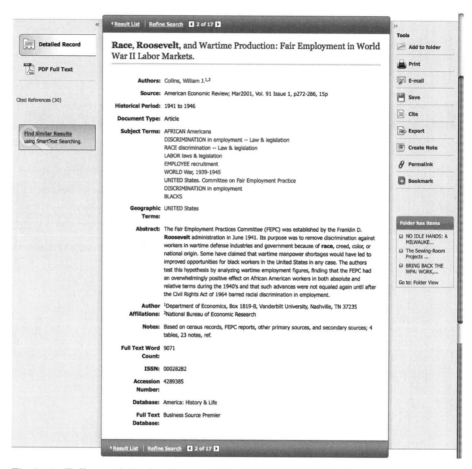

Fig. 7.10. Full record display for an article. © 2011 EBSCO Industries, Inc. All rights reserved.

are conveniently placed: in the results screen, each result has an Add to folder link, and in each full record the Add to folder icon appears first in the right panel, as in Figure 7.10. As you add items to the Folder, the latest three added are displayed in the right-hand panel, under the bar marked "Folder has items."

Output Options

Continuing down the right panel, on an individual full-record screen, you can print, email, save, see how to cite (in seven popular formats), or export the record to a citation manager program, as indicated by the icons in Figure 7.10. The Cite icon again uses a technology that superimposes a new screen over the current one (Ajax, as shown in Figure 7.4b). This technique saves a great deal of screen loading/refreshing time, and it leaves you right where you were when the superimposed screen is closed. The Export function now offers seven different formats, including XML, BibTex, and MARC21, as well as the more familiar RefWorks and EndNote. For extended research projects, you again have the ability to create a personal account with the database and add your own notes on records (Create note), obtain a perma-

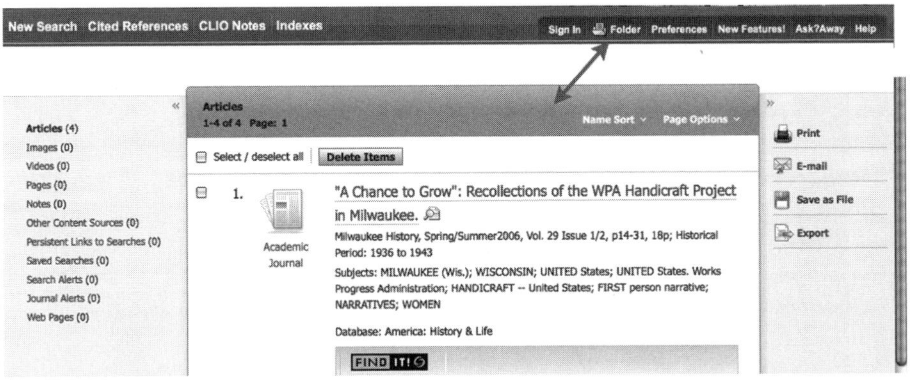

Fig. 7.11. Significant parts of the Folder interface: access link and display. © 2011 EBSCO Industries, Inc. All rights reserved.

nent link (Permalink) to the record, or share it via various social networking sites (Bookmark).

To output a group of records, you'll need to have added them in the Folder and then work from the Folder view (Figure 7.11). The Folder is accessed by the link in the topmost bar of the interface (indicated by the arrow in Figure 7.11). The options to print, email, save, or export to a citation management program are again available here, for all or selected records in the Folder.

The Folder includes detailed information about the types of materials that you've put in it (on the right), and you can retain your Folder items from session to session by creating a "My EBSCOhost" account; again, there is an emphasis on personalization and ongoing research.

Last, a word about the email function. The email interface lets you send to multiple recipients, specify the Subject line, and add comments. In addition, you can choose a standard format, a specific citation format, or create your own format by choosing exactly which fields you wish to send. The only drawback with the email program, as of the time of this writing, is that it does not allow you to fill in the "from" field; it is fixed at the vendor's address (which might cause a recipient to think it is spam).

Special Feature: CLIO Notes

You may have been wondering what in the world "CLIO Notes" is: if you click this option in the topmost bar, you'll be presented with a series of historical periods demarcated and named by the original database creators. Diving into any of these reveals a list of defining aspects of the era (such as Labor and Corporations, Grassroots Reform, Theodore Roosevelt, etc. for "The Progressive Era") and further topics associated with each of those aspects, as shown in the left panel of Figure 7.12. Clicking on any topic provides a useful, fairly brief essay, suggested research questions, and appropriate Subject headings for researching the topics; part of such a screen is shown in the right panel of Figure 7.12. It's an "I don't know what to write about" student's dream!

Quick Recap

America: History and Life (AHL), and its complement, *Historical Abstracts*, are the leading indexes to the literature of history. AHL provides

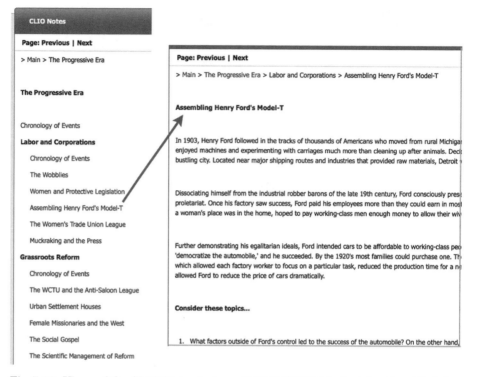

Fig. 7.12. Views of the CLIO Notes feature. © 2011 EBSCO Industries, Inc. All rights reserved.

indexing, abstracts, and some full text for articles as well as indexing for book and media reviews and dissertations. The scope of AHL is any period of American and Canadian history from prehistory to the present; *Historical Abstracts* covers the rest of the world. The Advanced Search interface offers field searching and limits, including the special purpose "Historical Period" limit. AHL offers a Cited References search that is friendlier to use but smaller in scale than that of the *Web of Science*. There are many options for changing the search on the Results screen, all easily reversible. Output of multiple records is done by adding them to the Folder and processing them from there. The output options are well developed, including good email features and output to citation management programs. Unique to the *America: History and Life* and *Historical Abstracts* databases is the CLIO Notes feature, which provides historically and thematically structured access to a wealth of research paper suggestions.

MLA International Bibliography

Background and Coverage

The *MLA International Bibliography* is produced by the Modern Language Association of America (MLA), and is one of the longest-running indexes still in existence. The Association itself was founded in 1883 and began publishing a printed index in 1921. This printed index was discontinued in 2009. The online database includes the indexing of records back to 1926; the addition of records for JSTOR journals has extended coverage for certain titles back to the 1880s,[6] however, providing another example of an electronic product that has expanded beyond its print counterpart (MLA 2010). In a situation similar to that at the National Library of Medicine, the staff of the MLA's Department of Bibliographic Information Services work with outside bibliographers from around the world to produce the *Bibliography* (ProQuest 2011a). It is a huge cooperative effort.

The *MLA International Bibliography* (MLA IB) is vast in many ways: the scope of topics included, sources, document types, number of records, and publication dates. Topical coverage is described broadly as "all forms of human communication": literature, folklore (including music and art), the study of linguistics and languages, literary theory and criticism, the dramatic arts, and the history of printing and publishing. Coverage of the "history, theory, and practice of teaching language, literature, and rhetoric and composition" from 1998 onward was added to the scope of the MLA IB in 2000 (MLA 2010). Over 100,000 subject-indexed records, representing the entire runs of the journals in JSTOR's Language and Literature collection, have been added to the index, extending the coverage of such journals as *Modern Language Notes* and *Publications of the Modern Language Association* (PMLA) back as far as the 1880s (ProQuest 2011a). As indicated in the title, sources from all over the world are reviewed for entry into the database. (The "Language of Publication" thesaurus list is probably the longest and most esoteric you will ever encounter.) Document types covered include types that you would expect, such as books, book chapters, and journal articles, but also indexed are reference works, published working papers, conference papers and proceedings, citations for dissertations listed in *Dissertations Abstracts International*, electronic publications, and works related to teaching—handbooks, textbooks, anthologies, etc. Note, however, that one common type of document that is *not* included is reviews (ProQuest 2011a).

The numbers for the MLA IB are equally impressive: there are "over 2.3 million records" in the database, and "over 66,000 citations" have been added each year since 2002. Subject terms used to describe records come from the *MLA Thesaurus*, which includes "over 49,000 topical terms and 327,000 names" (MLA 2010). A database about literature is, obviously, very concerned with names: the names of writers and of characters.

The MLA IB is the first database that we've encountered in this book that is purely an index. Full records are quite long owing to the number of fields included, but there are no abstracts.[7] On the other hand, opportunities for getting directly to full text are increasing: If your institution also subscribes to JSTOR and Project MUSE, your MLA IB subscription can be configured to include links to full text in those two databases. And as we have seen in other databases, the MLA IB is OpenURL compliant: It supports linking technologies for getting to full text in other sources as well. It is also possible to run the MLA IB in concert with, or as a module in, a full-text database called *Literature Online* (LION), as described briefly in the section that follows.

Relationship to Other Literature Resources

Any discussion of the MLA IB should also mention two other major literature resources: the *Annual Bibliography of English Language and Literature* (ABELL) and the previously mentioned *Literature Online* (LION). ABELL has a somewhat smaller scope than MLA IB in that it focuses on just English language materials and literature in English. ABELL also includes book reviews, unlike MLA IB. LION, the only full-text database of the three, also focuses on English literature, and it provides the texts of over 357,000 literary works, along with criticism and reference resources. At this time, Chadwyck-Healey, the specialist humanities imprint of ProQuest, is the sole publisher for LION and is also a supplier of ABELL. When the MLA IB was added to the set of Chadwyck-Healey databases, it became possible for sub-scribers to all three databases from this vendor to opt for integrated access using LION as the single point of access for all three literature databases—a very powerful combination (ProQuest 2011b). For the purposes of this chap-ter, however, we will consider the MLA IB as a stand-alone database.

Notes and Search Examples

Any consideration of humanities databases needs to look at the MLA IB, but the question then is: from which vendor? At the time of this writing, three database vendors are offering the MLA's database. (The MLA provides a very informative and helpful chart about the distributors of their database at http://www.mla.org/bib_dist_comparison.) I have chosen to look at Pro-Quest's Chadwyck-Healey version, because the interface seems to be nicely tuned to the subject matter,[8] and the possible integration with other data-bases (described earlier) is quite compelling. Let's take a look.

Standard Search Interface

The MLA IB as offered by Chadwyck-Healey provides three search in-terfaces: Standard, Advanced, and Directory of Periodicals. We'll work with the first two here; notes about the Directory of Periodicals appear under "Additional Feature" later in this chapter. The Standard Search (Figure 7.13) offers support for the kinds of searches users might need most often: a straight topical search (using Keyword[s], Title Keyword[s], or Subject—All), the ever-popular search for literary criticism or interpretation (Author as Subject, Author's Work), and the need to fill out a citation from incomplete information (using a combination of Keyword, Article Author, Journal, and Publication Year). If we are mentally ticking things off on our Searcher's Toolkit list, the ability to use Boolean operators is not obvious, although we assume that it's there. The "Help" confirms this, along with supplying information about the other tools we're used to looking for, such as proximity operators and wild-cards. There is an implied AND between fields on a page. A set of document types appears explicitly labeled Limit to; other fields commonly used as lim-its are also available: Language of Publication and Publication Year. Note too all the fields with a "select from a list" or "select from thesaurus" link: In all, this version of MLA offers a total of 29 searchable fields, 24 of which have searchable index lists of values. The ability to explore all the possible values for specific fields is something we are seeing less often in databases (WorldCat via FirstSearch is the only comparable one in this book), so this is rather special.

Search Example 1: A Subject–Keyword Search

Our first search example is a topic that receives continuing attention from the literary community: examples of the use of cross-dressing in the works of Shakespeare. Figure 7.13 shows our search ready to be run.

Just the first six results for this search (Figure 7.14) start to demon-strate the breadth of coverage, in terms of document types and international reach, of this database. Represented are two chapters from edited books, two

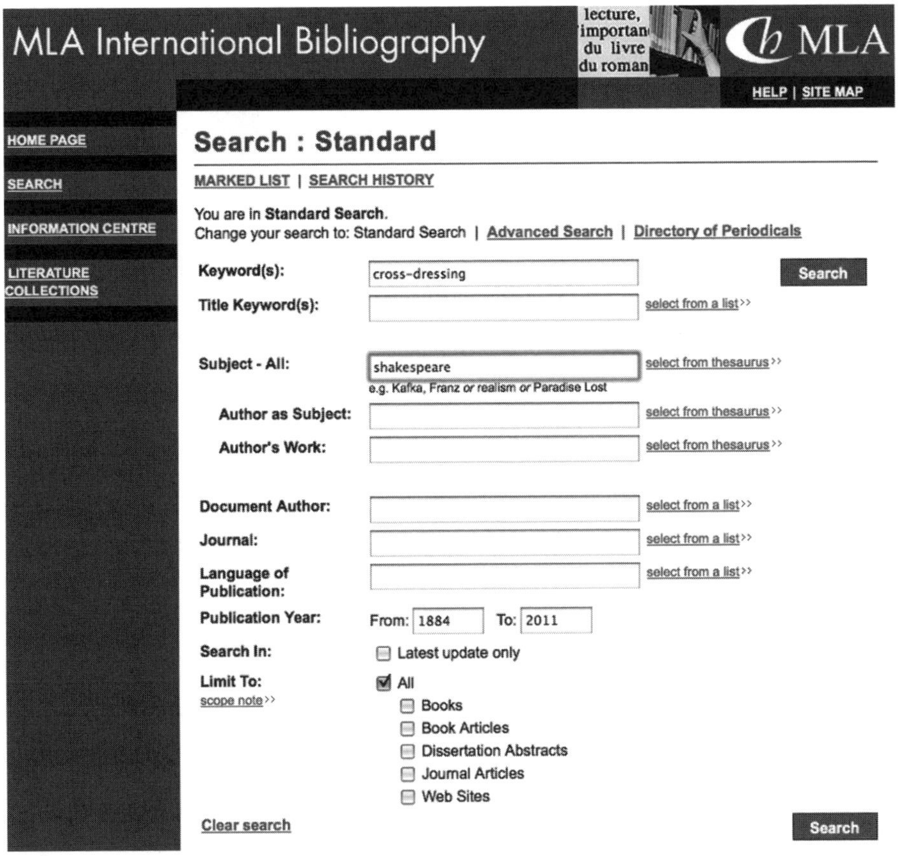

Fig. 7.13. Chadwyck-Healey MLA Standard Search Interface. The screen shots and their contents are published with permission of ProQuest LLC. Further reproduction is prohibited without permission.

dissertations, an article from a theater journal, and an article from a Chinese literary journal. Farther down the list you would see entries for books, records for articles and books in French, German, Romanian and Spanish, and an electronic journal article.

There are two additional points to notice about the results screen:

- First, several of these results have been selected in the usual way, by clicking their check boxes. These entries are automatically added to the Marked List; if you view a full record or page forward in the results, you won't lose your marked items.

- Second, the system reports that the search retrieved "70 entries" and "90 hits." The entries count refers to the total number of citations, or records. The second, larger hits count measures the number of times that search terms appeared in records. A record in which a search term appears more than once causes the hit count to increase.

The Full Record display in Figure 7.15 should begin to give you a sense of the detailed indexing performed on records in the MLA IB, and the degree to which the record structure in this version of the database supports and makes explicit the subject fields. In this record alone there are 13 subject

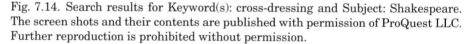

Use the checkboxes to add/remove individual records from a Marked List. From the Marked List you can email, download, print or save your selection of records.

Select all records on this page | Clear all records on this page

☑ 1   Camilleri, Anna: "The Androgynous Antics of Byron and the Bard"
       In (pp. 67-80) Cochran, Peter (ed. and introd.) , Byron and Women (and Men).
       Newcastle upon Tyne, England: Cambridge Scholars, 2010. lxix, 302 pp.. (2010)
       Find@UR

☐ 2   Craig, Susan: "'Show Me...Like a Queen': A Study of the 'New' Globe Theatre's Cross-
       Dressed Productions of 'Antony and Cleopatra' (1999) and 'Twelfth Night, or What You
       Will' (2002)"
       Dissertation Abstracts International, Section A: The Humanities and Social Sciences,
       (71:5) 2010 Nov, 1499. Drew U, 2010. DA3407080 . (2010)
       Find@UR

☐ 3   Thomas, Chad Allen: "On Queering Twelfth Night"
       Theatre Topics, (20:2), 2010 Sept, 101-111. (2010)
       Find@UR

☐ 4   Thomas, Chad Allen: "Performing Queer Shakespeare"
       Dissertation Abstracts International, Section A: The Humanities and Social Sciences,
       (71:2) 2010 Aug, 573. U of Michigan, 2009. DA3392942 . (2010)
       Find@UR

☑ 5   Baumgärtel, Stephan: "Body Politics between Sublimation and Subversion: Critical
       Perspectives on Twentieth-Century All-Male Performances of Shakespeare's As You
       Like It"
       In (pp. 248-269) Bradshaw, Graham (ed.); Bishop, Tom (ed.); Wright, Laurence (guest
       ed. and introd.) , The Shakespearean International Yearbook 9: Special Section, South
       African Shakespeare in the Twentieth Century. Farnham, England: Ashgate, 2009. vii,
       301 pp.. (Farnham, England: Shakespearean International Yearbook 9). (2009)
       Find@UR

☑ 6   Cheang, Wai Fong: "A Crossdressed Judith Shakespeare?-Reconceptualizing the
       Representation of Women's Predicaments in Three Contemporary Shakespeare-related
       Movies"
       Wenshan Review of Literature and Culture, (2:2), 2009 June, 71-103 (Chinese
       summary; English summary.). (2009)

Fig. 7.14. Search results for Keyword(s): cross-dressing and Subject: Shakespeare. The screen shots and their contents are published with permission of ProQuest LLC. Further reproduction is prohibited without permission.

fields, including eight Literary Feature fields, two Period fields, the Author as Subject field we used in our search, and so forth. (For an even more dramatic example, take a look at the record for "A Crossdressed Judith Shakespeare?"—it has 33 Subject fields associated with it!)

Two Additional Search Samples

Returning to the Standard Search screen, we see an example of a type of search that students frequently need to do, but frequently do incorrectly, in the partial screenshot in Figure 7.16. Students are used to searching for authors as authors, but when they need to find analysis or discussion *about* an author, they often fail to grasp that they must now search the author's name as a Subject. The "Author as Subject" field in the Standard Search screen is helpful for addressing this need.

Figure 7.17 is very similar, demonstrating a strategy for finding materials that discuss a specific work by an author. It also provides the opportunity for a discussion of non-English names.

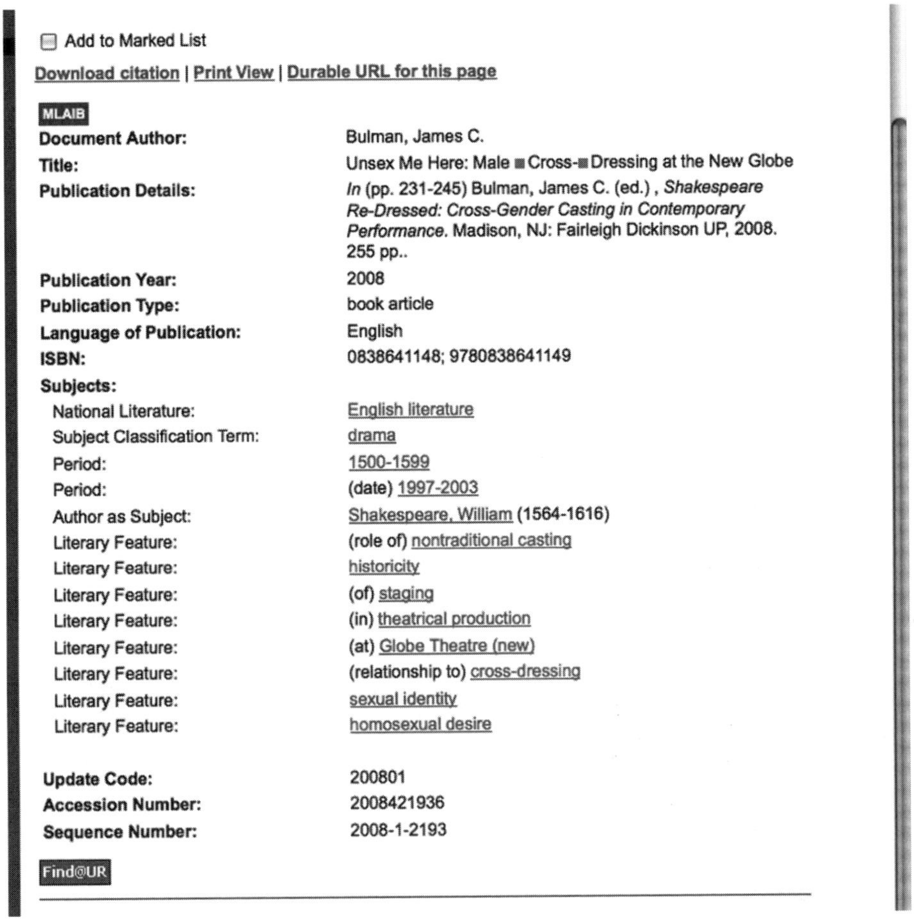

☐ Add to Marked List

Download citation | Print View | Durable URL for this page

MLAIB

Document Author:	Bulman, James C.
Title:	Unsex Me Here: Male ■ Cross-■ Dressing at the New Globe
Publication Details:	*In* (pp. 231-245) Bulman, James C. (ed.) , *Shakespeare Re-Dressed: Cross-Gender Casting in Contemporary Performance*. Madison, NJ: Fairleigh Dickinson UP, 2008. 255 pp..
Publication Year:	2008
Publication Type:	book article
Language of Publication:	English
ISBN:	0838641148; 9780838641149
Subjects:	
National Literature:	English literature
Subject Classification Term:	drama
Period:	1500-1599
Period:	(date) 1997-2003
Author as Subject:	Shakespeare, William (1564-1616)
Literary Feature:	(role of) nontraditional casting
Literary Feature:	historicity
Literary Feature:	(of) staging
Literary Feature:	(in) theatrical production
Literary Feature:	(at) Globe Theatre (new)
Literary Feature:	(relationship to) cross-dressing
Literary Feature:	sexual identity
Literary Feature:	homosexual desire
Update Code:	200801
Accession Number:	2008421936
Sequence Number:	2008-1-2193

Find@UR

Fig. 7.15. Full Record display from the cross-dressing search. The screen shots and their contents are published with permission of ProQuest LLC. Further reproduction is prohibited without permission.

Subject - All:		select from thesaurus ››
	e.g. Kafka, Franz *or* realism *or* Paradise Lost	
Author as Subject:	Bellow, Saul	select from thesaurus ››
Author's Work:		select from thesaurus ››

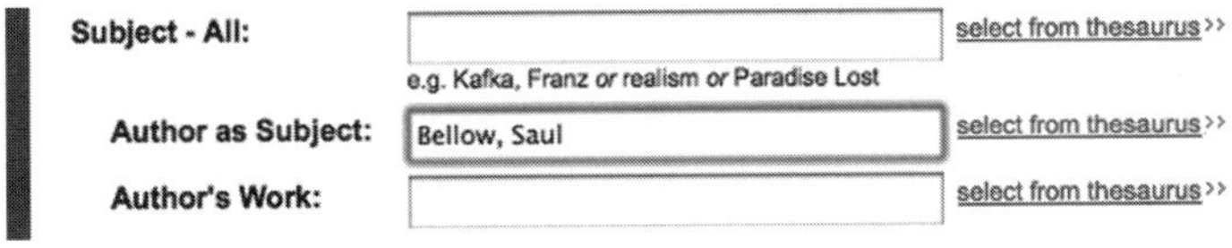

Fig. 7.16. Use of the Author as Subject field. The screen shots and their contents are published with permission of ProQuest LLC. Further reproduction is prohibited without permission.

Subject - All:		select from thesaurus ››
	e.g. Kafka, Franz *or* realism *or* Paradise Lost	
Author as Subject:	tolstoi	select from thesaurus ››
Author's Work:	"war and peace"	select from thesaurus ››

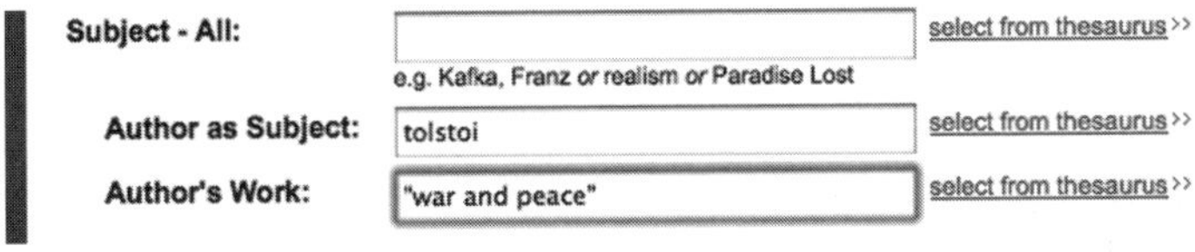

Fig. 7.17. Use of the Author as Subject and Author's Work fields. The screen shots and their contents are published with permission of ProQuest LLC. Further reproduction is prohibited without permission.

Non-English Names in the *Bibliography*

As has been pointed out several times, the scope of the *Bibliography* is international, and among those 327,000+ names in the Thesaurus are thousands of names from scores of nationalities, including names transliterated from non-Roman alphabets. For example, the MLA indexers prefer the spelling *Tolstoi*, not *Tolstoy*, for the author of *War and Peace*. The only problem is that if you look up Tolstoy in the Thesaurus, you will find it— but there is no "see" reference to guide you to the other spelling. To discover the Preferred Term, you need to select the entry Tolstoy, Leo, and then click the Related Terms button. Then you'll be told that the Preferred Term is: Tolstoi, Lev Nikolaevich. Working with Eastern European, Russian, and Chinese names (including place names) can be particularly tricky. For example, the controlled heading for the former leader of Communist China is *Mao Zedong*, not *Tse-tung, Mao*, or *Zedong, Mao*, forms and spellings that Westerners might be likely to try. If you can figure out a search that at least lets you see similar entries in the Thesaurus (for example, by searching on simply "mao" and then scanning), then you will see a listing for Mao Tse-tung that you can select, and *then* the Related Terms button will tell you that this is a "Nonpreferred Term(s)" and to use Mao Zedong instead. With so many names it is probably not realistic to ask the indexers to anticipate all the ways people

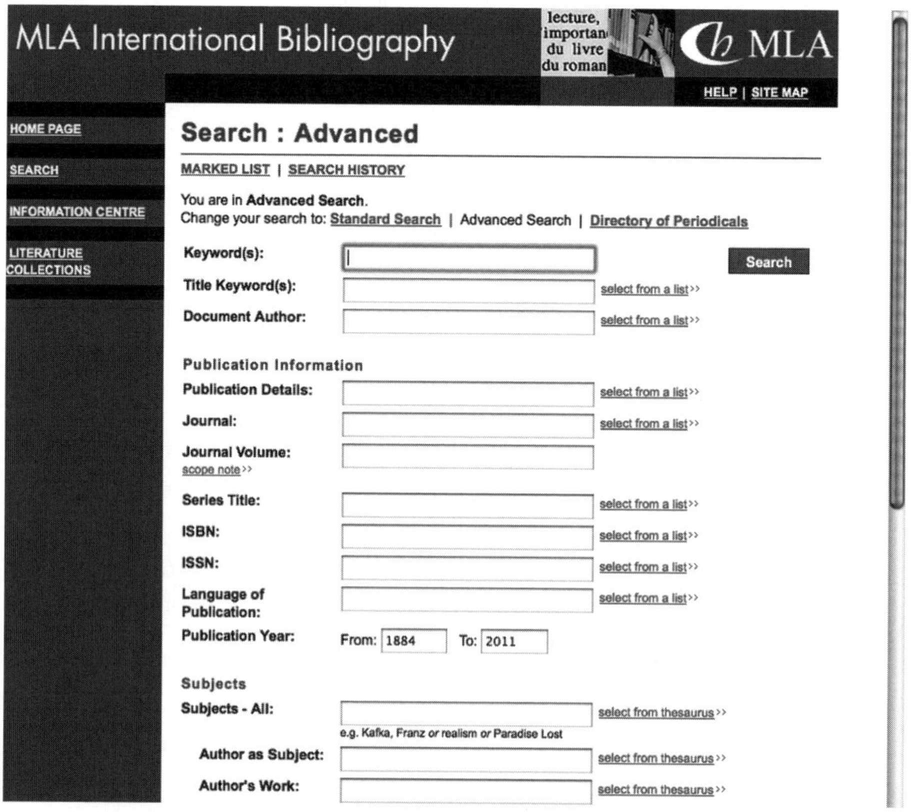

Fig. 7.18a. Advanced Search interface, upper half. The screen shots and their contents are published with permission of ProQuest LLC. Further reproduction is prohibited without permission.

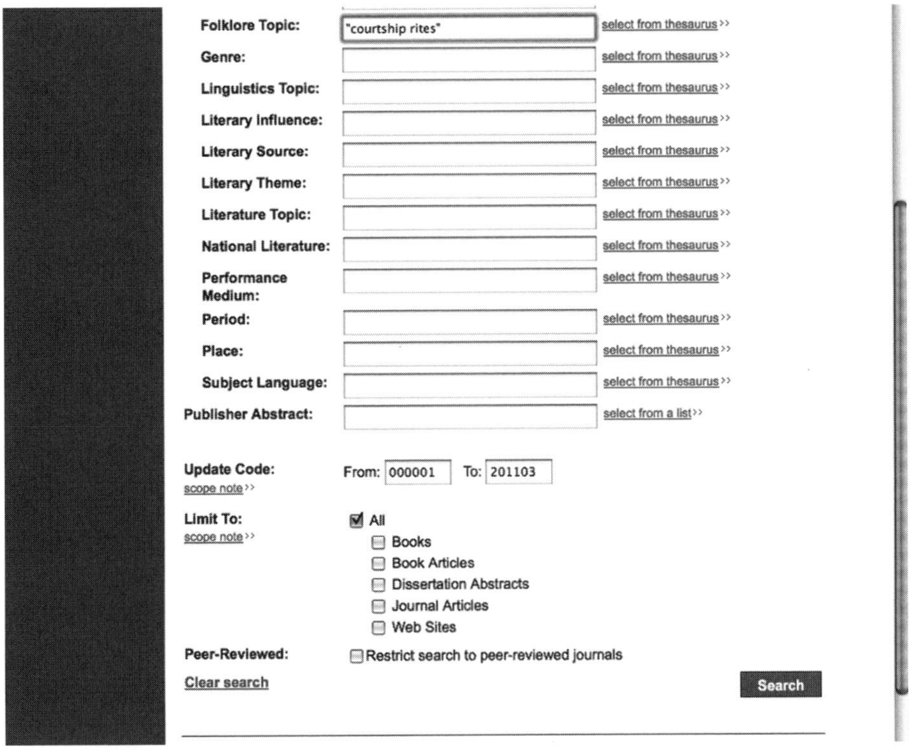

Fig. 7.18b. Advanced Search interface, lower half. The screen shots and their contents are published with permission of ProQuest LLC. Further reproduction is prohibited without permission.

might search for them, but getting the right version of a non-English name can be a bit tricky.

When working with names, be prepared to be flexible: use the Thesaurus if possible, but if the answer still isn't clear and you're getting frustrated, try searching the form of the name you're familiar with as Keyword(s), search parts of the name, or use truncation. You are likely to find records on the person you are after from a record where that form of the name appears in the title, and you can then see how that name is listed in the Subject fields of the record.

Advanced Search

Let us move on to the Advanced Search screen. Chadwyck-Healey has made a deliberate decision to display all the searchable database fields in a list rather than using drop-down menus. The advantage is that the number and names of all the fields are obvious at a glance; the disadvantage is that it does make for a rather long screen! Figures 7.18a and 7.18b provide the complete picture.

What a wealth of fields are available: every possible aspect of a publication has a searchable field, and now we see some of the other topical areas of this database being brought out, such as Folklore, Linguistics, and Performance. (I've left a search in the Folklore Topic field; we'll see a couple of results from that search later on.) Note that you can search by "Language of

Publication," but in keeping with the Linguistics aspect of this database, there is also a field to search by "Subject Language," that is, the language being discussed in the article. For example, you could find articles written in French on the Kumak language. Another Limit, for restricting to Peer-Reviewed journals, also appears on the Advanced Search screen.

Search Example 2: Finding Materials by Genre

Our search objective now is to find some materials discussing dystopias in the literatures of various countries. We could just type "dystopian" into the Genre field, but it's interesting and useful to see all of the possible headings that appear in the Thesaurus (Figure 7.19).

In the Thesaurus list for Genre we find "dystopian fiction" and "dystopian novel," which are both good. After checkmarking the desired headings, the Select button transfers the information to the Search screen, appropriately ORed together. Because the patron is interested in how dystopias are depicted across cultures, we will simply search for this Genre and see what this very international database can give us.

The first 5 of our 31 results for this search appear in Figure 7.20. Just within these results the international scope of this database is very evident, with records for works in Turkish and Russian. In this screen, some entries have again been selected to add to the Marked List, which already has some records from various other searches not depicted in the text. Let's see what that Marked List has accumulated.

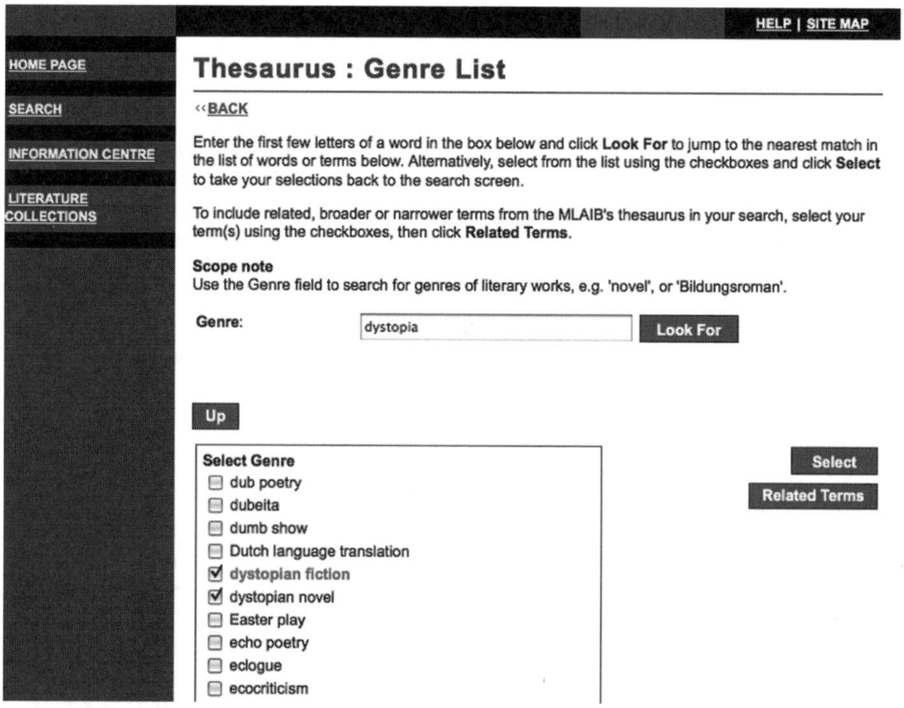

Fig. 7.19. The Genre List Thesaurus. The screen shots and their contents are published with permission of ProQuest LLC. Further reproduction is prohibited without permission.

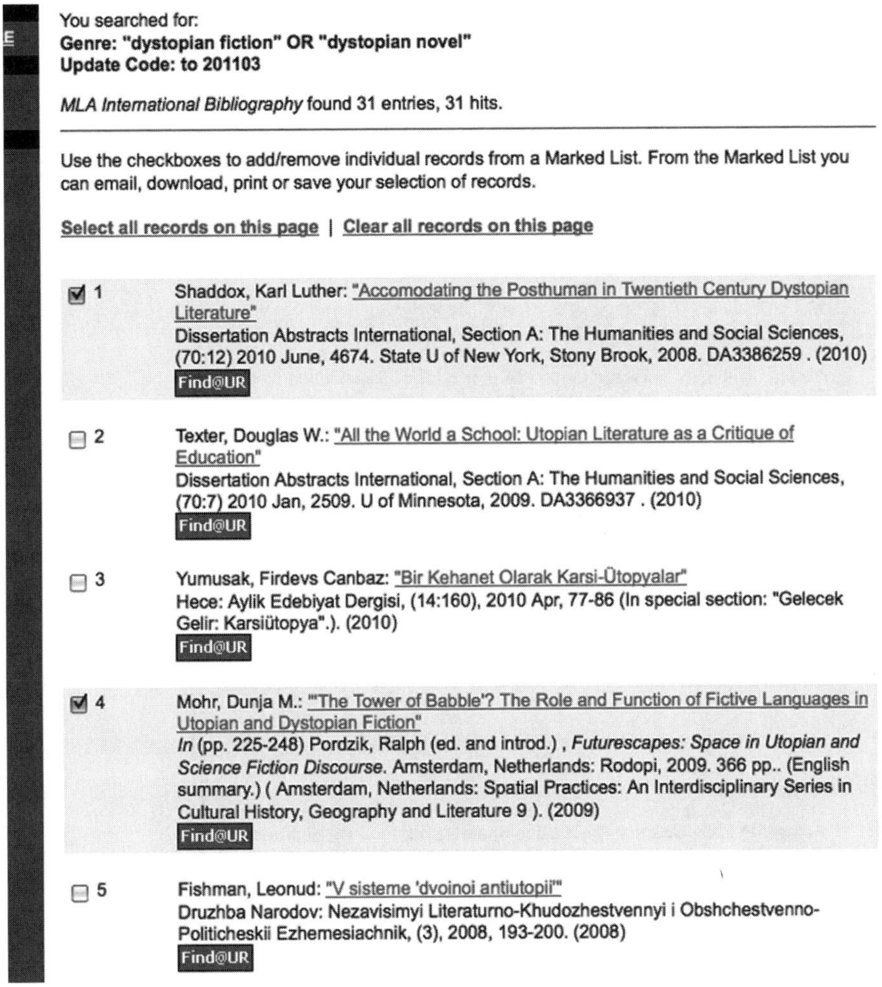

You searched for:
Genre: "dystopian fiction" OR "dystopian novel"
Update Code: to 201103

MLA International Bibliography found 31 entries, 31 hits.

Use the checkboxes to add/remove individual records from a Marked List. From the Marked List you can email, download, print or save your selection of records.

Select all records on this page | **Clear all records on this page**

☑ 1   Shaddox, Karl Luther: "Accomodating the Posthuman in Twentieth Century Dystopian Literature"
Dissertation Abstracts International, Section A: The Humanities and Social Sciences, (70:12) 2010 June, 4674. State U of New York, Stony Brook, 2008. DA3386259 . (2010)
`Find@UR`

☐ 2   Texter, Douglas W.: "All the World a School: Utopian Literature as a Critique of Education"
Dissertation Abstracts International, Section A: The Humanities and Social Sciences, (70:7) 2010 Jan, 2509. U of Minnesota, 2009. DA3366937 . (2010)
`Find@UR`

☐ 3   Yumusak, Firdevs Canbaz: "Bir Kehanet Olarak Karsi-Ütopyalar"
Hece: Aylik Edebiyat Dergisi, (14:160), 2010 Apr, 77-86 (In special section: "Gelecek Gelir: Karsiütopya".). (2010)
`Find@UR`

☑ 4   Mohr, Dunja M.: "'The Tower of Babble'? The Role and Function of Fictive Languages in Utopian and Dystopian Fiction"
In (pp. 225-248) Pordzik, Ralph (ed. and introd.) , *Futurescapes: Space in Utopian and Science Fiction Discourse.* Amsterdam, Netherlands: Rodopi, 2009. 366 pp.. (English summary.) (Amsterdam, Netherlands: Spatial Practices: An Interdisciplinary Series in Cultural History, Geography and Literature 9). (2009)
`Find@UR`

☐ 5   Fishman, Leonud: "V sisteme 'dvoinoi antiutopii'"
Druzhba Narodov: Nezavisimyi Literaturno-Khudozhestvennyi i Obshchestvenno-Politicheskii Ezhemesiachnik, (3), 2008, 193-200. (2008)
`Find@UR`

Fig. 7.20. Results for search on Genre: dystopian fiction or dystopian novel. The screen shots and their contents are published with permission of ProQuest LLC. Further reproduction is prohibited without permission.

The Marked List and Output

The first five entries in my Marked List appear in Figure 7.21a. The first two are from the most recent search on dystopian literature. The next two are from a Folklore Topic search on "brewing" (not mentioned in the text), exemplifying the broad topical reach of the database, which extends into culture (food) and history. The next three results are from the Folklore Topic search on "courtship rites" that was shown in Figure 7.18b.

In Figure 7.21b, the last three entries are from the first "Shakespeare and cross-dressing" search. Take a moment to appreciate the range and international variety of sources and authors represented in these results.

Note: If you are wondering about the order of the results, the entries accumulate in the exact sequence in which they were checked off in a Results screen, not in order by publication date. If you select the sixth result, then the first, and then the tenth, then look at your Marked List, you'll see

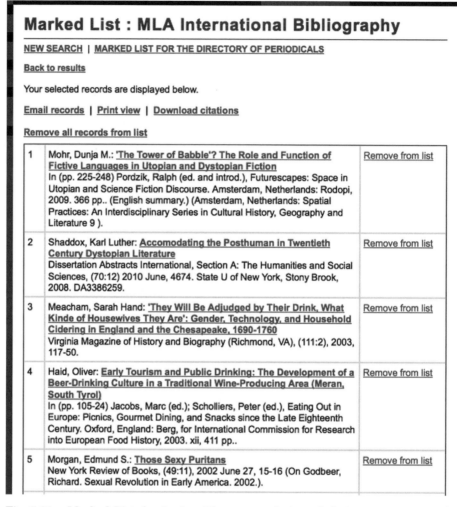

Marked List : MLA International Bibliography

NEW SEARCH | MARKED LIST FOR THE DIRECTORY OF PERIODICALS

Back to results

Your selected records are displayed below.

Email records | Print view | Download citations

Remove all records from list

1	Mohr, Dunja M.: 'The Tower of Babble'? The Role and Function of Fictive Languages in Utopian and Dystopian Fiction In (pp. 225-248) Pordzik, Ralph (ed. and introd.), Futurescapes: Space in Utopian and Science Fiction Discourse. Amsterdam, Netherlands: Rodopi, 2009. 366 pp.. (English summary.) (Amsterdam, Netherlands: Spatial Practices: An Interdisciplinary Series in Cultural History, Geography and Literature 9).	Remove from list
2	Shaddox, Karl Luther: Accomodating the Posthuman in Twentieth Century Dystopian Literature Dissertation Abstracts International, Section A: The Humanities and Social Sciences, (70:12) 2010 June, 4674. State U of New York, Stony Brook, 2008. DA3386259.	Remove from list
3	Meacham, Sarah Hand: 'They Will Be Adjudged by Their Drink, What Kinde of Housewives They Are': Gender, Technology, and Household Cidering in England and the Chesapeake, 1690-1760 Virginia Magazine of History and Biography (Richmond, VA), (111:2), 2003, 117-50.	Remove from list
4	Haid, Oliver: Early Tourism and Public Drinking: The Development of a Beer-Drinking Culture in a Traditional Wine-Producing Area (Meran, South Tyrol) In (pp. 105-24) Jacobs, Marc (ed.); Scholliers, Peter (ed.), Eating Out in Europe: Picnics, Gourmet Dining, and Snacks since the Late Eighteenth Century. Oxford, England: Berg, for International Commission for Research into European Food History, 2003. xii, 411 pp..	Remove from list
5	Morgan, Edmund S.: Those Sexy Puritans New York Review of Books, (49:11), 2002 June 27, 15-16 (On Godbeer, Richard. Sexual Revolution in Early America. 2002.).	Remove from list

Fig. 7.21a. Marked List, beginning. The screen shots and their contents are published with permission of ProQuest LLC. Further reproduction is prohibited without permission.

them in the order: tenth, first, sixth. If you revisit some previous search results using the Search History, any additional records you mark will be added to the top of your Marked List; that is, they won't be automatically grouped with the earlier marked records from that search. There is nothing wrong with this, but it is worth mentioning because it might be somewhat confusing the first time you look at the Marked List.

Records in the Marked List, as indicated by the links across the top, can be emailed, printed, or downloaded. The output interface for the email function is shown in Figure 7.22, and it includes a particularly nice feature: You can add an annotating note to *each* record in the list. The links associated with each citation point back to the corresponding record in the database.

The "Download citations" function is very bibliographic-management-software savvy. There are options to export directly to RefWorks, or to Pro-Cite, EndNote, or Reference Manager, to download a file compatible with importing into any of these four programs, or to download short or long versions of the citation records in plain text format.

6	Vosmeier, Sarah McNair: <u>Picturing Love and Friendship: Photograph Albums and Networks of Affection in the 1860s</u> In (pp. 207-19) Tucker, Susan (ed. and introd.); Ott, Katherine (ed. and introd.); Buckler, Patricia P. (ed. and introd.), The Scrapbook in American Life. Philadelphia, PA: Temple UP, 2006. x, 332 pp..	Remove from list
7	Humphreys, Margaret: <u>Gender Relationships, Matching, and Marriage Customs in an Irish Rural Community</u> Folk Life: Journal of Ethnological Studies, (48:1), 2010 May, 13-34 (English summary.).	Remove from list
8	Cheang, Wai Fong: <u>A Crossdressed Judith Shakespeare?-Reconceptualizing the Representation of Women's Predicaments in Three Contemporary Shakespeare-related Movies</u> Wenshan Review of Literature and Culture, (2:2), 2009 June, 71-103 (Chinese summary; English summary.).	Remove from list
9	Baumgärtel, Stephan: <u>Body Politics between Sublimation and Subversion: Critical Perspectives on Twentieth-Century All-Male Performances of Shakespeare's As You Like It</u> In (pp. 248-269) Bradshaw, Graham (ed.); Bishop, Tom (ed.); Wright, Laurence (guest ed. and introd.), The Shakespearean International Yearbook 9: Special Section, South African Shakespeare in the Twentieth Century. Farnham, England: Ashgate, 2009. vii, 301 pp.. (Farnham, England: Shakespearean International Yearbook 9).	Remove from list
10	Camilleri, Anna: <u>The Androgynous Antics of Byron and the Bard</u> In (pp. 67-80) Cochran, Peter (ed. and introd.), Byron and Women (and Men). Newcastle upon Tyne, England: Cambridge Scholars, 2010. lxix, 302 pp..	Remove from list

Fig. 7.21b. Marked List, continued. The screen shots and their contents are published with permission of ProQuest LLC. Further reproduction is prohibited without permission.

Cautionary Note

Although this section of the chapter is obviously enthusiastic about the many subject-specific search fields available in the Advanced Search screen, at the same time, do not hesitate to fall back on a simple keyword search if a field search doesn't seem to be working. For example, a search on "women" as a Folklore Topic and "animals" as a Keyword made sense to me, but this retrieves no results. (Reversing the terms doesn't help.) Searching "women and animals" as Keywords, however, retrieves many results, which can then be browsed for the most on-target citations. (Information from those citations might then be used for pearl growing a slightly better search.) The MLA indexers are governed by many principles in choosing and assigning terms for entries, as indicated in the overview provided on the MLA website (MLA 2004), but an overarching theme is that the indexing depends on *explicit* content. That is, a term will not be assigned to a record unless it is specifically mentioned in the content of the item. As the MLA indexers have seen the materials and you haven't, being too specific can lead to frustration. Always be ready to throw your net wider by simplifying your search.

Additional Feature: Directory of Periodicals

The third search option in the MLA IB is the Directory of Periodicals. (This is implemented in various ways by different database vendors: Sometimes the Directory of Periodicals content is integrated with the rest of the database, and sometimes it is necessary to search it as a separate database.) The Directory of Periodicals provides extensive, detailed information on over

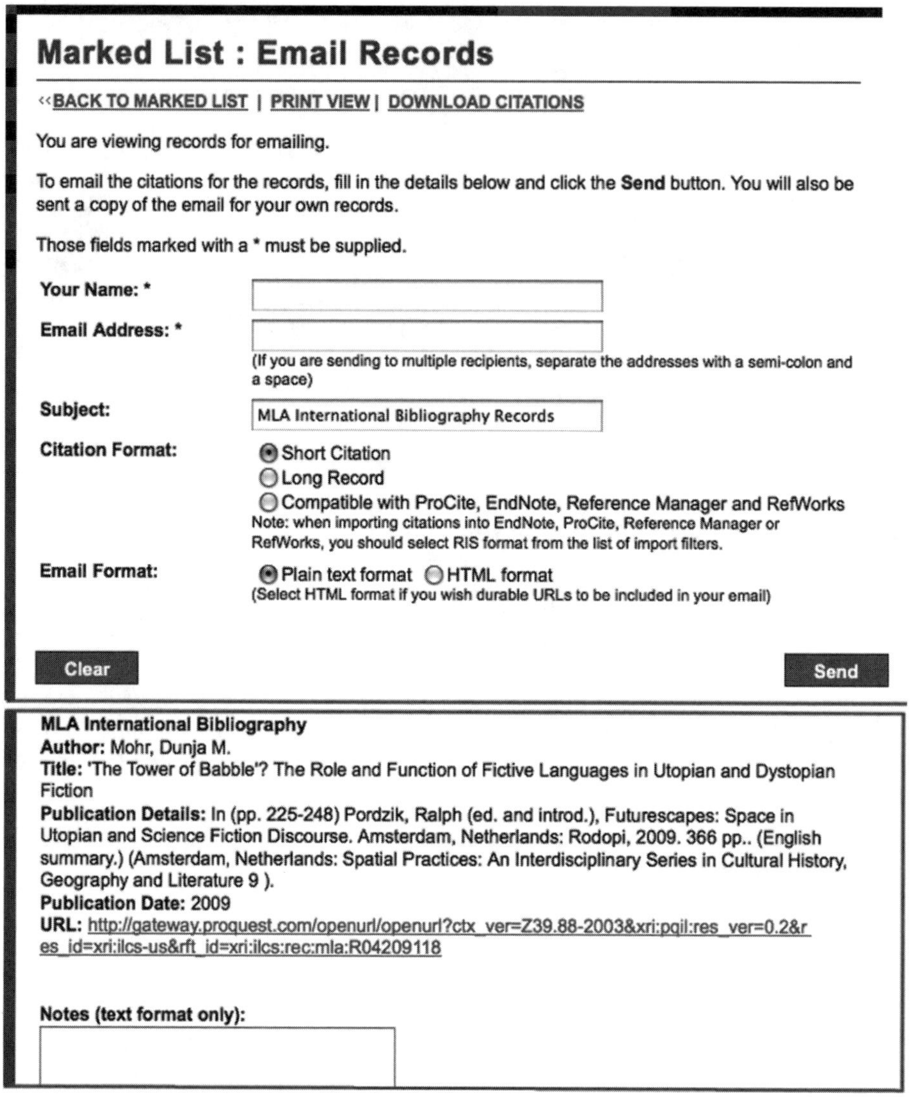

Marked List : Email Records

<<BACK TO MARKED LIST | PRINT VIEW | DOWNLOAD CITATIONS

You are viewing records for emailing.

To email the citations for the records, fill in the details below and click the **Send** button. You will also be sent a copy of the email for your own records.

Those fields marked with a * must be supplied.

Your Name: *

Email Address: *

(If you are sending to multiple recipients, separate the addresses with a semi-colon and a space)

Subject: MLA International Bibliography Records

Citation Format: ⦿ Short Citation
○ Long Record
○ Compatible with ProCite, EndNote, Reference Manager and RefWorks
Note: when importing citations into EndNote, ProCite, Reference Manager or RefWorks, you should select RIS format from the list of import filters.

Email Format: ⦿ Plain text format ○ HTML format
(Select HTML format if you wish durable URLs to be included in your email)

Clear   Send

MLA International Bibliography
Author: Mohr, Dunja M.
Title: 'The Tower of Babble'? The Role and Function of Fictive Languages in Utopian and Dystopian Fiction
Publication Details: In (pp. 225-248) Pordzik, Ralph (ed. and introd.), Futurescapes: Space in Utopian and Science Fiction Discourse. Amsterdam, Netherlands: Rodopi, 2009. 366 pp.. (English summary.) (Amsterdam, Netherlands: Spatial Practices: An Interdisciplinary Series in Cultural History, Geography and Literature 9).
Publication Date: 2009
URL: http://gateway.proquest.com/openurl/openurl?ctx_ver=Z39.88-2003&xri:pqil:res_ver=0.2&r es_id=xri:ilcs-us&rft_id=xri:ilcs:rec:mla:R04209118

Notes (text format only):

Fig. 7.22. E-mail output interface. The screen shots and their contents are published with permission of ProQuest LLC. Further reproduction is prohibited without permission.

6,000 journals and book series. The information provided is aimed both at users as *readers*—fields such as topical scope (subject), types of articles included, and subscription address—but even more at users as *writers*, as indicated by the extensive series of fields devoted to instructions for authors: charge for submission, preferred editorial style, copyright holder, time from submission to decision, and time from decision to publication, to name just a few. If you were a graduate student specializing in Renaissance literature, the Directory of Periodicals would provide a very easy way to produce a list of journals or book series to which you might submit your work for publication. If you were an established scholar, you could quickly refresh your memory of the submission guidelines for the journal(s) in which you usually

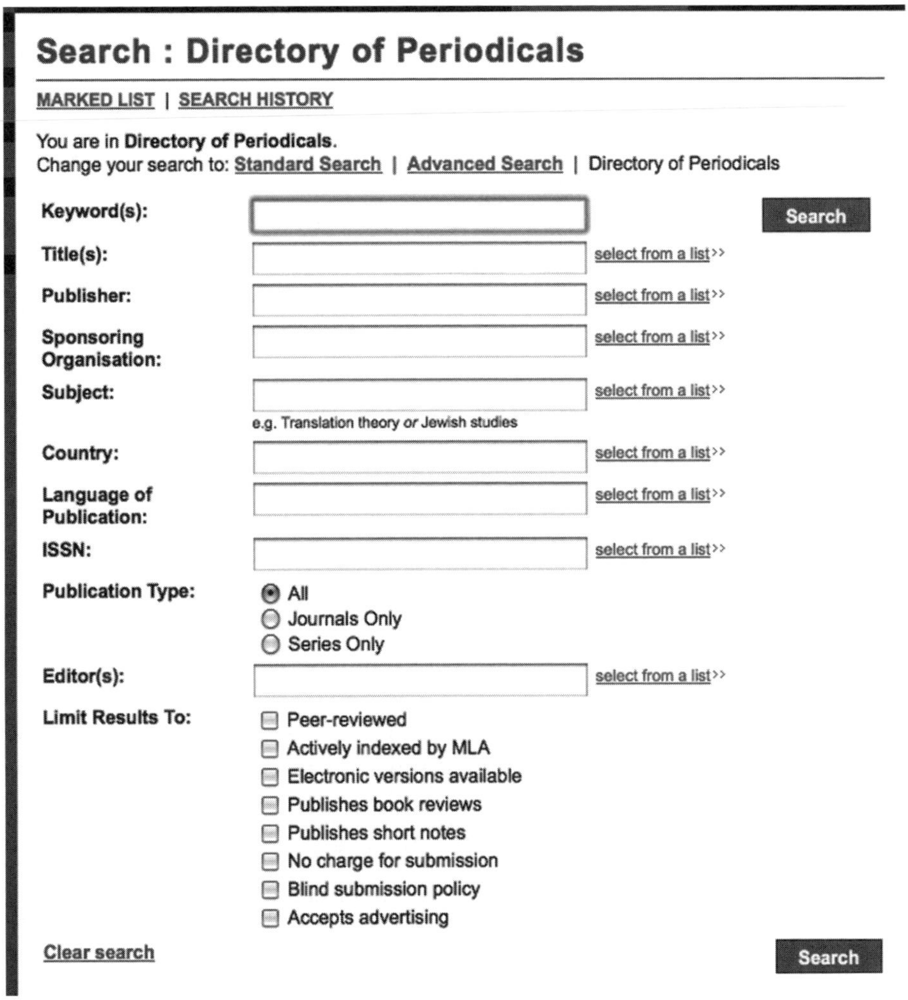

Search : Directory of Periodicals

MARKED LIST | SEARCH HISTORY

You are in **Directory of Periodicals**.
Change your search to: Standard Search | Advanced Search | Directory of Periodicals

Keyword(s):		**Search**
Title(s):		select from a list››
Publisher:		select from a list››
Sponsoring Organisation:		select from a list››
Subject:		select from a list››
	e.g. Translation theory *or* Jewish studies	
Country:		select from a list››
Language of Publication:		select from a list››
ISSN:		select from a list››
Publication Type:	● All ○ Journals Only ○ Series Only	
Editor(s):		select from a list››
Limit Results To:	☐ Peer-reviewed ☐ Actively indexed by MLA ☐ Electronic versions available ☐ Publishes book reviews ☐ Publishes short notes ☐ No charge for submission ☐ Blind submission policy ☐ Accepts advertising	
Clear search		**Search**

Fig. 7.23. The Directory of Periodicals Search interface. The screen shots and their contents are published with permission of ProQuest LLC. Further reproduction is prohibited without permission.

publish. Take note especially of all the new Limit options in Figure 7.23; they all have to do with the user as a writer.

Quick Recap

The *MLA International Bibliography* (MLA IB) is produced by the Modern Language Association of America. The topical scope of the *Bibliography* is very broad, encompassing almost anything that could be described as human communication, for example, from literature and linguistics to folklore, dramatic arts, and teaching. Types of materials indexed include journal articles, books, book chapters, reference works, conference papers, dissertations, electronic publications, and works related to teaching, such as handbooks. Book reviews are *not* included. The MLA IB database is available from several different vendors; the version considered here is from Chadwyck-Healey, the specialist humanities imprint of ProQuest. This version supports special-purpose search fields, such as Author as Subject and Author's Work (as subject), in the Standard interface. The Advanced Search interface offers a long list of discipline-specific search fields, including Literary Influence, Literary Theme, Genre, and Performance Medium. An unusual feature in the email output option is that a "Notes" field is supplied for *each* record being sent, allowing the user to individually annotate the citations. An additional feature of the MLA IB is the Directory of Periodicals, which contains detailed publication, subscription, and submission information for over 6,000 journals and book series. Authors seeking to publish their work can use the Directory of Periodicals to identify appropriate publications and obtain submission instructions.

Exercises and Points to Consider

Check the book companion website, www.LibrariansGuide.info, for supplementary materials.

1. If you also have access to the *Web of Science* citation databases, try the cited reference search for Doris Kearns Goodwin's *No Ordinary Time* there. Compare the overall experience, specific capabilities, and results with search example 3 in *America: History and Life* (AHL). (Hints: search just on the author's name, and for year, put in 1994–1995.)

2. What are some archival sources being used by current historians that can provide a *Mexican* perspective on the U.S. war with Mexico (1846–1848)? Think about this carefully for a few moments: How are you going to get at that "Mexican perspective" part of the search? See the Endnotes for a Hint.[9]

3. A faculty member comes and asks for some titles of U.S. military history journals that would be likely candidates for a scholarly article on Gen. George S. Patton Jr. How many possible sources can you discover in AHL?

4. Many features of EBSCO's AHL did not fit into this discussion: find, explore, and discuss them. Which ones would you have included that I didn't?

5. Compare the version of MLA described here with the version at your school, if available (and different). What are advantages and disadvantages of each?

6. In the MLA Subject list (Thesaurus), how is the author of *Huckleberry Finn* listed? As Samuel Clemens, or under his pseudonym, Mark Twain? Compare this to your OPAC—which name is used there?

7. Consider the name of this Spanish author who was active in the late 16th and early 17th centuries: Lope Félix de Vega Carpio, often referred to simply as "Lope de Vega." Try searching "Lope de Vega" as Keyword(s)—how many results are there? Then choose a record, and see the form of his name used by the MLA indexers. Search on that, and compare the number of results with your previous search. (The Search History link is very handy if you forget to write down the number from the previous search.)

8. How many people have written their dissertation on Tolstoi's *War and Peace* (that MLA knows about)?

9. Look up Saul Bellow as an Article Author, then as the Subject of other people's articles, and observe the difference in the number of results. Explore the longer list, and come up with a way to focus your search.

10. The aforementioned searches focused on "classic" authors. What can you find about a modern author, Terry Pratchett, and his Discworld novels? Has anyone written a dissertation on them yet?

Beyond the Textbook Exercises

Exercises requiring other humanities databases

1. A divinity student is looking for articles discussing Luke 18:1–8. (This is a passage from scripture, which is known as a "scripture citation.") Choose the most subject-specific database you can find for this, and figure out a search that will retrieve exactly the type of articles he wants. Hint: Examine the list of fields available for searching. Do any of them match something in this description?

2. A faculty member from the history department stopped by our reference desk and asked for "An article on the proper way for a Victorian Lady to faint." Look through your institution's list of databases and come up with as many as you can that look (from the description) like they might be helpful. Note that the Victorian era was in the 19th century; also, note that there's a database for PhD dissertations, and PhDs write about all kinds of weird, obscure things. Have fun with this one.

3. What can you find about the origins of the tune "Twinkle Twinkle Little Star"? A student from our music school once contacted our chat service about this: She had just been playing Smetana's "Die Moldau," and thought she detected some similarities between that and "Twinkle." Have any research articles been written about "Twinkle"? A database in the right subject area, even if it only provides abstracts, should help with this question. If your institution provides links from A&I databases to sources of full text, see if you can access the text of any likely looking articles.

Notes

1. Note that it's not "American"; this is a mistake people frequently make.

2. Note: BCE stands for "Before the Common Era"; CE stands for "Common Era." Political correctness comes to history.

3. I find the evolution of the terminology used in these interfaces interesting: A couple of years ago, these panels were all labeled "Narrow by." Now the wording is "Refine." How nice, we are getting more refined rather than narrower!

4. One does wonder where the "full words" come from, however, and one suspects possibly OCR (optical character recognition) scanning technology, given the number of "Worm War" and "Worm War H" (i.e., places where the words World War or World War II have been incorrectly interpreted by the OCR software) entries in the cited

reference database. References are frequently wrong, and people mistype things, but not *that* much. Try searching just "worm war" (with quotes) in the Cited Source field to see what I mean.

5. Your reaction to the output of the "Find Similar Results" link may vary; to me, SmartText searching simply produces A LOT of results, not necessarily better than what is produced in the course of a regular search.

6. The MLA deep-date coverage isn't just lip service, either: if you search simply the date range 1884–1885, there are sixty entries (as of July 2011)! Note also that it is interesting that you can do that, i.e., simply search a year range without entering any kind of keywords or other values at all.

7. Having written that, of course I just encountered the first instance I've ever seen of an MLA IB record with an abstract. I can't find any explanation at the MLA website, in the literature, or on the Web; we'll have to just accept it as an anomaly for now.

8. Each vendor, of course, has its own user interface that is based on that vendor's field structure, so your experience searching the same database offered by different vendors can vary a great deal. If your institution subscribes to MLA from a different vendor, you will see distinct differences between that version and the one described here. For example, other versions may not offer as many document types or as many search fields, such as the specialized search for "Author as Subject." Another difference you might notice is that other vendors implement field searching as drop-down menu choices (e.g., EBSCO), rather than listing all the fields. Be ready for differences, and use them as a constructive exercise: Which implementation seems to work better, either for specific types of searches or overall?

9. Hint: If you were writing about something from the Mexican perspective, in what language would you probably be writing? Search "Mexican War" as a Subject and limit it by language.

8
Numerical Databases

This chapter takes us into some very different territory. Rather than citations to textual materials, we're going to explore the idea of searching for numerical information: data, statistics—*numbers* about things. There are very few commercial databases that have tackled the issue of providing numerical information, but a great many websites have done so. We'll look at one of the major players in the commercial world, ProQuest's *Statistical Insight*, and two free government websites, American FactFinder (from the Census Bureau), and the Bureau of Labor Statistics. Before leaping into the databases, however, let's set the stage with some thoughts about finding numbers.

Finding Numbers

If you are not a specialist with years of experience—and even sometimes when you are—reference questions that involve finding statistics or data are probably the most challenging ones that you'll face. Let's be honest: for most of us, numbers are scary! There was a reason we weren't math majors. Don't be discouraged, however. Numbers questions don't always have to give you that deer in the headlights look: as with all of the other subject areas, my intent in this chapter is to try to give you some basic tools to help you to approach the question in an informed fashion, and to increase your chances of connecting the patron with the information requested. To begin with, I'm going to share with you my worldview about some basic number concepts: what determines the collection of numbers, how they can be categorized, who does the collection, and what sources to try for various categories.

Sidebar 8.1: Numerical Terminology

Data refers to individual numbers, for example, the original computer file of all the numerically coded responses to a survey, which usually looks like just a series of numbers. This is a *data* file, usually called a *data set*. Data are actual values. One value in a data set is a data point.

When you process data, grouping like data points and expressing them as percentages, then you have *statistics*, which are groups of numbers, usually expressed in terms of percentages. The data (number) and the statistical percentage it represents both appear in the following sentence: "Almost 9 million (data) young Americans, or about 15 percent (a statistic) of all children, are overweight."

In my experience, people who are not in numerically oriented fields (economics, business, sociology, etc.) tend to use the terms *data* and *statistics* almost interchangeably. They will ask for *data* about something, when they are really interested in statistics. (This is good, because statistics are usually easier to find.) If a person really does want a series of values to analyze, then he or she really does want a data set. A person in this position is usually quite aware of the difference between data and statistics, and you should be, too.

Concepts about Numbers

Collection of Numbers

First and foremost in working with a numerical question is to consider whether it will have been worth someone's time and effort to collect the information and make it available in the way the user desires. Numbers take a lot of time and effort to collect: real effort, often by real people. For example, the year 2000 Census cost a total of $4.5 billion, or $15.99 per person counted. By 2010, the estimated costs had ballooned to $13 billion, or $42.11 per person counted (Beine 2011). The first reports based on 2010 Census data only began to appear in May 2011, because collecting the numbers is only the beginning. Next, the data have to be analyzed and formatted into some kind of useful reports that either benefit the collecting organization (e.g., for planning or allocating) or are interesting enough to outside parties that they'll pay money for them.

In my experience on the job as a data librarian, I am frequently faced with people who feel they have an absolutely reasonable and rational numerical request, and that "certainly the information should be out there." And while what they're looking for might sound reasonable and rational to me too, it doesn't mean that the information actually is out there, or that it exists in exactly the way they envision. If the government doesn't have it (our best free source), and a nonprofit organization such as the Inter-university Consortium for Political and Social Research (ICPSR) or possibly a trade organization[1] doesn't have it, then it means it would have to be information collected by a for-profit organization. Obviously, it was collected to help the company make that profit, so they have no incentive to disseminate it for free while it is still relevant. If the information isn't strategically vital or tactically important, and the company thinks it can sell the data (or reports based on the data) for more than the cost of collecting and analyzing the information, then those numbers might be available (for a fee). Again, as stated at the beginning of this section: if it's not worth somebody's time and effort, it probably won't be counted, and then exactly *because* it's worth time and effort, it might not be freely available.

Categories of Numbers

It can be helpful to think of collected numbers as falling into three broad categories: people, business, and financial. Numbers that get collected about People are things such as population counts, demographics (race, income, etc.), and vital statistics (births, deaths, etc.). Business numbers include broad information *about* business, such as numbers of companies, production, and workers in various industries, as well as numbers related to *doing* business, for example, market research or sales figures for a particular company. There are certainly business numbers that are financial (e.g., historical stock prices), but my third category, financial numbers, has to do with money or monetary equivalents (e.g., stocks) in a broader sense: information such as gross domestic product, banking data (total currency in circulation, total value of money in savings accounts, etc.), exchange rates, and aggregate numbers associated with the stock market, such as the Dow Jones Industrial Averages.

Fitting a numbers question into one of these categories helps to organize my plan of attack, because the categories tend to be associated with certain kinds of collection agents. This means that I'll get some ideas of where to look first, and that I'll have a sense of whether the information might be freely available or fee based.

Who Collects Numbers

In the United States, the U.S. government is probably the largest collector and publisher of numbers. This can probably be said of other developed countries as well. These organizations are termed the *public sector* and usually the information that they make available is free (your tax dollars at work).

At the opposite extreme, we have the *private sector*: trade or business organizations, professional associations, market research companies, and polling and surveying organizations. Usually information produced by a private-sector organization isn't free, although some trade and professional groups may provide some statistics on their websites. In general, however, numerical information collected by the private sector ranges from possibly affordable (say, from $20 to $500, which would probably be acceptable to a small-business owner or to a library buying a reference book), to prices meant for large corporations (e.g., $4,000 market research reports).[2]

Between the public and private sectors is the nonprofit area of academic researchers. Mentioned earlier, the ICPSR was organized specifically to gather and archive the data collected in the course of social science research conducted by scholars across the United States. ICPSR is probably the largest social science data archive in the world. Your institution must be an ICPSR member for you to download their data. The membership fees reflect the magnitude of their organization and offerings (but for high-volume users, the cost per data set becomes quite inexpensive). If your institution is a member, it is likely that you will have a data librarian on staff, and ICPSR probably is his or her first or second most frequently used resource for serious number requests (i.e., for raw data that needs statistical processing, usually for advanced research). Although ICPSR is always working to make its resources more understandable to nonexpert users, it is still an advanced resource, and not as commonly found on institutional subscription lists as most of the databases in this book. Because I wish to keep the discussion at the beginning to intermediate level, using resources that are fairly common, I won't go into more details about ICPSR here. If you are interested in finding out more, their website is very helpful and informative: http://www.icpsr.umich.edu.

Try the Public Sector for . . .

When a reference question involves numbers having to do with people, my first move would be to try a government source (as long as the question is about people as *people*, and not as *consumers*). A government exists to govern people, and governing bodies are quite interested in information about their constituents. Governments are also very interested in the businesses in their countries: these companies are, after all, what keep the country solvent. For questions involving numbers of businesses, shipments of product X, employment, etc., try government sources. There are public-sector sources for some financial numbers questions as well: For questions involving monetary figures in a nationwide sense, try the Federal Reserve Bank, or for economic data, the Bureau of Economic Analysis.

Try the Private Sector for . . .

As mentioned previously, the government is my first choice for questions about people as people (heads that get counted). If someone wants to know about people as consumers, however, or what people are thinking, then it's more likely that the answer will come from a private-sector source: a market research report, a survey report from a company such as Harris Interactive, or perhaps a Gallup Poll. (It will probably also cost money.)

Questions about numbers for specific businesses almost always come from private-sector sources: trade organizations or publications that specialize in a particular line of business. Who cares most about home appliance manufacturing? The Association of Home Appliance Manufacturers. Hosiery? The National Association of Hosiery Manufacturers. Oil, airlines, and milk? They all have trade associations devoted to (among other things) collecting numbers pertinent to their mission, purpose, etc. Certain private-sector publishers specialize in trade reports: Crain Communications (e.g., *Advertising Age, Plastics News*), Ward's Communications (*Ward's Automotive Yearbook*), and Adams Media (beer, wine, and liquor handbooks). For any line of business, remember to consider associations as a source of information. This is perhaps especially true for service businesses, that is, any line of work that does not involve producing a product: be sure to check for a related professional organization, because this might be the only source of statistics about the profession.[3] (For example: Want to know what butlers earn? Try the website of the International Guild of Professional Butlers at http://www.butlersguild.com/.)

There are two types of business numbers that are, surprisingly, freely available on the Web. One is stock quotes for particular companies: current quotes are available from any of several websites, and Yahoo! Finance offers a remarkably deep historical stock quote reporting system (the catch is that it works only for companies currently in business and trading on U.S. stock exchanges). Also accessible on the Web are the financial statements of public companies, which must be filed with the Securities and Exchange Commission (SEC) and are public documents. This information is available in a number of places, including the SEC's Edgar system (http://www.sec.gov/edgar .shtml), and the company's own website,[4] where the figures appear in the company's annual report.

Financial number questions that can involve a fee-based source tend to be ones that require a series of historical values (e.g., an exchange rate for a particular currency over a 30-year period), or financial information for another country, or a combination of the two (e.g., a table of 20 years of debt values for Nigeria). *Global Financial Data* is a commercial database product that deals in extended time series data and other specialized data series. The International Monetary Fund also charges for access to its data. In a rather jaw-dropping development in 2010, however, the World Bank opened its entire data archive for free access on the Web: see http://data.worldbank .org/. The United Nations is another likely source for financial and other numbers about countries; some of their data is freely available and some isn't. It's worth a try: http://www.un.org/en/databases/.

Quick Recap

This section has provided some background to the whole idea of finding numbers, and has given an overview of the major free and fee-based resources for numbers. A basic premise is that it takes time and effort to collect, format, and publish data or statistics. Without a financial or other strong motivation to prompt the process, data are unlikely to be collected. If information has been collected, it may not be available for free. In the United States, the government (the *public sector*) is probably the largest collector and provider of freely available data about people, industries, and economics (national-level financial information). Nongovernmental organizations, notably the World Bank, may also offer their data for free on the web. Numbers relating to businesses that can also be found at no charge on the web are financial statements (balance sheet, income statement, etc.) for public companies and current stock quotes. Information that is rarely, if ever, free includes market research and data about specific businesses, which are most likely to be collected by survey companies, trade associations, or trade publishers (the *private sector*). One exception is trade associations, which occasionally make data related to their organization available on their websites.

A Comment about Searching for Numbers

One of the frustrating things about searching for numbers is that, all too often, whatever the person asks for, the numbers that you can find won't be exactly the ones that the patron wants:

> You: "Here are some great figures about spotted hyenas!"
> Patron: "Oh. Thanks, but I really wanted *striped* hyenas . . ."

Remember that this does not represent a failure on your part: if you have done a rigorous search, it probably means that no one has cared enough yet about striped hyenas to collect and publish numerical data about them. Don't be discouraged. It is amazing, on the other hand, the numbers that you *can* find! Let's learn about the first of the three sources that we'll cover, ProQuest's *Statistical Insight*.

Statistical Insight from ProQuest

Background and Coverage

Originally known as "Statistical Universe," this database was first reviewed in 1998 by Mary Ellen Bates. She described it as a "recently created" joint effort by LexisNexis and Congressional Information Service, Inc. As Bates says, the new database addressed "the need for value-added access to Web-based information" (Bates 1998). Indeed, LexisNexis saw how useful it would be if the wealth of statistical material produced by the many agencies and offices of the U.S. government could be brought together under one search interface, enhanced with indexing, and with the tables provided in a format that would keep their integrity intact (e.g., GIF images rather than ASCII renditions). Even though much of this information is freely available on the Web, the task of locating it amid the plethora of government websites can be frustrating and difficult. In addition, the need to preserve and continue to provide access to earlier editions of files is not consistent across all government websites. Putting the materials into a database increases the chances of preserving a historical series of reports. A print indexing and abstracting service for U.S. government statistics already existed: the Congressional Information Service *American Statistics Index* (ASI). By adding GIF images of the tables cited in the index, the service gives users immediate access to the information. Adding in selections from the Congressional Information Service's two other statistical A&I (abstracting and indexing) subscription series—*Statistical Reference Index* (SRI, which indexes statistical information published by state governments, private sector publishers, and universities) and the *Index to International Statistics* (IIS, which covers international intergovernmental organizations, e.g., the United Nations, World Bank, and Organisation for Economic Co-operation and Development), adds depth of coverage and takes the concept even further. In 2010, the whole data division of LexisNexis was purchased by ProQuest. Efforts to add more data, more quickly, were initiated: Data are now added weekly instead of monthly, and the source list is continually expanding. Changes to the interface, inaugurated under LexisNexis, have been tweaked and finalized under ProQuest. I have noticed a distinct increase in more recent content, and more frequent availability of full-text PDFs, than ever before. The change in ownership augurs well for this unique and much-needed statistical product.

"Much-needed" is the key term because *Statistical Insight* is still, as of this writing, the most broadly based, general-purpose numerical database on the market. In early 2006, Cambridge University Press published the *Historical Statistics of the United States Millennial Edition* in both print and online formats. This is a wonderful resource for very-long-time series of strictly American data, in fairly broad topic areas (it is based on Census data)—a wonderful tool, but not a substitute for *Statistical Insight*. Also in 2006, a free Web resource called DataPlace appeared, which also aggregates data from federal sources to make them easier to find; it also provides tools to help in analyzing and presenting the data. Mick O'Leary gave it a very favorable review but admitted that DataPlace "has little or nothing on some important subjects, including prices, finance, economic sectors, politics, and any foreign data" (O'Leary 2006). In 2008, Mr. O'Leary reviewed a pair of statistical resources, NationMaster and StateMaster (also freely available online), but again found them lacking (O'Leary 2008). There simply is no substitute for *Statistical Insight* in the marketplace or the free options on the Web.[5]

Subscription Options

Subscription options for *Statistical Insight* are somewhat complex, starting with a base service of full-text tables to which an institution can add optional modules representing the three indexes mentioned briefly earlier: ASI, SRI, and IIS. Within the modules, one can opt for just indexing and abstracts, or that plus full-text PDFs. It is beyond the scope of this book to go into subscription options in detail, but I wanted to comment on it because it is somewhat unusual, and yet another reminder that dealing in numbers is different.

Related Subscriptions: Statistical Datasets

We cannot leave a discussion of subscription options without mentioning *Statistical Datasets*, the highly interactive, graphical, and visual baby brother to *Statistical Insight*. The content of *Statistical Datasets* is more limited than *Statistical Insight*, but all of the available sets of data can be immediately graphed, multiple series can be overlaid, and the user can choose and control the variables to some extent. Because the product is highly customized, the interface and how to interact with it are different from the usual database, so an introduction can be helpful (the database itself provides a video tutorial). Once they understand how it works, undergraduates in economics and related disciplines are immediate fans. It's an amazing tool.

Date Coverage

Date coverage has somewhat different connotations in a numerical database than it does in a bibliographic or citation database. The range of *publication* dates—how far back the database goes—is not necessarily as important, because in the world of numbers it's very common to find recently published material that deals with the distant past, for example, "crop losses . . . 1948–1997" (published in 1999) or "acres harvested . . . 1930–1998" (published in 2006). There may be times when someone needs numbers published in a particular historical time period, but often it doesn't matter so much *when* the document was published as long as it has the right data. That said, to make the description of this database consistent with descriptions in the other chapters, we'll note that the basic *Statistical Insight* subscription provides records with tables from 1999 to the present. Adding on the ASI, SRI, and IIS modules provides indexing and abstracts back to 1973, 1980, and 1983, respectively (with recent options for full text as well). Any of these records can refer to information that is much older, however, so if you need to know the effect of weather and technology on corn yields in the Corn Belt, 1929–1962, this is the place to go. The options for the Publication Date limit recognize this difference: After doing a search, you have the option to filter your results by Date *Published* (anywhere from 1973 to 2011) or by Date *Covered* (1700–2089—yes, you read that right![6]). This is a far cry from the typical date-limit field in a database, so pause and ponder it for a moment. Having said all this, I will admit I tend to avoid using date filters when searching for data; my preference is to try and identify (any and all) sources first, and simply see what date coverage is available in the results.

Notes and Search Examples

Perhaps surprisingly by now, we are going to spend our whole search experience in *Statistical Insight* in the Basic search mode. The Filter options on the results page work so well that it is seldom necessary to go into the Advanced Search mode. Searching for numbers is just *different* from searching for words: Getting too specific in the Advanced Search can actually end up being frustrating and detrimental to your searching, unless you are searching for a known item (e.g., a specific report title or similar). For once, a simple keyword or broad subject heading approach that you then filter usually works more successfully.

Search Example 1: Finding Data on Occupations

As a first dip into *Statistical Insight*, we will demonstrate how to find data on a particular occupation. Feel free to try substituting whatever occupation you are interested in pursuing. Here, we will see what kinds of numbers we can find about librarians.

The Basic search screen for *Statistical Insight* is shown in Figure 8.1. It is very clean, very simple. Even the "filter panel" on the left is totally unintimidating: The filters won't become available until you've performed at least one search. You search, then you apply filters. Easy!

As you start to type in the Basic search box, after three letters the system starts suggesting things, a kind of auto-complete function such as we saw in PubMed (and that was first used by Google—what else?). But in this case, the suggestions are not just things other people have searched for: They are *programmed* suggestions, and include Subject headings, as shown in Figure 8.2. Words above the dashed line in the suggestion list are keywords; terms below the dashed line are labeled Subject (alerting us that Basic Tool No. 2, controlled vocabulary, is very much a part of this database). There's no need to go do a special look up in a list; if we get close enough, the system will simply tell us if a word or phrase is a Subject heading. If you start typing: informat . . . you will get a rich list of Subject headings, including Information industries, Information sciences, Information services, and if you keep typing, Information technology (for those of you who want to go into IT).

For this example, we will choose Subject: Librarians, and then click the Go button. Just hitting enter will not run your search, even though with only one search box it seems like it should: You must always click Go.

Filters

With our results, now all of our Filter options are available, as shown in Figure 8.3. The filters are organized into broad categories starting with the

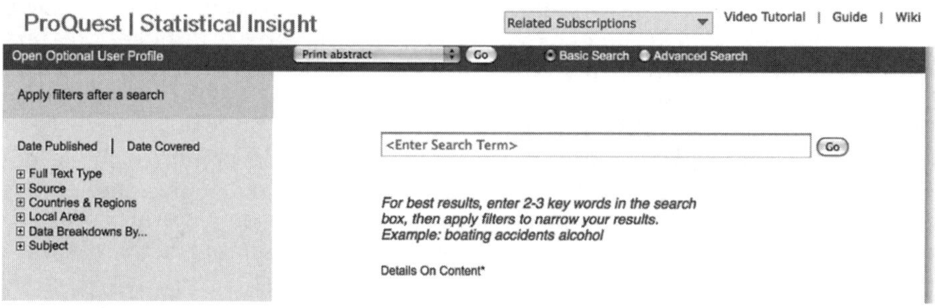

Fig. 8.1. *Statistical Insight* Basic search screen before any searches have been done. The screen shots and their contents are published with permission of ProQuest LLC. Further reproduction is prohibited without permission.

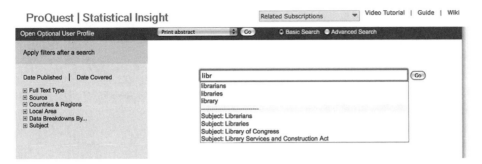

Fig. 8.2. The auto-complete suggestion system in action. The screen shots and their contents are published with permission of ProQuest LLC. Further reproduction is prohibited without permission.

Date Published / Date Covered options, then Full Text Type, Source, Countries & Regions, Local Area, Data Breakdowns By . . . , and Subject, some of which contain subcategories (a "+" box next to a term indicates that more detailed levels are available). For a search like this, you might want to drill down under Source and choose only reports from certain associations (such as the American Library Association or the Special Libraries Association—after all, who cares more about librarian salaries than they do?). The "Data Breakdowns By . . ." offerings are always very useful; these tend to be the things people are interested in most often, such as data by age, educational attainment, sex, race, industry, etc. Note that the entries under Subject are sorted by frequency by default, but you can change the sort to alphabetical. Each entry in every category includes a number, indicating how many records you will have if you choose that filter: a wonderful feature. As you choose filters, the numbers will change—you'll always know the point at which your results are about to go to zero.

Say we try filtering by Source: Associations: All Associations, and Data Breakdowns: By educational attainment. This gives us just 16 results, as shown in Figure 8.4. Sorting these by Date Published ("A" in Figure 8.4), we see that the newest information is from 2007. Not recent enough? Simply remove the Applied Filters by clicking specific ones or clearing them all, in the area marked "B" in Figure 8.4. Maybe it would be better to look for information from a federal agency: If you open that list under the Source filters, you'll see the Bureau of Labor Statistics listed, which we will visit later in this chapter. Maybe that source would have more recent information. If not, simply remove it and try something else. The bottom line is, it is extremely easy to try one or more filters, see if you are getting what you want, reverse your process, and try other filters if you aren't. You can slice and dice your results with just clicks.

Search Example 2: Exploring Subjects and Filters

This example is actually an interactive exercise: It depends on your having access to *Statistical Insight* and being able to get online and experiment. Start by typing the following into the search box:

Earn

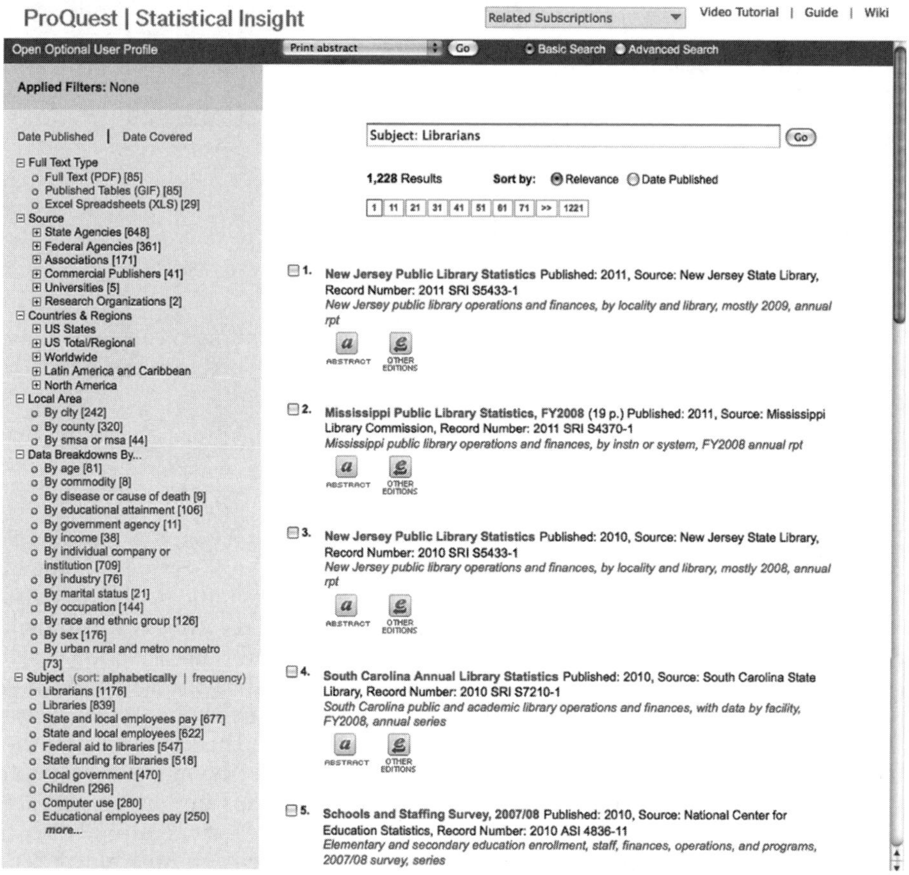

ProQuest | Statistical Insight

Related Subscriptions ▼   Video Tutorial | Guide | Wiki

Open Optional User Profile   Print abstract ▾ [Go]   ○ Basic Search ● Advanced Search

Applied Filters: None

Date Published | Date Covered

⊟ Full Text Type
  ○ Full Text (PDF) [85]
  ○ Published Tables (GIF) [85]
  ○ Excel Spreadsheets (XLS) [29]
⊟ Source
  ⊞ State Agencies [648]
  ⊞ Federal Agencies [361]
  ⊞ Associations [171]
  ⊞ Commercial Publishers [41]
  ⊞ Universities [5]
  ⊞ Research Organizations [2]
⊟ Countries & Regions
  ⊞ US States
  ⊞ US Total/Regional
  ⊞ Worldwide
  ⊞ Latin America and Caribbean
  ⊞ North America
⊟ Local Area
  ○ By city [242]
  ○ By county [320]
  ○ By smsa or msa [44]
⊟ Data Breakdowns By...
  ○ By age [81]
  ○ By commodity [8]
  ○ By disease or cause of death [9]
  ○ By educational attainment [106]
  ○ By government agency [11]
  ○ By income [38]
  ○ By individual company or
    institution [709]
  ○ By industry [76]
  ○ By marital status [21]
  ○ By occupation [144]
  ○ By race and ethnic group [126]
  ○ By sex [176]
  ○ By urban rural and metro nonmetro
    [73]
⊟ Subject (sort: alphabetically | frequency)
  ○ Librarians [1176]
  ○ Libraries [839]
  ○ State and local employees pay [677]
  ○ State and local employees [622]
  ○ Federal aid to libraries [547]
  ○ State funding for libraries [518]
  ○ Local government [470]
  ○ Children [296]
  ○ Computer use [280]
  ○ Educational employees pay [250]
  more...

Subject: Librarians [Go]

1,228 Results   Sort by: ● Relevance ○ Date Published

[1] [11] [21] [31] [41] [51] [61] [71] [»] [1221]

☐ 1. **New Jersey Public Library Statistics** Published: 2011, Source: New Jersey State Library,
Record Number: 2011 SRI S5433-1
New Jersey public library operations and finances, by locality and library, mostly 2009, annual rpt
  ABSTRACT OTHER EDITIONS

☐ 2. **Mississippi Public Library Statistics, FY2008** (19 p.) Published: 2011, Source: Mississippi
Library Commission, Record Number: 2011 SRI S4370-1
Mississippi public library operations and finances, by instn or system, FY2008 annual rpt
  ABSTRACT OTHER EDITIONS

☐ 3. **New Jersey Public Library Statistics** Published: 2010, Source: New Jersey State Library,
Record Number: 2010 SRI S5433-1
New Jersey public library operations and finances, by locality and library, mostly 2008, annual rpt
  ABSTRACT OTHER EDITIONS

☐ 4. **South Carolina Annual Library Statistics** Published: 2010, Source: South Carolina State
Library, Record Number: 2010 SRI S7210-1
South Carolina public and academic library operations and finances, with data by facility, FY2008, annual series
  ABSTRACT OTHER EDITIONS

☐ 5. **Schools and Staffing Survey, 2007/08** Published: 2010, Source: National Center for
Education Statistics, Record Number: 2010 ASI 4836-11
Elementary and secondary education enrollment, staff, finances, operations, and programs, 2007/08 survey, series

Fig. 8.3. Results display with Filter options. The screen shots and their contents are published with permission of ProQuest LLC. Further reproduction is prohibited without permission.

☒ Clear All Filters

Applied Filters: [B]

☒ ASR||All Associations
☒ Data Breakdown By educational attainment

Date Published | Date Covered

⊟ Full Text Type
⊟ Source
  ⊟ Associations [16]
    ○ All Associations [16]
    ○ Special Libraries Association [14]
    ○ American Federation of Labor and
      Congress of Industrial
      Organizations [2]
⊟ Countries & Regions
  ⊞ US Total/Regional
  ⊞ North America
⊟ Local Area
  ○ By smsa or msa [14]
⊟ Data Breakdowns By...
  ○ By age [5]
  ○ By educational attainment [16]
  ○ By industry [15]
  ○ By occupation [2]
  ○ By race and ethnic group [14]
  ○ By sex [11]

Subject: Librarians [Go]

16 Results   Sort by: ○ Relevance ● Date Published   [A]

[1] [11]

☐ 1. **SLA Annual Salary Survey and Workplace Study 2007** (262 p.) Published: 2008, Source:
Special Libraries Association, Record Number: 2008 SRI A8965-1
Librarians (special) salaries, by location, work setting, and personal characteristics, for US, Canada, UK, and/or Europe, mostly 2007, annual survey rpt
  ABSTRACT PDF DOCUMENT OTHER EDITIONS

☐ 2. **SLA Annual Salary Survey and Workplace Study 2006** (218 p.) Published: 2007, Source:
Special Libraries Association, Record Number: 2007 SRI A8965-1
Librarians (special) salaries, by location, work setting, and personal characteristics, for US and Canada, mostly 2006, annual survey rpt
  ABSTRACT OTHER EDITIONS

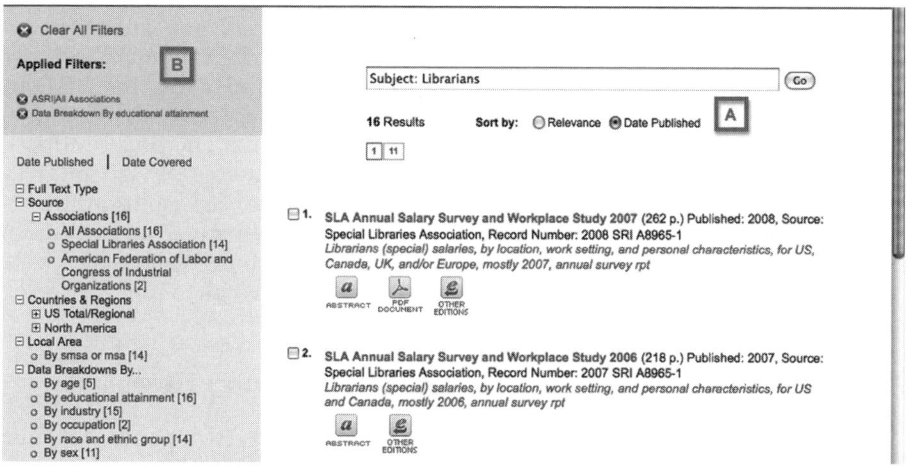

Fig. 8.4. Results after applying some filters. The screen shots and their contents are published with permission of ProQuest LLC. Further reproduction is prohibited without permission.

Then, see what comes up in the suggestions. The suggestion: "Subject: Earnings" will retrieve the largest set of results, thus giving you the greatest number of filters with which to experiment.

Using the large result set for "Subject: Earnings," start experimenting. Change the overall "Sort by:" order from Relevance to Date Published. Try selecting various options under the "Data Breakdowns By . . ." and/or Subject filters. Then see if you can add filters from the Countries and Regions, or Local Area lists. Add in Full Text Type filters at any point in your explorations. How about finding projections and forecasts for earnings? (Hint: Look under Subjects.) If a filter (or combination of filters) produces no results, simply remove one or more and try something else. One variation with some interesting results is shown in Figure 8.5. Note that filters of the same name can appear under Data Breakdowns By and Subject (in this case, educational attainment), and that you can apply them both, steadily reducing and focusing your results.

Search Example 3: Searching by Keyword

The emphasis so far has been on starting with a fairly broad search, typing a single word or phrase into the search box, observing what the system suggests, going with a suggested Subject heading, and then using the Filters to focus your results. Please do not get the impression that this is the only good approach, however. You can try keywords and the tools you've

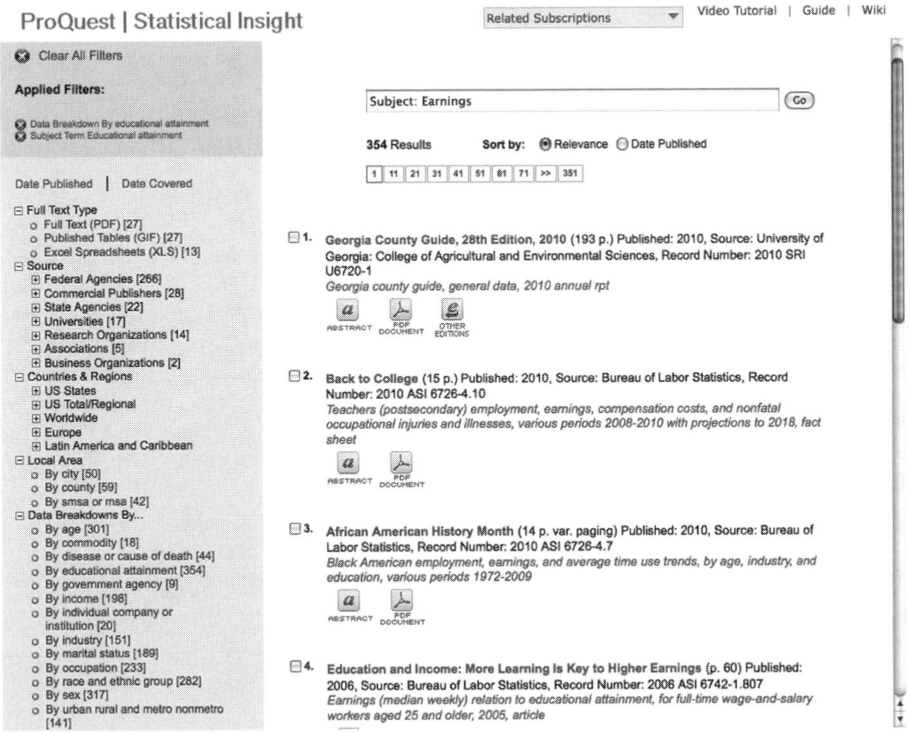

Fig. 8.5. Subject: Earnings—results after applying some filters, sorted by Relevance. The screen shots and their contents are published with permission of ProQuest LLC. Further reproduction is prohibited without permission.

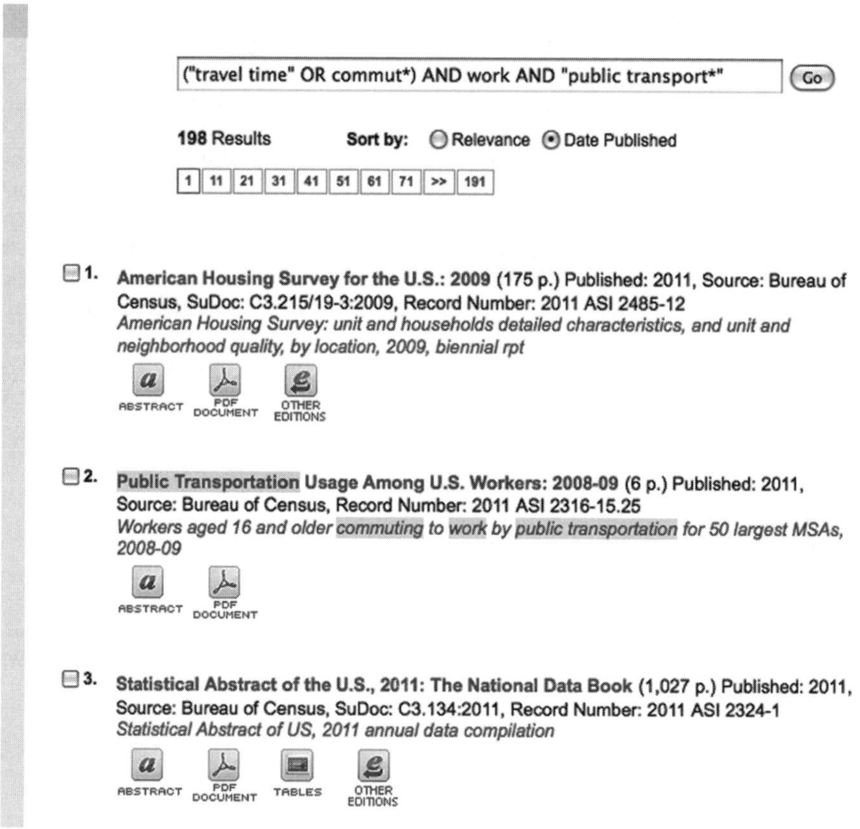

("travel time" OR commut*) AND work AND "public transport*"   (Go)

198 Results   Sort by: ○ Relevance ● Date Published

[1] [11] [21] [31] [41] [51] [61] [71] [>>] [191]

☐ **1.** **American Housing Survey for the U.S.: 2009** (175 p.) Published: 2011, Source: Bureau of Census, SuDoc: C3.215/19-3:2009, Record Number: 2011 ASI 2485-12
American Housing Survey: unit and households detailed characteristics, and unit and neighborhood quality, by location, 2009, biennial rpt

a   📄   *e*
ABSTRACT   PDF   OTHER
           DOCUMENT   EDITIONS

☐ **2.** **Public Transportation** Usage Among U.S. Workers: 2008-09 (6 p.) Published: 2011, Source: Bureau of Census, Record Number: 2011 ASI 2316-15.25
Workers aged 16 and older commuting to work by public transportation for 50 largest MSAs, 2008-09

a   📄
ABSTRACT   PDF
           DOCUMENT

☐ **3.** **Statistical Abstract of the U.S., 2011: The National Data Book** (1,027 p.) Published: 2011, Source: Bureau of Census, SuDoc: C3.134:2011, Record Number: 2011 ASI 2324-1
Statistical Abstract of US, 2011 annual data compilation

a   📄   🔲   *e*
ABSTRACT   PDF   TABLES   OTHER
           DOCUMENT   EDITIONS

Fig. 8.6. Most recent results for "travel time" search, not showing the Filter panel. The screen shots and their contents are published with permission of ProQuest LLC. Further reproduction is prohibited without permission.

learned about in this basic search box: double quotes to indicate phrases, truncation with the asterisk, Boolean operators, and parentheses to nest statements. Figure 8.6 shows such a search, constructed to find material about travel time or commuting (or commute or commuters) to work using public transport. Note that the sort order in the figure is by Date Published. Record three in Figure 8.6 is an entry for the *Statistical Abstract of the United States, 2011*, one of the best all-around data sources for anything "U.S."[7] We will go over the icons associated with this record in the next section.

Statistical Insight Results and Records

Records in *Statistical Insight* can have up to four icons associated with them:

- Abstract
- PDF Document
- Tables
- Other Editions

Clicking an icon opens that option within the same page; you never need to leave your results display. All records have at least an Abstract, of varying length depending on the length of the publication the record is referring to. The Abstract display includes the complete publication information (e.g., citation), the index (Subject) and category terms applied to the record, as well as a description of the content.

Figure 8.7 shows features of the next two possible icons. Clicking the PDF Document icon brings up two choices: Preview (the magnifying glass

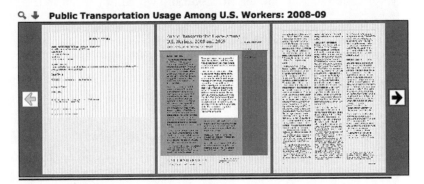

Fig. 8.7. Examples of the PDF Document and Tables icons open within the results display. The screen shots and their contents are published with permission of ProQuest LLC. Further reproduction is prohibited without permission.

icon) and Download (the down arrow icon). Preview provides the opportunity, shown in Figure 8.7, to page through a miniature version of the document—not enough to actually see the text, but enough to get a sense of whether the document contains tables or graphs and, if so, how many. Then you can decide whether you want to download it. The Tables icon, opened in the *Statistical Abstract* record, provides direct access to the list of tables from that document containing one or more of your search terms; in this case these tables are available in both XLS and GIF formats. Notice how far down the scroll bar in the Tables window is: The table that might be most pertinent ("Commuting to Work by State") is fairly far down in the list. Keep your eyes open for scroll bars, and remember that persistence can be a virtue.

Last, we have the Other Editions icon, shown expanded for the fifth result in our list in Figure 8.8. With this feature the *Statistical Insight* designers have come up with a very elegant way to provide information that was not handled very elegantly before. An icon, an "e" with a back arrow, alerts us to the fact that earlier editions of the same publication are available to us, should that be of interest, and we can drill into an earlier edition via the Show Abstract link. In the earlier incarnation of this database, there were simply multiple records, one for each edition, which appeared in the results

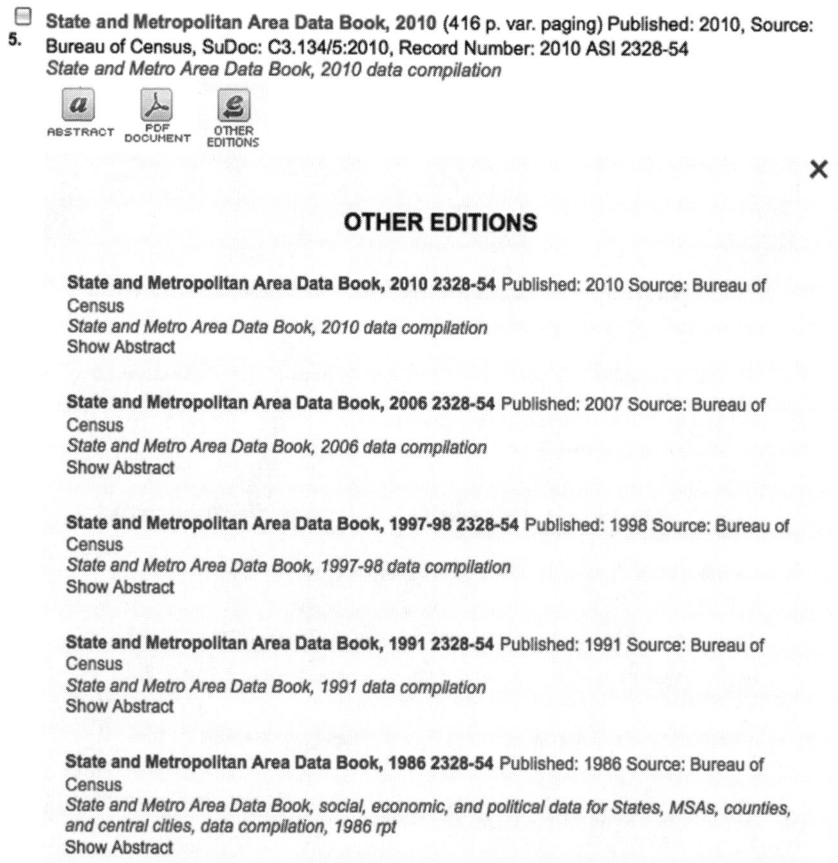

5. State and Metropolitan Area Data Book, 2010 (416 p. var. paging) Published: 2010, Source: Bureau of Census, SuDoc: C3.134/5:2010, Record Number: 2010 ASI 2328-54
State and Metro Area Data Book, 2010 data compilation

ABSTRACT　PDF DOCUMENT　OTHER EDITIONS

✕

OTHER EDITIONS

State and Metropolitan Area Data Book, 2010 2328-54 Published: 2010 Source: Bureau of Census
State and Metro Area Data Book, 2010 data compilation
Show Abstract

State and Metropolitan Area Data Book, 2006 2328-54 Published: 2007 Source: Bureau of Census
State and Metro Area Data Book, 2006 data compilation
Show Abstract

State and Metropolitan Area Data Book, 1997-98 2328-54 Published: 1998 Source: Bureau of Census
State and Metro Area Data Book, 1997-98 data compilation
Show Abstract

State and Metropolitan Area Data Book, 1991 2328-54 Published: 1991 Source: Bureau of Census
State and Metro Area Data Book, 1991 data compilation
Show Abstract

State and Metropolitan Area Data Book, 1986 2328-54 Published: 1986 Source: Bureau of Census
State and Metro Area Data Book, social, economic, and political data for States, MSAs, counties, and central cities, data compilation, 1986 rpt
Show Abstract

Fig. 8.8. The Other Editions icon. The screen shots and their contents are published with permission of ProQuest LLC. Further reproduction is prohibited without permission.

and frankly made the list both cluttered and difficult to understand. This approach is clean, efficient, and useful.

In these icons we have seen two possibilities for getting to the full text, either by a PDF or by GIF images of Tables being available. But there are still many records where the full text is not right there. Or you find the perfect report, but it's a little old, and you wish there was a newer one. Then what?

Getting to Full Text

Continuing the "travel time to work" theme, one could find the following record in *Statistical Insight*, which does not offer Tables or a PDF:

> Journey-to-Work Trends in the U.S. and Its Major Metropolitan Areas, 1960–2000 (225 p. +errata.) Published: 2005, Source: Federal Highway Administration, SuDoc: TD2.30/5:03-058, Record Number: 2005 ASI 7558-104
>
> *Commuting patterns, by mode of transport and central-suburban location, for 49 MSAs, 2000 with trends from 1960, decennial rpt*

Notice first that this is a "decennial rpt," that is, it is only published every 10 years and is undoubtedly based on information from the census (long form). This report was not published until 2005, five years after the 2000 census. However . . . we have the source, the Federal Highway Administration, so we know who cares about this information; we know where to go looking. And we have the title of this report.

To be honest, the first thing I always do is to Google the title. I have had incredible luck getting to the full text online this way.[8] This tactic has also been very effective in getting me to more recent editions of the same reports from their source websites. You could also Google the name of the federal agency to get to their website, and then search the website for the pertinent phrase from the title ("journey to work") to see if you can find similar reports, the original report, or more recent reports.

Next, with anything that appears to be a book-length document, try looking up the title in your institution's online catalog; your library may simply own it. Finally, look for evidence of identifying numbers: this item has a SuDoc number (a government document identifier) and the mysterious annotation "Record Number: 2005 ASI 7558-104." The former indicates that this was published as a government document; if your institution has a gov docs collection, it's time to visit it. The latter number is an indicator that the whole publication is available on microfiche, part of a huge set of microfilmed documents behind the ASI (American Statistics Index, mentioned in the "Background and Coverage" section). The ASI's companion indexes, SRI and IIS, also have attendant fiche collections. Many university libraries own these fiche collections; go and consult your friendly microform collection librarian to find out more. When all else fails, there is always Interlibrary Loan.

Outputting Records

As you can see in Figure 8.6, the results lists in *Statistical Insight* have the familiar check boxes for selecting those entries that you wish to output. Simply click the ones you want, and then go to the drop-down menu in the top bar, as shown in Figure 8.9. "Print abstract" is the default value. The other choices are things we've come to expect: Print citations, Email

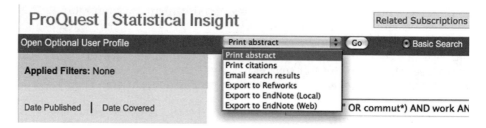

Fig. 8.9. Output options for *Statistical Insight*. The screen shots and their contents are published with permission of ProQuest LLC. Further reproduction is prohibited without permission.

search results, or Export to various bibliographic management systems. But wait . . . what if you have several records that offer Tables or the PDF Document?

Unfortunately, there isn't a way to mass output Tables or PDFs (at least not at this time, but who knows what may happen in the future?). For those, you'll need to download each one separately, and then attach them to an email to yourself (or print them). If you are in a hurry or not on your own computer, the easiest thing might be to mark the records you're interested in, then use the Email search results option to email yourself. You'll get a message containing a single link to "View ProQuest Statistical Search Results," which will take you to a page showing all the records you marked, complete with their Abstract, Table, PDF Document, or Other Editions icons. Now you're ready to crunch some numbers.

Quick Recap

The beginning of this chapter has introduced the whole topic of searching for "numbers" rather than articles, and introduced ProQuest's *Statistical Insight* as the only currently available multipurpose, entry-level subscription database for identifying numerical data (there are no free websites that compare). A companion subscription, *Statistical Datasets*, provides a more limited selection of data, but it offers the ability to interact with the data and see the results immediately in a graph (which can be exported for use in research papers, etc.).

The basic search in *Statistical Insight* is sufficient in almost all cases, although an Advanced Search is available. Typing into the basic search box causes suggestions to appear, including Subject terms. You can choose a Subject term or compose your own search strategy, and then easily apply and remove Filters from the extensive set provided on the left side of the screen. Each filter option includes the number of results that will be available when that filter is applied. Each record in the results list can have up to four icons: an Abstract, a PDF Document, Tables, or Other Editions. PDF Document and Tables provide access to full text; the Other Editions icon lists earlier editions of the same document that are also available in the database. To try and get to full text for items not directly available in the database, doing a Google search for the report title (or the issuing agency and then searching there) is a good approach; searching the local online catalog for the document title or consulting with a government documents librarian, if available, are other good strategies.

Even if the *Statistical Insight* database does not contain the full text of the data you are interested in, it is a far more efficient way of searching for and *identifying* what data might work and where it comes from, because it is custom built for that purpose. Having identified a report or an agency, one can then do a Google search for that known information. *Statistical Insight* provides a controlled entry into the crazy, messy world of numbers.

American FactFinder

Leaving the safety of the commercially crafted *Statistical Insight*, our first stop out on the wild frontier of numbers is the U.S. Bureau of Census (http://www.census.gov), home of *American FactFinder.*

Background and Coverage

In addition to everything else it provides, the Census Bureau website is home to a wonderful resource called *American FactFinder.* This is a good tool that keeps getting better. Reviews when it initially launched were highly positive (Jacsó 2000; Gordon-Murnane 2002), and subsequent reviews no less so. In 2006 Durant declared that: "All but the smallest academic and public libraries should link to it" and summed up his review of *American FactFinder* as "Highly recommended" (Durant 2006). Having used it since the early days, I can attest that this site has steadily gotten easier to use and understand, at least up to the latest release. With the third edition of this book we are on the cusp between the new *American FactFinder* and the legacy version, which is going offline late in 2011. I have to admit, my initial impression is that searching and using the latest iteration of *American FactFinder* is somewhat more complex, but then, compared with entering a zip code and receiving a detailed Fact Sheet, anything would seem more complex. Nonetheless, the folks at the Census Bureau deserve a lot of credit for continuing to work at understanding their users better, and making the incredible, complex wealth of information they collect more accessible to the public.

The data accessible through *American FactFinder* includes the current and previous decennial Census (i.e., from 2000 and 2010). The 2000 Census data has been completely processed, and includes sample data (from the long form) as well as the data from the short form everyone is asked to fill out (in data-speak, "100% data"). The 2010 Census used only the short form, and the information gathered will not be fully processed until sometime in 2013.[9] Keep in mind that the Census short form is literally short. It's only 10 questions, covering only the most basic information: age, sex, race, living arrangements (e.g., type of housing, own or rent, how many people in the household). You can find the form and much more about the 2010 Census at http://2010.census.gov/2010census/. Supplementing this information in *American FactFinder* is the more detailed information gathered by the American Community Survey (ACS), which is administered annually, but only to a subset of the population. The results are used to create estimates for the larger population. At the time of this writing, the ACS data has not yet been added to the new *American FactFinder*, making what we can find there rather limited. Thus, the following section only provides an introduction to using the *American FactFinder* interface, in order to help you explore and experiment on your own with the interesting data provided by this tool.

Accessing *American FactFinder*

The U.S. Census Bureau home page has many options but is laid out clearly enough to be navigable (Figure 8.10). It's very hard not to comment on all of the other interesting things available here, but I'm going to try to restrain myself. (Don't hesitate to explore on your own, however, especially some of the links associated with "People & Households" or "Business & Industry." Not to mention you can watch their videos on YouTube, follow them on Twitter, or friend the site on Facebook. The Census Bureau is thoroughly modern, Millie!)

The link to *American FactFinder* (http://factfinder2.census.gov) is located in the list on the left side of the page. The *American FactFinder* home page, as of July 2011, is shown in Figure 8.11.

Search Modes in *American FactFinder*

There are several ways to search on the *American FactFinder* home page. In the *Quick Start* area in the middle ("A" in Figure 8.11), you can enter a keyword and a "geography" (e.g., the name of a city, county, or state). As in *Statistical Insight*, as you type the system offers valid entries that match. This is very useful and important because "Census-speak" is not always quite like normal usage. Figure 8.12 shows the suggestions offered as the word "rent" is entered; the term Gross Rent is going to be selected. You could then start typing the name of a city in the geography field (again, the system will offer suggestions, guiding you to the correct entry) to get a list of all the data tables that have something to do with gross rent values for that area.

Figure 8.12 also shows the *Address Search* option: a very nonthreatening way to access the data by simply entering an address. Go and try it.

Fig. 8.10. The U.S. Census Bureau home page, as of July 2011.

Fig. 8.11. The American FactFinder home page, as of July 2011.

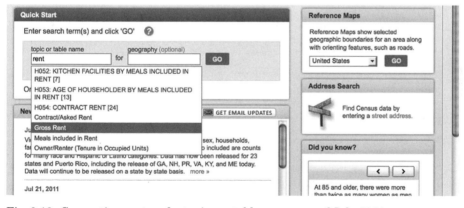

Fig. 8.12. Suggestion system for topics or table names, as of July 2011.

Don't be put off by the list of Geography Types that appear in response to your address; choose any of them and see what tables (what data) you get.

You can also go after data in *American FactFinder* in more of a browsing mode, using the buttons on the left (indicated with the bracket in Figure 8.11). Clicking the *Topics* button from the Main screen takes you to the Search screen with the Topics box displayed, as shown in Figure 8.13. You can drill into each main topic area (e.g., People, Housing, etc.), or, again, use the search box. At this point, the *Search Results* panel in the main part of the screen represents *all* the tables available in the system; try to ignore the mental disconnect of not actually having done a search—and yet having a huge result set.

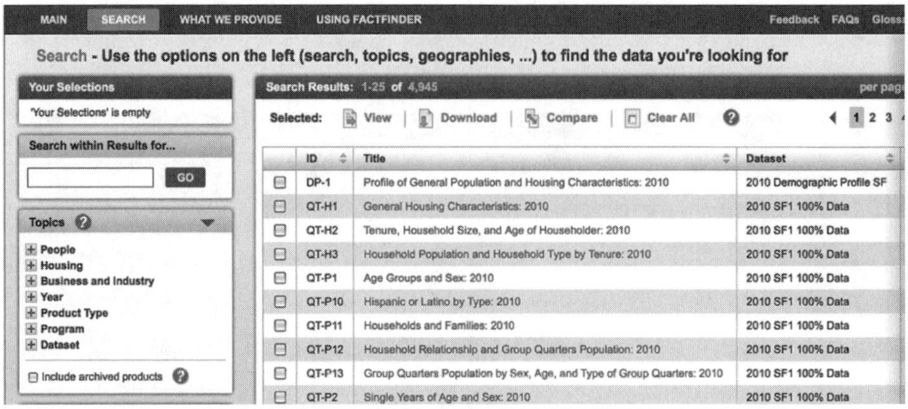

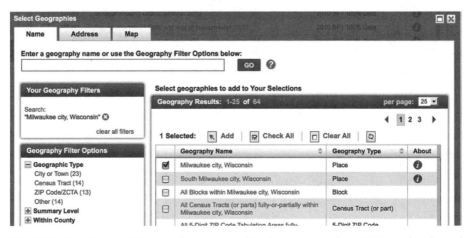

Fig. 8.13. Browsing access to Topics, as of July 2011.

Fig. 8.14. The Geographies overlay screen after doing a search on "Milwaukee," as of July 2011.

Clicking any of the other three buttons (*Geography, Population Groups,* or *Industry Codes*) brings up what the Census Bureau calls an "overlay screen," the same Ajax technology that was pointed out in EBSCO's *America: History and Life.* The initial Geographies overlay screen offers an almost overwhelming set of options. Do not panic. You can always just start typing the name of a place into the search box (a bit slowly so the system can keep up and offer suggestions), and then pick the option that best matches what you had in mind. Figure 8.14 shows the result of searching on "Milwaukee" and choosing the suggestion "Milwaukee city, Wisconsin." The check box for this entry is selected in the *Geography Results* panel, making the *Add* button go live. Clicking Add puts this geography into the *Your Selections* box in the main screen, and the Geographies overlay can then be closed. The Search screen is now displaying your search criteria (Your Selections), and the Search Results for those criteria: in this case, all the tables about Milwaukee, WI (1,939 as of July 2011) as shown in Figure 8.15.

To narrow these results to a specific topic (e.g., rent, marital status, travel time) for this geography, you can type the term of interest into the "Search

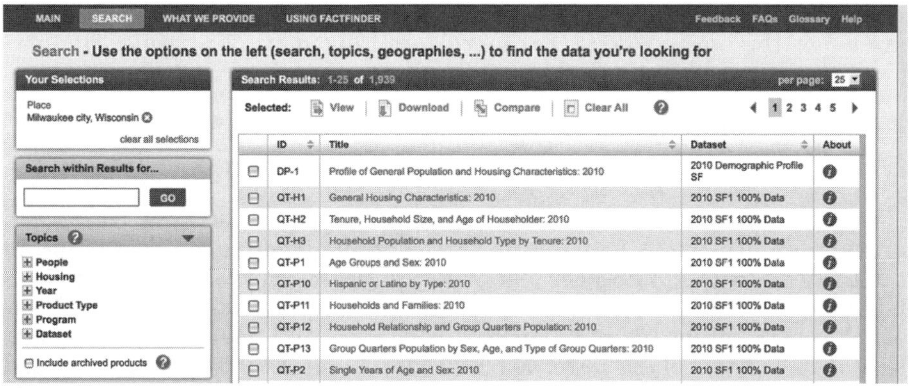

Fig. 8.15. Results of the geography selection, all the tables for Milwaukee, WI, as of July 2011.

within Results for . . ." box. The search criteria in the Your Selections box will stay there until you specifically remove it; if you start a new line of inquiry be sure to remove the current selections.

This is as much information as I am comfortable providing about *American FactFinder* in its current, transitional condition. By the time this book reaches your hands, there will be more (and more interesting) data available; I hope this introduction has given you at least enough of a grasp of the search options to explore it. The site itself also offers useful tutorials: see the Using FactFinder link on the Search page.

Quick Recap

This section has looked at *American FactFinder*, the interactive system created by the Census Bureau for accessing data from the decennial Census and the annual American Community Surveys. We looked at three ways to search *American FactFinder*: Quick Search by keyword and geography; Address Search; and detailed options for Topic, Geographies, Population Groups, and Industry Codes. Three suggestions for success in using *American Factfinder* are the following:

1. All of the search boxes in the system are designed to offer suggestions as you type; you are advised to type more slowly (so the system can keep up) to take advantage of those suggestions.

2. The Geographies, Population Groups, and Industry Codes options cause an overlay screen to appear; when you have made your selections and used the Add button to add them to Your Selections, close the overlay screen.

3. If you change the direction of your research, be sure to remove your previous criteria from the Your Selections box.

From "People" to "Workers"

The Census Bureau keeps track of the state of people in the United States: that is, how many people there are, how old they are, what sex they are, what race they belong to, where they live, and so forth. The Census Bureau notes whether people are employed or not, their income, and whether they are below the poverty level. For more detail about working America, however, we need to go to the Bureau of Labor Statistics.

Bureau of Labor Statistics

The Bureau of Labor Statistics, or BLS (http://www.bls.gov), tracks and provides exactly what the name says: everything about labor—working—in the United States. And it does mean *everything*—as of this writing, the BLS home page is featuring all sorts of current news, regional information, "Latest Numbers," other topics in various categories, and finally tiny additional lists at the bottom of the page, as pictured in Figures 8.16A and 8.16B. (And just wait until we mouse over "Subject Areas" at the top of the page.) Dearly as I love the BLS (how can you not love a government agency that uses a little green dinosaur icon to indicate "historical" data?), I understand that this page can be pretty overwhelming to look at. If you invest some time in studying it, however, you'll find that the designers have done their utmost to lay it out in a sensible and well-organized way, to try and connect you with

Fig. 8.16a. Bureau of Labor Statistics home page, upper half, as of July 2011.

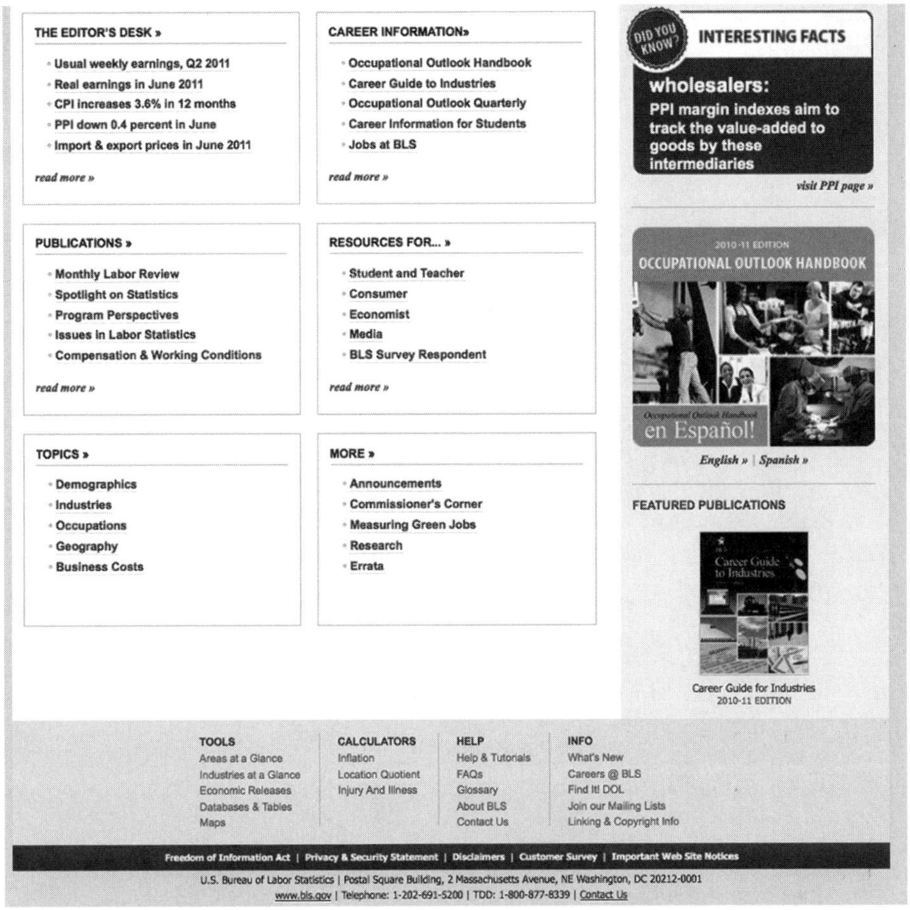

Fig. 8.16b. Bureau of Labor Statistics home page, lower half, as of July 2011.

the information you want as easily as possible. You will almost always find something new and useful, too.

For our first example, we will focus on one section, about wages.

Pay & Benefits at the Bureau of Labor Statistics

Search Example 1: Part 1—Finding Salary Information

Suppose the person closest to you has announced that as soon as you get done with your degree, he wants to go back to school and pursue *his* lifelong dream of becoming a registered nurse. This causes you to wonder about job prospects, and especially salaries for nurses.

On the BLS home page, mouse over words "Subject Areas" in the row menus just below the agency name, as shown in Figure 8.17. Blam! Don't panic at the myriad choices; simply look under the heading "Pay & Benefits" for the "Wages by Area & Occupation" link.

The next thing to decide is for what geographic area you want wage information: national, regional, state, or metropolitan area. When you're doing

Fig. 8.17. Subject Areas menu on the BLS home page, as of July 2011.

research for a particular person, it makes the most sense to look at data for a particular metropolitan area, since you'll be living and working in some specific place. (The other categories are more appropriate for more theoretical, comparative research purposes.) So let's try the option that lists "For 375 metropolitan statistical areas (MSAs), 34 metropolitan divisions, and over 170 nonmetropolitan areas," because it seems to offer more than the "major metropolitan areas" option (which only offers "80 metropolitan areas").

Clicking this link takes us to a straightforward page where you simply have to scroll to the state you want and choose a city name (or do a "find in page" for a city name). For instance, the "Occupational Employment and Wage Estimates" Web page for the metroplex of Portland-Vancouver-Beaverton, OR-WA, is shown in Figure 8.18.

Oh no! more numerical codes and broad category headings to choose from—or is that really true? Note how tiny the scroll bar is in this screenshot, indicating that this is a very long page. Here is a beautiful thing: you *don't* have to figure out that registered nurses fall under the heading "29–0000 Healthcare Practitioners and Technical Occupations." All you need to do is search the page for the word "nurses," using the Web browser's Find function. (Find is listed under the Edit menu, or can be invoked with "Ctrl-f" on a PC or with the Apple (⌘) key-f on a Mac.

Occupational Employment Statistics

OES 🔲   FONT SIZE: ⊖ ⊕   PRINT: 🖨

BROWSE OES
OES HOME
OES OVERVIEW ▶
OES NEWS RELEASES
OES DATABASES
OES TABLES
OES PUBLICATIONS
OES FAQS
CONTACT OES

SEARCH OES
[   ] Go

OES TOPICS
ARCHIVED DATA
CHARTS & MAPS
INFORMATION FOR RESPONDENTS
TECHNICAL DOCUMENTATION ▶

May 2010 Metropolitan and Nonmetropolitan Area Occupational Employment and Wage Estimates

Portland-Vancouver-Beaverton, OR-WA

For metropolitan and nonmetropolitan area definitions used by the OES survey, see the Metropolitan and nonmetropolitan area definitions page.

These estimates are calculated with data collected from employers in all industry sectors in Portland-Vancouver-Beaverton, OR-WA, a metropolitan statistical area that includes parts of Oregon and Washington.

Additional information, including the hourly and annual 10th, 25th, 75th, and 90th percentile wages and the employment percent relative standard error, is available in the downloadable XLS files.

Links to OES estimates for other areas and States

Major Occupational Groups in Portland-Vancouver-Beaverton, OR-WA (**Note**--clicking a link will scroll the page to the occupational group):

- 00-0000 All Occupations
- 11-0000 Management Occupations
- 13-0000 Business and Financial Operations Occupations
- 15-0000 Computer and Mathematical Occupations
- 17-0000 Architecture and Engineering Occupations
- 19-0000 Life, Physical, and Social Science Occupations
- 21-0000 Community and Social Service Occupations

29-1069	Physicians and Surgeons, All Other	3,630	8.4 %	3.777	1.634	(5)	$81.85	$170,240	11.1 %
29-1071	Physician Assistants	440	13.2 %	0.460	0.718	$49.05	$50.16	$104,330	4.0 %
29-1111	Registered Nurses*	19,610	6.6 %	20.387	0.976	$37.71	$37.59	$78,180	1.0 %
29-1122	Occupational Therapists	610	5.2 %	0.639	0.810	$35.30	$34.55	$71,870	1.2 %
29-1123	Physical Therapists	1,420	5.7 %	1.471	1.037	$36.01	$36.08	$75,050	1.3 %

Fig. 8.18. BLS page for Occupational Employment and Wage Estimates for Portland-Vancouver-Beaverton, OR, selected portions, as of July 2011.

Occupation Information at the Bureau of Labor Statistics

Search Example 1: Part 2

Continuing with the search example started earlier, your second concern was about the job outlook for nurses.

Back on the BLS home page, what we want is the *Occupational Outlook Handbook*. If you mouse over Publications (as we did Subject Areas), you'll find it listed there; it is also the first thing listed in the Career Information box (Figure 8.16b). The *Handbook* is a classic source of career guidance, first in hard copy and for many years now on the Web. The online version is getting a whole new look in late 2011; by the time this book reaches you the beta preview will have been finalized, and may be slightly different.

There are various ways to use the *Handbook*, depending on your interest (e.g., if you have a specific position in mind, as in this case, or you only want to browse a job category to get ideas). To find information on a specific line of work you can use the search box or browse the A–Z Index. If you are looking for a very specific job title, or the sorts of trendy titles that crop up in the tech industry ("chief creative officer"), you might not find an entry in the *Handbook*. But for a great many occupational titles, it brings together an extremely useful package of information: a Summary page, and then detailed information under tabs labeled What They Do, Work Environment, How to Become One, Pay, Job Outlook, Similar Occupations, and Contacts

Fig. 8.19. Preview of new interface for the *Occupational Outlook Handbook*, as of July 2011.

for More Info (as of the preview in July 2011). An example of how the BLS plans to present an occupation page is shown in Figure 8.19.

The current *Occupational Outlook Handbook* content for registered nurses gives us the encouraging news that "Overall job opportunities for registered nurses are expected to be excellent, but may vary by employment and geographic setting" and that "Employment of registered nurses is expected to grow by 22 percent from 2008 to 2018, much faster than the average for all occupations." This could be a good career move!

The only bad news is that this information is provided at the nationwide level only. Finding information on job outlook by state or city is, regrettably, beyond the entry-level scope of this text, and you are encouraged to go talk to your friendly local business librarian.

Quick Recap

The *Bureau of Labor Statistics* tracks and provides information about employment and occupations in the United States, along with limited international information. Other topics covered by the BLS are pricing, inflation, consumer spending, and time use. We looked at only two of the hundreds of resources at the BLS: wage information by occupation, based on geographic location (e.g., salaries for librarians in Boston versus Omaha), and the *Occupational Outlook Handbook* (OOH). The OOH pulls together a range of useful information for each job described to provide a clear picture of what work in that field is like, prospects for employment and pay, and organizations or websites to visit for more information. The BLS is a vast and incredibly rich resource for data of every kind about working in the United States.

Numbers and the Reference Interview

Numeric Reference is somewhat of a specialty, involving a lexicon all its own. Information from surveys gets turned into data sets, which are then defined in terms of four distinct characteristics. I have listed here four specific things to try to find out during a reference interview with any patron requesting "data."

- The *population*, often referred to as the "universe" in data-speak: Whom is the patron interested in? All of the people who live in rural areas of the United States? Nurses? Railway workers in the 19th century?

- *Date*: Most current available? One particular date (usually a year) in the past? Or a "time series," that is, a set of values over a particular period? (e.g., the gross national product for the United States from 1948 to now).

- *Frequency* (for a time series): Annually? Quarterly? Monthly?

- *Place, or geographic region*: The whole United States? Alabama? Spain?

It would be nice to provide you with a succinct, complementary list of actions to take based on the answers to these questions, but that probably requires a book unto itself. Suffice it to say that these definitely *are* the four questions to ask, and that eliciting information about these four things is useful in several ways, both practically and psychologically:

- The answers to these questions should help to determine if the patron really does want a data set, or just some statistics.

- If the request is vague, obviously the questions should help to clarify it, and asking them collects useful information (while also buying some time in which to rack your brain).

- Going through the process also provides a structured approach to fall back on (e.g., go back and ask the *right* questions), if you thought you understood the question and could get an answer pretty quickly, but your first resource isn't working out.

- Finally, answers to these questions are intended to help *you* to decide where to go looking for the information, but they will be equally helpful if you need to refer the patron to someone else in the library. Capturing the answers is a useful thing to do that makes the patron feel that a help process has been started, and forwarding the information will make the next librarian's task much easier, as well as saving time for both the librarian and the patron.

Exercises and Points to Consider

Check the book companion website, www.LibrariansGuide.info, for supplementary materials.

1. In the opening to this chapter, some broad categories of the following types of numbers were mentioned. If you are using this book in

a class, have a class discussion and see how many specific types of the following sorts of numbers or statistics you can come up with:

"People" type

"Business" type

"Financial" type

2. Similar to search example 1 in *Statistical Insight*, start typing "immigration" into the search box, and observe the suggestions that appear. Choose the one for "Subject: Immigration and emigration," and then again spend time experimenting with the filters and with sorting by Date Published as opposed to Relevance. For fun and amazement, before applying any filters, take a look at the values on the Date Covered Range Selector for this topic.

3. In *American FactFinder* click the Topics button, then open the Dataset subtopic. Click on "2010 SF1 100% Data," then "2000 SF1 100% Data" to add both of these to Your Selections. Then use the "Search within Results for . . ." box to search for "households and families" with the quotes (you are ignoring any system suggestions this time). You should be looking at a list of about 45 results. Find the option to change the number of results shown "per page" and change it to 50, so you can see all your results on one page. Now choose these tables from your results: "Households and Families: 2010" and "Households and Families: 2000." Click View. Notice that you are viewing "Result 1 of 2"; click the pointer so you are viewing Result 2 of 2. What happens if you click the View All button? Now experiment: click Back to Search, and see if you can get data on Households and Families for a specific U.S. state. Next click the Geographies button, then look up and add a state to Your Selections. (Your previous selections should still be there.) What about at the county or the city level? If you get no results when you choose View, it simply means the data (for 2010) have not yet been processed.

4. As mentioned in the Quick Recap for the BLS, this agency also conducts surveys and provides data on time use, that is, how Americans spend their days. Find the link to this information under Subject Areas, and take a look at the HTML version of the latest American Time Use Survey. You are after something called "Table 1. Time spent in primary activities (1) and percent of the civilian population engaging in each activity, averages per day by sex, [latest year annual averages]." Take a look at the categories, gender differences, etc.—does this "look like you"?

Beyond the Textbook Exercises

1. An article titled "Stuck in Jobs: The New Swing Voters" appeared in the June 16, 2011, issue of *Bloomberg BusinessWeek*. It discusses peoples' reluctance to quit their jobs since the recession hit in 2008: "Since January 2009, an average 1 million fewer Americans per month have quit their jobs than in previous years. Through April, the most recent data available, that adds up to 28 million Americans stuck in jobs they would have left in ordinary times" (Dorning 2011). The article includes a graph of the number of workers who

quit their jobs from April 2006 to April 2011. The graph is labeled
"Data: Bureau of Labor Statistics." Go to the BLS and see if you can
find this data for yourself. Hints: Your entry point is listed under
"Employment: Job Openings and Labor Turnover." Then use your
eyes. You want something about quitting, and you're after "Historical Data."

2. If your institution subscribes to *Statistical Datasets* (click the "Related Subscriptions" at the top of the *Statistical Insight* screen to
find out), here are some activities to try in that database. You will
need to let the database install a Java applet in order to run. First,
simply click on one of the topics listed for the "In the News" folder
in the frame on the left, for example, Gasoline Prices – All Grades.
This produces an instant graph of the results (how many years of
data does it offer?). Find the box labeled Time, and experiment with
changing the sampling frequency—Week, Month, Year—and notice
how the chart changes as you do so. Click the Export option above
the chart; the array of possibilities is wonderful. Now look back in
the left frame: if the Browse by Subject folder isn't open, click it to
open it. Then click the folder called Education. The first subfolder
under Education is called Library Statistics. Click the item Number of ALA-MLS on Staff. You should see a steady upward trend,
but how current is the data? In the boxes above the chart, find the
one called Type. Figure out how to get a chart for the county you
live in. Then change the Type back to All, and turn your attention
back to the left frame. Hold down the Control key, and select Staff
Salaries (also in Library Statistics). Shazam! Two sets of data showing in one graph. Neat, eh?

Suggested Readings

Anything that Stephen Woods has written for *DttP: Documents to the People*. His
articles on various number-finding questions and resources appear regularly,
and are useful, timely, and completely accessible. One of his series is "By the
numbers: [topic]," another is "What everyone should know about [x]." Search
by his name and the journal name to be sure of getting everything. Gems,
every one of them.

Google, Inc. 2011. *Think Quarterly*: Think Data [special issue on data]. http://
thinkquarterly.co.uk/ June 27, 2011. Get the unique "Google view" on data:
interesting, thought-provoking articles, such as "Data for Change" ("Can you
do business while doing good in the developing world? The answer is yes, but
only if you focus on the data that matters.") and "From Sticks to Clouds" ("A
visual history of data capture through the ages."). And the one you'll want to
look at first: The Knowledge ("Simon Rogers picks the 10 best places to see
'sexy' data online.").

Kellam, Lynda M., and Katharin Peter. 2011. *Numeric Data Services and Sources
for the General Reference Librarian*. Cambridge, UK: Woodhead Publishing
Limited. The perfect gentle introduction to working with "data questions" for
the nonspecialist. The authors are members of IASSIST, the professional
organization for data librarians.

Ojala, Marydee. 2004. "Statistically Speaking." *Online* (Weston, Conn.) 28 (March/
April): 42–44. A more in-depth look at "where numbers come from," similar to
the opening discussion in this chapter. Full of good advice and strategies from
a master in the field.

Notes

1. Note that nonprofits and trade organizations usually do not provide data for free; *nonprofit* does not mean "no fee" (and trade organizations need to recoup their costs too).

2. What one might call the "ha ha, you must be kidding!" price category.

3. Obviously, Google does a good job of finding websites for organizations, but *Associations Unlimited*, the database equivalent of that reference staple, the *Encyclopedia of Associations*, is handy for identifying associations—especially the international ones, whose website might not be in English.

4. Look for links with the word "Investor" in them: Investor Relations, Investor Center, etc.

5. A pretty close approximation to a comprehensive list of currently available data and statistics resources can be seen at the library website of a well-endowed university, such as Princeton. The Subject List of databases for "Economics & Finance" at Princeton (further subdivided by "Economic Data" and "Financial Data") is impressive. Still, the only general-purpose, usable-by-ordinary-mortals data database is *Statistical Insight*.

6. The year range you get for this limit will depend on what you search, of course. This was a simple search on the word "corn." Most searches would not produce such an amazing "date covered" range, but this is fun for its shock value.

7. In extremely disturbing news, as of May 2011, the branch of the Census Bureau that produced the *Statistical Abstract* has been "eliminated" as part of the effort to curb "non-essential administrative spending." The 130th edition may be the last (Griffiths 2011).

8. This one works. The second Google result as of June 2011, titled: [CTPP] Journey to Work Trends 1960–2000, turns out to be a message posting pointing you to an ftp site where the full report is available. Incredible, really!

9. A table of scheduled release dates for the 2010 data is available at http://www .census.gov/population/www/cen2010/glance/.

9
Focus on People

This entire book so far has been concerned with the mechanics of databases: what they are, how to use them, and how they differ by discipline. But at any time it's important to pause and reflect on the ultimate reason *why* we're interested in learning this: to assist other people in their research process. Understanding the people who might benefit from using these databases and how they feel about doing research (there are a lot of emotions involved, it turns out) can inform how you interact with them. This chapter provides an examination of the general theoretical underpinnings of what your users are going through: the whole process of *information seeking*. Indeed, information seeking is all around us, "always embedded in the larger tasks of work, learning, and play" (Nel 2001). Whether you're motivated by the question of locating the nearest coffee shop or a desire to find information on a rare form of cancer, although you might not have thought of it this way, those who study information seeking behavior see you as engaged in a complex set of interacting dimensions of work tasks, search tasks, time, and "individual, contextual, and environmental attributes"—all of which influence your information seeking and retrieval strategies (Xie 2009). If you are a librarian trying to facilitate information seeking, it's important to have the process in the back of your mind as you engage in a reference interview. Understanding the information seeking process also helps to inform your whole strategy of questioning in the reference interview (e.g., the use of "open" and "closed" questions) and helps to ensure greater satisfaction on both sides: librarian and patron.

This chapter is based on selected articles and other sources from the library literature that I found helpful for conveying the major points that I wish to make. These articles range from scholarly and erudite to down-home and practical (often the informal, one- or two-page pieces offer some of the best down-to-earth advice). This is by no means a comprehensive review of the literature; indeed, the examples listed in the section on Applied Studies are only selected articles that have been published since 2009 (when the previous edition of this book came out). The information seeking literature is vast and continually being added to. As of July 2011, there were 675 records that had been assigned the pure Thesaurus subject heading "Information Needs" ("used for: information-seeking behavior") in *Library Literature & Information Science*. The phrase "information needs" was used on its own or as part of other subject headings in a total of 2,871 records, representing articles dating from 1982 to July 2011. Entire journals are devoted to the study of information needs and seeking. *Information Research*, an "open access, international, peer-reviewed, scholarly journal" made its debut on the Web in 1995 and has been actively publishing ever since (Information Research home page 2011). This e-journal probably now offers the largest freely available body of research papers on this topic in the world. Interest in information seeking has a remarkably long history, as demonstrated by a study of the reference interview dating from the 19th century (Green 1876). Countless other studies have followed, continually analyzing how people go about fulfilling information needs and how librarians can better assist in the process.

Part 1: Information Seeking Behavior

The information seeking literature can generally be characterized as belonging to one of two groups: the *theoretical*, which discusses the topic in abstract terms and seeks to define it in terms of structured models, and the *applied*, which discusses it in terms of real-world observations and interactions. This section provides an introduction to some of the theory and the applied studies on people's information seeking behaviors.

Some Theoretical Background on Information Seeking

Robert S. Taylor's 1968 article is a classic in the area of theoretical information seeking studies. In it, he presents a model that identifies four levels of questions:

- Q1   the visceral need
- Q2   the conscious need
- Q3   the formalized need
- Q4   the compromised need

According to Taylor, information seeking can range from an unconscious, not-even-expressible information need, to a very fuzzy but vaguely discussible need, to a point at which the person can clearly voice the question, and finally to the compromised need—the question "*as presented to an information system*" (emphasis mine). An example of the question as presented to an information system is what a person types into the Google search box. (The source quoted lists "library or librarian" as the first kind of possible "information system," but as we know, and as is amply demonstrated in the literature, after friends or colleagues, the Web is by far the first choice of information seekers today.)

In his 2001 article, Johannes Nel surveys the subsequent theoretical literature and the models of information seeking with an emphasis on the emotional states that accompany the various stages of the search process. He describes the classic model of the "information search process" by Carol

Table 9.1. Information Search Process Stages in Kuhlthau's Model (1991).

Stage	Task	Emotions
Initiation	Recognize a need for information (result of awareness of lack of knowledge).	Uncertainty, apprehension
Selection	Identify and select general topic or approach.	Optimism (upon achieving task)
Exploration	Need to locate information about topic, become informed, integrate new information with previously held constructs, reconcile sources providing inconsistent or incompatible information	Confusion, uncertainty, discouragement, frustration, sense of personal inadequacy
Formulation	Focus, personalize topic by identifying and selecting ideas from all the information retrieved.	Increased confidence, sense of clarity
Collection	Gather information related to the restated, focused topic; clearer sense of direction allows for more efficient, relevant interactions with information systems.	Confidence increases, interest in project increases, uncertainty subsides.
Presentation	Prepare presentation of findings.	Relief, satisfaction (or disappointment if search has not gone well)

Kuhlthau (1991) in detail; it has many stages and affiliated emotions, as indicated in Table 9.1.

(This model was revisited in the very different world of 2008 by Kuhlthau and her colleagues, and found to be still valid [Kuhlthau, Heinström and Todd].) Taken overall, this process amounts to quite an emotional roller coaster for the poor information seeker. Looking over the stages, we could envision it as in Figure 9.1.

A study by Ethelene Whitmire (2003) demonstrates that when it comes to undergraduates faced with writing research papers, Kuhlthau's model fits

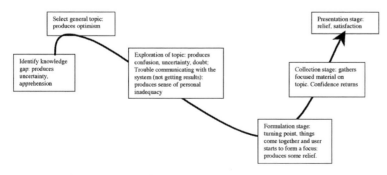

Fig. 9.1. The research roller coaster.

exactly. This model also fits with my own experience with academic information seekers, although the process doesn't necessarily progress steadily from one stage to another. Such seekers frequently go through several iterations of the select, explore, formulate, collect stages. Kulhthau's model has also been applied to adolescent information seeking by Ross J. Todd (2003). His version of the model also pulls in the associated cognitive processes (thoughts: from vague to focused to increased interest), and physical actions (exploring to documenting).

Dr. Jannica Heinström, who has worked closely with Todd and Kuhlthau, has published several articles on her research in this area. Her work brings the ideas in Kuhlthau's model (i.e., stages, tasks, and emotions in information seeking) to a next step (i.e., testing the influence of disciplinary area, study habits, and personality on information seeking in students) within the current, online-dominant information world. She has looked at patterns in information seeking both in master's level students and in middle and high school students. She has identified three characteristic information seeking patterns relating to the students' preferences for exploration or specificity, which she has named *fast surfing*, *broad scanning*, and *deep diving*. She found these various styles to be "grounded in personality traits" and could be "linked to the students' study approaches." In only one area, the social sciences, did discipline appear to have an influence on information seeking style (Heinström 2006). Table 9.2 attempts to capture the results of her studies on master's level students in a shorthand format. (Note the "good critical evaluation skills" of the broad scanners. In related research, the importance of critical thinking skills in determining a user's level of library anxiety—and, ultimately, information seeking success—has been studied and is usefully discussed in Kwon, Onwuegbuzie, and Alexander 2007.) In looking over this table, don't you find it easy to recognize fellow students or patrons of any kind that you have worked with?

Lopatovska and Arapakis (2011) provide a useful review of the theoretical literature concerning emotions in the information seeking and retrieval process. Theory, in all these cases, seems to accord well with reality, and the "reality" of information seeking behavior is a favorite topic of library literature.

Applied Research on Information Seeking Behavior

Literally hundreds of studies have been done on information seeking behaviors in academic settings. Wildemuth and Case (2010) provide an excellent, succinct history of the study of information seeking behavior and the literature it has produced. The topics covered in the following selection of articles published since the previous edition of this book was composed in 2008 demonstrate the breadth, depth, and international scope of this research:

- Undergraduates and other scholars in the social sciences and humanities (Ge 2010, Head 2008)

- Faculty, including basic science researchers (Haines et al. 2010), computer science and engineering faculty (Tucci 2011), and physics and astronomy faculty (Jamali and Nicholas 2010)

- National studies of academic researchers in the United States (Niu et al. 2010) and the United Kingdom (Nicholas et al. 2009)

- International studies: undergraduate humanities students in Nigeria (Baro, Onyenania, and Osaheni 2010), Greek graduate students

Table 9.2. Information Seeking by Fast Searchers, Broad Scanners, and Deep Divers.

	Fast Surfers	**Broad Scanners**	**Deep Divers**
Amount of effort	Minimal	Active, but highly spontaneous; serendipitous	Considerable, strong search engagement
Information acquisition pattern	Hasty, unstructured	Unstructured exploration	Focused and structured, systematic: preference for precision over recall
Preferred types of content	Easily accessible and digestible: overviews, restatements of views already held	Inspiring, challenging, presenting new ideas	High scientific quality, specific
Discipline (area of study)	No influence	Significant connection found between social sciences students and this approach	No influence
Study approach	Surface, low motivation	No influence	Focused, structured; desire for thorough understanding; deep or strategic approaches to studying; high motivation
Personality traits	Low conscientiousness: "easily distracted, impatient, easygoing"; low openness to experience and high sensitivity result in "avoidance of challenging information content"	Extroversion but low agreeableness, openness to experience: "outgoing, curious, and competitive"; good critical evaluation skills	No "significant influence of personality" but a positive connection between openness and conscientiousness to deep diving

Based on Heinström 2006.

(Korobili, Malliari, and Zapounidou 2011), Australian PhD candidates (Du and Evans 2011), faculty at various Indian universities (Khan and Shafique 2011; Mahajan 2009), faculty in Spain (Pinto and Fernández-Ramos 2010), and various studies at universities in China (Zhang, Ye, and Liu 2011; Gao, Guo, and Duan 2011)

- Very specific groups or themes, such as business students (Dubicki 2010), LGBTQ (lesbian, gay, bisexual, transgender, queer) college students (Schaller 2011), users of education literature (Wright 2010), and the impact of social marketing on the information-seeking behavior of college students (O'Connor and Lundstrom 2011)

Medical librarians and others have published a great many articles on information seeking in health care, often focusing on the professional side: clinical staff in a large health care organization (Hider et al. 2009), junior doctors (Cullen, Clark, and Esson 2011), veterinarians (Sewell, Funkhouser, and Foster 2011), and nurses and health professionals in the United Kingdom (Bertulis and Cheeseborough 2008). Cranley and colleagues (2009) provide a complete literature review of the role of uncertainty in information seeking among nurses.

There seems to be an increasing interest in studying how patients seek and use information, however, with research being carried out by a broader spectrum of the medical community. Researchers are studying information seeking behaviors as a public health issue (Weaver et al. 2010), looking at the sources people use (Cutilli 2010, Kunimoto 2010) and how prescription advertising affects information seeking (Rollins et al. 2010). Studies range far afield, as shown by an examination of information seeking behaviors in rural versus urban Peruvians (Garcia-Cosavalente, Wood, and Obregon 2010). Specific studies have looked at cancer patients and survivors in the United States (Lambert, Loiselle, and Macdonald 2009, Roach et al. 2009) and in South Korea (Noh et al. 2009), chronic pain sufferers (Corcoran et al. 2010), persons with diabetes (Longo et al. 2010), people with HIV/AIDS (Samal et al. 2010), and smokers (Rutten et al. 2009).

School media specialists and public librarians have also actively contributed their observations and advice about the information seeking behaviors that they observe in the clientele of their libraries. Andrew Shenton has a long history of writing about information seeking by young people; he added three more articles to this theme in 2010. Other authors writing on the topic of information seeking by children, youth, or adolescents include Large, Nesset, and Beheshti (2008); Spowage (2008); Dresang and Koh (2009); and Bowler (2010). Crow (2009) is interested in fostering an "intrinsic motivation" for information seeking, while Newell (2009) wants to improve instruction for information problem solving. At the other end of the spectrum, there seems to be a flurry of interest within the public library community in the information seeking behaviors of baby boomers (Decker 2010; Williamson, Bannister, and Sullivan 2010) and people in the "fourth age" (i.e., senior citizens) (Williamson and Asla 2009). Public librarians are also considering the issues of health information seeking from their clients (Harris et al. 2010), and information seeking behavior patterns observed in their online users (Ruthven 2010).

Scanning the recent literature, at the time of this writing we find studies of other groups ranging from seekers of music information (Lee 2010; Laplante and Downie 2011), practicing visual artists (Hemmig 2009), and theatre artists (Medaille 2010) to farmers in Ohio (Diekmann, Loibl and Batte 2009), backpackers (Chang 2009), the clergy (Wicks 2011), women's investment club members (O'Connor 2011), and Second Life users (Ostrander 2008). Internationally, studies of information seeking behavior have included policy makers in Pakistan (Ansari 2011), rural Chinese people (Zhang and Liangzhi 2009), women cement workers in India (Machendranath and Kamble 2010), and rural women in Borno State, Nigeria (Saleh and Lasisi 2011). Moving beyond human subjects, even dogs (McMahon, Macpherson, and Roberts 2010) have been the objects of scrutiny of their information seeking behaviors.

Information Seeking in the Internet Era

The recent applied research on information seeking behavior in wired societies has consistent themes: people tend to turn first to the Internet or to friends or colleagues when they have an information need. As much as they love the Internet, they still do like interacting with humans. Given the choice between someone they know—a friend, a teacher, or a colleague—and a librarian (whom they do not know), they'll start with the former. As Stephen Abram notes about millennial students, "Need help? Ask the MySpace community" (Abram 2007). With social networking sites, users now have the best of all worlds: doing their information seeking with friends and doing it conveniently, online. Another finding has to do with time: in the studies, users consistently complain about lack of time. Information seekers try to save time whenever possible, which leads to opting for convenience over quality to the point of convenience as the governing factor in their information seeking (Connaway, Dickey, and Radford 2011). In a study of gender differences in information seeking, the researchers found that men deal with this time problem by having a stronger preference for fast retrieval tools and are slightly more likely to go to the Internet as their first resource, but that women "perceived lack of time more intensely" (Steinerová and Šušol 2007).

Although a major obstacle to doing research that is repeatedly mentioned is "knowing where to start," at the same time, elementary school children, teenagers, and undergraduates consider themselves skilled and quite capable of doing their own research. Users are also increasingly aware of the enormous amount of information available, and in conjunction with the lack of time problem, complain about information overload (Young and Seggern 2001). This phenomenon remains a frequent topic in the literature (Blair 2010; Blocker 2011; Davis 2011).

Participants in Young and Seggern's (2001) study described a "dream information machine" as something intuitive (a mind reader), a thing they can interact with in natural language. Their dream information machine is also a single source: comprehensive, complete, portable, and accessible 24 hours a day, 7 days a week (24/7). Although you can interact with librarians in natural language, we are not exactly portable or available 24/7. We tend to point you to several possible sources rather than "the one perfect answer," but we are sometimes rather good at mind reading. Given the earlier description, it is likely that these study participants would regard Google as the answer to their dream. This is a good place to pause and consider:

Why People Love the Internet

According to the literature, at the beginning stages of the research process information seekers are anxious and nervous (unless they are teenagers or undergraduates, born into the Web world and quite confident of their abilities to find things). One of the big problems is getting started. An information seeker gets very discouraged and might even quit if he or she doesn't get results. They prefer one source, they want it fast, and they want it everywhere, all the time. On the Internet you do it on your own. Among other things, your thoughts don't have to be as clearly formulated as they would be to express your question to someone whom you don't know well. Embarrassment is therefore avoided, and:

- Starting is easier because you simply type something in and almost always get results.

- Anxiety is immediately reduced, because you got *something* (you probably have gotten much more than just something—perhaps thousands of hits—but it is better, quite literally, than nothing).

- You feel like you must know what you're doing. Confidence is increased because you got something, so you don't need help.

- It appears to be "one source" because you can get something on practically any topic from one search engine.

- It's fast, it's available 24/7, and it's almost ubiquitous, especially now that you can get to it on your mobile device.

What's not to like? There are, however, many negative emotions connected with searching on the Internet.

Downsides of Internet Searching

Some of the negative emotions and aspects of doing one's own searching on the Internet include the following:

- Doubt, uncertainty
- Confusion
- Frustration
- Time pressure
- Being overwhelmed with results
- Never knowing when you're finished or if you've found all there is to find

Uncertainty in information seeking in the digital environment is a frequent research topic, for example (Chowdhury, Gibb, and Landoni 2011). You have undoubtedly encountered many of these negative emotions yourself when searching the Internet. (Even Google is only as good as the search you give it.) Having to sift through long lists of results, visiting various pages, evaluating, clicking deeper within a site to try to figure out why it was included in the results, then backtracking and trying not to get lost can definitely elicit all of these emotions. From the literature and my own experiences with users, the user mind-set appears to be something like this:

> Web searching can be very frustrating, but at least you suffer in private. You don't have to confess or try to explain your topic to a stranger: a librarian (especially if it isn't totally clear to *you* yet). Perhaps you've been working on this idea for a while and think you're quite on top of it, so how could someone (a librarian) totally unfamiliar with it be any help? You'd have to explain so much, and that would take too much time. Besides, you got results, so you obviously know how to search, and you're sure the information you want is out there. You want it, and it sounds reasonable to you that such information should exist, therefore it must be there, because you can find anything on the Internet, right? Somewhere. It must just be a matter of trying again, and again, frustrating as it is.

Effect of the "Internet Mind-set" on Information Seeking

For some years now the literature about information seeking behaviors has scarcely questioned that users go straight to the Internet; that is a given. Now what is studied is how the "Internet mind-set" affects their information seeking, or search, habits. The patterns that seem to be emerging are the use of very simplistic searches involving only one or two keywords, and many iterations: search and scan (the results), search and scan again, and again. Rather than trying to evaluate or analyze why a search didn't work, users immediately change a word and try again, rapidly abandoning searches that don't appear to work (Novotny 2004; Moulaison 2008). Users rarely, if ever, take advantage of advanced search features, and Boolean scarcely enters the picture. Presented with an advanced search interface, they still simply enter keywords (Novotny 2004; Moulaison 2008). Users either don't know how or can't be bothered to refine large result sets; instead, they scan quickly for one or two likely looking titles (Kim and Sin 2011). Overall, digital search habits seem to be characterized by a trial-and-error approach, and a general lack of critical, analytical skills (Todd 2003)—or at least, a failure to employ same (Kim and Sin 2011). The title of Eric Novotny's 2004 article captures it exactly: "I Don't Think I Click." Although Heinström's (2006) study was not about the specific actions of the research participants, the type of searching described here sounds very much like what fast surfers and broad scanners would do, although she notes that the broad scanners are better at critiquing their results.

Is all this a death knell for the powerful, sophisticated interfaces developed for subscription databases? My hope is no. I hope that features such as Boolean operators and field searching will continue to be available, to be used by those who know how (by Heinström's third group, the deep divers). At the same time, one can already see that the way keyword searches are handled behind the scenes in these databases is getting better and better, so that simple keyword searches in a sophisticated database produce useful results. We have also seen in previous chapters that many of the databases have started adding myriad features aimed at helping users to refine their outcome on the results page, if they don't choose to use the capabilities in the search interface. Is there any hope of teaching students and others to use more effective search methods, such as synonyms, Boolean logic, limits? In my opinion, trying to do this on the large scale, that is, teaching whole classes to be expert searchers, is probably not realistic. As teaching moments arise, one on one, introducing just one or two of these concepts with the appropriate hooks—"This will make your searching much more efficient, it'll be much easier to get the information you need, and you'll get a better grade on your paper"—can be a successful approach in my experience. Woo them gently; the carrot is much more effective than the stick. The occasion for most of these teaching moments is in the reference interview, our next topic.

Quick Recap

The information seeking process has been described in the theoretical literature with various models. Taylor's model uses levels of questions, whereas Kuhlthau's model describes it as a series of stages and tasks, each with a good deal of emotion attached. Heinström studies information seekers in the Internet era, and characterizes them as fast surfers, broad scanners, or deep divers. Applied studies of academic users support these models and show two major trends: a person seeking information tends to consult (1) the Internet or (2) friends and colleagues before turning to the library. Searching the Internet has many very appealing aspects, as well as frustrations, for information seekers. The predominance of Internet usage has affected how people of the Net generation search for information; their habits generally are characterized by speed, reliance on keyword searches rather than anything more sophisticated, and trial and error. The deep diver searchers are an exception, however.

Part 2: The Reference Interview

Certainly, what the literature tells us about how people look for information is borne out in our own realities every day:

People go straight to the Internet,

Or they ask other people.

Where do libraries and librarians fit in, then? It appears, for better or worse, that for most people librarians have become the resource of last resort. (Although women are more likely than men to seek out help from librarians, at least in Slovakia [Steinerová and Šušol 2007]). In a 2008 study of OPAC users, when asked, "What would you do next?" after an unsuccessful topic search, the authors observe repeatedly "not one student mentioned asking a library staff member for help" (Antell and Huang). (Ouch.) The exception is a person you have worked with and helped before: Once someone has experienced a good search that produces useful material fairly quickly, he or she is likely to consider returning to you rather than continue to engage in marathon, fruitless sessions on the Internet. Even if the answer with the librarian is a Web search, it may well be more efficiently done and produce the needed results faster. Being a resource of last resort means we are not, perhaps, asked as many questions (chronically overworked reference librarians can throw things at me now), but the ones that we are asked are often more difficult. Most of the time this makes the job more interesting. (The rest of the time—well, every job has its frustrations. It's better if you don't bash your head on the desk when people can see you.) Being a resource of last resort and having to work with more difficult questions means, however, that the topic of this section of the chapter, the reference interview, has only grown in importance.

To sort out these more difficult questions and elicit useful information from people who are convinced that they are already good searchers who have done everything possible, you need all your best communication and people skills. Indeed, the oft-quoted dilemma, as phrased by Robert Taylor in 1968, still applies:

> Without doubt, the negotiation of reference questions is one of the most complex acts of human communication. During this process, one person tries to describe for another person not something he knows, but rather something he does NOT know.

What Is the Real Question?

One of the most challenging things about the reference interview is simply that people do not ask for what they really want. This is a recurring theme in the literature: "inquirers seldom ask at first for what they want" (Taylor 1968), and "librarians have long recognized the tendency of library users to pose their initial questions in incomplete, often unclear, and sometimes apparently covert terms" (Dewdney and Michell 1997). Mary Ellen Bates (1998) expressed the issue succinctly as "finding the question behind the question." Catherine Ross (2003) is strongly in favor of a reference interview in "almost every" transaction, because even a very brief exchange helps people to "clarify in their own minds what their question really is." In some musings about his work on a Reference Desk, Sean Scott (2004) has a humorous example of the type of question that makes any reference librarian's blood run cold: "Do you have anything on that gal who died?" ("That gal" turned out to be Anne Frank.)

Why is this asking of a question so difficult? Why don't people simply ask what they really want to know? It turns out there's a lot more to *asking* a question (let alone answering one) than meets the eye. For example:

- The question might be used as a way to make contact, to see if you're available. Indeed, it has been suggested (Dewdney and Michell 1996) that the initial question actually be treated as "four unspoken questions":
  - Am I in the right place?
  - Are you available to help me?
  - Are you listening and willing to help me?
  - Have you understood my topic (in general)?

- People all have worldviews and their own ideas (mental models) of how things work, even if they have no actual experience on which to base that idea. Because of this, they ask a question that they think you can answer. They couch their need in terms of something they think that you can provide. This is what Taylor meant by his fourth type of question, the "compromised need." The person deliberately recasts the question "in anticipation of what the files can deliver" (Taylor 1968), or in the form he or she thinks "is the sort of thing one should ask" (Fister 2002).

- As illustrated by the extended quotation from Taylor at the beginning of this section, people don't ask an exact question because they might not know exactly what they want or know any better way to phrase what they want. If you were a 6-year-old trying to ask your school librarian for something to read that would explain why your parents always seemed to be taking your older brother to the doctor, how well do you think you could express it? You may discover that many people become about 6 years old on approaching a Reference Desk.

- Communication barriers—because of age, language, jargon, or mishearing or misinterpreting what was heard—can interfere in asking questions.

- Many questions can sound quite reasonable but just aren't. When you start to examine them more closely, they turn out to be impossibly broad.

- The exact information need might not be expressed because of embarrassment at having to ask or because of the nature of the question.

- Having to ask a question may bring up feelings of fear that are even stronger than embarrassment: fear from not knowing what to expect when they ask (What if it's a really stupid question and the librarian becomes angry or says. something belittling?). You can well imagine that patrons/information seekers in that situation would be very careful about the question they asked, and that it might be a long way from what they really want to know (Fister 2002).

"Not the Real Question": Some Examples

Here are some examples, drawn from real life and from the literature, of questions that were asked based on the motivations described earlier, or questions that are open to several interpretations.

- The totally misdirected question: "Could you read my paper and tell me if my arguments are right and if I've made any mistakes?" In reality, what the person wanted were some better, more scholarly sources.

- The question that they think you're more likely to be able to answer: "Where are the issues of *Mergers & Acquisitions* [*M&A*]?" The real question: The student's professor had suggested a particular article in *M&A*, and the student was going to browse until he found it.

- Here is a wonderful example of six possible situations that could be lurking behind the very simple question, "Where are the cookbooks?" (Peterson 1997):

  1. Polly wants to browse a wide range of cookbooks to get different recipe ideas.

  2. Edna is looking for a specific recipe on authentic Italian Alfredo sauce.

  3. Mary is considering modifying her diet for health reasons and could really use some books on health and nutrition.

  4. Jenny is conducting a cooking seminar and needs information on how to structure her classes.

  5. Joe wants to be a chef, but he really needs books on job-hunting strategies.

  6. Marty is looking for *The Anarchist's Cookbook*, which is not a cookbook at all and is located in a completely different section.

- The question that sounds reasonable and isn't: "I need a list of the top 50 undergraduate programs in math, computer science, and engineering worldwide." There are directories of such programs (in the United States), and one frequently sees lists in *Business Week* and similar publications of the top 50 or top 100 this or that, and so this seems like a reasonable request. (But it's not; don't try it!)

- The failure of communication question (mishearing the original information): An undergraduate asks for *Oranges and Peaches*, by Charles somebody, and gets more and more upset as the librarian can't find it. Finally, he happens to say, "but my professor said it was the Bible of evolution!" and the librarian realizes that what he meant was *Origin of Species* by Charles Darwin (Dewdney and Michell 1996).

Question Negotiation in the Reference Interview

It is possible to discover the real question, however. A combination of good communication skills, emotional intelligence, practice, and experience are the keys. The major component of good communication skills for the reference interview is known as *question negotiation*.

Question negotiation, which in reality is quite a complex process, sounds simple: You try to elicit information by asking questions. The questions have a particular style, known as open and closed. *Open questions* invite your interlocutor to tell you more, to expand on the topic in a free-form way (like the famous interview question: "Tell me about yourself"), whereas *closed questions* are used to request a specific piece of information and usually require only a yes or no, or a one- to two-word response.

Open and Closed Questions

Here are some examples of open questions that are good to use in the reference interview (they tend to begin with words such as how, where, what, why, and the useful phrase, "can you tell me . . ."):

- Can you tell me something more about (the class assignment, the topic, etc.)?
- How much material were you hoping to find?
- What would you like to find out (about the topic)?
- How are you intending to use the information?
- What have you tried already?
- What else have you found, or do you have any papers on this topic already that we could look at?
- Where did you find (example, if presented)?

Similar to these, but with some interesting variations, is a lovely set of questions suggested by Mary Ellen Bates (1998), a notable authority on searching:

- What do you mean by _____?
- What do you already know about ____?
- What do you expect me to find?
- Are there any sources you have already checked or that you would recommend?
- If you were writing an article about this subject, what would the headline be?
- If I can't find exactly _____, what would be second-best?
- How will you be using the information?
- So, in other words, what you'd like me to find is _____, right?

Following are some examples of closed questions:

- Are you looking for a specific item or a list of materials on a topic?
- Do you want a comprehensive search or a few good items?
- Did you try (the catalog, the Web, or a particular database)?
- When do you need this by?
- Do you need scholarly (research, journal) articles, or are popular (*Time*, *Newsweek*) articles okay?
- Are you looking for recent information, or are you doing historical research?
- Have you used (particular resource) before?

Both open and closed questions are important and useful in question negotiation; don't fall into the trap of equating open with good and closed with bad. Open questions are a good way to get things going, to start developing a big picture, and to get the user talking and thus providing subject words. Closed questions are useful for focusing the topic, making sure the interaction proceeds efficiently, and helping to rule out courses of action. Strive to avoid a question negotiation session that uses only closed questions; rather, try to employ a mix of both. If you encounter a situation for which closed questions seem to be all that is required, however, don't feel guilty. It can happen, especially around basic questions, or in an instant messaging environment. What you want to avoid is falling into the habit of asking only closed questions from laziness or disinterest.

In coming up with questions, keep in mind the ultimate goals for the reference interview:

- Understand the problem and its literature—the topic.
- Find out what the person has already done (if anything).
- Develop search vocabulary and alternatives (synonyms).
- Determine limits (date, etc.) and levels (research or popular literature?).
- Discuss retrieval goals (How much/How many? How soon?).
- Develop an overall strategy to help you to select appropriate resources (database, Web, etc.).

Overall, the question negotiation process in the reference interview should help you to understand the problem context, that is, *who* and *why*. Who is your questioner: a 5-year-old, your mom, an undergraduate, or a sales manager in your company? Your choice of words, your questions, your suggestions, and the amount of time spent—every part of your interaction—should be adjusted based on whom you are talking to. For example, most of the open questions suggested here aren't very appropriate for an elementary school student.[1] The second primary part of the context is *why* are they asking—what is motivating the search? Is it just exploratory, a personal interest? Is it specific, a class assignment or preparation for an upcoming interview? Again, this affects the whole nature and direction of the search.

Interpersonal Communication Skills
in the Reference Interview

Having lists of questions to ask will take you only so far, however. A successful reference interaction also requires a healthy amount of good interpersonal communication skills, such as the following:

- Active listening: verbally or nonverbally indicating interest, attentiveness (saying "uh huh," nodding), and empathy (facial expressions that mirror the other person's feelings, "ouch"), even humor (this seems to come up particularly in an instant messaging type of exchange [Fagan and Desai 2003]).

- Paraphrasing: "So you'd like (xyz); is that right?"

- Giving positive nonverbal cues: projecting an approachable attitude, using welcoming body language, such as smiling, making eye contact, and presenting an "interested face." The emotional underpinnings of the whole situation cannot be emphasized too much, and thus the need for "emotional intelligence" in conducting the exchange (Eidson 2000). People generally pick up on tones of voice and negative body attitudes quickly and unerringly (Ross 2003) and will be more satisfied with a helpful and friendly, even if incorrect or incomplete, answer than one that is correct but cold (Radford 1999; Fagan and Desai 2003).

As Tyckoson (2003) says: "It is the interaction, the process of communication, which is often more important than the content or a specific answer," an opinion that was codified a year later in the *Guidelines for Behavioral Performance of Reference and Information Service Providers*, which stated: "the success of the transaction is measured not only by the information conveyed, but also by the positive or negative impact of the patron/staff interaction" (ALA 2004). The importance of establishing "rapport" with patrons is so crucial that one author has suggested adopting techniques from neurolinguistic programming in order to enhance rapport and relationship-building in the reference encounter (Stock 2010).

A school librarian's list of important communication skills emphasizes the following points, which are definitely applicable to any situation (Riedling 2000):

- Positive, respectful responses

- Encouraging words

- Avoiding premature answers

The last point deserves extra attention, because it is a trap that is so easy to fall into. Even if students have been asking for the same thing for a week, it's important to treat each instance as if it were new. You never know—the fifteenth time it might actually be something a bit different.

In discussing communication skills and pitfalls, a public librarian is emphatic about not using library jargon, and points out terms that people frequently either mistake or use in a different sense from the "library" sense (Cramer 1998):

- Bibliography for biography
- Reference book for nonfiction work
- Equating "fiction" with "not true," and thus pejorative
- "Check out" for "look at"

This point also bears some further elaboration. We need to remember that we use a very specialized professional vocabulary that is unfamiliar to most people outside our profession. For many people, "entering a library is like going into a foreign country, where a foreign language is spoken" (Ross 2003). We should ask questions and provide an atmosphere that allows patrons to "describe their information need in their own terms" and in their own language (Ross 2003).

Concluding the Reference Interview

One of the most important criteria of a successful reference interview is how it is concluded. It is crucial to leave the user with the feeling that the door is open to further interactions, by saying "if you don't find it, come back" or "if this doesn't work, come back; we'll try again." If you have the opportunity of seeing the person a bit later, asking a follow-up question (e.g., "Did you find it?" "How did that work out?") is also very powerful in terms of the user's sense of satisfaction, even if the question wasn't answered! Willingness and interest seem to count for as much, or even more, than accuracy in a reference interview situation. What you want to avoid is *negative closure*: simply sending someone off to another part of the building to browse, not conducting any sort of question negotiation to determine the real need, not offering any sort of follow-up option, or any of several other negative verbal or body language tactics (Ross and Dewdney 1998).

Know When to Stop

Finally, although you may now have the impression that every reference interview is going to be a huge affair, that you'll need to ask all kinds of questions, and that you should follow up on each one if possible—relax. They definitely won't all be like that. Some will be quite simple and brief, and even so, satisfying to both you and the patron. It's not only important to know about all these skills but also to employ them wisely. Use your emotional antennae and your ability to read the other person's body language, and don't go overboard if the patron is obviously in a hurry or not very interested. Give her what she seems to need and let it go. Something that is every bit as true today as when it was written in 1982 is Somerville's advice: "Part of the skill in conducting an effective interview is to know when to stop."

Beyond the Face-to-Face Reference Interview

There are many modes in which the reference interview can take place nowadays: the in-person Reference Desk still exists, and of course, there is the telephone, but reference interviews increasingly are being carried out by email (an asynchronous exchange) and through reference chat, which uses instant-messaging software (a synchronous exchange), to the point that "virtual reference" has become "ubiquitous in academic libraries" (Breitbach and DeMars 2009). Each move away from the face-to-face situation presents some hurdles but also, surprisingly, some advantages.

Reference Interviews on the Telephone

On the telephone, you have no visual cues, but the auditory ones are still there. You can tell a lot about people's ages and situations by their voices, and because it's usually easier to talk than to type, you can ask and receive more information. On the negative side, you might find that conversing with a non-native–English speaker over the phone seems much harder than in person; perhaps we unconsciously rely much more on visual cues, facial expressions, and the like when it is difficult to understand what we are hearing. It can also be more cumbersome to explain a process (e.g., navigating through various computer screens and interacting with an interface) over the telephone, but it's not terrible if the other person is sitting in front of their computer. On the plus side, you don't have to control your facial expression as rigorously as you do in person (some questions really do make you wince)! Also, there seems to be something about our telephone expectations: people are usually quite accepting of an offer to be called back if you can't find what they need immediately. This gives you time to think and explore without the pressure of being watched or knowing that someone is on hold.

Electronic Reference Interviews: E-mail and Chat

With email and reference chat, even the auditory cues are gone, and all you have are words on a screen, which does present quite a challenge for nuanced communication. If you have no body language or gestures, and no voice intonation or accents, what do you do? In both email and reference chat, you can use emoticons,[2] descriptions of gestures, and language that is more like how you would speak than write (Ronan 2003). E-mail gives you plenty of time to think and compose a thoughtful, structured answer. You can attach files with screenshots to help explain something if needed. You can check your "script," and always remember to have positive closure by adding "let me know how this goes" or "ask again if this doesn't work out; we'll think of something else." In email, the requester may very well follow up with you, and depending on the email system, all of your exchanges might stay listed in the message, so you can quickly review what you've said and done so far. The typed environment can actually be a plus for people having to communicate in a foreign language, because accents are not in the way, and the people on both sides of the conversation have time to study the words to figure out what is being said. This typed environment is also such a part of our lives now that it is more nuanced than you would think: frustration and humor come through fairly obviously, and appropriate responses can be given. "[T]one and mood words, capital letters, and repeated punctuation reveal a lot about the writer's state of mind" (Fagan and Desai 2003).

Reference chat often implies to the chat operator that there is a greater immediacy to the question than if the patron had emailed, but that is not necessarily so. Either by asking up front, "do you need this right away?" (Ronan 2003), or by frequently communicating to the user that you are working on the question, the person at the other end may turn out to be fairly patient (Kern 2003; Fagan and Desai 2003). After all, it's likely that if the person is of student age, he or she is doing several other things at the same time and not just waiting for you (Carter 2002/2003; Oblinger and Oblinger 2005). The Reference and User Services Association (RUSA) *Guidelines for Behavioral Performance of Reference* were amended in 2004 to address the additional electronic forms of reference encounters (ALA 2004). Ronan does an excellent job of showing how to meet the RUSA *Guidelines* in a chat environment. She describes how to use the same time-honored techniques: open and closed questions, encouragement, interest, and follow up, but modify them for the medium. For example, try to keep both your questions and your responses brief and relatively informal (Ronan 2003). In a large study of chat reference transactions at a public library system, Kwon and Gregory found a definite correlation between following the RUSA *Guidelines* and patron satisfaction. The five behaviors most likely to result in user satisfaction were receptive and cordial listening, searching information sources with or for the patrons, providing information sources, asking patrons whether the question was answered completely, and asking patrons to return when they need further assistance (Kwon and Gregory 2007). You'll probably end up using mostly closed questions, and that's all right; it's appropriate here. Throwing out a big open-ended question can be a useful way to stall for time while you are thinking or looking and can provide additional useful information as well (Carter 2002/2003). Breitbach and DeMars (2009) offer a number of suggestions for enhancing the reference chat encounter by taking it beyond just text by incorporating images, video, or Web page annotation using free or low-cost software. More useful advice may be found in the description of the "best practices in chat reference" used by Florida's virtual reference librarians (Ward and Barbier 2010), and a detailed study of "query clarification" in chat reference based on a huge set of transcripts from the *QuestionPoint* cooperative virtual reference service administered by OCLC (Radford et al. 2011).

Both email and reference chat also offer some significant intangibles. Gone is the embarrassment at having to approach a desk, where other people can see and possibly hear the interaction. A 2010 study of adults and members of the Net generation revealed that both groups "found chat to be the least intimidating form of reference" (and the most convenient) (Connaway and Radford 2010[3]). In fact, the removal of inhibitions may work a little *too* well, causing users to make far more, and more personal, requests than they would in person (Westbrook 2009). Also gone is the reluctance to interrupt someone busily at work at something else. (If you're the chat operator, that's all you're doing, right? They can't see that you're multitasking as well.) Although there are no visual cues to use in positive ways, those same visual cues aren't there to influence either party in negative ways either: the librarian can't see that you have 29 body piercings, and you can't see that the librarian looks like the neighbor who always yelled at you for playing ball in the backyard—someone who can't possibly understand you. That anonymity can be very freeing.

Can a True Reference Interview Happen Online?

Librarians have questioned whether a decent reference interview can occur at all in an online situation, but more and more voices have come out in support of it, saying that it can (Tyckoson 2003; Fagan and Desai 2003). As the Oblingers (2005) point out, "Personal does not always mean 'in person' to the Net Gen. Online conversations may be as meaningful as one that is face-to-face." My own experience bears this out as well. You are simply meeting the users where they are, instead of making them come into your physical space: it's convenient, it eliminates some of the worst impediments to asking questions (fear and embarrassment), it can definitely work, and the key remains communication.[4] Communication in the different media is different, but skills exist that can make it equally effective. Verbal, nonverbal, and textual: all offer ways to communicate effectively and positively. And "[s]uccessful communication . . . regardless of the medium over which that communication takes place—implies success in the reference process" (Tyckoson 2003). And who knows? With technologies such as Skype and Google video chat, we could be right back to face-to-face reference service.

Why Is the Reference Interview So Important?

Obviously we can't all be subject specialists in everything, but we need to gain our patrons' confidence enough that they will work with us. Being attentive, asking questions, and taking an interest can help with this. You *are* a specialist in the search field. However, at the moment the person you are working with is the specialist in his field (i.e., what he wants), and you are a layperson. You can still "achieve an intelligent and collegial interest" in their work, and this is "the level the search specialist should try to achieve" (Harter 1986). This situation calls for good communication skills and rapport, because you're depending a great deal on the person you're working with to supply the terminology describing her search need. You need to get as much out of your patron as you can. You then work with him or her to think of synonyms, and using that knowledge, try to match the terminology against an appropriate database's thesaurus, or simply try the terms given to you as keywords in a multidisciplinary database (or the Web), and proceed to pearl grow. The initial set of terms describing the topic usually needs to come from the patron, however.

The reference interview is how you are going to connect people to the information they need. Through an exchange of questions, you help them to clarify what their question really is, which ultimately saves their time, because you haven't, through misunderstanding or lack of probing, pointed them at something that is not useful (Kern 2003). Tyckoson (2003) sums it up by saying: "The reference interview is the most important skill that a reference librarian can learn. Tools and sources will always change, but the process will always begin with the reference interview."

To me, it's really all about one simple thing:

You want them to come back.

A positive reference interaction, in person, on the phone, or online (accurate or not), helps that to happen.

Quick Recap

For several reasons, the questions that people ask in a reference situation frequently do not represent their real information need. The reference interview is meant to identify the real question and suggest terminology that can be used in a search. A good reference interview includes question negotiation, involving a good mix of open and closed questions, and good interpersonal skills, such as a positive, encouraging attitude, welcoming body language, and awareness of specialized vocabulary. How the interview is concluded and knowing when to stop are also important. Reference interviews over the phone, by email, or by chat each have their advantages and disadvantages, but techniques can be employed to make encounters that are not face to face equally successful. A good reference interview leaves the patron with positive feelings and more likely to return to the library with future questions.

Exercises and Points to Consider

1. School media specialists: What would be a good list of questions to use with your clientele?

2. Communication barriers were mentioned in a general way in this chapter, and a few examples were given (e.g., language, age differences). Can you elaborate on these? How many other communication barriers can you think of?

3. What would welcoming body language look like? How about unwelcoming?

4. How would you feel if you asked a question at a Reference Desk, and the librarian responded by turning immediately to his or her computer and typing?

5. Have you had many interactions with Reference Desks where you were the patron? Which ones do you remember? What do you remember about them?

6. Say that you were at the Reference Desk, and a woman approached and said she was looking for information about sign languages used with children who are *not* deaf. What are some questions you might try asking her? What are some other things you might do?[5]

Suggested Readings

The information seeking literature can quickly become overwhelming. Rather than reading the myriad articles cited in this chapter, you might find it more manageable to choose from the following short list of books on the topic:

Aspray, William, and Barbara M. Hayes. 2011. *Everyday Information: The Evolution of Information Seeking in America*. Cambridge, MA: MIT Press.

Case, Donald O. 2007. *Looking for Information: A Survey of Research on Information Seeking, Needs, and Behavior*. 2nd ed. Amsterdam: Academic Press.

Connaway, Lynn Silipigni, and Timothy J. Dickey. 2010. *The Digital Information Seeker: Report of the Findings from Selected OCLC, RIN, and JISC User Behaviour Projects*. Bristol, UK: Higher Education Funding Council for England.

Gunter, Barrie, Ian Rowlands, and David Nicholas. 2009. *The Google Generation: Are ICT Innovations Changing Information-Seeking Behaviour?* Oxford: Chandos Publishing.

Knoer, Susan. 2011. *The Reference Interview Today*. Santa Barbara, CA: ABC-CLIO.

Notes

1. For guidance on reference interviews with children, see Pattee (2008).

2. Emoticons, also known as *smileys*, are facial expressions created from punctuation, for example, :-) :-(:-p or abbreviated forms, without "noses" :) :(;)

3. It's terribly hard to pick just one article to recommend on the topic of chat reference, but if I *really* had to. this might be the one. It's a great balance of formal study, extremely important topic (especially because of the two groups of people in the study), and accessible writing.

4. In a review of nine discontinued chat reference services, the reasons for discontinuing were identified as low volume, funding, staffing, and technical problems, not the ability to conduct reference transactions online (e.g., librarians' communication skills). See Radford and Kern 2006.

5. Skilled questioning, or even more likely, a session with appropriate databases employing good pearl growing tactics, are needed to recast this question as "methods of nonverbal communication used with autistic children." Unless you're an expert in this field (in which case presumably you don't need help finding such information), this is not the language you are likely to use in everyday speech. To get the best results most efficiently, it helps tremendously to have the question reformulated into this language.

10
Choosing the Right Resource for the Question

By this point in this book, or in your course if the book is being used as your textbook, you may be feeling somewhat overwhelmed: there are so many databases, and there's the whole Internet. How are you supposed to know what to use when? Specifically, you might wonder:

1. Should you always try to use a database first?

   (What if you have no subscription databases?)

2. Is it wrong to use the Web?

3. Are there guidelines for when you should use a database and when you should use the Web?

4. Where do you start?

First and foremost: don't panic. Everybody feels this way at some point in his or her library school career, and frequently during the training on their first (and second, and third . . .) job as well. While there are no hard and fast rules for what to use when (like so many things, with time and experience you'll develop a style that is effective for you), there is an answer to the first two specific questions. Question 1: Should you always try a database first? Not at all. You should start with whatever seems most appropriate for the question and where you feel most comfortable starting, given the resources you have available. If you have no subscription databases, a growing number of high-quality resources are now available without a subscription on the Web: not only Google Scholar, but also a number of others. This chapter will devote a section to these resources. In answer to Question 2: It is never wrong to use the Web, as long as you also use database resources if the question suggests that they might be helpful (and you have databases available to you).

The rest of this chapter will address Questions 3 and 4, as well as discussing the range of situations you may encounter on the job: from having a huge selection of commercial databases available to none. In all cases, but especially the latter, the section on free, high-quality databases on the Web will be of interest. We will start with Question 4 because that is actually the beginning of the process, and the question "Where do I start?" has a simple and direct answer. It's the same answer that applies to anything in reference service: Start with a good reference interview.

Start With the Reference Interview

The reference interview, whether it is in depth or only a two- or three-line dialogue, is the key to everything that happens next. That is how you find out what the patron wants, which should then suggest to you what resource(s) would meet the need. The reference interview should reveal factors such as the following:

- What is the subject area?

- What is the person looking for? For example, a specific factoid, a few good articles, an overview, or some statistics?

- Does the requester want current or historical information?

- How much material is needed: a great deal, or again, a "few good articles"?

- Does the person require research-level material (also known as scholarly or peer-reviewed) or popular material?

These points are discussed in the reference interview section of Chapter 9. Your reference interview should also provide some keywords or phrases with which to start your search. You now have a body of information to work with (context, guidelines, intent, and subject) and can make an initial decision as to whether it sounds like a database question or a Web question. Note that I said "initial decision"—you can always change your mind and take a new approach as you work on the request; you don't have to get it right the first time.[1]

Now let's tackle the harder issue—guidelines for using databases or using Web search engines. What should you be looking for in the information that you gather during the reference interview to help address that issue?

Questions for Databases

When trying to decide when to use databases and when to use a Web search engine, remember that people are using the Web to answer many questions on their own, and by the time they approach a librarian, it's likely that more sophisticated techniques are called for. That said, in this section you'll find the hallmarks of questions that indicate *to me* that a database might be the answer, and questions for which a Web search might be a better approach. Never get the impression that any of this is carved in stone. As you gain experience, you will undoubtedly come to identify further or different indicators based on the clientele you are serving that will whisper to you: "database" or "Web." You will find yourself instinctively making good choices most of the time.

Why and When to Try a Database

Why choose a database over a Web search engine? (Note my terminology here: I am specifically referring to *search engines* such as Google or Bing, not Google Scholar. We will talk about Google Scholar in the context of free *databases* on the Web. Google Scholar will inevitably creep into the conversation in other places as well, no doubt.) The reasons are basic: authority and credibility. Databases can contain material with errors, but in general, there is a presumption that the material has been vetted somewhere in the process, and part of what you are paying the database vendor for is taking some responsibility for the quality of the material. Nancy Bloggs, writing Web pages in her bedroom, doesn't necessarily assume any responsibility at all. You can be more confident providing patrons with information from a commercial database than the free Web in many cases. Even with information such as a formula from a *CRC Handbook* or a dictionary definition, which can be readily available on the Web, if this material is being provided to *someone else*, it is better if it can be printed out from a database and handed over. No one is left wondering, "Who wrote this? Can I trust it to be right?" in situations in which the patron really wants to be sure of getting credible information. The Web is a useful tool for starting searches, but it is not generally the provider of choice for content to hand over formally to the patron as a final product.

Inevitably in the following descriptions of when to try a database you will find that Web searching is mentioned as well. It really is impossible to draw hard and fast lines between the two types of resources, because so often they do complement each other well, but I have tried to keep the discussions focused as much as possible on databases.

Requests Involving Articles

If your reference interview has shown that *articles* are involved in any way, it is usually a strong indicator to try a database. Articles represent content that has been formally published, usually in hard copy, and then distributed and made available for a fee. The publishers of the magazines, journals, and newspapers the articles appeared in are (usually) not giving them away free on the Internet. Yes, it's true that on the Web you can find papers that authors have posted on their websites or archived in their organization's institutional repository.[2] If you're after a known item, a Web search might work, but it's not as organized, efficient, and comprehensive as searching a good commercial database. Using your institutional databases also increases your chances of getting the full text, either directly or via a linking system. Google Scholar is rapidly closing the gap with commercial databases, but it doesn't have all the features and options they offer. (It can be a great place to start, however, especially in a subject area you are unfamiliar with, or when you want to figure out new terminology or places to look if you are having no luck in the databases you are trying.)

For example, in an academic situation involving a student writing a paper, in almost every case your best choice is an article or encyclopedia database. The ability to search by subjects, to use various limits, and to know that the material you'll retrieve has all made an appearance in the commercial press all firmly call for such a database. Again, the full text or links to full text in so many commercial databases is another obvious reason to go to a database.

Another way articles can be involved is as citations. In any setting, if someone were trying to track down a citation or flesh out an incomplete citation, you should try appropriate databases first. (If it seems to be a history article, try a history database.) If you don't find what you need there, however, turn to the Web (see notes in the Questions for the Web section, later in the chapter). If the patron wants to see who has *cited* an article recently, this is clearly a database question (and which database to search is fairly clear as well), although again, Google Scholar has links for "Cited by <number>." But how and where is Google getting that information? How accurate is that count? What does it include? (You can scan the list of citing items and try to figure that out; some of it is legitimate, some is hard to tell.) If the *Web of Science* is available to you, my advice is to try that first, every time. A person wanting to know where something has been cited is usually after high-quality, published, find-able articles.

Of course, articles come from journals. Although patrons seldom ask, "Where is the *Journal of XYZ* indexed?" this often becomes an implied question for the librarian in the course of answering the question they did ask. Usually the most efficient course of action is to check the *UlrichsWeb* database to see where the journal is indexed. (Of course, you can also simply go to a likely database and use its Publication Browse feature, to see if the requested journal is listed.)

Requests for an "Overview Article"

Patrons often want an article that provides an *overview* of some topic. There are a couple of problems with such a request. One is, you hear the word *article*, and you do think database, which is right. The problem is, it is not that easy to find general, overview-type articles in the periodical literature, unless the author is writing a review of the literature or a tutorial on the topic,[3] or the topic falls within a discipline that publishes special-purpose survey journals, such as *Computer Surveys*. In general, articles tend to focus on a particular, finite topic rather than providing a broad introduction. A better source for an introductory or overview treatment of a topic is often an encyclopedia entry (or a chapter in a prominent textbook for that field). Thousands of specific-topic encyclopedias are available, and more and more of them are being offered in online versions. Such a commercial encyclopedia database could indeed provide an authoritative, trustworthy overview.[4]

Book Questions

With the advent of mega online book vendors such as Amazon.com, Barnes & Noble (at http://www.books.com), or Powells.com (which covers the gamut of new, used, and out of print), and the availability of WorldCat on the Web at WorldCat.org, the line between whether to use a subscription database or a Web resource for book questions has grown much more indistinct. Obviously, if the patron wants to know if your library owns a particular book, you'll go to your library's OPAC. After that, it may depend on what resources you have available. If you have access to WorldCat via FirstSearch (and enjoy all the options that interface offers) and *Books in Print*, you might try those databases first for book-related questions (e.g., verifying or completing book citations, finding books on a topic, or identifying a particular title that might be old or unusual). Because the subscription databases are not trying to *sell* the books, there is less screen "noise" to ignore, and thus they can be more efficient. You cannot beat the comprehensiveness of WorldCat, which helps to avoid the possibility of having to look at several online book and out-of-print vendor websites. And if it's quicker and easier to type "worldcat

.org" into your browser than to click through a couple of library Web pages to find the link to the subscription version, by all means use the Web version. On the other hand, if the patron is a student who wants a textbook (and is surprised that you don't have all the textbooks on Reserve), head off to Amazon.com immediately, to show him the deals on used copies.

Business Questions

Just by the nature of the beast, if it's a business question, it is usually safe to assume that the answer is worth money and thus is less likely to be freely available on the Internet. Business questions frequently involve articles, which we have already discussed as a database indicator. Another typical business query is the request for lists of companies in a certain line of business or in a specific geographical area. Although there are free telephone directories and other similar resources on the Web, the best directories for companies are commercial databases, such as the *Million Dollar Database* or *Business and Company Resource Center*. Business documents such as market research reports or analyst's reports almost without exception come from subscription or other fee-based resources. A major exception to this general rule of using databases for business questions is in the case of certain business numbers, which we encountered in chapter 8. Stock quotes and the financial reports (e.g., annual reports) of current public companies can usually be found on the Web. Another exception has to do with research in the murky realm of "competitive intelligence," in which almost anything goes: almost any information could be valuable. Thus, information from blogs, wikis, newspaper websites (often providing content not available in their printed versions), etc. is becoming an important—although often frustrating—part of business research (Ojala 2008).

Law Questions

In this highly specialized area of reference, official legal databases are definitely your first choice. Although it is possible to find the text of some states' statutes (e.g., Texas Statutes) or laws (often referred to as "code," as in U.S. Code or N.Y. Code) online, it is probably easier to find the information needed using a commercial legal database. Especially in this topic area, the authority of a commercial, subject-specific database is very important. (And the assistance of a skilled law librarian is even more important.)

Medical Questions

Things become somewhat fuzzier when it comes to helping patrons with medical questions. Because, as with law, we are again working in a very serious and specialized topical area, you should start with databases if possible to take advantage of their authority and credibility. If you are working with medical professionals or medical students, obviously you'll use MEDLINE or PubMed. There is also a database called CINAHL, which is specifically aimed at nursing professionals. For the lay public, there is a very nice Gale database called *Health Reference Center Academic*. However, there is also an immense amount of medical information available on the Web that people are more than happy to tap into on their own, usually without recognizing the risks involved: the need to be very aware of the credibility of the source, the date of the information, etc. We'll revisit this issue in the Questions for the Web section.

Quick Recap

This section has attempted to address the issue of when you should try a database rather than a Web search engine. Questions for which you will want to try to use databases are those hallmarked by an underlying need for authority and credibility. Requests that mention a need for articles, either for research purposes such as writing a paper or tracking down a specific citation, are usually best answered by appropriate databases. Requests expressed as a need for an overview article are often better served by material from an encyclopedia entry. Questions about books are sometimes answered equally well by subscription databases and free websites, such as Amazon.com or WorldCat.org. Business-related questions usually involve material that has been expensive to collect, and such questions are usually better addressed with commercial databases. Preference should also be given to commercial databases for law and medical questions, due to the specialized and serious nature of the topic areas. The particular need in those situations for authority and credibility demands that only professionally produced and professionally acknowledged resources be used.

Choosing a Database

If you're faced with a question that seems like a database question, you could be in one of three situations: having many databases at your disposal (the assumption so far in this book), a few databases, or none at all. In this section we'll look at how to make a choice in each of those three scenarios.

Scenario 1: An Embarrassment of Riches

If you're at an institution that subscribes to literally hundreds of databases, the natural question is this: How do you decide which one to use? Determining which database to start with involves many of the factors you use to *evaluate* a database (a topic addressed again in chapter 11):

- What subjects does the database cover? (If the topic is well defined, definitely in one subject area, a subject-specific database such as *Art Index* or *EconLit* could be the right resource. If the topic seems fuzzy, or interdisciplinary, a multisubject database such as ProQuest's *Research Library* or EBSCO's *Academic Search* or *MasterFILE* may be a better answer.)

- What types of material are included? Magazines? Scholarly journals? Books or book chapters? "Working papers"? Other materials? Or do you need a numeric or directory database?

- What *level* of material? (Is it popular level or research level?)

- What is the date coverage of the database? Does it cover the right time period? If you are trying to find or verify a really recent article, you'll want to check how frequently material is added to the database you're thinking of using, and how up to date it is.

- If the database does not provide full text, are the sources mostly available in your library (or in another database)?

- How searchable is the database? Does it offer controlled vocabulary to focus your search, or does it offer keyword searching of all fields if you need to find a needle in the haystack? Which fields are searchable? If you only have one piece of information, but that field isn't searchable in the database you've picked out, you have a problem. If you're looking for a particular *kind* of article, like a book review, you want a database that lets you limit or search by article type, and one that includes book reviews. Is it possible to limit by scholarly or peer-reviewed articles, if that's what you need?

You also don't have to pick just one database. You could identify two or three candidates and test your most specific search term in each one to see which shows the most hits. Especially if you're venturing into a new subject area, try your most specific term in the database that you've chosen, and see how many hits there are. If the database has a subject list or a thesaurus, look up your term to see if it is listed, and how many records are associated with it.

This list of factors to consider probably sounds like it would take far too much time, while the patron is sitting there expecting immediate action. As you gain experience, however, you will find that you can do this analysis of "database or the Web?" quite quickly. If you're at a major university or large public library that subscribes to a large number of databases, it's very likely that library staff have already created Web pages that organize the databases into groups by subject, and often by whether or not they are full text. Start by looking at databases by subject, or look at guides developed by librarians that might suggest the best databases for different subject areas. Quickly scan the descriptions of the databases' *coverage*, *currency*, and *material* types. Go into the database(s) that seem most appropriate and test them for subject coverage, availability of appropriate fields, and limits, as mentioned in the earlier bulleted list. This all comes across as taking action on the question to the patron, and results will probably follow pretty quickly.

Of course, you have the free Web as well. Even when you have hundreds of subscription databases at your fingertips, it's a perfectly acceptable strategy to run a quick search in a Web search engine or in Google Scholar, just to see if the term is out there and in what context it is used, especially for an unfamiliar topic area (think of this as a reality check). As mentioned before, your subscription databases and the Web can complement each other well.

Scenario 2: A Few Good Databases

This scenario could apply to a school library with a handful of databases available, or to a corporate, law, or other special library. In each case, the limited number of databases was chosen for its appropriateness to your clientele and your mission, so in a way, you could consider this an advantage: some pre-selection has taken place, and these should already be the most likely databases for the questions that you expect to encounter. Given this, you can still look at your databases in light of the factors discussed earlier. Which one(s) might be most appropriate, given their *coverage*, *currency*, *searchability*, and ability to identify research? You can jump into one or more and test your search terms. Frankly, in many ways you have the advantage over those libraries that have hundreds of databases, because you can be thoroughly familiar with each of your resources, and have a much better idea which one is likely to be most useful for any given question, without any testing or analysis at all. And, of course, you have the free Web as well.

Scenario 3: No Subscription Databases at All

It would certainly be sad and frustrating, after learning about all these nifty fee-based resources, to find yourself in a situation in which you don't have any subscription databases available. There's no point in grousing and hand wringing, however: let's assume that at least you have an Internet connection. First, you may find there are some (subscription) databases provided at no cost to you through your local public library system. This is something to have explored ahead of time, so you'll have some idea of what is there, and what you need to do to gain access (e.g., a current library card with a barcode number). Next, as we have seen already in this book, many U.S. government agencies provide free versions of their database content on the Web: PubMed from the National Library of Medicine, ERIC from the Department of Education, and endless data from the Bureau of Census and the Bureau of Labor Statistics. Other free government databases not mentioned previously include Agricola, from the National Agricultural Library (http://agricola.nal.usda.gov/), and ToxNet, another database from the National Library of Medicine, covering toxicology, hazardous chemicals, environmental health, and toxic releases (http://toxnet.nlm.nih.gov/). You have the riches of OCLC's WorldCat now at your fingertips, at WorldCat.org. Google Scholar has also been mentioned several times. In the next section, we'll discuss Google Scholar in more detail, along with some other databases of subscription-quality content[5] available for free on the Web.

Free Databases on the Web

Google Scholar (http://scholar.google.com) is a true database of scholarly content: peer-reviewed articles from commercially published scholarly journals, conference proceedings, theses, patents, legal opinions and journals, book content from Google Books, scholarly content from the open Web (such as from institutional repositories), and who knows what else may have been added by the time you see this. It is a wonderful resource, incredible and vast (as everything to do with Google is), and is utterly nonsectarian in its approach to subjects: it includes material from any and every subject. (Google Scholar's effectiveness may vary according to the subject area of your search—definitely try it for an engineering literature search,[6] for example—but as with anything Google, you're almost guaranteed to find *something*.) It includes a fairly sophisticated Advanced Search, where you can limit by subject area if desired, and you can perform basic Boolean and field searches (for author, publication, or in a particular range of years). All of this, and it's completely free. So why do we pay for subscription databases?

First and foremost, at least to me, is that we have no idea what the content of Google Scholar actually is: There is no way to assess its *coverage*. For its commercially published content, Google does not provide lists of which publications are covered, for how many years, etc., something that is standard in any commercial database. Just because it's vast doesn't mean it's comprehensive. If you are looking for an article and aren't finding it—does it mean your information is wrong, or that Google Scholar's coverage of that journal doesn't go back that far? (Or doesn't include that journal? Or just didn't include that article?) The system is a complete black box in terms of content: You can search it, but there is no way to know what (if any) parameters are bounding your search. Google Scholar also offers no sorting functions (results are ranked, which is Google's preferred method of showing any results). You can limit to things published "since YYYY"—but you can't *sort* by date descending. There are no marking or output functions. And Google is a commercial venture: for years Google Scholar was marked "beta." It no longer is, but what if they get bored with it, or decide to start charging? It could vanish as suddenly as it appeared. Don't get me wrong: I love Google Scholar. I use it a lot, but I do not see it as an all-inclusive alternative if you also have subscription databases available.

Let us move on to some academic and .org sites that provide subject specific databases for free on the Web. A mix of long-standing and recent additions, this list demonstrates that the free Web is not just the purview of the sciences: there are social science and humanities databases out there as well.

- arXiv[7] (www.arXiv.org), hosted by Cornell University: It provides e-prints in all areas of physics, plus some mathematics, computer science, quantitative biology, quantitative finance, and statistics. Physicists generally do not need (or know of) any other database.

- BioMed Central (www.biomedcentral.com): Despite the .com website, this really is searchable, free access to over 200 open-access journals in biology and medicine.

- CiteSeer (citeseerx.ist.psu.edu), hosted by Pennsylvania State University: CiteSeer is to computer scientists as arXiv is to physicists. If you didn't have subscriptions to the IEEE and ACM databases, you would use this.

- Scitopia.org (www.scitopia.org/scitopia), launched in 2007: This is a collaborative effort on the part of about 20 leading science and technology societies to provide a search tool for all of their societies' publications, plus those of some government agencies and the U.S., European, and Japanese patent offices. It has good search capabilities and faceted results, and it provides bibliographic records with abstracts. If you couldn't afford INSPEC, between this and Google Scholar you might not miss it.

- Ideas (ideas.repec.org), hosted by the Federal Reserve Bank of St. Louis: This is the largest collection of economics materials on the Web. RePEc stands for Research Papers in Economics. It includes both citations and full text for working papers, articles, chapters, and books in every area of economics. If you don't have EconLit, this is the place to go.

- Library, Information Science & Technology Abstracts (LISTA; www.libraryresearch.com). This is a full-featured EBSCO database that the company provides for free to "anyone interested in libraries and information management." Indexing goes back to the mid-1960s for close to 600 periodicals and other materials, making its depth and breadth of coverage somewhat greater than that of *Library Literature*. If you had no access to *Library Literature*, a wealth of scholarly information and EBSCO's powerful search platform would still be at your fingertips with this resource.

- TRID[8] (trid.trb.org/): A joint effort of the Transportation Research Board of the National Academies and the OECD's Joint Transport Research Centre, this transportation research database includes over 900,000 records related to transportation research from around the world. (Who knew there was so much written on transportation?

Try browsing the Pedestrians and Bicyclists category—the titles are fascinating.)

- World Bank's Data Bank (databank.worldbank.org), including the World Development Indicators database: Formerly subscription-based, the World Bank has now made all of its data available, and searchable, for free online.

- Bibliography of the History of Art (BHA) and Repertoire de la litera-ture de l'art (RILA) (library.getty.edu/bha), hosted by the Getty Re-search Institute: This is an index to the literature of art from 1975 to 2007.

- IMDb—Internet Movie Database (www.imdb.com): We have to allow this .com into the list, since the IMDb is indeed a database, and it is a remarkable and rich source of information for films and television old and new.

- Stanford Encyclopedia of Philosophy (plato.stanford.edu), hosted by Stanford University: While not a database of articles, this is an ex-cellent example of a searchable, subject-specific, respected encyclo-pedia that has been online for over 10 years.

In late 2010, Mark Shores reported on a number of additions to the arena of "free range" databases, including Anthropological Index Online (http://schapera.kent.ac.uk/aio/) and a database devoted to reproductive health, POPLINE (www.popline.org), among many others. What is especially interesting is that his review notes whether or not each resource is "Indexed by Google?"—and in the case of the two databases mentioned here, the answer is "No" (Shores 2010). So despite evidence to the contrary, Google doesn't quite know about *everything* that's out there. Shores's article in-cludes tips for finding more such databases and for remembering them; it is listed as one of the Suggested Readings at the end of this chapter along with the "best of free reference" feature that appears annually in the print *Li-brary Journal*. Additional free databases specifically for science and technol-ogy are provided in the last article listed under Suggested Readings.

Quick Recap

This section has discussed the range of situations you might find your-self in once you leave school. If you work at another university or large pub-lic library, you are likely to have a full range of subscription databases available. At a school, smaller public, or special library, you may have a small collection of databases, but ones that are especially targeted at your user group and with which you are very familiar. At the farthest end of the spec-trum, you may be in a situation where there are no subscription databases. In that case, it is worth checking with your local public library to see if there are databases accessible to you as a library cardholder via a local or state consortium. We then looked at a number of free options, notably Google Scholar, as well as a number of subject-specific, mostly noncommercial op-tions, in the sciences, social sciences, and humanities. With a bit of digging, you will find there are a surprising number of databases with high-quality and scholarly content freely available on the Web.

Having looked at questions best answered by databases and database availability, it is time to consider what questions are best answered by the Web.

Questions for the Web

One is tempted to say, "What *isn't* a question for the Web?" because it seems that no matter what keywords you search for, they'll have appeared in some Web page, somewhere. There are certainly topics, however, that are much more likely, or only, answerable by a Web search.

Personal Uses of the Web

We use the Web endlessly for personal research: finding books at Amazon.com, getting weather reports, checking crossing delay times for the bridges to Canada, making travel plans, checking movie times, buying almost anything, filling in the missing parts of song lyrics, or trying to find an answer to a software question. It's quick, it's easy, and it's not the sort of information you'll find in databases. (For a review from *Consumer Reports* about something that we're thinking of buying, however, we wind up back at a database, because that's an article.) Because it's only for our personal information, we take the responsibility for deciding how authoritative the information is and whether that's important.

Professional Uses of the Web

Popular Culture, Local Information, and People

At the Reference Desk, questions about popular culture ("Who is the highest-paid player in the NFL?"), daily life or local information ("Where are all the HSBC bank branches in [city X]?" "Can I get a list of all the choral societies in [city Y]?"), or, one of my favorites, identifying the source of a song, poem, or quotation from a small fragment, are definitely Web search material. A question such as "Who did the music in the 2007 *Beowulf* movie?" is perfect for the IMDb; mentioned earlier as a free source of film and television information. The Web is also amazing (a little frighteningly so) for finding people. It doesn't always work, but we all know some pretty incredible stories about locating people by searching for them on the Web.

Citation Disambiguation

The Web is useful for tracking down citations. If you're not finding a citation in a database (even after leaving out part of what the patron has told you), don't hesitate to drop parts of the citation into Google (or your favorite search engine) to try to figure out where the problem lies. In doing a Web search, you are looking for the citation to appear on someone else's Web page (where one hopes that it's correct and complete), or at least to gain some sense of context that would indicate, for example, that you have chosen to look in a database in the wrong subject area. Maybe you can even find the author's Web page and see how he or she referred to the work in question. Try anything you can think of to provide a clue.

Rare or Obscure Topics

You can also start with a Web search when the patron indicates that what she is looking for is quite obscure, and you want the biggest haystack possible in which to look for that needle (think of the desperate parents in the movie *Lorenzo's Oil*). Of course, the patron has probably already searched on the Web, but perhaps you can do it better. Do a quick Web search if the topic is obscure *to you*, just to try for a quick sense of context and possibly some additional useful keywords.

Medical Questions from Laypeople

If you are working on a medical question with a patron who is not a member of the health services professions, it is hard not to use the Web in your research. As mentioned in the previous section about Medical Questions, the patron very likely has been searching the Web on his own, and one can't deny there is a great deal of medical information available there. What is imperative is that you impress on the patron that much of it is incorrect, misleading, and outright dangerous, unless it comes from a reputable source. Depending on the resources available in your library and the skill level of the patron, your approach might be to encourage a change not in *source* but in *methodology*. Rather than simply doing Web searches, you can try to get the patron to *browse* reputable sites, such as MedlinePlus.gov, WebMD.com, and the sites of, again, reputable organizations. Use Web searches to find those associations and organizations, but then urge the patron to go into those sites and browse or search within the site. You should be able to trust the authority of websites from the government (.gov), such as the Centers for Disease Control and Prevention (www.cdc.gov) or sites run by reputable organizations (.org), like the American Cancer Society (http://www.cancer.org). If at all possible, however, databases such as *Health Reference Center Academic* or the *Virtual Reference Library*, both from Gale, would be preferable.

Standard Facts and Statistics

For someone looking for a specific, standard fact (e.g., in what year did the Berlin Wall fall?), the authority of an encyclopedia database is attractive, but you may well simply try a Web search, because it's likely to be quicker and just as useful. (It's a standard date, after all; if the page comes from a credible source, it should be right. Wikipedia should be fine in this case.) Of course, if the patron then wants historical background for the falling of the Wall, you should get back to the encyclopedia or article databases very quickly. The area of quotations and definitions can be equally murky: in a situation in which it doesn't matter that much, you can probably just do a Web search. At the Reference Desk, if you have a resource such as *Oxford Online*, it would be more authoritative and professional to use that.

As we found in chapter 8, government agencies provide quite a wealth of statistical and numerical information on the Web. There aren't as many databases available in this area, so I often find myself using the Web as an equal partner when a question requires statistics or numbers to answer it. (But again, if I have access to an appropriate database, it almost always provides a much more *efficient* way of getting the information and is usually more authoritative as well.)

Quick Recap

The overarching themes in this Questions for the Web section have been issues of daily life, popular culture, people, and connecting with the "informal college," that is, tapping into the web of other people's knowledge (e.g., for software questions, obscure topics, or fragment questions—lyrics, quotations, etc.). The Web is useful for providing clues, context, or a reality check.

As discussed in the Free Databases section, it is rapidly becoming a viable place to do scholarly research as well. It is amazing—what *did* we do before?

Exercises and Points to Consider

1. What do *you* use the Web for? Try keeping a journal for a week in which you record every time you use the Web to answer a question, either at work or in your personal life. Can you detect any common themes in your Web use?

2. "Search madness" activity: If you are using this book as part of a class, have the group members come up with a list of questions that they have encountered in a library, in their studies, or in their daily life. Then add in questions from earlier chapters in this book, or from search assignments. For questions that required databases before, try them as Web searches. For the questions submitted by the class, decide which seem suitable for the Web, and which are for databases. Spend a class session just madly searching and comparing results.

3. Here is a research request that would lend itself well to a group search session: An upper-level undergrad wrote me an email saying she was "trying to find the percent of people that buy local, or try to buy local, or any type of data on numbers of people who buy local." You have now been exposed to a whole gamut of databases, including numerical ones and free, high-quality resources on the Web. Although it might look like she only wants numbers (so you could try *Statistical Insight* or the Department of Agriculture website), for this particular topic, you might be better off going for articles that *discuss* the topic, and hopefully drop a number or statistic here or there. So which databases? What about Google Scholar, or just Google? Decide how you'll divide up the work and how you'll share insights about search terms and tactics as you go along—and go to town!

Suggested Readings

Etkin, Cynthia, and Brian E. Coutts. Best of Free Reference. *Library Journal.* Since 2009, a list of free online reference resources has appeared as part of the annual feature on the best reference titles published during the preceding year. Different database vendors index this feature differently; in *Library Literature,* searching Library Journal as the journal name and "best of free reference" in the title works perfectly. In other databases, you may need to search for the title of the journal in the publication field, "best" AND "reference" in the title, and Coutts in the author field.

Shores, Mark L. 2010. "Resource Review: Free Range Databases." Library Journal.com, December 16. http://www.libraryjournal.com/lj/community academiclibraries/888511-265/resource_review_free_range_databases .html.csp.

Tenopir, Carol. 2002. "Sorting Through Online Systems." *Library Journal,* May 1, 32, 34. This is the shortest, sanest set of tips and advice for keeping the plethora of databases straight in your head. Even though some of the names have changed since 2002, the advice still applies. A must read.

Zdravkovska, Nevenka, and Bob Kackley. 2009. "Science/Engineering Bibliographic Databases' Future: Collection Development Issues at the University of Maryland. *IATUL Proceedings 2009.* http://www.iatul.org/conferences /pastconferences/2009proceedings.asp. Though it's specific to sci-tech, this is a very pertinent case study; the authors describe how they are shifting their reliance to free databases over subscription sources in the face of budget cuts. It provides an excellent list of free, high-quality resources for science and technology.

Notes

1. For the record, this is a sea change from the early days of searching on systems like Dialog, where you paid by the minute and often by each record displayed. Then you really did do your homework thoroughly before going online, and it was generally expected that you would get it right the first time. The advent of databases on CD-ROM and now on the Web has totally changed this aspect of searching (for the better).

2. Google the term "institutional repository" IR+ or DSpace or Eprints for more information on this topic.

3. This varies a great deal by discipline: tutorial articles (which can also appear under a title of "Review" or "Survey") are common in the engineering and computer science literature. There is a standard format for articles in medical journals that includes a literature review, and the more scholarly library science articles have this as well. A literature review might not be the same as an overview, however, and certainly in subject areas such as business, a real overview is fairly rare.

4. Unfortunately, I often find it hard to convince my patrons—who are generally undergraduates or graduate students—that an encyclopedia entry is a valid resource or way to start. I'm trying to point them to a specialized encyclopedia, but they seem to relegate anything with *encyclopedia* in the title to "little kid" status.

5. The *content* is definitely subscription quality, but the interfaces are not necessarily of the same caliber as the fee-based databases. Hence the careful wording here.

6. In a study published in May 2008 comparing coverage of the engineering literature in *Compendex* and Google Scholar, the researchers found an almost 90 percent matching rate in Google Scholar for materials published after 1990. See Meier, John J., and Thomas W. Conkling. 2008. "Google Scholar's Coverage of the Engineering Literature: An Empirical Study." *The Journal of Academic Librarianship* 34 (May): 196–201.

7. It's pronounced "archive"—the X is the Greek letter chi, pronounced "ki."

8. You may have been wondering why I didn't write out what TRID stands for. Are you ready? TRID is the union of the Transportation Research Board's *T*ransportation *R*esearch *I*nformation *S*ervices (TRIS) Database and the OECD's Joint Transport Research Centre's *I*nternational *T*ransport *R*esearch *D*ocumentation (ITRD) Database. So, TRIS + ITRD = TRID. It just seemed too insanely wordy for what was meant to be a brief and pithy list.

11
Evaluating Databases

This chapter provides a detailed list of issues to consider when evaluating a database: information to gather, factors to assess, and suggestions for benchmarking. It concludes with advice about how to use this information effectively in putting together a database purchase request. The previous chapter, on choosing the best resource for the question, also draws on this material; don't be surprised if you find yourself going back and forth between these two chapters.

In real life, occasions requiring an in-depth formal evaluation of a database are not going to arise that frequently. Institutions don't change their database subscriptions that often: getting anything new usually means giving up an existing service, and changing between relatively equivalent products tends to be held in check by the overall community's resistance to change. (Users generally prefer a status quo they are familiar with, rather than frequent changes. A replacement has to demonstrate obvious and significant improvements in ease of use or content to be accepted.) At the same time, you want to remain up to date on new databases in your subject area, and, therefore, familiarizing yourself with new and changing products may become a fairly steady undercurrent to your job (depending on the volatility of products in your subject area). Another motivation for doing a thorough study of a database is to write a review of it. Although reviewing is an excellent way to start getting published, it isn't something you do every day. Finally, you obviously want to master a database completely before teaching others about it, even though (as you'll find in the last chapter) you want to be judicious in how much of what you learn you choose to pass on to your audience.

This explains the position of this chapter in the book: almost at the end of the sequence rather than at the beginning. It's important, and I hope useful, but it is not information that you'll need to work through in its entirety very frequently. Note that I said, "in its entirety"—the information here is intended to be a fairly comprehensive list for the special situations listed earlier. Some of these are major considerations, some are minor, and some you might not be able to find any information on, but it's still interesting to be aware of all the potential factors. You certainly will find that you use selected elements from this list regularly in your daily reference activities, as mentioned in chapter 10. Factors of database evaluation such as topical coverage, date range, availability of full text, and usability of the interface, you'll find yourself assessing almost automatically, and even memorizing for the databases you use frequently. For those situations requiring an in-depth examination, such as conducting a database trial or writing a review for publication, the following two sections offer a list of categories and associated factors to consider in evaluating and testing databases.

Basic Facts and Figures

Initial Factual Information to Gather

Database Vendor(s)

As with anything else, the same databases are often available from different vendors, and it can pay to shop around. Vendors get the data in a raw format and then format and load it according to how they structure their database, what fields they want to use, whether those fields are searchable, etc. The search capabilities (and obviously the user interface) vary depending on the vendor, and you can have a really different experience searching the same database offered by different vendors. If you are seriously looking at a new database and more than one vendor provides it, be sure to try them all. Buying a database is a big investment, and you owe it to your organization, and especially to your users, to get the version that will best meet *their* needs.

Existing Reviews

Has anyone already written a review of this database? A thorough database review is a large task, requiring hours of research and testing. Although you may still need to check the latest facts and figures (number of sources, etc.) if the review is only a few years old, and you will always want to do your own testing, someone else's review is a useful place to start. The *Charleston Advisor* is an excellent source of reviews. If you are using a database such as *Library Literature & Information Science* to locate reviews, look for document type "review," and author names such as Gail Golderman, Péter Jacsó, Cheryl LaGuardia, Mick O'Leary, Barbara Quint, and Carol Tenopir (and for anything to do with searching, add Mary Ellen Bates and Mary Dee Ojala). If the database is offered by more than one vendor, look for comparative reviews or individual reviews for the different versions.

Coverage

There are many aspects to coverage, including the following:

Subject Coverage. This is also referred to as "scope." What is the subject emphasis of the database—what topical areas does it cover, or is it multidisciplinary? For the subject, what is the *level* of the material covered; that is, who is the intended audience? K-12 students? College students? Graduate students? Faculty? Specialists? The lay public?

Material Coverage. What types of material and formats are included? If only periodicals, what types? Popular or scholarly? Trade journals or newspapers? Is there one type that is emphasized; that is, are there mostly popular or trade journals, with only a few scholarly titles? For articles containing tables or graphics, are those elements included? If yes, how are they reproduced? (A formatted table reproduced in plain text can be almost impossible to interpret.) If other kinds of documents are covered, what are they? (Possibilities include books, book chapters, theses, conference proceedings, government documents, speeches, audio transcripts such as NPR interviews, and photos or visual materials such as would be found in an image archive.) Are any primary source materials included? What formats are offered for full text: HTML, PDF, or both?

Source Coverage. How many sources are indexed?[1] More important, if both popular and scholarly sources are included, approximately how many of each are there? What is the *selection policy*: Are the source publications indexed cover-to-cover, or only selectively? Is this policy universal for all titles in the database, or does it vary by title? Does the vendor have exclusive rights to any titles, for example, is there a journal whose content you will only find in So-and-So's databaseX? How much information is provided: citations only, citations with abstracts, or citations and full text? This is also referred to as the breadth and depth of coverage: more source titles would indicate greater *breadth*, and cover-to-cover indexing would provide greater *depth* of coverage.

Date Coverage. Does the database provide current, or retrospective coverage (e.g., how far back in time does indexing for most of the titles go)? Does the database use a "moving wall" date coverage system, wherein titles are covered up to a set number of years in the past (e.g., JSTOR titles are usually covered from the first issue up to issues from three to five years ago. Each year one more new year is added, but current issues are not available.)

Geographic Coverage. Does the database index just U.S. publications, or is the source list international? If it is international, are the materials in their original language? How many and which languages are represented? Are article titles and abstracts (if available) offered in translation?

Availability of Sources

A major consideration for any database is how accessible the material that it indexes will be to your users. How many, or what percentage, of the sources are available in full text? If the records are mainly or all citations, does the database support linking technologies such as SFX? (And if so, is your institution running such technology, and do you have other databases that might offer the content that is indexed in the database you are evaluating?) If the database is offered by multiple vendors, which ones support linking? Whether or not you can use a linking technology with a database that provides only citations, and how many of the sources indexed are physically available at your library, should be key elements in a decision to purchase. Interlibrary loan is always an option, but people usually prefer to be able to put their hands on what they want locally.

Currency

How often is material added? How soon after a journal is published do records for its content appear in the database? (This can be a hard question to answer, but it's worth asking.) Are there embargoes on certain titles (e.g., the publisher has decided not to make the most current issues available)? How many titles are embargoed and for how long? (Are they embargoed for weeks, months, a year or more?) If there are embargoed titles that are of significant interest to your library, do you have subscriptions to the print versions, or a separate online access arrangement, so that users have access to the current issues? Here again, if the database is offered by more than one vendor, check the updating and embargo schedules for each one. Both of these factors can vary considerably by vendor.

So far this discussion has focused mainly on periodical databases, but what about a directory database? A list of associations might remain fairly stable, but matters in the corporate world are fairly dynamic: companies change their names or get bought, sold, and merged into other companies. For both associations and corporations, names of officers, their titles, phone numbers, etc., are likely to change. You should try to find out how often such a directory type of database is updated (and where do they get the information from)? For example, if you live in a place where the area code has changed, and records in a business or association database don't reflect that change after a year, this is a red flag that there might be problems with the vendor's updating system.

Size

Mainstream commercial databases can probably all be described as huge in terms of number of individual records; that is, the number of records is so large as to be meaningless. (For more on the question of database size, see Péter Jacsó's useful article, "How Big Is a Database Versus How Is a Database Big" (2007).) What is likely to be more important is to find out how fast the database is growing. If the database is already very large, is it divided up into multiple sections? Are the sections by date (e.g., current, backfile), or by subject or material group? A database broken into sections can be annoying to use if you frequently have to rerun searches in each section. Last, a fairly uncommon concern: if the database is one that you load locally on your own server, how much space does it require?

Errors

Are you surprised to see this heading? Remember, databases are ultimately human creations, and therefore, errors are definitely a possibility. Unfortunately, errors or error rates in a database are hard to determine empirically. You simply need to keep your eye out for them as you work with the database and decide for yourself if you're seeing too many.

Generally, there are three kinds of errors: factual errors, typos, and indexing errors. Factual errors are nontypographical mistakes in numerical or other data (e.g., a date, an address, a phone number, or a name). Typos are things like transposition of letters or numbers, or inadvertent dropping or doubling of words. Usually fairly benign, typos become a big problem when you can't pull up an article because there's a typo in the title, author, etc., or if there is a typo in a supposedly stable URL link, so that the link does not function. Indexing errors are errors of judgment in assigning terms or categorizing records. This type of error is almost impossible to find deliberately; it is mentioned here only so that someday when you're looking at a record and thinking "Why in the world did they assign *that* term?"—you know that it could be an error. Some errors are acceptable, but when they start interfering with searching, or when they mean that the resource is simply providing wrong information, obviously you are moving into the unacceptable realm.

Unfortunately, it is very difficult to test for errors. In doing test searches, you can watch for typos to appear, or you can try keyword searching for words that are frequently mistyped (e.g., *serach* for *search*). In a directory database, you could randomly sample a few records and try to check the names and phone numbers against another source. Otherwise, the best thing to do is to tap the experience of all the other users out there: look for articles, even if not review articles, which mention the database. Do they say anything about errors? You could also post a question to an appropriate newsgroup or blog, and see what anecdotal evidence other users have to offer.

Database Aids

Database aids include both online and physical resources that provide help in using the database, teaching others to use it, and promoting it. You'll want to find out: Does the database have an online Help function? Is it easy to find, easy to understand, and easy to use? Is the help context sensitive, that is, different depending on which screen you are on, or always the same? Note that context sensitive is not necessarily always better than static: the system's interpretation of your context may leave you scratching your head and wanting to start at the beginning instead. Also, if this is a vendor supplying many databases, is the Help specific to the database at hand, or is it generic, a one-size-fits-all for all the databases they offer? (The latter can be very annoying if you are trying to find out something about a database-specific field or feature.) Is there an online tutorial, and is it useful? Is there a printed manual? (Usually not, but it never hurts to ask.) Are there "quick start" or similar brief "how to" cards or leaflets that the vendor can provide? Will the vendor send you promotional materials to help market the new database? Does the vendor offer any train-the-trainer services, either in person or by webcast seminars (webinars)?

Cost and Vendor Support

Vendors regularly experiment with new pricing models, and this can often be a more intricate question than you might think. In academic situations, the database cost is frequently based on FTE, or how many *full-time equivalent* students there are on campus. Such a charge model usually then means there is no limit to the number of people who can use the database at the same time. At the other end of the spectrum from this model, some databases charge by number of simultaneous users, or *seats*, that you opt for, meaning that only a limited number of people can use the database at the same time. Another model is to charge by the search, or to sell *blocks* or sets of searches. When the number of searches in the block is used up, access is suspended until you purchase more. A database with deep date coverage may be divided into sections, and it might be worth checking to see if you can purchase only the most recent section (if that would meet your needs). Price negotiation can be full of wheeling and dealing: discounts might be available based on the number of years that you sign on for or by the number of databases purchased from same vendor. No matter how you look at it, however, database subscriptions are expensive. Many libraries now participate in library consortia, which act together to negotiate pricing with vendors. Because there are so many possible factors, database prices are seldom (if ever) posted on vendor websites or listed anywhere (and that is the reason this book makes no attempt to provide pricing information on any of the databases discussed). The best way to determine the cost for a particular database is to start with the collection development or acquisitions librarian in your library. If you are not currently in a library, call the vendor directly and speak with a sales representative.

It's also useful to explore the kind of support that the vendor offers, in particular for usage statistics. Are usage statistics available? How detailed are they? How do you access them, or can a report be automatically sent to you on a regular basis? Do the statistics adhere to the standards suggested by Project COUNTER (Counting Online Usage of NeTworked Resources), that is, are they "COUNTER compliant"? (See http://www.projectcounter.org.) Standardized statistics allow you to really know what you are looking at, what has been counted, and what it means. If you decide to invest the money, it's very important to have some idea of how much the database is getting used.

Other vendor support issues to explore are the nature and availability of technical and search support (by phone? email? Web form? Is it 24/7 and 365 days a year?), and, as mentioned previously, train-the-trainer services. During your database trial period, besides working with the database itself, be sure to test the technical and search support services, not once, but a few times. Is it easy to reach a knowledgeable person? Were your questions answered accurately and in a timely fashion?

Finally, check to see if the database has any special platform (i.e., PC, Mac, Unix, or Linux) or Web browser requirements or limitations. Even if there is nothing in the vendor descriptions about requiring, say, Internet Explorer v. ##, be sure to try the database under all the current favorite browsers, on Macs, PCs, and Linux machines. If the database is only fully functional under IE on a PC, and most of your users have Macs and prefer Chrome or Safari, you have a disconnect. If any of these would mean upgrades or new equipment or software configurations in order to offer the database, it puts another cost consideration into your evaluation and planning.

Testing and Benchmarking

As mentioned earlier, prior to initiating a subscription request, you will want to get a database trial (or multiple trials if the database is offered by more than one vendor). This is a key component in your evaluation. I have never encountered a vendor who wouldn't offer some kind of trial access to their products. Do not abuse their good nature in this regard: don't ask for a trial if you aren't serious about the database for some reason (either for purchase or for review-writing purposes), or if you don't have the time to evaluate it properly. While you have the trial, make good use of it. If necessary, deliberately schedule several time slots on your calendar over the course of the trial to devote to working with the database. As they say, pound on it! You really need to know what you're talking about if you are going to recommend it for purchase. The following section describes aspects of the database to look for, assess, and compare (benchmark) during your database trial (your test period).

Testing

Record and File Structure

This topic takes us all the way back to the material in chapter 1. Factors to assess include the following: What fields are available? Are the fields appropriate and useful given the subject matter of the database? Sometimes when vendors simply apply their standard interface to a new database, the result is usually less than optimal. Of the fields you see in a full record display, how many are also searchable? (Some fields may be "display only.") Another way to think of it is this: How many ways can you look up same record? That is, how many "access points" do the records have? More fields aren't always better but can be helpful. Do the searchable fields each have their own index list, and can you browse that list? Think of the WorldCat database and its many indexes, which even distinguish single-word from phrase indexes. More indexes are great but not always better. The questions to have at the front of your mind at all times during an evaluation are these: Does this make sense for this database? Is it helpful? Does it help get me to better results more efficiently?

Linking is an aspect of record and file structure that you can divine simply by observation. In a record display, are there fields that are linked (e.g., Author or Subject), which allow you to pull up all other records with that author or subject immediately? Are there other linked fields in the record, and to what do they link?

Indexing and Cataloging Practices: Searchability

Don't be put off by the heading of this section: It is not a suggestion for you to try to find out the interior policies and work practices that the vendor uses. Rather, there are many things that you can observe during testing, or find out from the documentation, that reveal something about how the vendor has set up the indexes, and how much human intervention (cataloging) has been applied to the records. These things can be dubbed *searchability*, and you will find many of them familiar from earlier chapters:

- Are there stop words?

- Can you adjust the date range of your search?

- What limits are available? Are they useful?

- In regard to controlled vocabulary:

  - Does the database use a set of a controlled vocabulary (e.g., subject terms)?

  - Is it a subject list, a straight alphabetical list of terms, as in EBSCO's *MasterFILE Premier* or ProQuest's *Research Library*?

  - Or is it a thesaurus: a hierarchical system, with "broader," "narrower," and "related" headings that shows relationships between terms, as you find in *PsycINFO* or ERIC?

  - If it is a thesaurus, who created it—the original database *producer* (such as the American Psychological Association) or the database *vendor*? (Remember that these are often two very different organizations.)

  - With any kind of list of subject terms, can you browse the list?

  - Is there any kind of mapping functionality to help you to get to the right subject terms?

  - If subject terms are assigned to each record, how many are assigned? (2 to 3? 5? 10 or more?)

- Are the subject terms broad or very specific? (What is the specificity of the indexing language?)

- What about consistency of indexing? Has the subject list grown or changed over the years? If so, and if there are discarded headings, how is that handled? How do you know if a term has been discontinued?

- Has some form of mass search-and-replace been performed, or do you need to search on both the old and the new term? (These are good nitty-gritty questions to ask the vendor's search help desk.)

- With any browsable indexes, do they offer a "paste to search" function, so you don't have to retype the entry in the search interface? (This saves time and the risk of typing errors.)

- In regard to abstracts:

  - Do the records offer abstracts?

  - Are they simply replications of the first paragraph of the article, or are they actually evaluative or summarizing? (The former are more likely to have been machine generated, whereas the latter are most likely to have been written by a person.)

  - Are the abstracts generally long and detailed or short?

- In regard to title enhancements:

  - If titles in this subject discipline's literature are frequently cute or clever rather than straightforward, is a supplemental title added, to clarify what the article is really about (and to give you a better chance of retrieving it with a keyword search)?

  - If the database offers materials in different languages, are the article titles offered in translation?

- What about full text? If full text is available, is it searchable?[2] Are the better tools for searching full text available (e.g., proximity operators)?

- Does the database offer a "find more like this" function? If yes, does it pull up appropriate, useful material?

- Overall, does the database employ features and conventions that are similar to those in other databases?

An additional point that bridges both searchability and the next category, user interface, is the idea of search history. This is a user interface functionality that does not have to do with indexing or cataloging practices, but that certainly contributes to a database's searchability. Does the database keep track of your search history? Can you reuse previous searches? Can you combine searches with other previous searches or with new terms?

User Interface: Usability

This is an area that is open to both objective and subjective evaluation, and can be particularly important in the case of the same database offered by multiple vendors. As you work with the database, besides assessing the content and search function, keep track of your experiences and reactions to the interface—the *way* you access that content and those search functions. In the broadest sense you should ask, "Does it work? How well?" When you are comparing vendors, searching the same information through a different interface can feel like a totally different experience. Following are some specific things to be look for:

- Are different skill levels accommodated, such as novice and expert?

- Is the interface easily understood?

- Does the interface make it clear how to use it, both by layout and by the terminology used? For example, are field names clear and understandable to the user?

- If icons are used, are they meaningful?

- Is the interface so bare and simple that it's "naked," or is it cluttered, busy, or mysterious?

- Are there *too many* options (or too many ways to do the same thing)?

- How is color contrast used? Is color used to demarcate functional areas of the screen, or is everything uniform in color?

- Is the interface visually appealing? For instance, is the color scheme easy on the eyes? Are the fonts too small, too big, too hard to read, etc.? Are the colors or fonts adjustable, either on an individual basis by users to suit their personal preferences, or globally for the whole institution's account, by a local system administrator (or both)?

- Does it provide good navigation links? Is it well designed?

- How much control do the navigation links exert. For example, if you use the Back button rather than a "Modify search" link, does it wipe out your search? (This is very annoying.)

- Can you initiate a search by just pressing Enter, or is it necessary to always click a "Search" or "Go" button?

- How many clicks does it take to get to your goal (i.e., abstract, fulltext, etc.) and back?

- How easy is it to adjust or modify your search? Do you have to go back to a main search screen, or is a search interface (or other kinds of refine options) available on the results screen?

- How easy is it to find help? What terminology is used for help?

- Are functions such as save, email, and download easy to see and understand?

- If the database has a "time-out" function, that is, you get disconnected after a certain period of inactivity, does it provide a warning before disconnecting you? Can the time-out period be adjusted?

- If the subscription is based on a limited number of users, what sort of message is displayed if all the "seats" are in use when you try to sign on?

- Again, is the database browser or platform dependent, that is, will it work only with a specific Web browser, on a specific type of computer (usually Windows rather than Mac, Unix, or Linux)?

- If the database is browser dependent, what sort of warning does it provide if you attempt to use it with an unsupported browser?

- If you encounter nonfunctioning tools (i.e., buttons/features that don't work), is it because you are on an unsupported platform? This is another good excuse to call the vendor's tech support line and evaluate how they respond.

Treatment of Research

How research is treated is an important factor for any institution that works with students who are writing papers. Terms frequently used for research articles are *peer reviewed*, or *scholarly*. Databases such as ProQuest's *Research Library* or EBSCO's *Academic Search Complete*, which offer both popular and scholarly articles, provide a limit function for "Scholarly" or "Peer Reviewed."[3] Provision of such a limit or similar functionality only makes sense when a database includes a wide range of materials, however. Databases that consist almost entirely of scholarly materials, such as the *Science Citation Index* or *EconLit*, do not need this type of filtering functionality. Questions to ask in evaluating a multidisciplinary database are the following:

- Does the database provide research-level material?

- How can scholarly materials be identified? By a limit in the search interface?

- Is there a way to distinguish scholarly materials in search results, even if you haven't used a limit (e.g., by an icon in the record, or by a separate tab in the results display that filters for scholarly articles)?

- Is there anything in the product literature to indicate how many journals, or what percentage of the sources, are scholarly?

- One other point to check: Scholarly articles almost always have a bibliography of sources at the end. If the database provides full text in HTML rather than PDF format, check to be sure that such bibliographies are included.

Sorting/Display/Output Capabilities

The amount of control you have over the presentation and output of your results can make a big difference in the usefulness of those results. It affects the extent to which you can easily evaluate them, and the ease of working with them. Here are things you may want to assess for each function.

Sorting:

- What is the default sort order for displaying results? Can you change it?

- Where is the sort function offered: in the search interface, in the results display, or in both?

- What are the sort options?

- Is there a limit on the number of results that can be sorted? Some databases offer a sort option only on results sets of, for example, 500 or less.

- What fields can you sort by?

- If the database allows you to select certain records and create a list of just the selected or marked records, can those be sorted?

Displaying:

- How many results are displayed per page? Can you change the number?

- Are the search parameters (e.g., words searched, limits used) reiterated on the results list screen?

- What is the default record display: full or brief? Can you change it?

- Are search terms highlighted in the results display? If they are, is it possible to turn such highlighting off? (Many repetitions of high-lighted terms can sometimes turn out to be more annoying than helpful.)

- Are format options indicated for each record, for example, icons indicating HTML or PDF availability?

Output:

- What formats are offered for output, especially of full text? Plain text, HTML, or PDF?

- Can you email records? What email options are offered: for example, sending the information formatted as plain text, as HTML, or as a PDF attachment? How much can you customize the email: Can you enter your email as the return address, put in your own Subject line, or add a note? Can you choose to include the search history with the emailed results?

- When printing records, do you get to choose what is printed (which fields)? Note the following especially in databases that provide full text: Can you select a group of records, and then print the full records in one continuous stream? Or are you forced to print full-text records one by one?

- If you have reason to believe that many of the people who would use this database use software programs such as RefWorks or EndNote to keep track of their citations, does the database offer an export function for bibliographic management software programs?

Benchmarking

The first three types of benchmark activities listed here are, obviously, most important when you are trying to choose between two databases, especially if you already subscribe to one and are contemplating whether to change to the other. The next point addresses the fact that in academia, there is always a set of schools with which your school compares itself, and such comparisons are important to administrators. The final point here is perhaps not a realistic goal, but it is a significant concept.

Source List Comparisons

In choosing between rival databases, a good first step is to compare their lists of sources, that is, which journals (or other document types) does each one offer? How much overlap is there? How many unique titles are there? Among the unique titles, which list has more titles that are of interest to *your* institution? Among the titles that are the same in both databases, is the coverage the same? That is, how do the dates of coverage and the availability of full text (if any) compare? If you can obtain the source lists in Excel format and merge them into one spreadsheet, it can greatly facilitate this comparison process. This comparison is also almost entirely quantitative and objective, and therefore it carries more weight in a request for purchase. And you might not have to do this comparison by hand with your own spreadsheets: Check the recent library literature, and ask colleagues in the collection development, acquisitions, or cataloging departments to see if any comparison products are available to you.

Search Result Comparisons

Just as it sounds, you should run the same searches in the databases that you are comparing, and see how the number and nature of the hits compares. The number refers to how many results, and the nature refers to the quality of the results: If one database yields 10 more hits on a search, but of those extra 10, 8 are from popular magazines or are only brief articles, are you really getting any significant advantage? Absolutely equal searches are somewhat difficult to achieve, because each database could use differing subject terms, the default fields that are searched might be different, etc., but this is still a very useful exercise to do. Experiment with keyword searches, phrase searches, and field searches. If there are subject terms that are the same in both databases, those are ideal for benchmark searches. Simply spending some time with the two subject lists side by side on the screen can be useful, too. Try to get a sense of the level of detail of subject terms used and the nature of the language. Even in the realm of controlled vocabulary, there are some that are more formal, and others that sound more like natural language. Users are more likely to benefit by accident when the subject terms are less formal (e.g., because the terms they type in happen to match the subject vocabulary).

Be sure to keep a record of everything you do while you're benchmark searching: exactly what the search was, the number of results, and comments on the results. Don't count on your memory; by the next day the similarities and differences will be a blur. Keeping a good log helps this activity stay in the quantitative, objective realm, rather than the gut instinct, subjective realm.

Finally, be sure to test searching at different times of day to compare response times. Based on the vendor's location, figure out what represents peak hours and test during that time. Significantly slower response times or access refusals are not a good sign.

Technical Support Comparisons

If you are comparing two databases, come up with some questions for the technical support staff at both vendors. Compare the time required to get answers, how accurate the answers are, and the general effectiveness of the staff.

Peer Institution Holdings

As mentioned previously, administrators at colleges and universities are very aware of, and sensitive to, comparisons with other schools that are recognized as peers. It has nothing to do with the intrinsic worth of the database at hand, but if you can show that a significant number of your school's peer institutions already subscribe to this database, it may be helpful in persuading your administration to fund the purchase.

Ideal Assessment of Coverage

The ideal assessment of coverage is represented by this question: What is the percentage of the total literature in the discipline that is covered by this database? This is an ideal, because, frankly, I can't imagine how one would go about determining it with any kind of precision, but it is an interesting and thought-provoking point to raise. (If the database is subject specific, one strategy might be to see if there is a matching subject category in *Ulrich's*, and then compare numbers of titles. This is still bound to be somewhat crude, however.) It could be a good question for the database vendor.

Making a Request for Purchase

As mentioned as the beginning of this chapter, one of the reasons that you would choose to go through this much work is if you were considering a new database subscription. Now that you've done the work, what can you do to try to make the new subscription a reality? You've done your homework well, but keep in mind that administrators, like the rest of us, have limited time and attention spans. They don't want to read 10 pages of detail, they just want to see a succinct argument that shows why database XYZ is necessary, how it will benefit library users, and, quite likely, how you propose to fund the purchase. Most organizations have a process in place for making such requests, but the following list of points probably meshes with, or can be used to enhance, the existing process.

Elements to Include in the Request

What Does This Database Bring to the Institution?

Show what material this database offers that is not available from any other existing service (this could include topic areas, material types, specific publication titles, date ranges, etc.). Use numbers rather than text as much as you can. Relate the database directly to the goals of your organization, for example, to specific classes, areas of expansion (new programs), and so forth. If you need to highlight textual elements such as publication titles, provide at most four key titles, and list any additional titles you think are important in an appendix. Once you have demonstrated why this database is unique, it is also important to address the following consideration.

How Does This Database Complement the Existing Collection?

Although, of course, the database needs to bring something new to your organization (otherwise, why would you be interested in it?), it's also important to demonstrate how the material in this database could complement and extend the existing library collections. For example, if your institution has a strong language program, you could probably make quite a strong case for a database of international newspapers in the original languages as it would provide a wealth of language content without any of the knotty issues of getting such things in print. Conversely, if you are trying to make a case for a new religion database, but your school doesn't offer any kind of religion degree, you certainly can say it brings something new to your resources, but what exactly would be the point? There would be little complementary material in the collection, and, unless there were popular religion courses offered in another department, it would be difficult to identify a strong user base.

If you are proposing to change from an existing database to a rival product, obviously you'll do many comparisons, as mentioned in the first two types of benchmarking. You'll want to emphasize differences in the new version of the database that are important to your stated audience for the database. The following section discusses this key point, the potential database users.

Who Will Use the Database?

Who will be interested in the material in this database? How many potential users will it have? If at all possible, try to get some of those potential users involved during the database trial period. Have them test drive the database, or at least take a look at the source list. Comments from users (e.g., "it helped me with a paper," "I needed this for my thesis research," "it seemed easy to use"), or even better, purchase requests from users (i.e., "the library should definitely have this resource"), can be very persuasive. If you found a database review that included a strong comment relating to the audience for the database, which matches your potential audience, include it here.

How Will the Database Be Marketed?

If you get the database, how will you let people know that the new resource is available? As always, strive for brevity, but try to outline all the avenues you propose to use to market the database. For example, try a mass email to department faculty and students (possibly more than once) that includes links to appropriate Web pages or use posters, flyers, brown-bag (or better, free pizza) information or training sessions, etc. Put links to the new resource on as many pages of your website as are appropriate. People have a lot vying for their attention, and as vociferously as your users may have said they wanted this new database, you will still need to put out quite a bit of effort to get them to integrate the new tool into their work habits.

In addition, it's a good idea to include how you plan to evaluate database usage after a year. How well did your marketing work? Usage statistics are one obvious measure, but some kind of quick, informal survey (e.g., by email or a Web page) of your target communities shows a bit more initiative on your part. Besides, such a survey has the added benefit of providing additional marketing as well as assessing usage, usefulness, etc.

How Will the Purchase Be Funded?

Funding is usually the make-or-break factor: what is the cost, and where will the money come from? With the cost, indicate whether it includes any discounts, which pricing model was used (e.g., if you opted for only two simultaneous users rather than five), etc. If you have competing price quotes from multiple vendors, indicate that you've chosen the most economical one (or if you haven't, why). The money may come from canceling something else (another database, or several serial titles), or, if your accounting system permits, from a permanent transfer of funds from a monographic to a serial budget. If you believe your case is strong enough, there is always the option of simply requesting additional funds to be added to your budget line to pay for the new subscription.

What Else?

If the database has been favorably reviewed, include citation(s) to the review(s) in an appendix. Particularly useful or pertinent quotes might be included in appropriate sections of the main document. If in the course of your review and testing you have discovered features that you feel are particularly compelling, mention those now. Indicate that you can provide detailed title comparisons, or search logs, if requested.

Your overall goal is to present a succinct, clear, and quantitative case as well as a qualitative case. Your first attempt might not be successful, but you will have shown that you can perform a rational and cogent analysis. Your funding agents are more likely to trust you and try to do their best for you when you try again. So take a refusal like a good sport, and just keep gathering data for the next attempt.

Exercises and Points to Consider

1. This list of things to consider in evaluating a database is fairly comprehensive (perhaps daunting?), but no list can ever be absolutely complete. You've been working with databases a lot by now: What other points or issues have *you* encountered that you'd add to this list? What points do you think aren't as important or that you wouldn't need to bother with?

2. A major project: Choose a database that is new to you, either from the resources available at your institution, or by requesting a trial from a vendor. Do a thorough evaluation of it, from the point of view of either writing a review of the database for publication or writing up a purchase request for your management. (If you aren't currently employed in a library or other type of information center, make one up.) Then either:

    Write the review

    or

    Write up the purchase request.

If you choose the review option, write the review as if you were going to submit it for publication. Include the name of the publication to which you would submit the review, and follow its guidelines in terms of formatting, length, etc. (See "Instructions for authors" on the publication's website.) After your professor has seen it, she might well encourage you to follow through with the submission; this is a realistic goal.

If you choose the purchase request option, include a separate description of your (real or fictional) library or information center, to set the scene. Be sure to describe your user community and your institution's overall budget situation. Make it as realistic as possible. If you are currently working in a library or information center, choose a database you'd actually like to obtain: You may be able to put your work here to good use on the job.

In either case, do not feel compelled to work through every single point mentioned in this chapter: Choose the ones that make sense and are feasible for your chosen project.

Suggested Readings

Powers, Audrey. 2006. "Evaluating Databases for Acquisitions and Collection Development." In: *Handbook of Electronic and Digital Acquisitions* edited by Thomas W. Leonhardt, 41–60. Binghamton, NY: Haworth Press. Powers's chapter covers much of the same ground as this chapter, but with some interesting differences, including a case study. It can be very helpful to read similar material presented in a different voice. Other chapters in this *Handbook* are useful as well; for example, chapter 4 discusses the special issues around aggregator databases.

Carroll, Diane, and Joel Cummings. 2010. "Data Driven Collection Assessment Using a Serial Decision Database." *Serials Review* 36, no. 4: 227–239. This is a report on the serial database tool developed in-house and used for selection and cancellation projects, evaluation of electronic journal packages, and collection assessment by Washington State University librarians.

Notes

1. The number of sources is usually easily found in the vendor's promotional literature for the database, because—dearly as we love them—vendors do love to play the numbers game: that is, "we have more sources than vendor Y." Now, what really matters is what those sources *consist* of: Are they all quality publications, or are the numbers being padded with the sort of titles you find in your dentist's office? Still, the number of sources is worth finding, if only because it provides another quantifiable piece of information for your purchase request.

2. This is not as silly a question as it sounds. For example, the *Investext Plus* database used to consist of nothing but full-text PDF documents, but you could not search the full-text content. It doesn't hurt to check.

3. Tip: If a database includes both popular and scholarly materials, but doesn't provide any functionality for distinguishing between them but does use subject headings, then some subject terms that might help sift out research articles are "methodology," "sampling," "populations," "results," "variables," or "hypotheses."

12
Teaching Other People about Databases

If the thought of getting up in front of other people and speaking makes your blood run cold, and you were hoping that by becoming a librarian you could avoid having to do that kind of activity, I'm sorry to have to burst your bubble.[1] But *my* hope is that after reading through this chapter and getting some experience, you will change your mind and come to understand that teaching and presenting are a vital part of librarianship. Let us consider the importance and ramifications of presenting for a moment, and then we'll get into some more specific nuts and bolts.

The library profession needs spokespeople and champions. The focus of this book has been, of course, databases, but what good are a group of wonderful databases if you can't convey to others that they exist and how to use them? How long do you think funding for these expensive resources will last if you can't defend them? (Especially in competition with something like Google Scholar?) In the larger scheme of things, it's never too early to get used to the idea of justifying your existence: public, school, and state-employed librarians need to be able to talk to their communities and to local and state legislatures. Academic librarians make points for their libraries in the eyes of the budget controllers by successfully engaging in the academic game: by giving presentations at conferences and holding offices in state and national professional organizations. Our profession might not be in crisis, but we certainly are challenged by the Internet as almost no other profession is. The Internet is free, and libraries are expensive: we are cost centers, not profit centers. It's difficult to quantify the value we give back. If you've chosen to become a librarian, or are already in the profession, presumably you've made that choice because you enjoy and believe in the library as an institution and librarianship as a vocation. Isn't it worth it to learn to get up in front of people and talk for a short time to ensure that your chosen path has a future? *Any* kind of speaking you do—whether it's an information literacy session for a freshman writing class, an evening program for adults at a public library, a talk at a conference, three minutes of impassioned defense before a state

251

legislature, or even a brief discussion in an elevator—makes a difference. It makes a difference both for libraries in general, and for your own career, to be able to effectively tell others what we do, why our (expensive) tools are useful, and what benefits they bestow.

Teaching means getting up in front of people and talking. Humans like to communicate (look at the popularity and omnipresence of cell phones), and teaching is just another form of communicating. It's a wonderful improvement that all of the American Library Association–accredited library schools in the United States now offer at least one class on instruction (Roy 2011), but maybe that course didn't fit into your schedule, or maybe library school is a distant memory for you. Still, even if public speaking ranks right up there with getting a root canal in your list of favorite things to do, be assured that it can be done. It gets easier, and you might even enjoy it someday,[2] Honest. Maybe you enjoy teaching and presenting already; if so, good for you! If not, the following principles should help to make the experience at least manageable, if not totally enjoyable.

Teaching Principles

The second part of this chapter discusses the opportunities to teach people about databases that librarians commonly encounter. Of the four types of teaching or public speaking opportunities considered, I count myself as quite lucky to have experienced them all (with the exception of the public or school library versions of the second point). These experiences have informed my thoughts about what works and what doesn't, and what's important and what isn't, in the process of conveying skills or knowledge from one person to another, or from one person to a group. The process of writing up my thoughts for this chapter included double-checking my instincts against some representative examples from the teaching literature (see the Suggested Readings at the end of the chapter), including essays by two professors who have been recipients of the undergraduate teaching award at my university. It was gratifying to find my instincts borne out by this review. A particular acknowledgment goes to Celia Applegate, professor of history at the University of Rochester, whose list of rules both inspired and frequently informed the following list of principles.

These are guidelines that can be applied to any type of teaching, not just of databases, although there are underlying assumptions (e.g., in the emphasis on use of technology) that what is being taught is technical or online in nature. You'll find that the list ranges from the more philosophical "teach to your audience" to the very directive and practical "wait for someone to answer when you ask a question." You will be able to use these principles as a kind of checklist and support system as you strive to acquire all the hallmarks of an effective teacher. Repeated studies have shown that "concern for students, knowledge of the subject matter, stimulation of interest, availability, encouragement of discussion, ability to explain clearly, enthusiasm, and preparation" are the qualities that students cite most often in describing effective teachers (Feldman 1976). Those are your goals, and these suggestions will help you achieve them.

Principle 1: Teach to Your Audience

Be very clear who your audience is, and keep them firmly in mind as you prepare the session. Make your teaching objectives, material, and handouts—

Sidebar 12.1: Teaching the "Millennial" Audience

Millennials, *Net gens*, or *Generation Next* are the various terms used to refer to people born between 1981–1982 and 2002 (also frequently spelled *millenials*).

Characteristics of Millennials	Effective Teaching Strategies for Millennials
• Don't like being passive recipients of information	• More self-directed
	• Very little lecture
• Like trial and error (they have no fear of failure)	• Relaxed and informal
• Like to learn from each other	• Lots of student engagement and activity; for example, they like competition
• Don't like formal instruction	
• Like to be engaged and entertained	

From Carter and Simmons (2007).

everything about what you're doing—appropriate to the needs and interests of *that* audience. It's quite easy to decide what you want to tell people, but it takes a good deal more effort to determine how to deliver your message in a way they will really *hear* and perhaps remember. Ten-year-olds, undergraduates, lawyers, or the PTA are all very different groups of people, and your approach needs to be different in each case.

Principle 2: Avoid Lecturing

Avoid pure lecture at every opportunity. As Professor Applegate (1999) puts it: "Never miss an opportunity to keep your mouth shut." You probably thought that if you were asked to teach or present, you should fill every moment, but silence truly can be golden. Do not be afraid of silence (Applegate 1999). People need time to process what you're saying, which means that you need to stop speaking from time to time. Give people time to "think about what they have been told" at regular intervals (Felder and Silverman 1988). Something as simple as pausing to write a point on the board, and not talking while you do it, can provide a moment of needed silence. We're lucky in our subject matter, too, in that when you're teaching about databases, you have all kinds of ways you can stop lecturing and give your audience time to *use* what they've heard as well as think about it. For example:

- In a hands-on situation, have people start doing their own searching. Try to make the searching, not your lecture, fill the majority of the class time. Talk about one idea, then have people try it, then go on to another idea, and have them try it. Alternate between talking and activity.

- In a demonstration (not hands-on) situation, you might present people with a search statement, and then have them work alone or with the person next to them, to come up with as many synonyms as they can for each of the concepts in the search.

- Use the projector to display a search request, or hand out a paragraph describing a search request, either in the form of discursive text, or as a dialogue between a patron and a librarian. Have the class—individually, in groups, or as a whole—figure out one or more search strategies to try. Then have members of the audience come up and type in the chosen searches.

- If you are going over a computer function of some kind (e.g., looking materials up in the online catalog), ask the class if anyone has done it before. (*Wait* for an answer.) Then have one or two volunteers come up and demonstrate how they do it.

- Use questions such as "What are all the uses you can think of for (XYZ)?" to start discussions. To get even the quiet people involved, hand out brightly colored Post-it notes to everyone, and have them *write* their ideas, one per note. Stick them up on a wall or a white board, in categories, and start a discussion from there.

In general, look at the list of concepts you wish to get across, and come up with alternatives to straight lecturing. Students in the "Net gen" or "millennial" generation (1981–2002) seem to be especially adverse to lecture, and even the students' faculty have noticed that they learn more effectively from discussing issues with each other (Viele 2006). Small groups, discussion, writing on the board, Post-its, other hands at the instructor keyboard, any kind of physical activity or acting out (you can do some fun things with people acting out Boolean logic)—all of these are lecture alternatives. People learn best when they are developing and putting concepts into practice themselves, so aim for that if possible. You don't have to come up with all these teaching ideas on your own. Brainstorm with a colleague; it will be fun for both of you.

Principle 3: *Wait* for Answers

When you ask questions (which is definitely a good thing to do), first, ask with a purpose, that is, ask a question for which you really want an answer, and second, *wait* for someone to answer. Give your audience a chance to marshal their thoughts and come up with a response. Resist with every fiber of your being the desire to answer your own question. The moment you do, the audience will decide your questioning is all a sham, and they won't bother to make any further effort. You will have no chance of getting them to answer any subsequent questions.

Waiting for someone to answer is definitely one of the hardest things to do in a teaching situation. That silence seems to stretch out forever, but try to remember two things. One, the time seems much longer to you than it does to your audience. Two, the silence will eventually start to bother the people in your audience as well, and they will realize that you really mean it; you *do* want to hear from them. Sooner or later someone will crack and say something. If you really can't stand it, pick someone in the group and push the matter by asking, "What do you think?" in a friendly way.

Of course, the kinds of questions that you ask make a difference, too. Questions that ask people to relate things to their own lives or experience are generally more comfortable, and can usually get *someone* to pipe up. Once they do, if you're looking to foster more group discussion, don't immediately respond yourself—look around for someone else who looks on the verge of speaking and give that person an encouraging look, or just ask, "What do you think?" Try not to be the arbiter, the touchstone, for every response from the group. It is not necessary to "respond to every response" (Applegate 1999).

Principle 4: Less Is More

Don't overwhelm your audience by trying to do too much. Guided by Principle 1, choose only a limited number of concepts or instructions that you feel will be the most useful information for *that audience*. Take two or perhaps three things you think would be most helpful for *that audience* to remember or learn, and build your presentation around those items. One of the biggest pitfalls for new professors—and this extends to anyone new to teaching—is that they tend to over-prepare lectures and try to present too much material too rapidly. Successful teachers, however, present material "paced in a relaxed style so as to provide opportunities for student comprehension and involvement" (Boice 1992).

This may well sound like an advocation that you set your sights pretty low, and you may feel that it's a disservice to show only a few features of a wonderful database that is loaded with functionality. The problem is, you can't possibly cover as much material in interactive, nonlecture classes as you can if you are only lecturing; such classes aren't very efficient in that sense. If you are adhering to Principle 2, sincerely trying to avoid pure lecture (which is the most ineffectual form of instruction anyway), and instead trying to foster discussion and engagement and active learning, you can't go over every bell and whistle. It will be frustrating at times. You'll find yourself worrying, "They should know this! They should know that, too! And this other thing!" Consider this, however: If you show them two or three things that get their interest enough so that they go back on their own, don't you think they might discover some of the other "things they should know" on their own? It's likely that they can. Motivated, interested people are pretty smart that way.

Overall, the outcomes of a nonlecture style of teaching can be much more useful and rewarding to your students. If you cover only two or three things in an interesting way that shows, "here's how this will benefit you," the participants are much more likely to remember at least some of the content. And, if you manage *not* to alienate your audience, and *not* make the session one they can't wait to get out of, they are much more likely to seek you out again for help later, in what is probably a more useful one-on-one situation at the Reference Desk or in an appointment in your office.

Principle 5: Transparency in Teaching

Don't be inscrutable (Applegate 1999). Lay out clearly the goals and objectives for the class, the assignment, or the exercise—whatever you are doing. Always keeping in mind Principle 1, relate the goals and objectives to your audience. Do your best to make them feel that it's worth their while to be there. Keep things simple, straightforward, and honest—you are not a god(dess) or keeper of keys to special mysteries, you just happen to have some useful knowledge you'd like to share that you believe will make your audiences' lives better in some way. Honesty is important because of the next principle.

Principle 6: You Have the Right to Be Wrong

It is acceptable to be wrong occasionally, or not to know the answer to every question. Acting inscrutable is often allied with trying to be infallible, and both are terrible ideas. Of course you will have done your best to master your material (Principle 8), but it is still inevitable that someone will ask you a question to which you don't know the answer, or that some alert person will point out something you've gotten wrong, pure and simple. Laugh at yourself, thank the person (sincerely) for noticing, make a note to fix it for next time, and get over it. No one is perfect, and most audiences will relate to you more easily if they think that you're human rather than a remote and infallible being. Consider this wonderful quotation:

> Arnold Schoenberg wrote in the introduction to his 1911 text on musical harmony that ". . . the teacher must have the courage to be wrong." The teacher's task, he continued, "is not to prove infallible, knowing everything and never going wrong, but rather inexhaustible, ever seeking and perhaps sometimes finding."
> The more we can involve the students with us in this task, "ever seeking and . . . sometimes finding," the better . . . (Applegate 1999)

Ever seeking and perhaps sometimes finding—what a perfect expression for librarianship. So don't get upset if you make a mistake; you are in excellent company.

Principle 7: Teaching with Technology

If working with technology of any kind, there are two things to keep in mind: (1) slow down, and (2) anticipate technology failure.

When you are working with technology, that is, either a projected computer screen or a hands-on computer classroom, you need to build more time into presentation plans. Especially in a hands-on situation, in which people are looking back and forth from your (projected) screen to their own (and maybe back to yours yet again), *slow down*. It's essential to take more time. You know where you're going, but your audience doesn't. It is all uncharted territory for them. You must give the people who are trying to follow you time to process. Even if they are not trying to replicate what you are doing on their own computers and are just watching the screen, take your speed down a few notches. Don't scroll rapidly up and down, and practice mousing from point A to point B without a lot of whizzing around on the screen. These may sound like small details, but again, your audience is madly trying to follow you (and might also be trying to take notes); this is new territory for them, and their minds will be doing a lot more processing than yours. Excessive scrolling and mousing in that situation is distracting, if not downright annoying, so work on keeping it to a minimum.

The other thing about technology: Be ready for things to go wrong. Plan for how you will handle it if the projector bulb burns out, or you can't get on the Net, or the computer crashes. For example, if you're leading a hands-on session and the projector malfunctions, simply designate one or two of the people in the class as your hands, and have them follow your directions while the other students gather around those computers. Invite all the students to help as backseat drivers. They'll probably all have more fun and get more out of it than if things had gone according to plan! If you're presenting in a non–hands-on situation and your projector fails, start a discussion instead. Ask the group something about what you have just been trying to cover. As noted earlier, questions that relate the material to their own experience ("What do you folks usually do when you need to find XYZ?") are good for getting the ball rolling.

If you're presenting somewhere other than your home location and intend to show something live on the Internet, take a PowerPoint file (with screenshots of what you intended to show live) along as backup. It's a fair amount of extra work (depending on the length of your presentation), and you might not need it, but oh, if you do need it, you will be intensely thankful that you took the time. So take the time. It also gives you a way to rehearse (if you take a laptop with you) on the plane or in the hotel room the night before.

If you're in your home situation and something goes wrong: first, call tech support (if you have it); second, restart the computer; and third, start some kind of discussion.[3] With students, ask them about their assignment (or whatever has brought them to you today), what they've done so far with it, and their familiarity with the library and its systems. In a nonacademic situation, ask them what brought them to the session, what they hope to get out of it, etc.

Above all, in a technology failure situation, do not betray your anxiety. Don't wring your hands and whimper helplessly. Groaning is permitted, as long as you also laugh. Maintain your aplomb. This is much easier to do if you've rehearsed in your mind what you'll do if the technology lets you down. Because it will: not every time, but at least sometimes. Dave Barry says that your household plumbing makes plans in the middle of the night for how it will go wrong and disrupt your big party. These devices—computers, projectors, servers, etc.—undoubtedly do the same thing. And speaking of rehearsal . . .

Principle 8: Practice

There is an old gag that asks, "How do you get to Carnegie Hall?" Answer: "Practice, practice, practice." Practice is essential. If you are not used to presenting, or are uncomfortable with it, I cannot emphasize enough the importance of rehearsal. Practice is crucial for several reasons. First and foremost, the time you are allotted will always be limited, and a live run-through is the only way to find out how long the session you have planned actually lasts (and usually you will find that you have more material than you think). Practicing also helps you to become more comfortable, and can help identify bugs in your presentation, saving embarrassment later. Let's look at the "limited time" issue in more detail.

No matter what sort of group teaching or presentation situation it is (information literacy, staff development, etc.) you will always be working within a specified time limit. Until you have run through what you plan to say—actually spoken the words *out loud*—you won't know how long your presentation really takes. Unless you have a lot of experience, you cannot mentally run through a talk at a slow enough pace to mimic a verbalized version reliably. Especially when a presentation or sample class is part of a job interview, practice it to be sure it fits within the time allotted. If you practice and find that your presentation is too long, the only option is reducing the amount of information that you attempt to convey. When in doubt, cut it out. Talking faster is *not* an option, nor is running over. Both things will irritate your audience. If you simply keep talking and have to be cut off before you're finished, you will look unprepared. Practice by yourself (but aloud!), even if it means talking to the wall and feeling like an idiot. If possible, the best option is to round up some classmates, friends, or family, and give your talk to them. Especially if you are trying to simulate a class situation, with questions and back and forth, practicing with friends is extremely helpful in determining your timing and pacing. They can also help identify any non sequiturs or outright errors in your talk. In a job interview situation, if you teach only one thing but do it well, appear relaxed, interact with your audience, and stay within your time limit, your prospective employers will feel as if you've taught them much more, and will, in general, have far more positive feelings about you than if you try to cram in every last nuance, are forced to rush, and lecture the entire time. Unless you are unusually gifted in this area, your audience will almost always be able to tell whether or not you have practiced.

At the same time, being well rehearsed doesn't mean rattling off your script like—well, like a memorized script. Rather, it means full mastery of your material, so that you are talking about your topic naturally and easily, you are able to field questions or take small side trips (or encounter technical difficulties) without getting flustered or derailed from your main intent, and your enthusiasm and enjoyment of your topic come through. If you are suffering, your audience will suffer as well. Take some lessons from Hollywood: rehearse, know your lines, and deliver them with sincerity and enthusiasm. Act like you're enjoying it, even if you aren't. Your audience will enjoy it a great deal more (and you might too). Remember to smile occasionally (write yourself a note about it if necessary) and breathe. You can't panic when you're breathing deeply and slowly. So practice, then breathe, smile, open your mouth, and share the wonderful information you have with your audience. You'll be great!

Database Teaching Opportunities

Let's take a look at the kinds of opportunities for teaching or presenting information about databases that you are likely to encounter as a librarian. In order of frequency of occurrence (from most to least), these can be summarized as follows:

- One on one, with a patron over a question at the Reference Desk.

- One-off, one-time sessions, often known as information literacy classes (or sometimes *bibliographic instruction*) in college and university settings. Presenting such a class is a common part of an academic job interview. In a school library, these are usually referred to simply as classes and tend to be quite brief: 15 to 20 minutes. The public library equivalent might be an evening or noontime continuing education session.

- A database introduction or review, such as one would present at a staff meeting or staff development session.

- A sustained, semester-long class.

These are all quite different sorts of encounters, yet you'll find that many of the principles given here apply to them all. What follows are some thoughts about applying the principles in each case to make your database instruction more effective.

Teaching at the Reference Desk

This is probably the type of teaching encounter[4] that people generally find most comfortable. It's intimate, one on one; you only have to deal with one person and can focus entirely on him or her. It's also reactive, rather than proactive; the person has *chosen* to approach you, and after you focus on the topic of the moment the encounter is over. True, you can't prepare (Principle 8) exactly, but that can be a plus: you won't be overprepared. You have your life knowledge, your library science education, and your professional experience, and you simply apply these in various ways to meet each person's individual information needs.

Introducing a patron to a database at the Reference Desk provides an opportunity for a teaching moment, but if you take advantage of that, keep it to a moment. Don't overwhelm (Principle 4, less is more). Pick one or two things to try to teach the patron, such as "This is how you get to the list of databases on (subject X)" and "See this drop-down? If you change it to Subject, the articles you get should be right on target." *Suggest* the power of the database, but don't try to impart all your knowledge. (As Carol Kuhlthau [1988] says in more formal terms, the reference encounter represents the ideal in terms of teaching, because it offers "intervention that matches the user's actual level of information need.") Go through the process with the patron, asking questions about the topic, etc., and explaining in a general way what you're doing, but without necessarily going into all the details. In other words, try to be transparent (Principle 5) without being overwhelming or lecturing (Principle 2). For example: "Let's try this database—it's got psychology articles" rather than "Well, first you should go to the list of psychology databases, and then read the descriptions to decide which one to use. . . ." Attempt to engage the patron gently, and be quiet from time to time. A good time to be quiet is when you're looking at a list of results together, so that the patron can study the screen and process. It's much better to hold back a bit and have the patron ask "How did you do that?" than to overwhelm him or her with information. Let's face it, not everyone is that interested, or *needs* to do this kind of research again (Principle 1, Teach to Your Audience). Dropping a limited number of teaching seeds is more likely to result in further questioning and ultimate skill flowering than 10 minutes of unmitigated, and probably unappreciated, lecture.

Teaching an Information Literacy Session

The classroom situation a librarian is most likely to encounter is really quite the hardest: the one-off, limited time (usually only around an hour) class, whose purpose might range from the typical information literacy, or "library," session for freshman English students, to how to search the Internet in an evening class for adults at the public library. Now you as an instructor are facing a roomful of people who may or may not wish to be there, and with whom you will probably only have one class session. You are supposed to have some idea of what makes them tick, make contact with them, communicate, and impart two or three chunks of useful knowledge about a fairly sophisticated topic (i.e., database or Web searching) in the limited time allotted. Certainly it is a challenge, but by keeping the principles in mind, you can meet that challenge.

Even in this situation, you can still teach to your audience: You will have advance notice that the session is coming, which gives you time to find out something about who your audience is going to be. In any kind of school situation, the instructor should be willing to tell you the reason that he or she has requested an instruction session in the library, and something about the class (personalities, skill levels, etc.). In a community education situation, talk to other librarians who have taught such classes before: Who tends to show up? What are they usually most interested in? How are their skills? If you feel you need more information, do some reading: Plenty of research has been done on teaching adults (and every other age group). Here's your chance to go to ERIC and get "a few good articles."

We'll assume that, based on your research, some demonstration or hands-on training with a database will be part of your session, or possibly two databases, or a database and the library's online catalog—but that is probably pushing the limits of Principle 4 (less is more). It depends on the point that you are trying to make with each resource. For example, for a first freshman introduction to the library, you might decide that a multidisciplinary database that offers mostly full text is the resource most attuned with their needs and interests, and therefore you will show them the pertinent features of that database. For an upper-level course, you might opt to demonstrate a subject-specific, abstracts-only database (or one of the *Web of Science* Citation Indexes), along with the library catalog, with an explanation of how the two can be used in concert. Here is where you can use self-exploration to great advantage: you could divide the class into small groups and have each one explore and report back on a different resource, allowing the class as a whole to cover a lot more ground. (A scenario based on this idea is described later.) One thing you can almost be sure of, no matter who is in your class, is that while they may be vaguely aware of databases, they won't have used them nearly as much as they have Google (or whatever search engine is hot at the moment). Use this to your advantage. You know one thing that represents familiar ground to them, so work it in: Compare and contrast the search engine with the properties of databases to introduce what databases are. (What is frustrating is that if you have to explain that there are such things as databases, it uses up one of the precious two to three learning objectives.)

Examples of Class Scenarios

Here is a step-by-step scenario that might be used in an introductory session for students (my experience is with undergraduates, but this might well work with high school students or graduate students as well). You will need to have prepared the handouts with the assignment for each group, and if possible, a Web page specifically for the class, with links to the database(s) that you want them to use. If your school uses a course management system and you have rights to add material there, that's ideal.

- Explain that the students' instructor has told you about their assignment, and you want to familiarize them with some resources that will help with the research for that assignment—make it go faster, be more efficient, and provide better-quality information—so that they can write better papers. They are going to do most of the work, however, and need to do a good job, because they will be teaching the rest of the class. (Transparency, and some motivation.)

- If your school uses a course management system such as Blackboard (and you have rights to add material there), ask, "Have any of you used course pages on [whatever your institution calls the course system]?" Don't forget to wait for an answer. If anyone has, ask if they have looked at the library resources section for this course.

- If you are simply using a Web page you have created that is not part of a course management system, show the students how to get there.

- Divide the class into small groups of three or four, and give each group a handout with its assignment. (Avoid lecturing; encourage active learning.) For the assignments, give each group a search topic appropriate to the class, and have them search it in a subscription database. Ask them two to three "how do you . . .?" types of questions about the resource. (Less is more.) Then ask them to do the same things in a Web search engine, Google Scholar, or another appropriate database. Here are some examples of activities

  - Here are two examples of handouts for a freshman composition class:

    (1) In *Project MUSE*, search for "fairy tales and strong women."

    Questions: How many results do you get? Are these articles scholarly or popular? How can you tell? Working from one result, how might you find more like this? (The purpose of the "more-like-this" question is to get them to notice and use subject headings.)

    Try the same search and answer the same questions using Google.

    (2) In *MLA International Bibliography*, search for criticism or interpretation of Grimm's fairy tales.

    Questions: Does the database have any special fields that might help you do this search? What are the different kinds of publications included in the *MLA International Bibliography*? How would you get from these records to the full text?

    Try the same search and answer the same questions using Google Scholar.

  - Here is an example for use in an upper-level computer science course:

    In the *ACM Digital Library*, search on "wearable computers."

    Questions: How many results do you get? How recent are they? Can you sort the results in different ways? How might you use one result to "find more like this"?

    Try the same search and answer the same questions using CiteSeer (citeseer.ist.psu.edu). (For other groups, substitute *IEEE Xplore* and Google Scholar or Scirus.)

  - And the following example would work for any class:

  - In [your library's catalog], try a keyword search on [appropriate topic].

  - Questions: (two to three things you'd really like your audience to "get" about your online catalog, such as finding and using Subject Headings from records, how to interpret Location information, or how to access special features you think will be particularly useful to them.

  - Try the same search and questions using Google Books and/or WorldCat.org. Which do you like better? What are the advantages and disadvantages of each?

- Even if you have enough computers for everyone, in your groups of three to four, have only one to two people working the keyboards. Tell the others they are in charge of taking notes, because they will be presenting their group's results. (Active learning, engagement.)

- When the groups are finished, have each group come to the front and present their results. Only jump in and point things out or add material if they really seem to have missed something; you may be very surprised at how little you need to add. (Avoid lecturing.) Ask the rest of the group if they have any questions (wait for answers). Use your talk time to ask questions about their perceptions of similarities or differences among the various subscription resources.

Overall, you should find that this kind of hands-off, active learning approach will definitely be "teaching to your audience." You have done your "practicing" in coming up with the assignment handouts (obviously, you need to test drive them all and make sure they support whatever points you are trying to make, which counts as "practice"). Here are two additional variations on this theme, this time concerning a common teaching objective:

One of the most difficult things to convey to undergraduates seems to be how to identify and obtain scholarly articles, especially when the full text has to be tracked down from physical copies of journals in the library. You might decide that all you want to make sure the students come away with are the ideas (1) that special-purpose databases exist, and (2) that databases provide an efficient means to identify articles on a topic. If you are at an institution that subscribes to many databases that offer full text, or that has implemented a link resolver system such as SFX, you might limit your goals to just those two basic ideas, and tell the students to ask at the Reference Desk when they need help accessing the physical journals. Then structure the session along the lines described earlier, but focusing on databases that do not provide full text. Have every group address this question: How do you get from a citation to the full text? See if anyone knows, and have that person explain how she does it.

Alternatively, you could start with the idea that (1) special-purpose databases provide an efficient means of identifying articles. Then you might demonstrate a sample search (without trying to explain Boolean concepts, or the importance of synonyms or other searching concepts), for which the results include a perfect article that is not available in full text online. Ask the students what they would do at this point. (Remember to *wait* for somebody to say something—anything!) Then go for your point (2): how to get from a citation to a physical bound journal on a shelf. If it's possible to have the class all look up the journal, get its call number, and head out into the stacks in search of it, all the better. Give hints, but don't lead. Let them work together; perhaps divide the class into two or more teams and turn it into a competition (at this point, it would be even better to supply each group with a different citation on a slip of paper, so that they are heading in different directions). If all that isn't possible, bring the appropriate volume into class with you, and give it to one of the students to find the actual article within the bound volume. Encourage him to get help from a friend if he wants, and discuss something else while they work on that. Basically, don't try to do too much, and if possible, try to make what you *do* do interactive, collegial, and physical. If you should be lucky enough to have someone ask a question (and don't forget, of course, to solicit questions), that's great—explain, but otherwise remember the thought in Principle 2: never miss an opportunity to keep your mouth shut. Resist the urge to data dump to your audience. (For even more nifty ideas for active-learning exercises to use with undergraduates, be sure to consult Burkhardt and colleagues (2003) or simply look at the latest crop of articles in *Library Literature* under "Subject: Bibliographic instruction—College and university students." There are more and more great ideas out there.)

My examples are heavily oriented to undergraduates, since that is the group with which I am most familiar, but you should be able to turn the basic ideas, and the principles outlined earlier, to your advantage for whatever group you are teaching. For example, a class of adults from the community will, of course, have quite different learning objectives. Rather than finding articles to support research papers, they may want to learn how to find reputable health information on the Web, or how to assess the validity or quality of any Web resource. You might decide that your goals are to introduce the idea of advanced search, and how to use it to limit a Web search to .gov or .edu sites. If you are introducing article databases, it's probably for different purposes, for example, current events, genealogy, business, or investment research. No matter what the subject matter, the principles still apply: Try to determine what information will be most pertinent to *that* audience; don't just lecture; definitely ask questions (an adult group might actually answer, and it can be easier to get an interesting discussion going); don't try to do too much; and finally, be extra careful to take it slow in a hands-on session. An adult group is also probably more likely to point out a mistake, or ask you a new question, and that's great: You'll learn something, and they'll secretly enjoy the idea that they stumped the teacher. It's a win-win situation.

In general, although a brief, one-off session[5] can be challenging, it is challenging in a good way. (For an even greater-but-good challenge, consider doing such a session in 15 minutes. Arant-Kaspar and Benefiel [2008] demonstrate a real mastery of "knowing their audience" and "less is more" in their description of their successful outreach program of brief instructional visits to classrooms.) True, you don't have the opportunity to establish much rapport with the group, to see their growth or progress, or to repair any blunders in this week's class next week. On the other hand, you are forced to be really rigorous in developing your one class (draw up your list of learning objectives, and then cross most of them out), so that what your attendees receive is a carefully honed, very targeted product. The quality is just as high, if not higher, than that of many of their regular classes, and the session is likely to be more interactive and memorable as well. If nothing else, the class will come away knowing that (1) you exist, (2) something other than Google exists, and (3) you were trying to show them something that would enhance some aspect of their life. Just as we discussed in the Reference Interview chapter, if you can leave them with a positive impression, it's more likely that individual students will later seek you out at the Reference Desk, in your office, or by email, chat, etc.

Teaching a Class in a Job Interview

Presenting a class as part of a job interview has been mentioned a few times already, but let me add some specific notes about it here. First, the time will probably be shorter (20–30 minutes) than in any real class. This will tend to force you into more of a lecture style of presentation, which your audience is expecting, but try to surprise them by working in at least one of the interactive, nonlecture approaches suggested under Principle 2. Second, though this may sound obvious: do your homework. The library where you will be interviewing most likely has a website. If the library is part of an institution of higher education or a corporation, the organization probably has a website. Study these, and use them to inform your presentation. Make the class you create look as if you already work there. Base your presentation on a database available at that library, and make your audience a group at that institution (a particular class, with a real class number and professor's name, or a real group within the company or organization). For a public library, study the schedule of classes already on offer, and try to come up with a session that would augment or complement an existing class. If you decide that you want to demonstrate a database that is available only at your target library, and not wherever you currently are, call up the vendor and ask for a trial so that you can learn it, and use the library's link when you are on site. (Create a PowerPoint as a backup just in case.) Create one or more appropriate handouts to go with your presentation, and again, don't be shy about copying the library or organization's logo off their website to brand your handouts. In as many ways as possible, act like you're already on board. With this kind of preparation, perhaps you soon will be!

A Staff Presentation

Teaching your colleagues about a database is quite different from all of the other situations described here. For one thing, knowing your audience shouldn't be an issue; even if you are a new hire right out of library school, you should have a pretty good sense of what librarians are interested in and want to know. Because they are your peers and colleagues (which can make the whole thing both more and less comfortable), it should be much easier to plan and deliver your message. Note, however, that if your group includes members from throughout the library and not just reference librarians, it changes the playing field a good deal. Staff from departments outside of reference, including computer support, may have little or no idea that databases exist or how they are used, and teaching in this situation is much more akin to teaching a group of adults from the community. But teaching a group of reference librarians about a database turns many of the formerly stated principles upside down.

- Principle 2—Avoid Lecturing. You might be able to get away with more lecture here than in any other situation. It will still be appreciated if you try to break things up, however, and give your audience time to absorb what you're saying from time to time. I think you'll find, however, that a lecture naturally devolves into a more participatory session, for the reason noted in the next point.

- Principle 3—Wait for Answers. You probably won't have to wait for answers or need to work at fostering discussion; your colleagues likely will be very forthcoming with comments and questions. This is a group that is truly interested in what you are talking about and eager to explore it with you. (They are glad that you've done the work to master this database, so that they can ask *you* questions.)

- Principle 4—Less is More. You can set higher goals for the amount of information you plan to impart. Again, this audience is *interested* and does want the details. They are already knowledgeable, and will be more interested in salient differences from what they know, rather than the basics. You can start at a much higher level of discussion. However, take some guidance from Principle 4 and don't overwhelm them. A rule of thumb might be to master as much of the database as you can, plan to present 50 to 60 percent of that (all of which is beyond the basics), and let questions bring out whatever else people want to know.

The other principles do not change much. Principle 5, Transparency in Teaching, still applies. These librarians are likely to have chosen to attend your session, and so they are willing participants, but it's still a good idea to outline clearly the goals and objectives of your talk; that is, give them good reasons to stay and listen. You will very likely get a good workout of Principle 6, You Have the Right to be Wrong. You are talking to a very knowledgeable audience, who will undoubtedly catch something or know something that you don't. Don't worry about it! It's a benefit, not a contest. The two technology points of Principle 7 (go slower, and be ready for it to fail), both apply as in any other situation. Just because they are librarians doesn't mean they can look from their screen to your projected screen (or from your projected screen to their notes) any faster than anyone else. In fact, it may take them longer, because they are studying all the details more closely. So give everyone plenty of time. If the technology fails, you probably will have a whole roomful of people ready to jump in and help, so it's not all up to you. Still, you will want to show that you can stay calm, and have a plan in mind for what to do if the technology lets you down. Of course, Principle 8 applies to every situation: *practice* your database demonstration, in as realistic a situation as possible (e.g., out loud, in front of people if possible), before heading off to your staff development meeting.

If an information literacy session presents the most challenging *format* for teaching, a session for your colleagues undoubtedly presents the most challenging *audience* for your teaching. But again, let it be a good challenge. Learn the database, practice, but don't kill yourself preparing. You'll never remember it all anyway, and you'll just make yourself nervous. If one of your "students" knows something that you don't, let him or her teach you. If someone asks a question that you don't know the answer to, and neither does anyone else in the room, make it an opportunity to explore and find out together. It's really much more interesting that way.

The Full Semester Class

Here at last we have a chance to aspire to what is truly important in teaching, that is, "connection, communication, and the stimulation of critical thinking" (Brown 1999). Instead of one session, you'll see this class over and over, get to know your students, and get beyond the limits of just a few how-tos of only one database. You'll be able to explore many databases and broader philosophical and technical considerations of databases and information seeking. Sadly, these opportunities are quite rare for librarians, so I will not spend much time on this topic. I would like to say enough to indicate that this is a *feasible* project, however. Should you ever get offered the chance to develop and provide such a class, think seriously about taking it on.

A full semester class, obviously, requires considerable planning, and there are entire books devoted to teaching and curriculum planning (the Suggested Readings include two titles, and a search of WorldCat or Amazon .com reveals many, many more). However, it is not an insurmountable effort. Consider these six steps that are recommended in planning a course (Davidson and Ambrose 1994):

- Assess the backgrounds and interests of your students.

- Choose the course objectives (note that these are often set by the department, and you simply need to determine how to achieve them).

- Develop the learning experiences within the course.

- Plan how to seek feedback and evaluate student learning.

- Prepare a syllabus for the course.

You are already familiar with the concept in the first point: know your audience. With a full semester to work with, you can now choose overall course objectives, as well as objectives for each session. In both cases, however, you still need to be careful not to overwhelm your students. In each individual class meeting, you shouldn't try to deliver too much, and the sum total of all the sessions ultimately determines the amount of material that you can get through in a semester. You may find it useful to approach a semester-long course as an organizational activity: to work from large, overarching ideas, to the components of those ideas, and finally to the steps needed to teach those components. As you work out the steps, you can plan the best learning experiences to support them. As you determine the components, you can then plan ways to assess mastery of them. When all of that is done, you will have enough material to write up a syllabus.

A discouraging aspect of a whole semester's course for many people is that it seems like you have to come up with *so much material*. But, at least in the area of databases and research techniques, the large ideas—the overall objectives—can be broken down into many component parts. If you start analyzing, breaking down the knowledge or skills that you take for granted into a series of intellectually manageable chunks, you'll be surprised at the amount of material this represents. (Students like clearly defined chunks of information.) As you present the course, those component ideas build on each other, heading toward the overall course objectives. Along the way you are presenting learning experiences to convey those ideas, assessing to see if the ideas have been conveyed, and giving feedback. It's an organic, iterative, growing process. Go for it.

Exercises and Points to Consider

1. Think back over all your schooling. Which teachers do you remember most vividly (both good and bad)? See if you can come up with a list of reasons why those instructors either worked (or didn't) for you. Use this information to form your own list of teaching principles.

2. A major effort: Decide what type of library you would be most likely to apply for a job in, then develop a 20-minute mock teaching session that could be used in your interview. This could be an academic, school, public, corporate, law, or medical library.

   In real life, outreach is an increasingly important aspect in the services of all of these types of libraries (their very survival could depend on proving their value to the overall organization), so even if such a session is not listed as part of your interview schedule, be proactive and offer a session as an added extra to your interview.

Suggested Readings

Accardi, Maria, Emily Drabinski, and Alana Kumbier. 2010. *Critical Library Instruction: Theories and Methods*. Duluth, MN: Library Juice Press.

Applegate, Celia. "Teaching: Taming the Terror." Chapter 2 in *How I Teach: Essays on Teaching by Winners of the Robert and Pamela Goergen Award for Distinguished Achievement and Artistry in Undergraduate Teaching*. Rochester, NY: University of Rochester, 1999. http://hdl.handle.net/1802/2864.

Booth, Char. 2011. *Reflective Teaching, Effective Learning: Instructional Literacy for Library Educators*. Chicago: ALA Editions.

Lippincott, Joan K. 2005. "Net Generation Students and Libraries." In *Educating the Net Generation*, edited by Diana G. Oblinger and James L. Oblinger. Boulder, CO: EDUCAUSE. http://www.educause.edu/educatingthenetgen/. An excellent source for learning more about and achieving a better understanding of this particular audience.

McKeachie, Wilbert J. 1994. *Teaching Tips: Strategies, Research, and Theory for College and University Teachers*. 9th ed. Lexington, MA: D.C. Heath and Company. A totally practical, down-to-earth guidebook covering every aspect of teaching. Although oriented toward the creation and delivery of a semester-long class, chapters 4 and 5, on Organizing Effective Discussions, and Lecturing; chapter 13, on Peer Learning, Collaborative Learning, Cooperative Learning; and chapter 19, Teaching in the Age of Electronic Information, are all universally applicable. Ignore the date; this book is timeless.

Veldof, Jerilyn. 2006. *Creating the One-Shot Library Workshop: A Step-by-Step Guide*. Chicago: American Library Association. If you didn't have the good fortune to have taken a course in instructional design, here is the ideal alternative. Veldof's guide is meant to address the need for a library session that is "one shot," but frequently requested, and that can be taught by different people. This book will help you design a session that can be consistently taught by different people and consistently received by any group of students, but the instructional design principles are useful for improving any kind of class development.

Notes

1. My opening statement to this chapter is based on years of informal observation and interactions with librarians from many different libraries; an excellent study by Kaetrena Davis now provides empirical evidence for it as well. In her survey, she found that most of the time people don't go into librarianship specifically with teaching in mind: "more than two-thirds of the respondents (64%) chose librarianship with a desire to help people, followed by a love of reading and literacy (52%)" (Davis 2007).

2. The magic time for jettisoning pre-class nervousness and anxiety seems to be between 51 and 60 years of age according to Davis's study (2007).

3. Tech support people may hate me for presenting these actions in this order, but if you restart the computer and that *doesn't* solve the problem, you've lost a lot of precious time before initiating contact with tech support, who will inevitably take some time to respond.

4. Frankly, it had never occurred to me to question that what happens at the Reference Desk is teaching, but if you have any doubts, there is a quantity of literature available to support the idea. See Eckel (2007), Elmborg (2002), and Gremmels and Lehmann (2007), all of which have strong "review of the literature" sections.

5. Actually, you might find that you get invited back to give a library session every time the professor teaches the class, so definitely keep your notes and whatever materials (e.g., PowerPoint) you used.

References

Preface

Tennant, Roy. 2003. *Metasearching: The Promise and the Peril*. Ithaca, NY: New York Library Tour 2004. http://roytennant.com/presentations/older /2004newyork/metasearch.pdf.

Tenopir, Carol, Gayle Baker, and Jill Grogg. 2010. "Feast and Famine: Database Marketplace 2010." *Library Journal* 135 (May 15): 32–36, 38.

Chapter 1

Computer History Museum. 2004. *Timeline of Computer History—Networking*. http://www.computerhistory.org/timeline/?category=net.

Dialog (a Thomson Reuters business). 2005. *Company Background—Dialog History Movie Transcript*. http://www.dialog.com/about/history/transcript.shtml.

Encyclopædia Britannica. 2008. s.v. "digital computer." Encyclopædia Britannica Online. http://www.britannica.com/EBchecked/topic/163278/digital-computer.

Lexikon's History of Computing. 2002. *Master Chronology of Events*. http://www .computermuseum.li/Testpage/01HISTORYCD-Chrono1.htm.

Chapter 2

Walker, Geraldene, and Joseph Janes. 1999. *Online Retrieval: A Dialogue of Theory and Practice*. 2nd ed. Englewood, CO: Libraries Unlimited, p. 63.

Chapter 4

American Psychological Association. 2011. *PsycINFO Facts*. http://www.apa.org /pubs/databases/psycinfo/index.aspx.

Tenopir, Carol. 2003. "Databases for Information Professionals." *Library Journal* 128 (October 1): 32.

Tenopir, Carol. 2004. "Eric's Extreme Makeover." *Library Journal* 129 (September 1): 36.

Viadero, Debra. 2004. "ERIC Clearinghouses Close; New System in Works. *Education Week* 23 (January 14): 20–21.

Chapter 5

Tenopir, Carol. 2001. "The Power of Citation Searching." *Library Journal* 126 (November 1): 39–40.

Thomson Reuters. 2005. "Dr. Eugene Garfield, Pioneer of Citation Indexing and Analysis, Celebrates 80th Birthday." Press Release Archives Sept. 12, 2005. http://science.thomsonreuters.com/scientific/press/2005/8289850/.

Thomson Reuters. 2011. "Products A-Z: Web of Science." http://thomsonreuters.com /products_services/science/science_products/a-z/web_of_science/.

U.S. National Library of Medicine. 2011a. "Medical Subject Headings (MeSH)." Fact Sheet. http://www.nlm.nih.gov/pubs/factsheets/mesh.html.

U.S. National Library of Medicine. 2011b. "MEDLINE®." Fact Sheet, http://www .nlm.nih.gov/pubs/factsheets/medline.html.

U.S. National Library of Medicine. 2010. "What's the Difference between MEDLINE and PubMed?" Fact Sheet. http://www.nlm.nih.gov/pubs/factsheets/dif_med _pub.html.

Chapter 6

Flagg, G. 2006. "New WorldCat Search Site Offers Public Access." *American Libraries* 37 (September): 12–13.

Hane, Paula J. 2006. "OCLC to Open WorldCat Searching to the World." *NewsBreaks* Information Today, Inc. http://newsbreaks.infotoday.com/nbreader .asp?ArticleID=16951.

Helfer, Doris Small. 2002. "OCLC's March into the 21st Century." *Searcher: The Magazine for Database Professionals* 10 (February): 66–69.

Hogan, Tom. 1991. "OCLC Looks to End-User Market with FirstSearch." *Information Today* 8 (November): 1, 4.

Jordan, Jay. 2003. "Cooperating During Difficult Times." *The Journal of Academic Librarianship* 29, no. 6: 343–345.

OCLC. 2011a. *WorldCat: A global catalog.* http://www.oclc.org/us/en/worldcat /catalog/default.htm.

OCLC. 2011b. *WorldCat: Facts and statistics.* http://www.oclc.org/us/en /worldcat/statistics/default.htm.

"OCLC Launches Eserials Holdings." WorldCat.org. 2006. *Advanced Technology Libraries* 35 (August): 1, 8–9.

"WorldCat.org Adds New Features, Functionality." 2007. *Advanced Technology Libraries* 36 (March): 2–3.

"WorldCat.org Adds List-Building Features, User Profiles." 2007. *Advanced Technology Libraries* 36 (August): 4.

Chapter 7

Golderman, Gail. 2008. "History E-Reference Ratings." November 15. *Library Journal.com.* http://www.libraryjournal.com/article/CA6612291.html.

MLA. 2004. *Descriptors and Indexing.* Modern Language Association. http://www.mla.org/publications/bibliography/bib_descriptors.

MLA. 2010. *Frequently Asked Questions.* Modern Language Association. http://www.mla.org/publications/bibliography/bib_faq.

ProQuest LLC. 2011a. *Information Centre: About MLA International Bibliography. Chadwyck-Healey Literature Collections.* http://collections.chadwyck.com/infoCentre/products/about_ilc.jsp?collection=mla.

ProQuest LLC. 2011b. *Literature Online with MLA Add-On Module.* http://www.proquest.com/en-US/catalogs/databases/detail/lit_online_mla.shtml.

Chapter 8

Bates, Mary Ellen. 1998. "Statistical Universe." *Database* 21 (October/November): 96.

Beine, Joe. "The Cost of the U.S. Census." http://www.genealogybranches.com/censuscosts.html. Quoting Gauthier, Jason G. 2002. *Measuring America: The Decennial Censuses From 1790–2000.* U.S. Bureau of the Census/Dept of Commerce. Washington, DC: U.S. Government Printing Office. Appendix A, p. A-1. Cost per person calculated and added by Mr. Beine; 2010 data is from the GAO and U.S. Census Bureau websites.

Dorning, Mike. 2011. "Stuck in Jobs: The New Swing Voters." *Bloomberg Business-Week*, June 16: 35–36.

Durant, D. 2006. "American FactFinder." *Choice* 43 (August): 177.

Gordon-Murnane, Laura. 2002. "Digital Government: Digital Tools for the Electronic Dissemination of Government Information: FirstGov and American FactFinder." *Searcher* 10, no. 2: 44–53.

Griffiths, David N. 2011. "Notable Government Documents 2011: Digital Diamonds & Budget Cuts." *LibraryJournal.com.* May 15. http://www.libraryjournal.com/lj/home/890105-264/notable_government_documents_2011_.html.csp

Jacsó, Péter. 2000. "Peter's Picks & Pans." *Econtent* 23 (August/September): 84–86.

O'Leary, Mick. 2006. "DataPlace to the Rescue." *Information Today* 23 (December): 47, 52.

O'Leary, Mick. 2008. "NationMaster and StateMaster Solve Great Statistics Problem – Almost." *Information Today* 25 (November): 37, 43.

Chapter 9

Abram, Stephen. 2007. "Millennials: Deal with Them! Part II." *School Library Media Activities Monthly* 24 (October): 55–58.

American Library Association (ALA). 2004. *Guidelines for Behavioral Performance of Reference and Information Service Providers. Reference and User Services Association, American Library Association.* http://www.ala.org/ala/mgrps/divs/rusa/resources/guidelines/guidelines behavioral.cfm.

Ansari, Munira Nasreen. 2011. "Information Seeking Behavior of Policy Maker, Policy Executor and Worker Media Practitioners of Pakistan." Pakistan *Library & Information Science Journal* 42, no. 1: 12–20.

Antell, Karen, and Jie Huang. 2008. "Subject Searching Success: Transaction Logs, Patron Perceptions, and Implications for Library Instruction." *Reference & User Services Quarterly* 48, no. 1: 68–76.

Baro, Emmanuel E., George O. Onyenania, and Oni Osaheni. 2010. "Information Seeking Behaviour of Undergraduate Students in the Humanities in Three Universities in Nigeria." *South African Journal of Library and Information Science* 76, no. 2: 109–117.

Bates, Mary Ellen. 1998. "Finding the Question behind the Question." *Information Outlook* 2 (July): 19–21.

Bertulis, Ros, and Jackie Cheeseborough. 2008. "The Royal College of Nursing's Information Needs Survey of Nurses and Health Professionals." *Health Information & Libraries Journal* 25, no. 3: 186–197.

Blair, Ann. 2010. "Information Overload, Then and Now." *The Chronicle of Higher Education* 57, no. 15: B4–B5.

Blocker, LouAnn. 2011. "Information Overload . . . @ Your Library." *Georgia Library Quarterly* 48, no. 1: 6–9.

Bowler, Leanne. 2010. "A Taxonomy of Adolescent Metacognitive Knowledge During the Information Search Process." *Library & Information Science Research* 32, no. 1 (November 8): 27–42.

Breitbach, William, and J. Michael DeMars. 2009. "Enhancing Virtual Reference: Techniques and Technologies to Engage Users and Enrich Interaction." *Internet Reference Services Quarterly* 14, no. 3–4: 82–91.

Carter, David S. 2002/2003. "Hurry Up and Wait: Observations and Tips about the Practice of Chat Reference." *The Reference Librarian* 79/80: 113–120.

Chang, S. 2009. "Information Research in Leisure: Implications from an Empirical Study of Backpackers." *Library Trends* 57, no. 4: 711–728.

Chowdhury, Sudatta, Forbes Gibb, and Monica Landoni. 2011. "Uncertainty in Information Seeking and Retrieval: A Study in an Academic Environment." *Information Processing & Management* 47, no. 2: 157–175.

Connaway, Lynn Silipigni, Timothy J. Dickey, and Marie L. Radford. 2011. "'If It Is too Inconvenient I'm Not Going After It': Convenience as a Critical Factor in Information-Seeking Behaviors." *Library & Information Science Research* 33, no. 3: 179–190.

Connaway, Lynn Silipigni, and Marie L. Radford. 2010. "Virtual Reference Service Quality: Critical Components for Adults and the Net-Generation." *Libri* 60, no. 2: 165–180.

Corcoran, Tomas B., Fran Haigh, Amanda Seabrook, and Stephan A. Schug. 2010. "A Survey of Patients' Use of the Internet for Chronic Pain-Related Information." *Pain Medicine* 11, no. 4: 512–517.

Cramer, Dina C. 1998. "How to Speak Patron." *Public Libraries* 37 (November/December): 349.

Cranley, L., D. M. Doran, A. E. Tourangeau, A. Kushniruk, and L. Nagle. 2009. "Nurses' Uncertainty in Decision-Making: A Literature Review." *Worldviews on Evidence-Based Nursing* 6, no. 1: 3–15.

Crow, Sherry R. 2009. "Relationships that Foster Intrinsic Motivation for Information Seeking." *School Libraries Worldwide* 15, no. 2: 91–112.

Cullen, Rowena, Megan Clark, and Rachel Esson. 2011. "Evidence-Based Information-Seeking Skills of Junior Doctors Entering the Workforce: An Evaluation of the Impact of Information Literacy Training During Pre-clinical Years." *Health Information & Libraries Journal* 28, no. 2: 119–129.

Cutilli, C. C. 2010. "Seeking Health Information: What Sources Do Your Patients Use?" *Orthopaedic Nursing* 29, no. 3: 214–219.

Davis, Nathaniel. 2011. "Information Overload, Reloaded." *Bulletin of the American Society for Information Science and Technology* 37, no. 5: 45–49.

Decker, Emy Nelson. 2010. "Baby Boomers and the United States Public Library System." *Library Hi Tech* 28, no. 4: 605–616.

Dewdney, Patricia, and Gillian Michell. 1996. "Oranges and Peaches: Understanding Communication Accidents in the Reference Interview." *RQ* 35 (Summer): 520–535.

Dewdney, Patricia, and Gillian Michell. 1997. "Asking Why Questions in the Reference Interview: A Theoretical Justification." *Library Quarterly* 67, no. 1: 50–71. Quoted in Marshall Eidson, 2000.

Diekmann, F., C. Loibl, and M. T. Batte. 2009. "The Economics of Agricultural Information: Factors Affecting Commercial Farmers' Information Strategies in Ohio." *Review of Agricultural Economics* 31, no. 4: 853–872.

Dresang, Eliza T., and Kyungwon Koh. 2009. "Radical Change Theory, Youth Information Behavior, and School Libraries." *Library Trends* 58, no. 1: 26–50.

Du, Jia Tina, and Nina Evans. 2011. "Academic Users' Information Searching on Research Topics: Characteristics of Research Tasks and Search Strategies." *The Journal of Academic Librarianship* 37, no. 4: 299–306.

Dubicki, Eleonora. 2010. "Research Behavior Patterns of Business Students." *Reference Services Review* 38, no. 3: 360–384.

Eidson, Marshall. 2000. "Using Emotional Intelligence in the Reference Interview." *Colorado Libraries* 26 (Summer): 8–10.

Fagan, Jody Condit, and Christina M. Desai. 2003. "Communication Strategies for Instant Messaging and Chat Reference Services." *The Reference Librarian* 79/80: 121–155.

Fister, Barbara. 2002. "Fear of Reference." *Chronicle of Higher Education* 48 (June 14): B20.

Gao, Shi-Jian, Jin Xiu Guo, and Xiao-Ling Duan. 2011. "The Study of Library Use and Document Gathering Behavior: A Survey of Geomatics Faculty at Wuhan University, China." *Library Collections, Acquisitions, and Technical Services* 35, no. 1: 19–28.

Garcia-Cosavalente, H. P., L. E. Wood, and R. Obregon. 2010. "Health Information Seeking Behavior Among Rural and Urban Peruvians: Variations in Information Resource Access and Preferences." *Information Development* 26, no. 1: 37–45.

Ge, Xuemei. 2010. "Information-Seeking Behavior in the Digital Age: A Multidisciplinary Study of Academic Researchers." *College & Research Libraries* 71, no. 5: 435–455.

Green, Samuel Swett. 1876. "Personal Relations between Librarians and Readers." *Library Journal* (October): 74–81. Quoted in David Tyckoson, 2003.

Haines, Laura L., Jeanene Light, Donna O'Malley, and Frances A. Delwiche. 2010. "Information-Seeking Behavior of Basic Science Researchers: Implications for Library Services." *Journal of the Medical Library Association* 98, no. 1: 73–81.

Harris, Roma, Flis Henwood, Audrey Marshall, and Samantha Burdett. 2010. "'I'm Not Sure If That's What Their Job Is': Consumer Health Information and Emerging 'Healthwork' Roles in the Public Library." *Reference & User Services Quarterly* 49, no. 3: 239–252.

Harter, Stephen P. 1986. *Online Information Retrieval: Concepts, Principles, and Techniques*. Orlando, FL: Academic Press, p. 149.

Head, Alison J. 2008. "Information Literacy from the Trenches: How Do Humanities and Social Science Majors Conduct Academic Research?" *College & Research Libraries* 69, no. 5: 427–445.

Heinström, Jannica. 2006. "Broad Exploration or Precise Specificity: Two Basic Information-Seeking Patterns among Students." *Journal of the American Society for Information Science and Technology* 57, no. 11: 1440–1450.

Hemmig, William. 2009. "An Empirical Study of the Information-Seeking Behavior of Practicing Visual Artists." *Journal of Documentation* 65, no. 4: 682–703.

Hider, Philip N., Gemma Griffin, Marg Walker, and Edward Coughlan. 2009. "The Information-Seeking Behavior of Clinical Staff in a Large Health Care Organization." *Journal of the Medical Library Association* 97, no. 1: 47–50.

Information Research home page. 2011. *Information Research: An International Electronic Journal*. http://informationr.net/ir/.

Jamali, Hamid R., and David Nicholas. 2010. "Interdisciplinarity and the Information-Seeking Behavior of Scientists." *Information Processing & Management* 46, no. 2: 233–243.

Kern, Kathleen. 2003. "Communication, Patron Satisfaction, and the Reference Interview." *Reference & User Services Quarterly* 43 (Fall): 47–49.

Khan, Shakeel A., and Farzana Shafique. 2011. "Information Needs and Information-Seeking Behavior: A Survey of College Faculty at Bahawalpur." *Library Philosophy and Practice* (January). http://www.webpages.uidaho.edu/~mbolin/khan-shafique.htm.

Kim, Kyung-Sun, and Sei-Ching Joanna Sin. 2011. "Selecting Quality Sources: Bridging the Gap Between the Perception and Use of Information Sources." *Journal of Information Science* 37, no. 2: 178–188.

Korobili, Stella, Aphrodite Malliari, and Sofia Zapounidou. 2011. "Factors that Influence Information-Seeking Behavior: The Case of Greek Graduate Students." *Journal of Academic Librarianship* 37, no. 2: 155–165.

Kuhlthau, Carol C. 1991. "Inside the Search Process: Information-Seeking from the User's Perspective." *Journal of the American Society for Information Science* 42, no. 5: 361–371. Quoted in Johannes G. Nel, 2001.

Kuhlthau, Carol C., Jannica Heinström, and Ross J. Todd. 2008. "The 'Information Search Process' Revisited: Is the Model Still Useful?" *Information Research* 13, no. 4. http://informationr.net/ir/13-4/paper355.html.

Kunimoto, C. 2010. "How People Initiate Information Seeking Behavior: Case Studies of Medical Information Seeking." *Library and Information Science* (64): 55–79.

Kwon, Nahyun, and Vicki L. Gregory. 2007. "The Effects of Librarians' Behavioral Performance on User Satisfaction in Chat Reference Services." *Reference & User Services Quarterly* 47, no. 2: 137–148.

Kwon, Nahyun, Anthony J. Onwuegbuzie, and Linda Alexander. 2007. "Critical Thinking Disposition and Library Anxiety: Affective Domains on the Space of Information Seeking and Use in Academic Libraries." *College & Research Libraries* 68 (May): 268–278.

Lambert, Sylvie D., Carmen G. Loiselle, and Mary Ellen Macdonald. 2009. "An In-depth Exploration of Information-Seeking Behavior Among Individuals With Cancer Part 1: Understanding Differential Patterns of Active Information Seeking." *Cancer Nursing* 32, no. 1: 11–23.

Laplante, Audrey, and J. Stephen Downie. 2011. "The Utilitarian and Hedonic Outcomes of Music Information-Seeking in Everyday Life." *Library & Information Science Research* 33, no. 3: 202–210.

Large, Andrew, Valerie Nesset, and Jamshid Beheshti. 2008. "Children as Information Seekers: What Researchers Tell Us." *New Review of Children's Literature & Librarianship* 14, no. 2: 121–140.

Lee, J. H. 2010. "Analysis of User Needs and Information Features in Natural Language Queries Seeking Music Information." *Journal of the American Society for Information Science and Technology* 61, no. 5: 1025–1045.

Longo, Daniel R., Shari L. Schubert, Barbara A. Wright, Joseph LeMaster, Casey D. Williams, and John N. Clore. 2010. "Health Information Seeking, Receipt, and Use in Diabetes Self-Management." *Annals of Family Medicine* 8, no. 4: 334–340.

Lopatovska, Irene, and Ioannis Arapakis. 2010. "Theories, Methods and Current Research on Emotions in Library and Information Science, Information Retrieval and Human–Computer Interaction. *Information Processing & Management* 47, no. 4: 575–592.

Machendranath, S., and V. T. Kamble. 2010. "Information Use Among Working Women in the Associated Cement Company (ACC) Wadi, Gulbarga: A Survey." *Library Philosophy and Practice* (March). http://www.webpages.uidaho .edu/~mbolin/machendranath-kamble.htm.

Mahajan, Preeti. 2009. "Information-Seeking Behavior: A Study of Panjab University, India." *Library Philosophy and Practice* (March). http://www.webpages .uidaho.edu/~mbolin/mahajan4.htm.

McMahon, S., K. Macpherson, and W. A. Roberts. 2010. "Dogs Choose a Human Informant: Metacognition in Canines." *Behavioral Processes* 85, no. 3: 293–298.

Medaille, Ann. 2010. "Creativity and Craft: The Information-Seeking Behavior of Theatre Artists." *Journal of Documentation* 66, no. 3: 327–347.

Moulaison, Heather L. 2008. "OPAC Queries at a Medium-Sized Academic Library: A Transaction Log Analysis." *Library Resources & Technical Services* 52, no. 4: 230–237.

Nel, Johannes G. 2001. "The Information-Seeking Process: Is There a Sixth Sense?" *Mousaion* 19, no. 2: 23–32.

Newell, Terrance S. 2009. "Examining Information Problem-Solving Instruction: Dynamic Relationship Patterns Mediated by Distinct Instructional Methodologies." *School Libraries Worldwide* 15, no. 2: 49–76.

Nicholas, D., D. Clark, I. Rowlands, and H. Jamali. 2009. "Online Use and Information Seeking Behaviour: Institutional and Subject Comparisons of UK Researchers." *Journal of Information Science* 35, no. 6: 660.

Niu, Xi, Bradley M. Hemminger, Cory Lown, Stephanie Adams, Cecelia Brown, Allison Level, Merinda McLure, Audrey Powers, Michele R. Tennant, Tara Cataldo. 2010. "National Study of Information Seeking Behavior of Academic Researchers in the United States." *Journal of the American Society for Information Science and Technology* 61, no. 5: 869–890.

Noh, H. I., J. M. Lee, Y. H. Yun, S. Y. Park, D. S. Bae, J. H. Nam, C. T. Park, C. H. Cho, S. Y. Kye, Y. J. Chang. 2009. "Cervical Cancer Patient Information-Seeking

Behaviors, Information Needs, and Information Sources in South Korea." *Supportive Care in Cancer* 17, no. 10: 1277–1283.

Novotny, Eric. 2004. "I Don't Think I Click: A Protocol Analysis Study of Use of a Library Online Catalog in the Internet Age." *College & Research Libraries* 65 (November): 525–537.

Oblinger, Diana G., and James L. Oblinger. 2005. "Is it Age or IT: First Steps Toward Understanding the Net Generation." In *Educating the Net Generation*, edited by Diana G. Oblinger and James L. Oblinger, 2.1–2.20. Boulder, CO: Educause. http://www.educause.edu/ir/library/pdf/pub7101b.pdf.

O'Connor, Lisa G. 2011. "Duct Tape and WD-40: The Information Worlds of Female Investors." *Library & Information Science Research* 33, no. 3: 228–235.

O'Connor, L., and K. Lundstrom. 2011. "The Impact of Social Marketing Strategies on the Information Seeking Behaviors of College Students." *Reference & User Services Quarterly* 50, no. 4: 351–365.

Ostrander, Margaret. 2008. "Talking, Looking, Flying, Searching: Information Seeking Behaviour in Second Life." *Library Hi Tech* 26, no. 4: 512–524.

Pattee, Amy S. 2008. "What Do You Know? Applying the K-W-L Method to the Reference Transaction with Children." *Children & Libraries* 6, no. 1: 30–31, 34–39.

Peterson, Lisa C. 1997. "Effective Question Negotiation in the Reference Interview." *Current Studies in Librarianship* 21 (Spring/Fall): 22–34.

Pinto, M., and A. Fernández-Ramos. 2010. "Spanish Faculty Preferences and Usage of Library Services in the Field of Science and Technology." *Portal: Libraries and the Academy* 10, no. 2: 215–239.

Radford, Marie L. 1999. "The Reference Encounter: Interpersonal Communication in the Academic Library." Chicago: Association of College and Research Libraries. Quoted in Catherine Sheldrick Ross, 2003.

Radford, Marie L., and M. Kathleen Kern. 2006. "A Multiple-Case Study Investigation of the Discontinuation of Nine Chat Reference Services." *Library & Information Science Research* 28, no. 4: 521–547.

Radford, Marie L., Lynn Silipigni Connaway, Patrick A. Confer, Susanna Sabolci-Boros, and Hannah Kwon. 2011. "'Are We Getting Warmer?' Query Clarification in Live Chat Virtual Reference." *Reference & User Services Quarterly* 50, no. 3: 259–279.

Riedling, Ann Marlow. 2000. "Great Ideas for Improving Reference Interviews." *Book Report* 19 (November/December): 28–29.

Roach, A. R., E. L. B. Lykins, C. G. Gochett, E. H. Brechting, L. O. Graue, and M. A. Andrykowski. 2009. "Differences in Cancer Information-Seeking Behavior, Preferences, and Awareness Between Cancer Survivors and Healthy Controls: A National, Population-Based Survey." *Journal of Cancer Education* 24, no. 1: 73–79.

Rollins, B. L., K. King, G. Zinkhan, and M. Perri. 2010. "Behavioral Intentions and Information-Seeking Behavior: A Comparison of Nonbranded Versus Branded Direct-to-Consumer Prescription Advertisements." *Drug Information Journal* 44, no. 6: 673–683.

Ronan, Jana. 2003. "The Reference Interview Online." *Reference & User Services Quarterly* 43 (Fall): 43–47.

Ross, Catherine Sheldrick. 2003. "The Reference Interview: Why It Needs to Be Used in Every (Well, Almost Every) Reference Transaction." *Reference & User Services Quarterly* 43 (Fall): 38–42.

Ross, Catherine Sheldrick, and Patricia Dewdney. 1998. "Negative Closure: Strategies and Counter-Strategies in the Reference Transaction." *Reference & User Services Quarterly* 38, no. 2: 151–163.

Ruthven, Joan. 2010. "The Information-Seeking Behavior of Online Public Library Clients: A Conceptual Model." *Australian Library Journal* 59, no. 1/2: 30–45.

Rutten, L. J. F., E. M. Augustson, K. A. Doran, R. P. Moser, and B. W. Hesse. 2009. "Health Information Seeking and Media Exposure Among Smokers: A Comparison of Light and Intermittent Tobacco Users with Heavy Users. *Nicotine & Tobacco Research* 11, no. 2: 190–196.

Saleh, Adam Gambo, and Fatima Ibrahim Lasisi. 2011. "Information Needs and Information Seeking Behavior of Rural Women in Borno State, Nigeria." *Library Philosophy and Practice* (February). http://www.webpages.uidaho.edu/~mbolin/saleh-lasisi2.htm.

Samal, L., G. Chander, R. Moore, M. C. Beach, T. Korthuis, S. Saha, V. Sharp, and J. Cohn. 2010. "Internet Health Information Seeking Behavior and Antiretroviral Adherence in Persons Living with HIV/AIDS." *Journal of General Internal Medicine* 25 (Suppl. 3): 316–317.

Schaller, Susann. 2011. "Information Needs of LGBTQ College Students." *Libri: International Journal of Libraries & Information Services* 61, no. 2: 100–115.

Scott, Sean Cunnison. 2004. "Process, Practice, and Psychic Stress at the Reference Desk." *OLA Quarterly* 10 (Fall): 19–23.

Sewell, R. R., N. F. Funkhouser, and C. L. Foster. 2011. "Reaching Beyond Our Walls: Library Outreach to Veterinary Practitioners." *Journal of Veterinary Medical Education* 38, no. 1: 16–20.

Shenton, Andrew K. 2010a. "Uniting Information Behaviour Research and the Information Professional: Identifying the Key Journals." *Library Review* 59, no. 1: 9–23.

Shenton, Andrew K. 2010b. "Etic, Emic, or Both? A Fundamental Decision for Researchers of Young People's Information Needs." *New Review of Children's Literature & Librarianship* 16, no. 1: 54–67.

Shenton, Andrew K. 2010c. "How Comparable Are the Actions of a School-Based Intermediary Responding to Inquiries and the Information-Seeking Behavior of Young People?" *Reference Librarian* 51, no. 4: 276–289.

Somerville, Arleen N. 1982. "The Pre-Search Reference Interview—A Step by Step Guide." *Database* 5 (February): 32–38.

Spowage, Michelle. 2008. "Detailed Look at How Young People Search." Book Review. *Library & Information Update* 7, no. 4: 46.

Steinerová, Jela, and Jaroslav Šušol. 2007. "Users' Information Behaviour—A Gender Perspective." *Information Research* 12 (April). http://informationr.net/ir/12-3/paper320.html.

Stock, Matt. 2010. "The Three R's: Rapport, Relationship, and Reference." *The Reference Librarian* 51, no. 1: 45–52.

Taylor, Robert S. 1968. "Question-Negotiation and Information Seeking in Libraries." *College & Research Libraries* 29, no. 3: 178–194.

Todd, Ross J. 2003. "Adolescents of the Information Age: Patterns of Information-Seeking and Use, and Implications for Information Professionals." *School Libraries Worldwide* 9, no. 2: 27–46.

Tucci, Valerie K. 2011. "Assessing Information-Seeking Behavior of Computer Science and Engineering Faculty." *Issues in Science & Technology Librarianship* 64 (Winter). http://www.istl.org/11-winter/refereed5.html.

Tyckoson, David. 2003. "Reference at Its Core: The Reference Interview." *Reference & User Services Quarterly* 43 (Fall): 49–51.

Ward, Joyce, and Patricia Barbier. 2010. "Best Practices in Chat Reference Used by Florida's Ask a Librarian Virtual Reference Librarians." *The Reference Librarian* 51, no. 1: 53–68.

Weaver, J., D. Mays, S. Weaver, G. Hopkins, D. Eroglu, and J. Bernhardt. 2010. "Health Information-Seeking Behaviors, Health Indicators, and Health Risks." *American Journal of Public Health* 100, no. 8: 1520–1525.

Westbrook, Lynn. 2009. "Unanswerable Questions at the IPL: User Expectations of E-mail Reference." *Journal of Documentation* 65, no. 3: 367–395.

Whitmire, Ethelene. 2003. "Epistemological Beliefs and the Information-Seeking Behavior of Undergraduates." *Library & Information Science Research* 25: 127–142.

Wicks, Don A. 2011. "New Horizons: A Center for Research into Information and Religion." *Journal of Religious & Theological Information* 10, no. 1/2: 1–4.

Wildemuth, B., and D. Case. 2010. "Early Information Behavior Research." *Bulletin of the American Society for Information Science and Technology (Online)*, February 1, 35–38. http://www.asis.org/Bulletin/Feb-10/FebMar10 _Wildemuth_Case.html.

Williamson, Kirsty, and Terryl Asla. 2009. "Information Behavior of People in the Fourth Age: Implications for the Conceptualization of Information Literacy." *Library & Information Science Research* 31, no. 2: 76–83.

Williamson, Kirsty, Marion Bannister, and Jen Sullivan. 2010. "The Crossover Generation: Baby Boomers and the Role of the Public Library." *Journal of Librarianship and Information Science (Folkestone, England)* 42, no. 3: 179–90.

Wright, Carol. 2010. "Information-Seeking Behaviors of Education Literature User Populations." *Teachers College Record* 112, no. 10: 2537–2564.

Xie, Iris. 2009. "Dimensions of Tasks: Influences on Information-Seeking and Retrieving Process. *Journal of Documentation* 65, no. 3: 339–366.

Young, Nancy J., and Marilyn Von Seggern. 2001. "General Information-Seeking in Changing Times: A Focus Group Study." *Reference & User Services Quarterly* 41 (Winter): 159–169.

Zhang, Liyi, Pinghao Ye, and Qihua Liu. 2011. "A Survey of the Use of Electronic Resources at Seven Universities in Wuhan, China." *Program* 45, no. 1: 67–77.

Zhang, Yao, and Yu Liangzhi. 2009. "Information for Social and Economic Participation: A Review of Related Research on the Information Needs and Acquisition of Rural Chinese." *International Information & Library Review* 41, no. 2: 63–70.

Chapter 10

Ojala, Marydee. 2008. "Business Research 2.0." *Online* 32 (March/April): 45–47.

Shores, Mark L. 2010. "Resource Review: Free Range Databases." *LibraryJournal .com,* December 16. http://www.libraryjournal.com/lj/community academiclibraries/888511-419/resource_review_free_range_databases .html.csp.

Chapter 11

Jacsó, Péter. 2007. "How Big Is a Database Versus How Is a Database Big." *Online Information Review* 31 (August): 533–536.

Chapter 12

Applegate, Celia. 1999. "Teaching: Taming the Terror." In *How I Teach: Essays on Teaching by Winners of the Robert and Pamela Goergen Award for Distinguished Achievement and Artistry in Undergraduate Teaching*, 23–36. Rochester, NY: University of Rochester. http://hdl.handle.net /1802/2864.

Arant-Kaspar, Wendi, and Candace Benefiel. 2008. "Drive-by BI: Tailored In-class Mini-instruction Sessions for Graduate and Upper-level Undergraduate Courses." *Reference Services Review* 36, no. 1: 39–47.

Boice, R. 1992. *The New Faculty Member: Supporting and Fostering Professional Development*. San Francisco, CA: Jossey-Bass. Quoted in Richard M. Reis, *Tomorrow's Professor: Preparing for Academic Careers in Science and Engineering*. New York: IEEE Press, 1997, p. 276.

Brown, Theodore M. 1999. "Connection, Communication, and Critical Thinking." In *How I Teach: Essays on Teaching by Winners of the Robert and Pamela Goergen Award for Distinguished Achievement and Artistry in Undergraduate Teaching*, 9–20. Rochester, NY: University of Rochester. http://hdl.handle .net/1802/2862.

Burkhardt, Joanna M., Mary C. MacDonald, and Andrée J. Rathemacher. 2003. *Teaching Information Literacy: 35 Practical, Standards-based Exercises for College Students*. Chicago: American Library Association.

Carter, Toni, and Beverly Simmons. 2007. "Reaching Your Millenials: A Fresh Look at Freshman Orientation." *Tennessee Libraries* 57 (1): 1–4. http://www.tnla .org/displaycommon.cfm?an=1&subarticlenbr=124&printpage=true.

Davidson, C. I., and S. A. Ambrose. 1994. *The New Professor's Handbook: A Guide to Teaching and Research in Engineering and Science*. Bolton, MA: Anker Publishing. Quoted in Richard M. Reis, *Tomorrow's Professor: Preparing for Academic Careers in Science and Engineering*. New York: IEEE Press, 1997, p. 277.

Davis, Kaetrena D. 2007. "The Academic Librarian as Instructor: A Study of Teacher Anxiety." *College & Undergraduate Libraries* 14, no. 2: 77–101. http://digitalarchive.gsu.edu/univ_lib_facpub/29.

Eckel, Edward J. 2007. "Fostering Self-Regulated Learning at the Reference Desk." *Reference & User Services Quarterly* 47 (Fall): 16–20.

Elmborg, James K. 2002. "Teaching at the Desk: Toward a Reference Pedagogy." *Portal: Libraries and the Academy* 2 (July): 455–464.

Felder, R. M., and L. K. Silverman. 1988. "Learning and Teaching Styles in Engineering Education." *Journal of Engineering Education* 77, no. 2. Quoted in Richard M. Reis, *Tomorrow's Professor: Preparing for Academic Careers in Science and Engineering*. New York: IEEE Press, 1997, p. 265.

Feldman, K. 1976. "The Superior College Teacher from the Students' View." *Research in Higher Education* 5, no. 3: 243–288. Quoted in Richard M. Reis, *Tomorrow's Professor: Preparing for Academic Careers in Science and Engineering*. New York: IEEE Press, 1997, p. 261.

Gremmels, Gillian S., and Karen Shostrom Lehmann. 2007. "Assessment of Student Learning from Reference Service." *College & Research Libraries* 68 (November): 488–501.

Kuhlthau, Carol C. 1988. "Developing a Model of the Library Search Process: Cognitive and Affective Aspect." *RQ* 28 (Winter): 232–242. Quoted in Edward J. Eckel, 2007.

Roy, Loriene. 2011. "Library Instruction: The Teaching Prong in the Reference /Readers' Advisory/Instruction Triad." *The Reference Librarian* 52, no. 3: 274–276.

Viele, Patricia T. 2006. "Physics 213: An Example of Faculty/Librarian Collaboration." *Issues in Science and Technology Librarianship* 47 (Summer). http://www.istl.org/06-summer/article2.html.

Index

About the Author

SUZANNE S. BELL is an adjunct instructor for the School of Information Studies at the University of Wisconsin-Milwaukee, and business librarian and administrator for the institutional repository at the University of Rochester. Previous positions have included economics and data librarian at the University of Rochester, Internet education specialist at the University of Rochester Medical Center, and computer science librarian at Carnegie-Mellon University and the Rochester Institute of Technology.